MAYBE WE SHOULD BE LEARNING HOW TO PROGRAM A VCR INSTEAD.

PSHOOO

...

和月伸宏

NOBUHIRO WATSUKI

IT'S BAZAAR

NOT THAT I FELL PREY TO THEIR "( )ZAAR DE GOZARU" AD CAMPAIGN OR ANYTHING, BUT ABOUT HALF A YEAR AGO, I GAVE IN AND BOUGHT A PC. ONE YEAR TO E-MAIL—ONE YEAR TO WORD PROCESSING— ONE YEAR TO A GRAPHICS PAINT PRO- GRAM. THAT WAS THE PLAN...BUT, WHEN LAST SEEN, THE COMPUTER WAS STILL IN A CORNER OF THE STUDIO, COLLECTING DUST. CAST NOT GOLD COINS TO CATS, PEARLS BEFORE SWINE, OR PC'S TO WATSUKI— THOSE OF YOU WHO AREN'T UP ON YOUR TECHNOLOGY, JUST BE RE-A-A-ALLY SURE YOU KNOW WHAT YOU'RE GETTING INTO....

Rurouni Kenshin, which has found fans not only in Japan but around the world, first made its appearance in 1992, as an original short story in *Weekly Shonen Jump Special*. Later rewritten and published as a regular, continuing *Jump* series in 1994, *Rurouni Kenshin* ended serialization in 1999 but continued in popularity, as evidenced by the 2000 publica- tion of *Yahiko no Sakabatô* ("Yahiko's Reversed-Edge Sword") in *Weekly Shonen Jump*. His most current work, *Busô Renkin* ("Armored Alchemist"), began pub- lication in June 2003, also in *Jump*.

RUROUNI KENSHIN
VOL. 11: OVERTURE TO DESTRUCTION
The SHONEN JUMP Graphic Novel Edition

STORY AND ART BY
NOBUHIRO WATSUKI

English Adaptation/Gerard Jones
Translation/Kenichiro Yagi
Touch-Up Art & Lettering/Steve Dutro
Cover, Graphics & Layout/Sean Lee
Editor/Avery Gotoh

Supervising Editor/Kit Fox
Managing Editor/Elizabeth Kawasaki
Director of Production/Noboru Watanabe
Editorial Director/Alvin Lu
Executive Vice President & Editor in Chief/Hyoe Narita
Sr. Director of Licensing & Acquisitions/Rika Inouye
Vice President of Sales & Marketing/Liza Coppola
Vice President of Strategic Development/Yumi Hoashi
Publisher/Seiji Horibuchi

Printed in the U.S.A.

Published by VIZ, LLC
P.O. Box 77010
San Francisco, CA 94107

SHONEN JUMP Graphic Novel Edition
10 9 8 7 6 5 4 3 2 1
First printing, January 2005

www.viz.com

THE WORLD'S
MOST POPULAR MANGA

SHONEN JUMP
GRAPHIC NOVEL
www.shonenjump.com

SHONEN JUMP GRAPHIC NOVEL

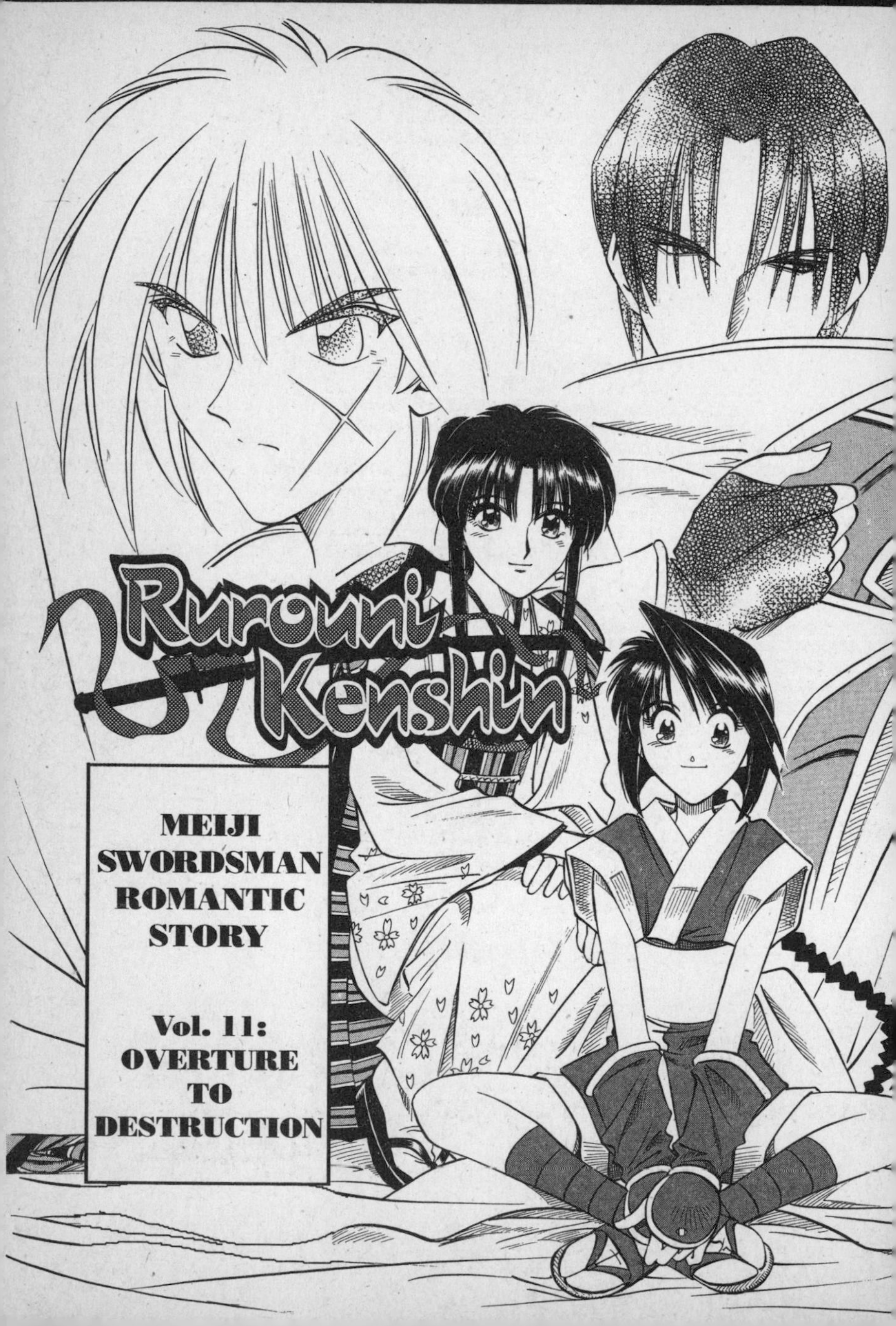
Rurouni Kenshin
MEIJI SWORDSMAN ROMANTIC STORY
Vol. 11: OVERTURE TO DESTRUCTION

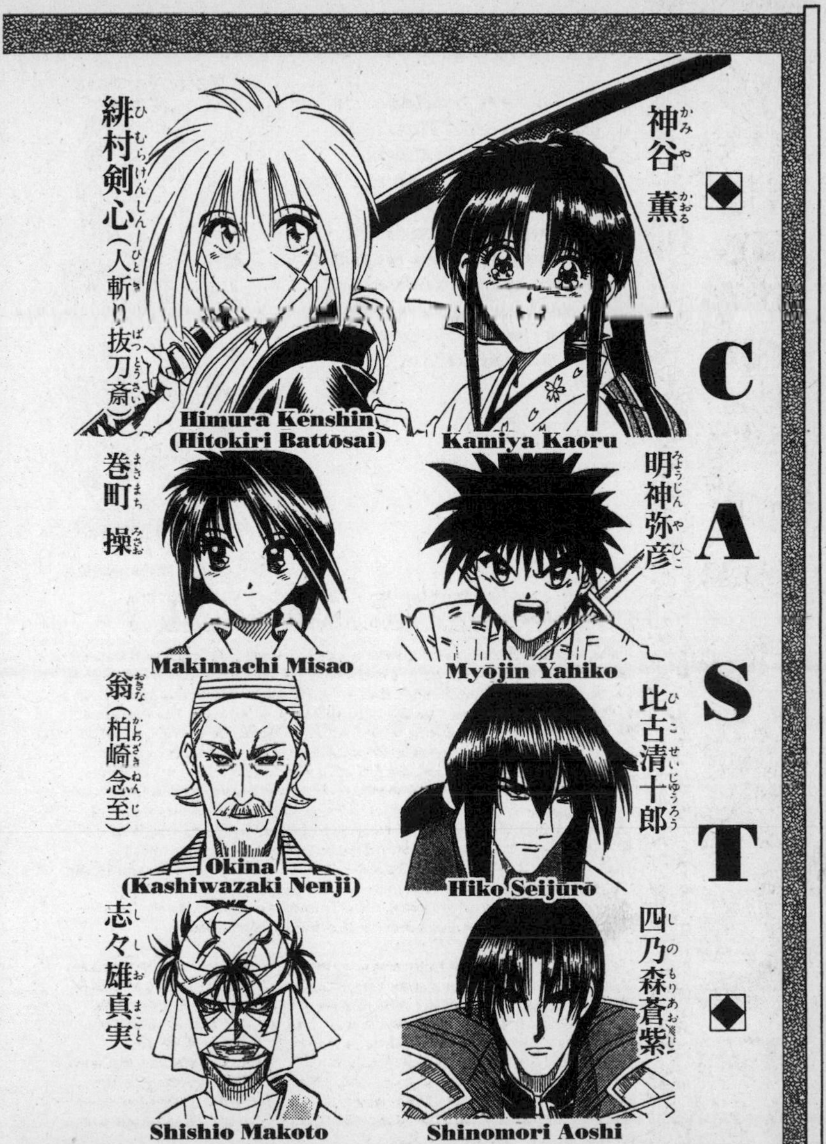
CAST
神谷薫
Kamiya Kaoru
緋村剣心（人斬り抜刀斎）
Himura Kenshin (Hitokiri Battōsai)
明神弥彦
Myōjin Yahiko
巻町操
Makimachi Misao
比古清十郎
Hiko Seijūrō
翁（柏崎念至）
Okina (Kashiwazaki Nenji)
四乃森蒼紫
Shinomori Aoshi
志々雄真実
Shishio Makoto

Once he was *hitokiri*, an assassin, called Battōsai. His name was legend among the pro-Imperialist or "patriot" warriors who launched the Meiji Era. Now, Himura Kenshin is *rurouni*, a wanderer, and carries a reversed-edge *sakabatō* to prohibit himself from killing.

Saitō Hajime

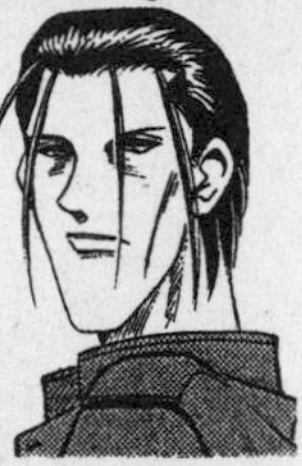

斎藤一（さいとう はじめ）

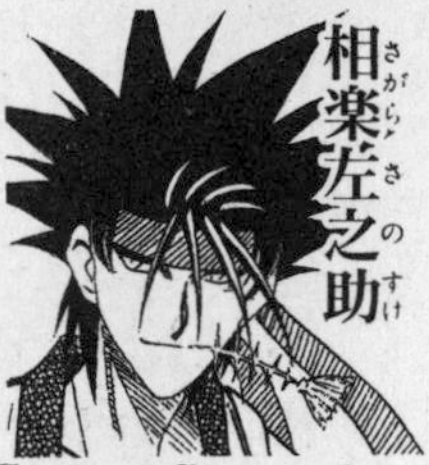

相楽左之助（さがら さのすけ）

Sagara Sanosuke

THUS FAR

Ōkubo Toshimichi, head of the government's "Internal Affairs," tries to hire Kenshin to assassinate Shishio Makoto, the successor to "Hitokiri Battōsai." But it is Ōkubo who is assassinated, and Kenshin sets out for Kyoto to find his killers. On the East Sea Road, Kenshin meets a girl named Misao and travels with her to a village occupied by Shishio's men—where he reconnects with Saitō Hajime, an intelligence agent for the police and ex-member of the Shinsengumi. There, they encounter Shishio himself, but the assassin refuses to fight Kenshin and vanishes. Behind him Shishio leaves Sōjirō—the "Sword of Heaven"—to fight, and Kenshin's *sakabatō* is shattered. Arriving in Kyoto, Kenshin asks the ex-Oniwabanshū surrogate father of Misao to find the swordsmith, Arai Shakkū. But Shakkū is dead, and the son who inherited his skills desires only peace and has abandoned the making of blades.

Chō, one of Shishio's *Juppongatana* or "Ten Swords" assassins, kidnaps Seikū's son to force the handing-over of the final blade. Kenshin rescues the boy and draws Shakkū's last blade himself—seemingly about to break his vow never to kill—but the sword turns out to be another *sakabatō*! With the blade, "Shinuchi," in hand, Kenshin leaves Aoi-Ya to seek out the master of the Hiten Mitsurugi school, Hiko Seijūrō. Asking to be taught the technique's final move, Kenshin is told that he does not "deserve" the secret. Just then, Yahiko and Kaoru arrive on the scene, led by Misao....

CONTENTS

RUROUNI KENSHIN
Meiji Swordsman Romantic Story
BOOK ELEVEN: OVERTURE TO DESTRUCTION

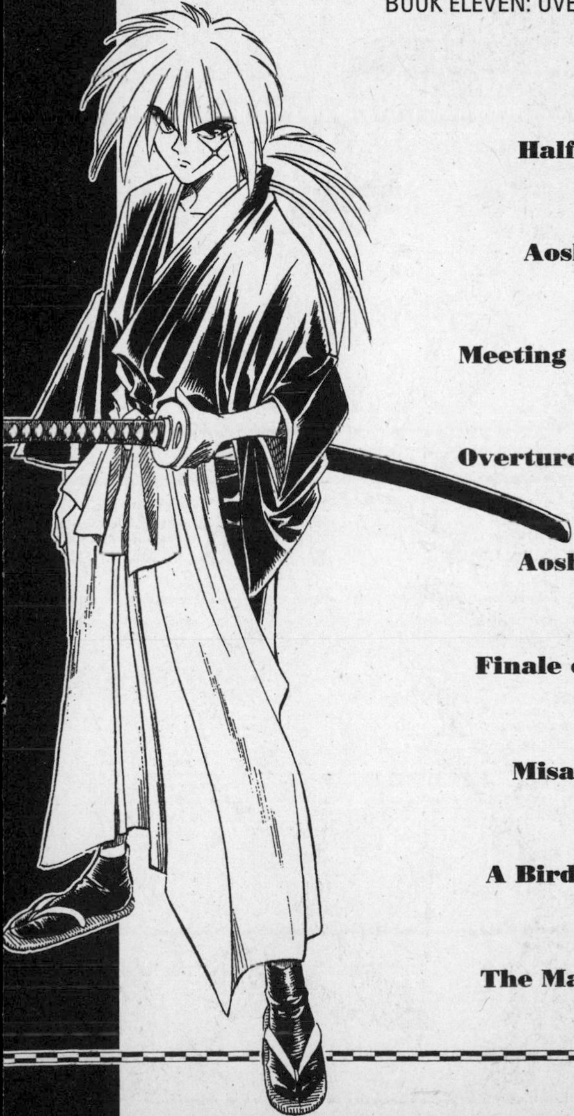

Act 85
Half the Feeling

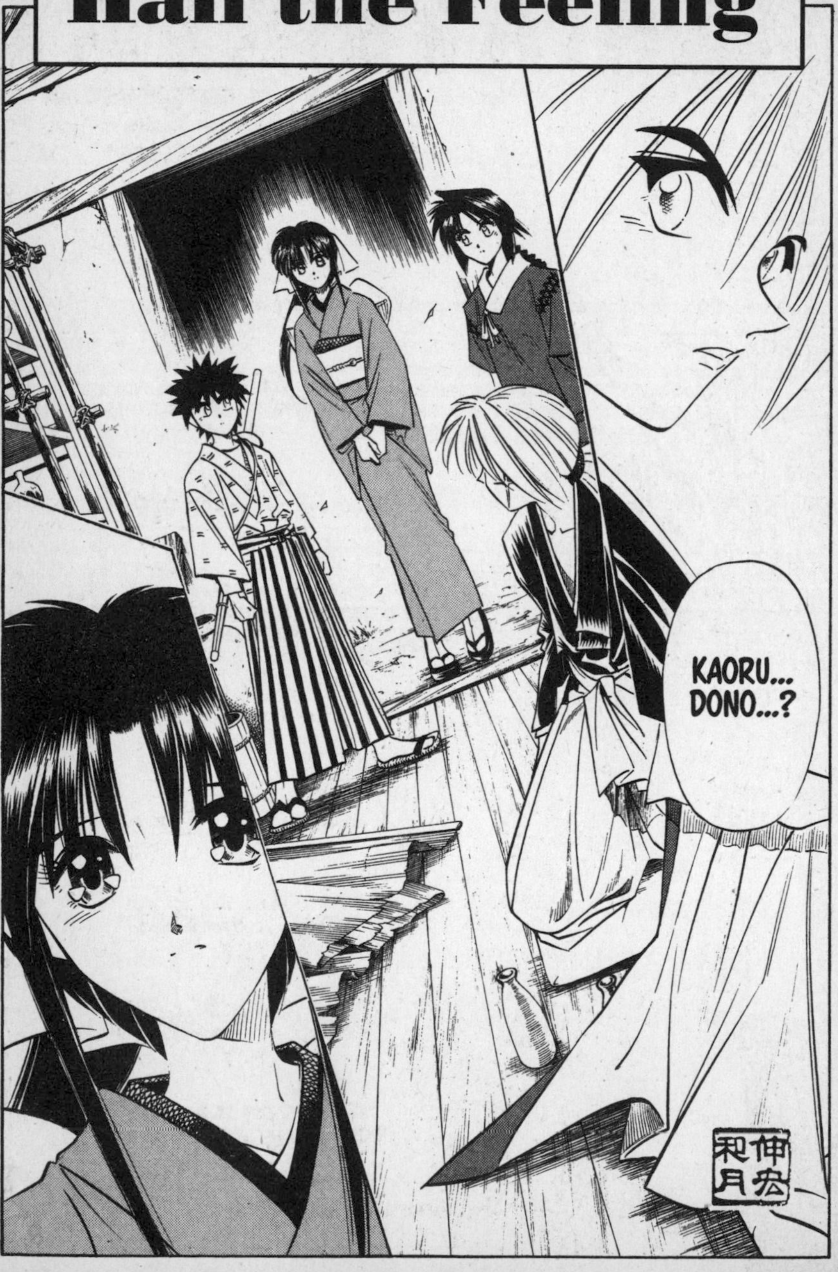
KAORU... DONO...?

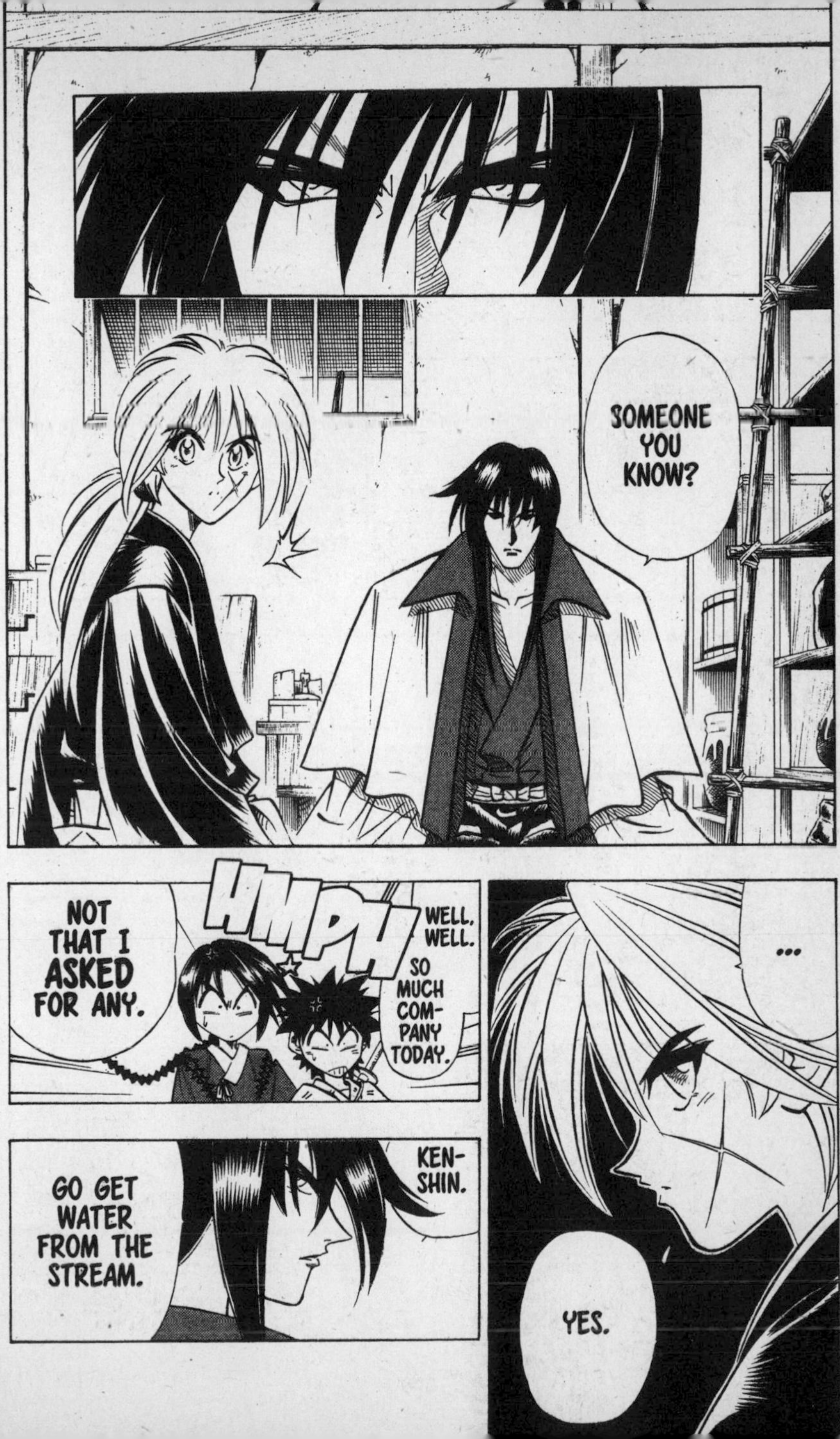
SOMEONE YOU KNOW?
...
YES.
WELL, WELL. SO MUCH COM-PANY TODAY.
HMPH
NOT THAT I ASKED FOR ANY.
KEN-SHIN.
GO GET WATER FROM THE STREAM.

READ THIS WAY

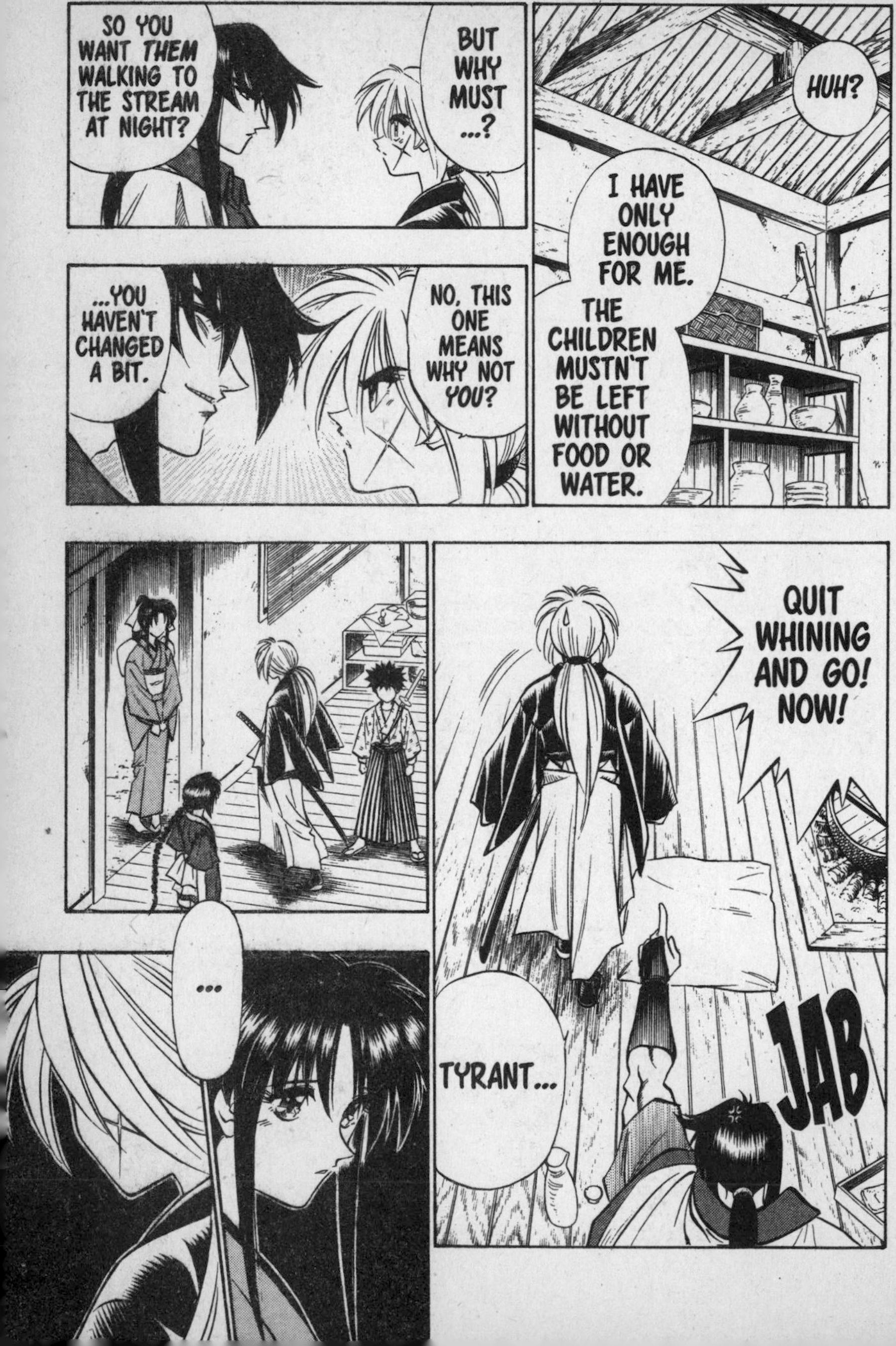
HUH?
I HAVE ONLY ENOUGH FOR ME.
THE CHILDREN MUSTN'T BE LEFT WITHOUT FOOD OR WATER.
BUT WHY MUST ...?
SO YOU WANT *THEM* WALKING TO THE STREAM AT NIGHT?
NO, THIS ONE MEANS WHY NOT *YOU*?
...YOU HAVEN'T CHANGED A BIT.
QUIT WHINING AND GO! NOW!
TYRANT...
JAB
...

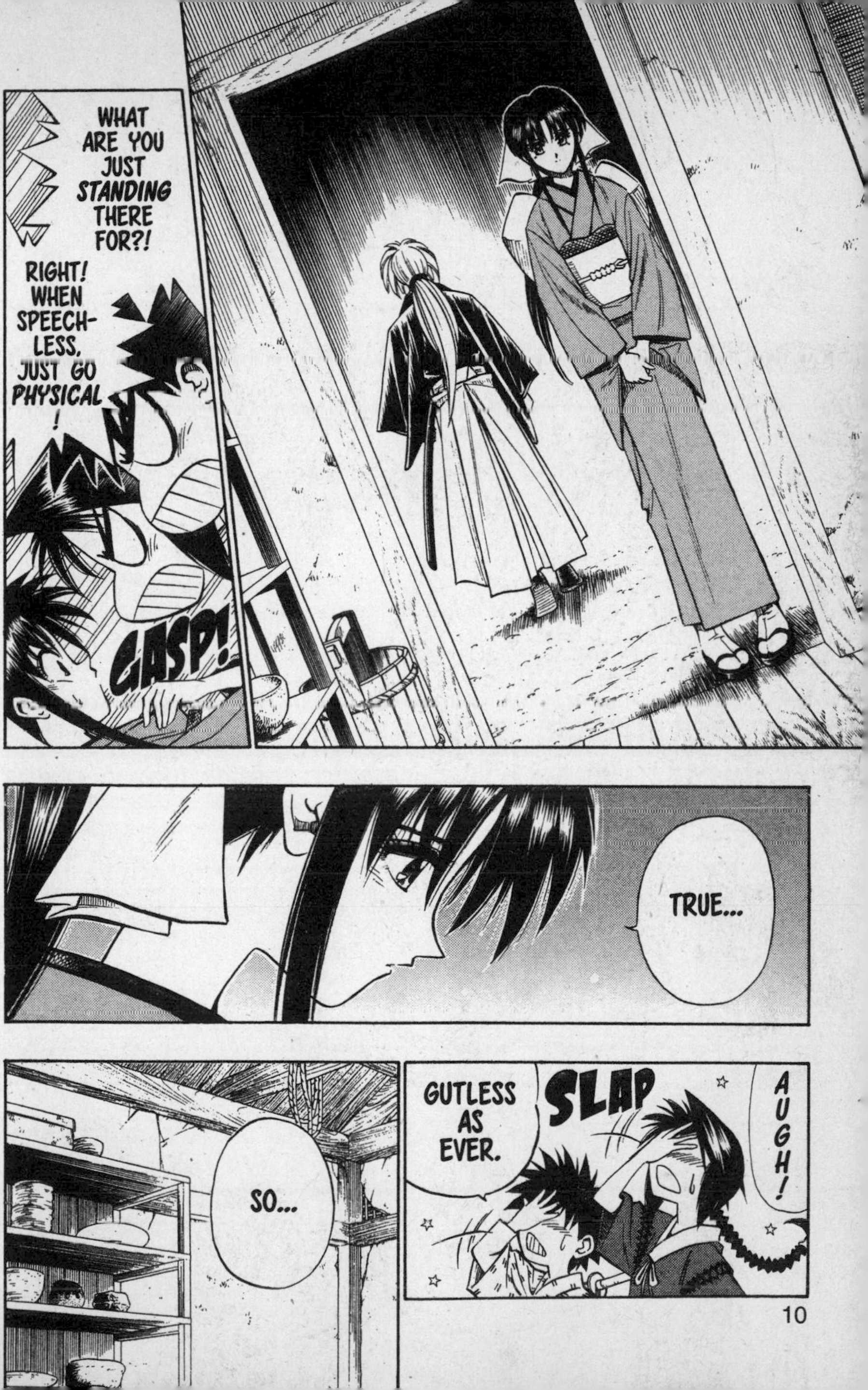
WHAT ARE YOU JUST STANDING THERE FOR?!
RIGHT! WHEN SPEECH-LESS, JUST GO PHYSICAL!
GASP!
TRUE...
AUGH!
SLAP
GUTLESS AS EVER.
SO...

READ THIS WAY

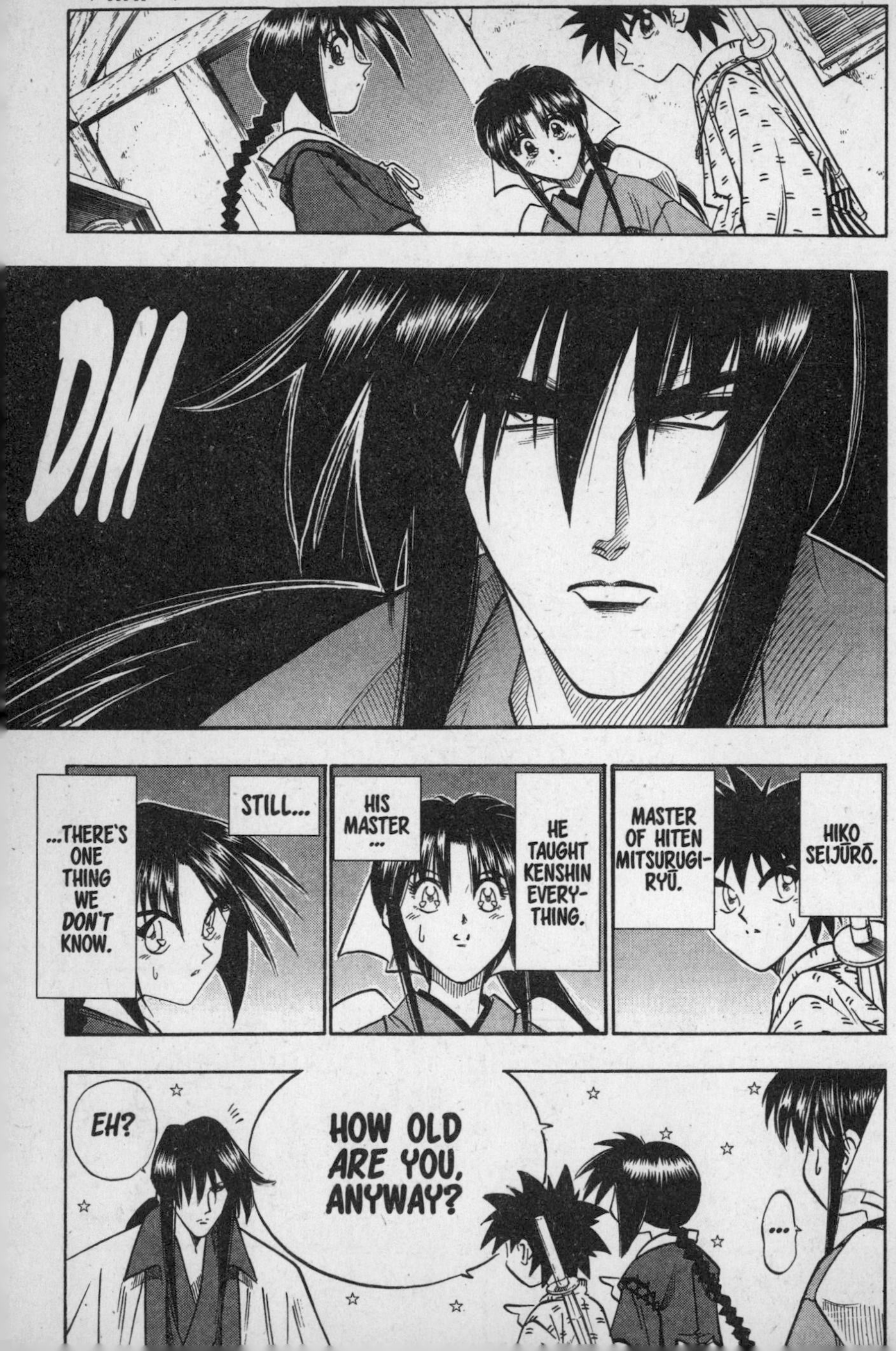
DM
HIKO SEIJŪRŌ.
MASTER OF HITEN MITSURUGI-RYŪ.
HE TAUGHT KENSHIN EVERYTHING.
HIS MASTER...
STILL...
...THERE'S ONE THING WE DON'T KNOW.
...
HOW OLD ARE YOU, ANYWAY?
EH?

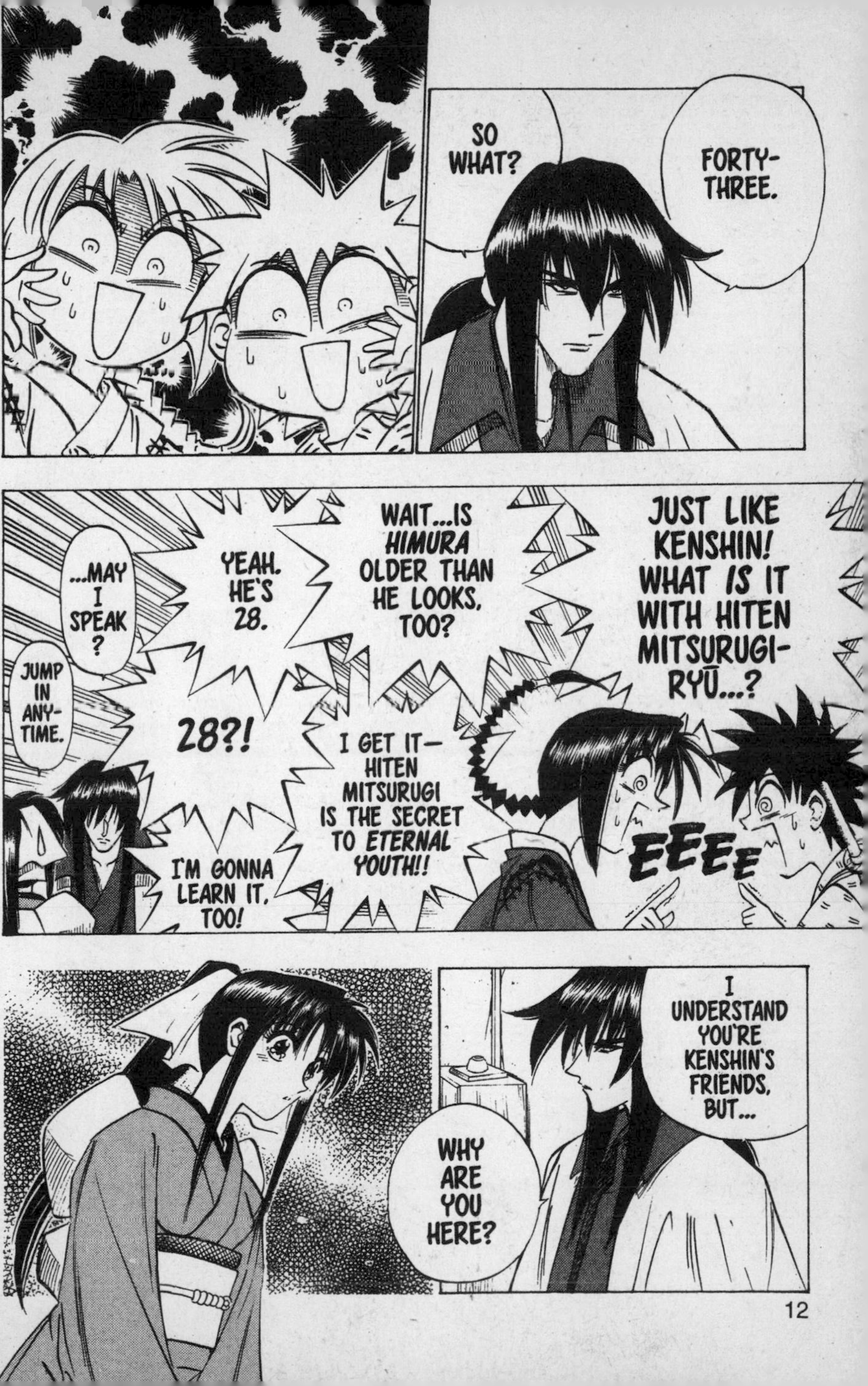
FORTY-THREE.
SO WHAT?
JUST LIKE KENSHIN! WHAT IS IT WITH HITEN MITSURUGI-RYŪ...?
WAIT...IS HIMURA OLDER THAN HE LOOKS, TOO?
YEAH. HE'S 28.
...MAY I SPEAK?
JUMP IN ANYTIME.
EEEE
I GET IT— HITEN MITSURUGI IS THE SECRET TO ETERNAL YOUTH!!
28?!
I'M GONNA LEARN IT, TOO!
I UNDERSTAND YOU'RE KENSHIN'S FRIENDS, BUT...
WHY ARE YOU HERE?

READ THIS WAY

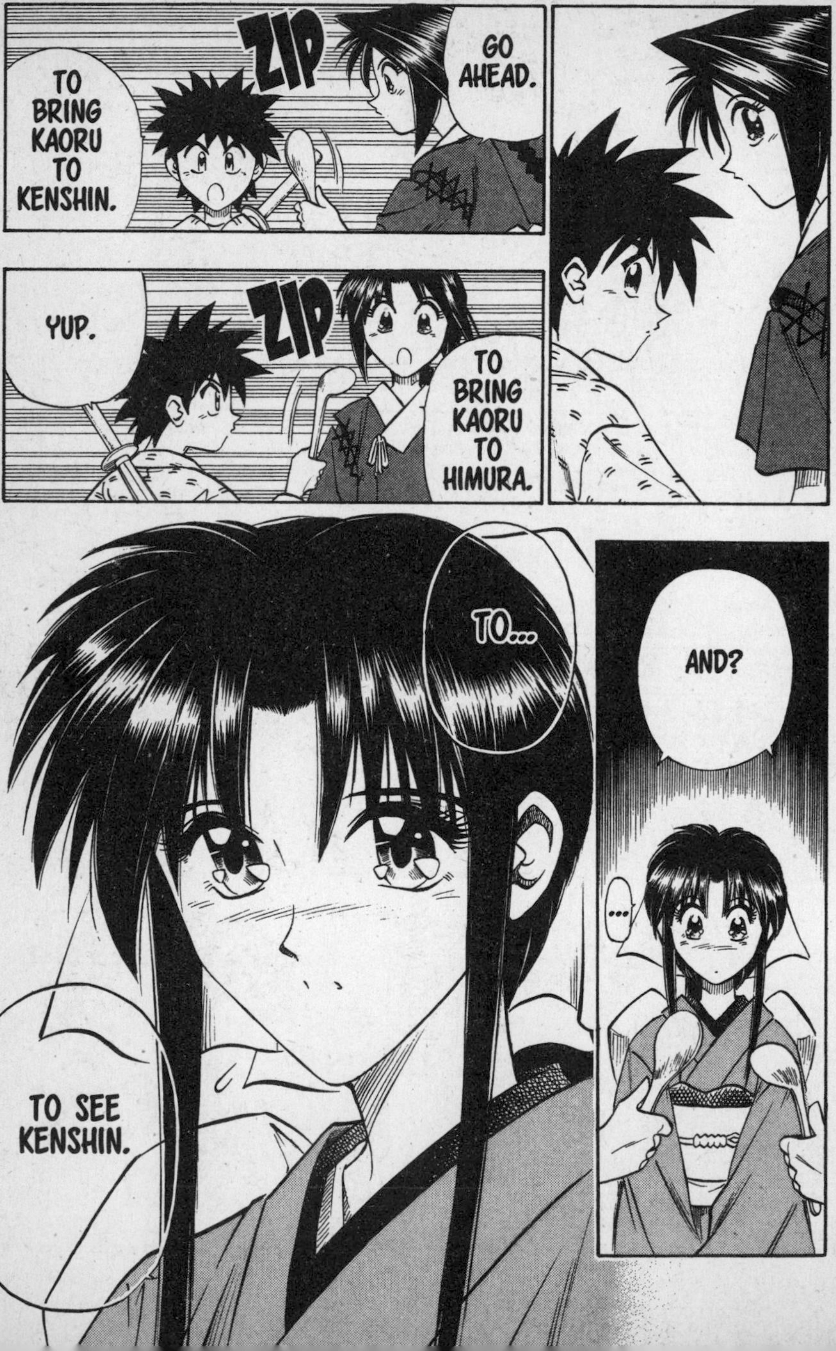
GO AHEAD.
ZIP
TO BRING KAORU TO KENSHIN.
TO BRING KAORU TO HIMURA.
ZIP
YUP.
AND?
...
TO...
TO SEE KENSHIN.

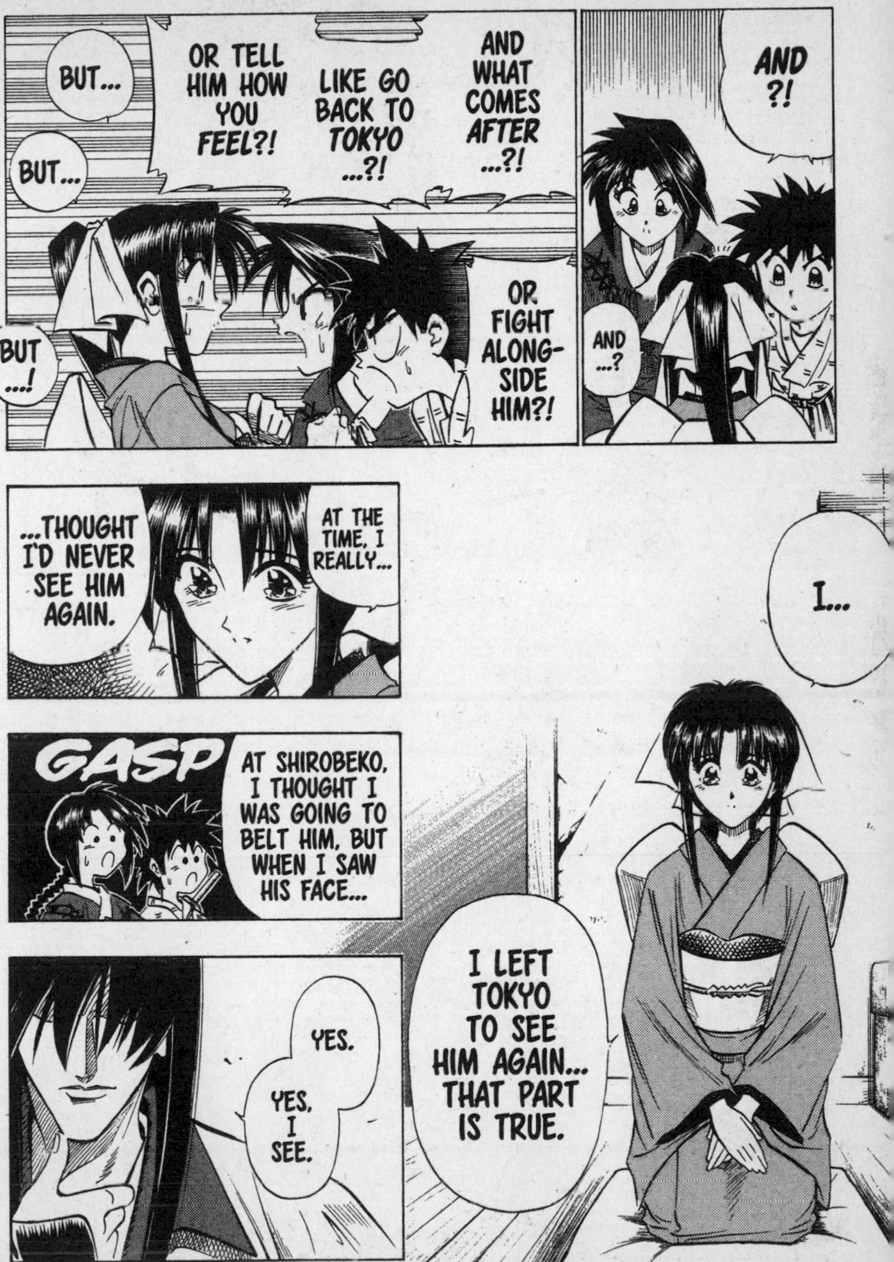
AND ?!
AND ...?
AND WHAT COMES AFTER ...?!
LIKE GO BACK TO TOKYO ...?!
OR TELL HIM HOW YOU FEEL?!
BUT...
BUT...
OR FIGHT ALONG-SIDE HIM?!
BUT ...!
I...
I LEFT TOKYO TO SEE HIM AGAIN... THAT PART IS TRUE.
AT THE TIME, I REALLY...
...THOUGHT I'D NEVER SEE HIM AGAIN.
GASP
AT SHIROBEKO, I THOUGHT I WAS GOING TO BELT HIM, BUT WHEN I SAW HIS FACE...
YES.
YES, I SEE.

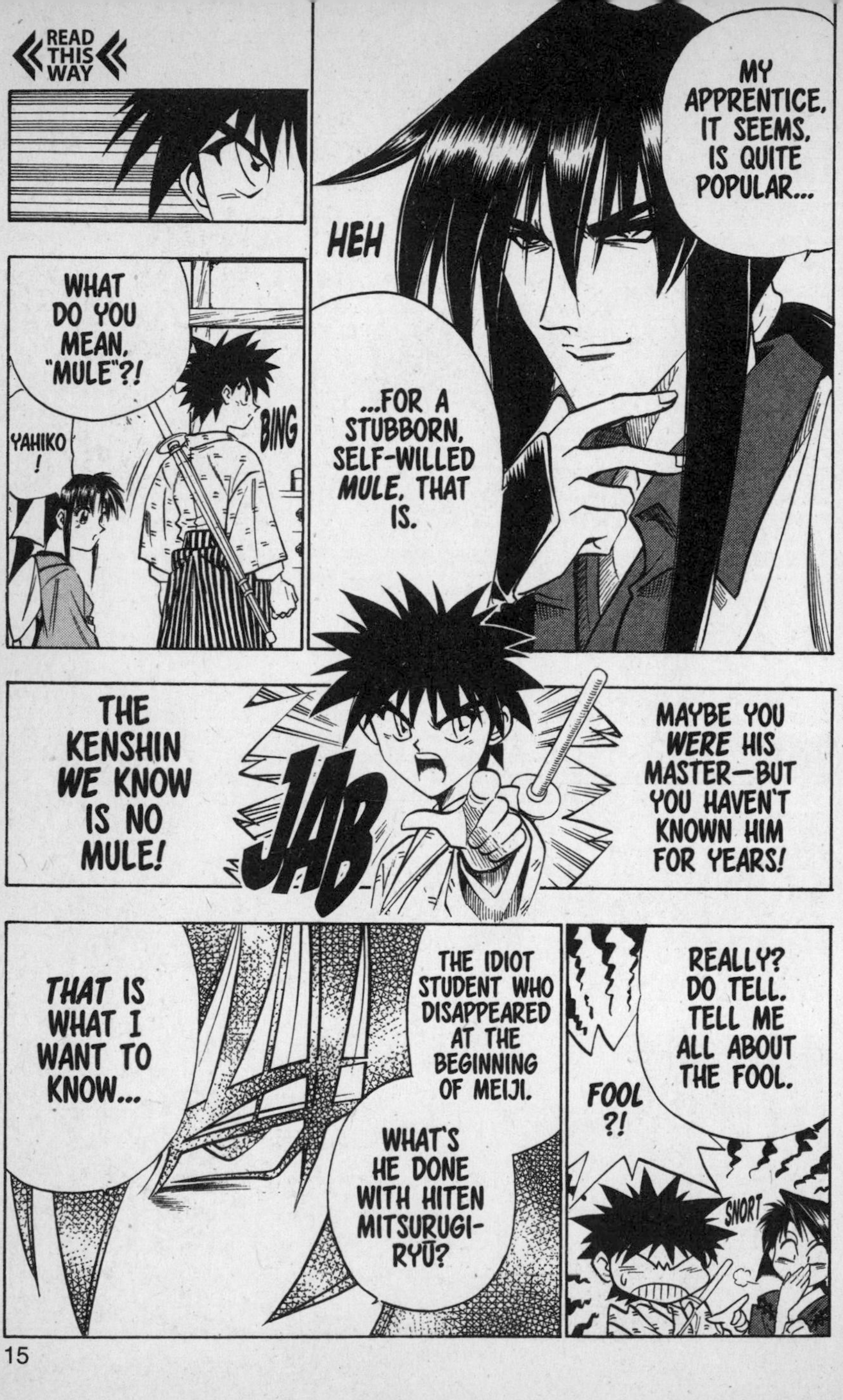
READ THIS WAY
MY APPRENTICE, IT SEEMS, IS QUITE POPULAR...
HEH
...FOR A STUBBORN, SELF-WILLED *MULE*, THAT IS.
WHAT DO YOU MEAN, "MULE"?!
BING
YAHIKO!
MAYBE YOU *WERE* HIS MASTER—BUT YOU HAVEN'T KNOWN HIM FOR YEARS!
JAB
THE KENSHIN *WE* KNOW IS NO MULE!
REALLY? DO TELL. TELL ME ALL ABOUT THE FOOL.
FOOL?!
SNORT
THE IDIOT STUDENT WHO DISAPPEARED AT THE BEGINNING OF MEIJI.
WHAT'S HE DONE WITH HITEN MITSURUGI-RYŪ?
THAT IS WHAT I WANT TO KNOW...

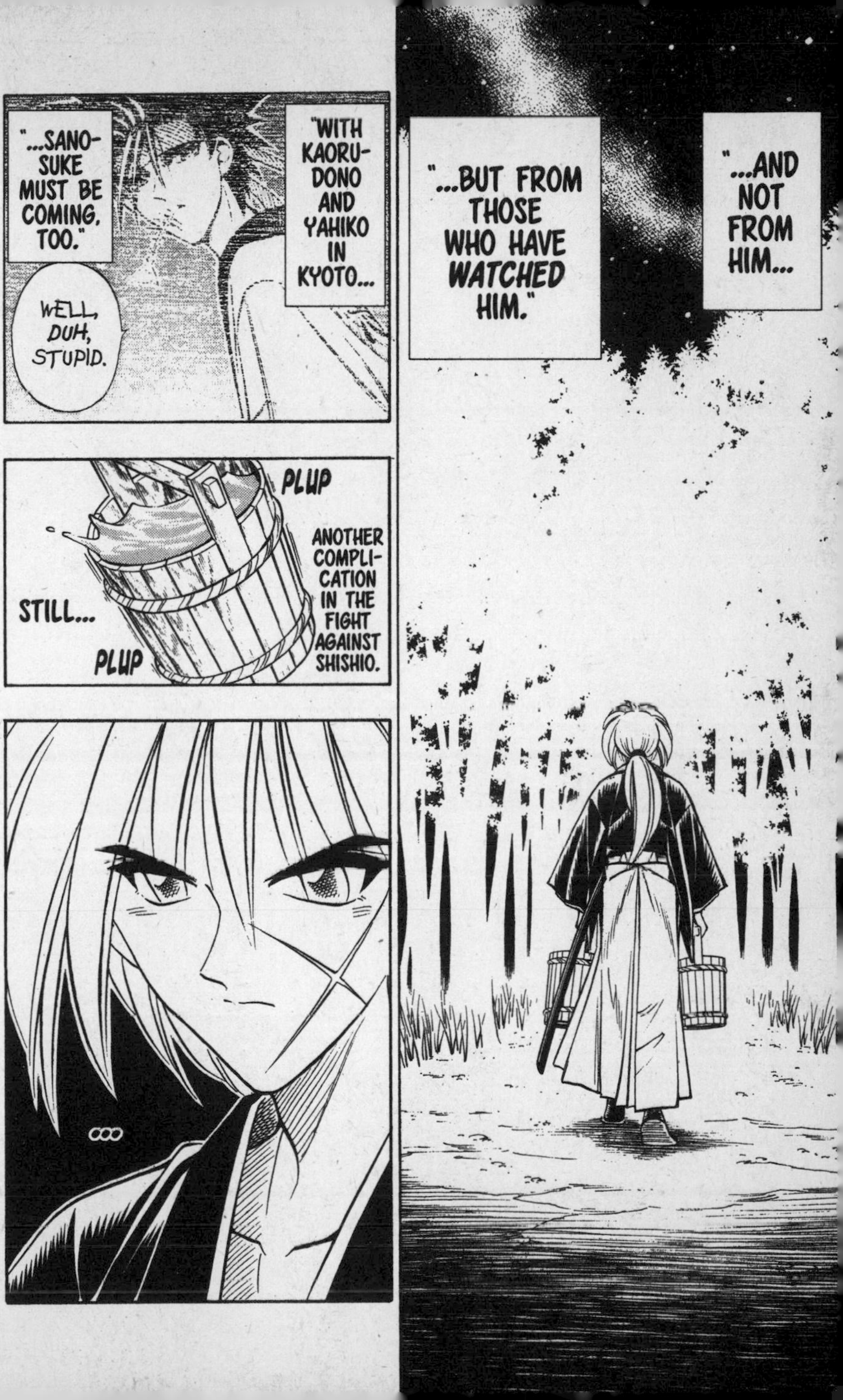
"...AND NOT FROM HIM...
"...BUT FROM THOSE WHO HAVE *WATCHED* HIM."
"WITH KAORU-DONO AND YAHIKO IN KYOTO...
"...SANO-SUKE MUST BE COMING, TOO."
WELL, *DUH*, STUPID.
PLUP
ANOTHER COMPLICATION IN THE FIGHT AGAINST SHISHIO.
STILL...
PLUP

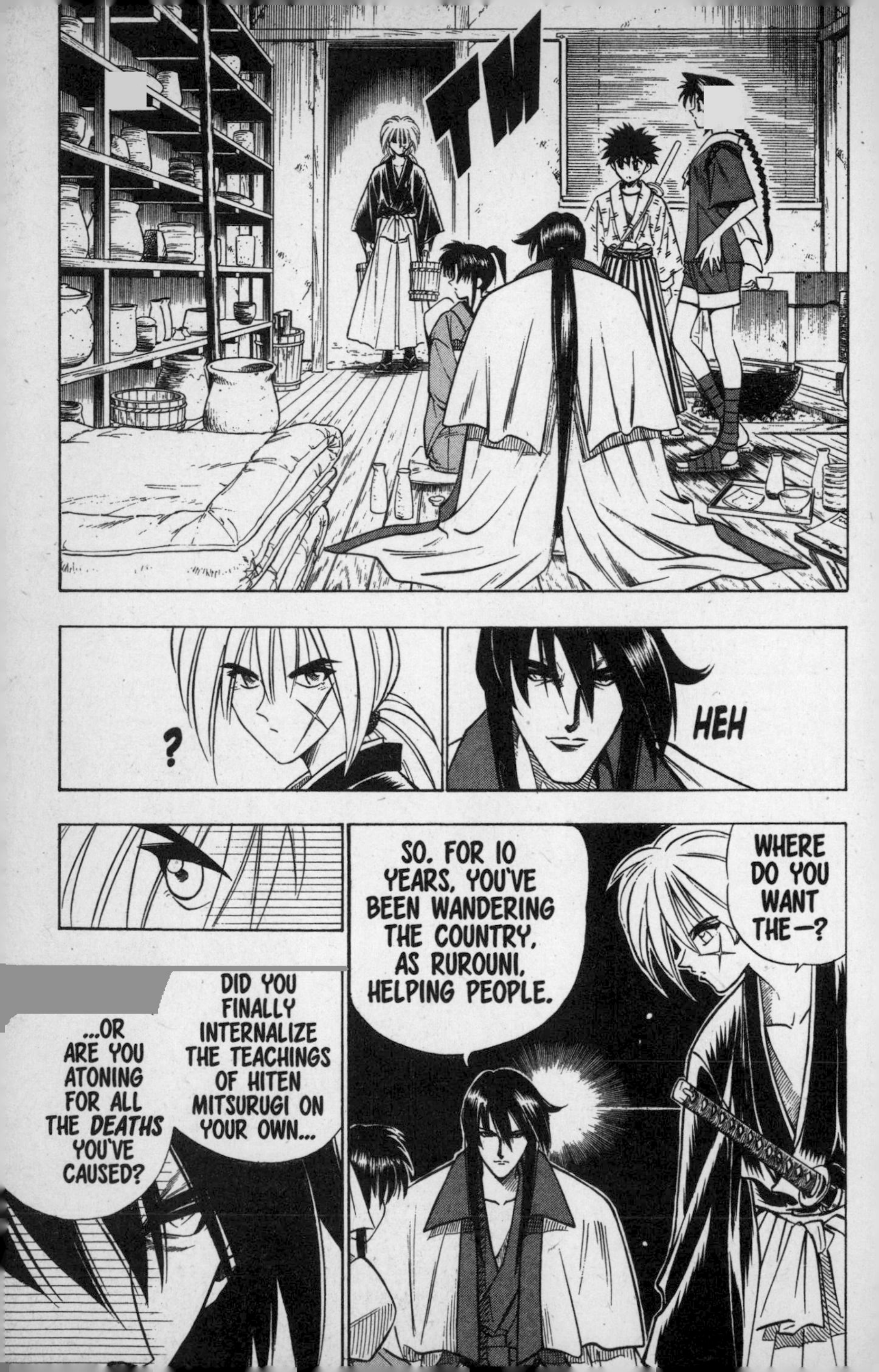
TM
HEH
?
WHERE DO YOU WANT THE—?
SO. FOR 10 YEARS, YOU'VE BEEN WANDERING THE COUNTRY, AS RUROUNI, HELPING PEOPLE.
DID YOU FINALLY INTERNALIZE THE TEACHINGS OF HITEN MITSURUGI ON YOUR OWN...
...OR ARE YOU ATONING FOR ALL THE *DEATHS* YOU'VE CAUSED?

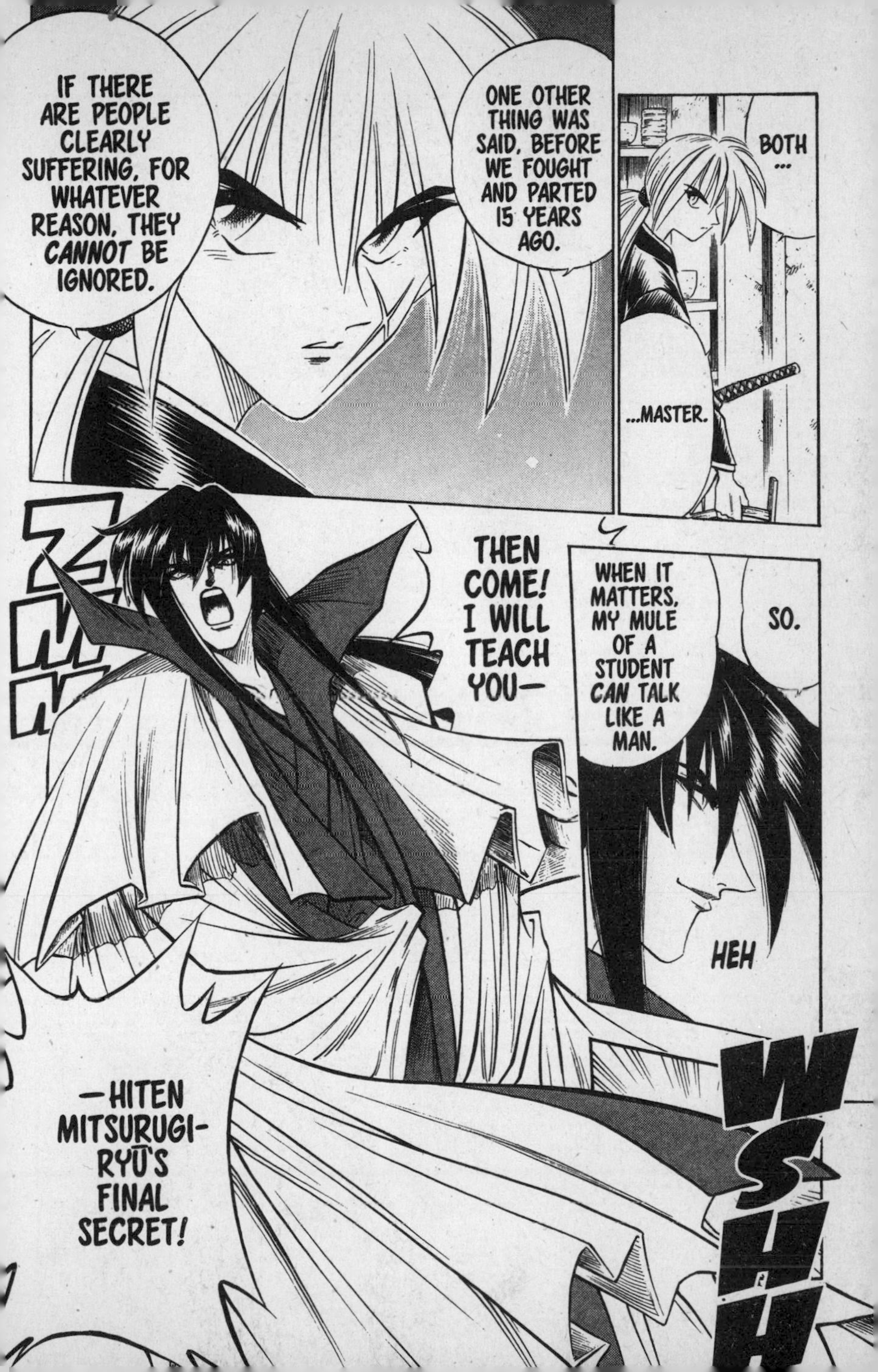
BOTH ...
...MASTER.
ONE OTHER THING WAS SAID, BEFORE WE FOUGHT AND PARTED 15 YEARS AGO.
IF THERE ARE PEOPLE CLEARLY SUFFERING, FOR WHATEVER REASON, THEY *CANNOT* BE IGNORED.
SO.
WHEN IT MATTERS, MY MULE OF A STUDENT *CAN* TALK LIKE A MAN.
HEH
THEN COME! I WILL TEACH YOU—
WSHH
—HITEN MITSURUGI-RYŪ'S FINAL SECRET!

READ THIS WAY

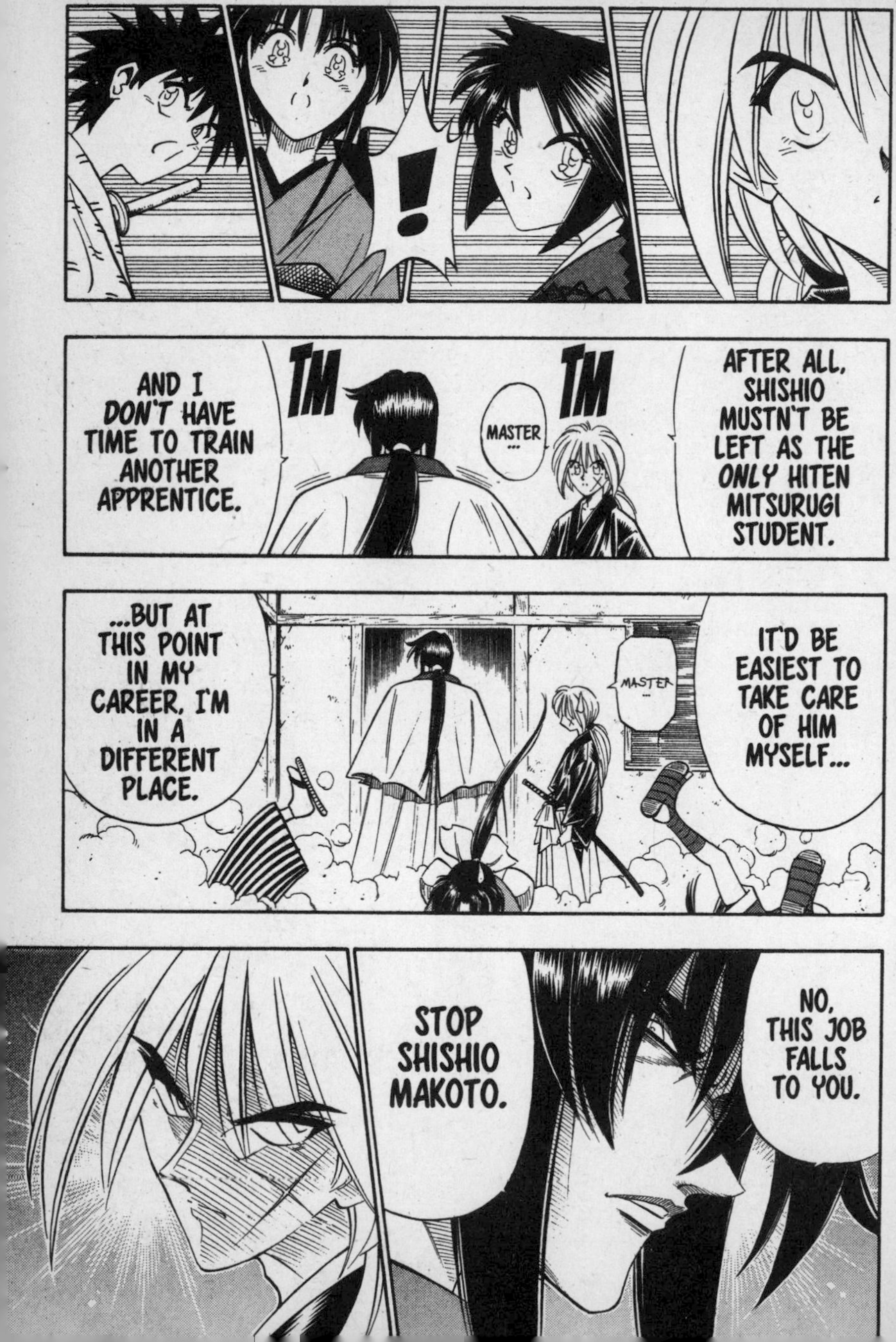
!
AFTER ALL, SHISHIO MUSTN'T BE LEFT AS THE *ONLY* HITEN MITSURUGI STUDENT.
TM
MASTER ...
TM
AND I *DON'T* HAVE TIME TO TRAIN ANOTHER APPRENTICE.
IT'D BE EASIEST TO TAKE CARE OF HIM MYSELF...
MASTER ...
...BUT AT THIS POINT IN MY CAREER, I'M IN A DIFFERENT PLACE.
NO, THIS JOB FALLS TO YOU.
STOP SHISHIO MAKOTO.

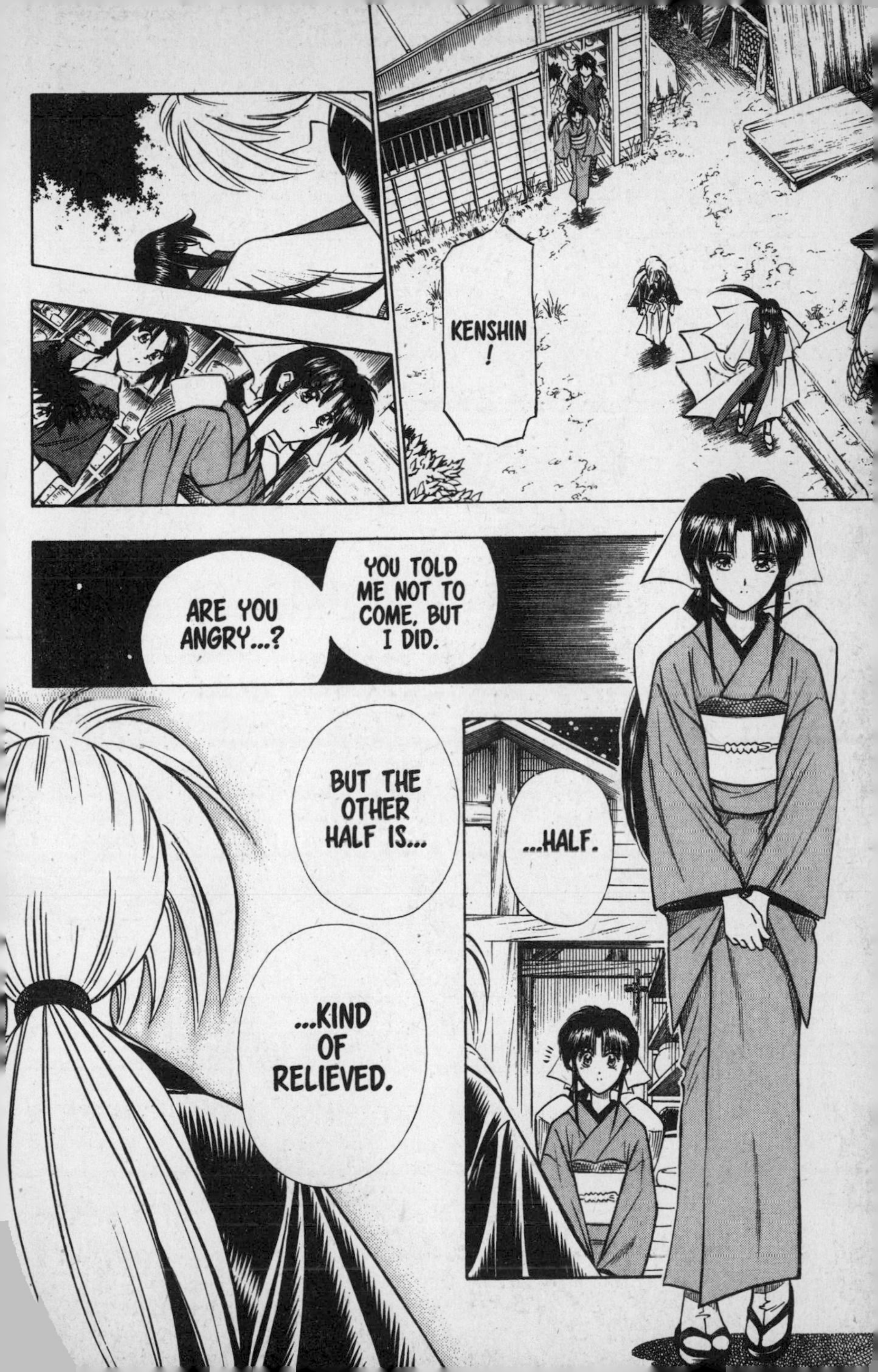
KENSHIN!
YOU TOLD ME NOT TO COME, BUT I DID.
ARE YOU ANGRY...?
...HALF.
BUT THE OTHER HALF IS...
...KIND OF RELIEVED.

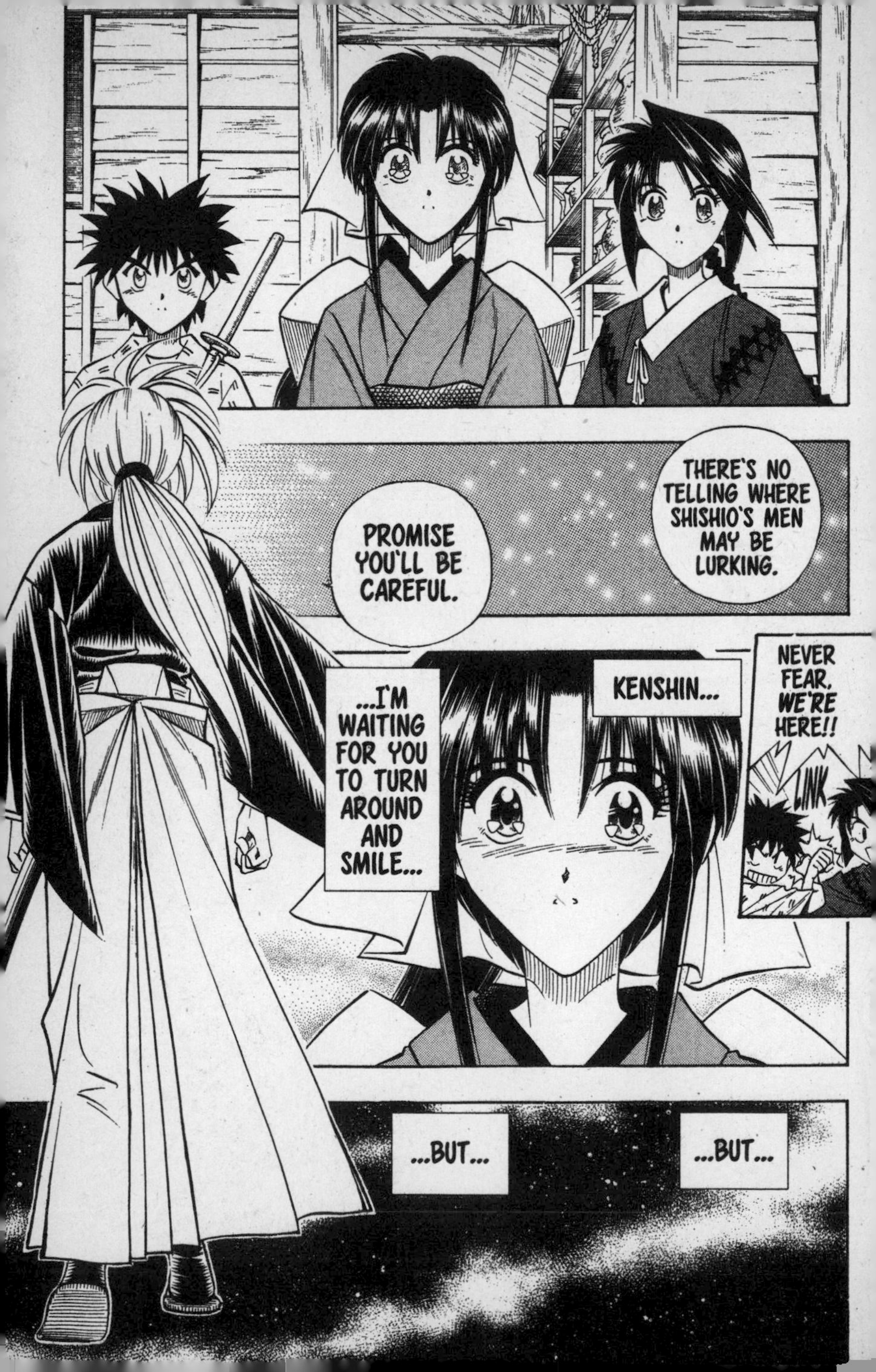

THERE'S NO TELLING WHERE SHISHIO'S MEN MAY BE LURKING.
PROMISE YOU'LL BE CAREFUL.
NEVER FEAR, WE'RE HERE!!
LINK
KENSHIN...
...I'M WAITING FOR YOU TO TURN AROUND AND SMILE...
...BUT...
...BUT...

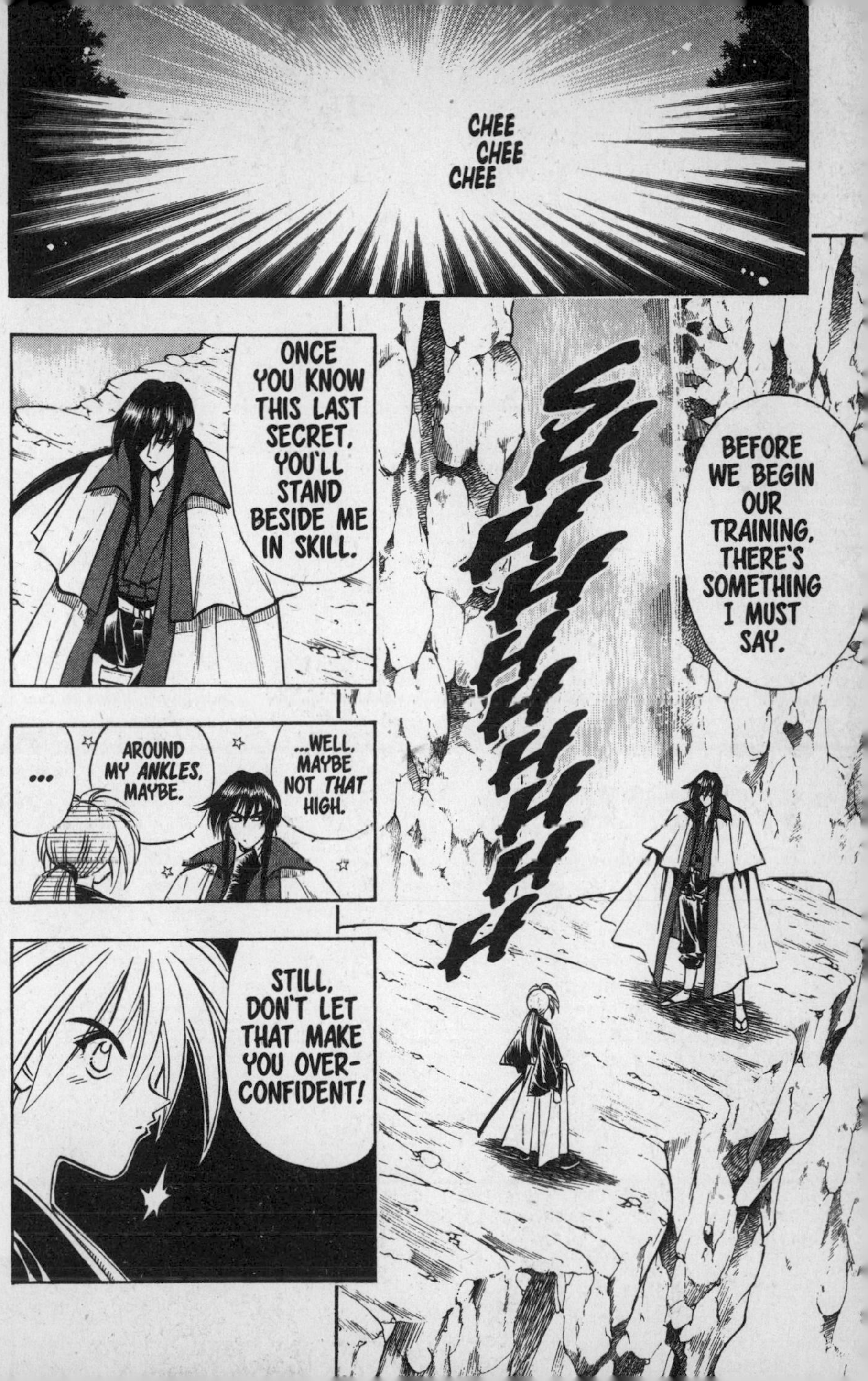
CHEE CHEE CHEE
BEFORE WE BEGIN OUR TRAINING, THERE'S SOMETHING I MUST SAY.
SHUHHHHHHHHH
ONCE YOU KNOW THIS LAST SECRET, YOU'LL STAND BESIDE ME IN SKILL.
...WELL, MAYBE NOT *THAT* HIGH.
AROUND MY *ANKLES*, MAYBE.
...
STILL, DON'T LET THAT MAKE YOU OVER-CONFIDENT!

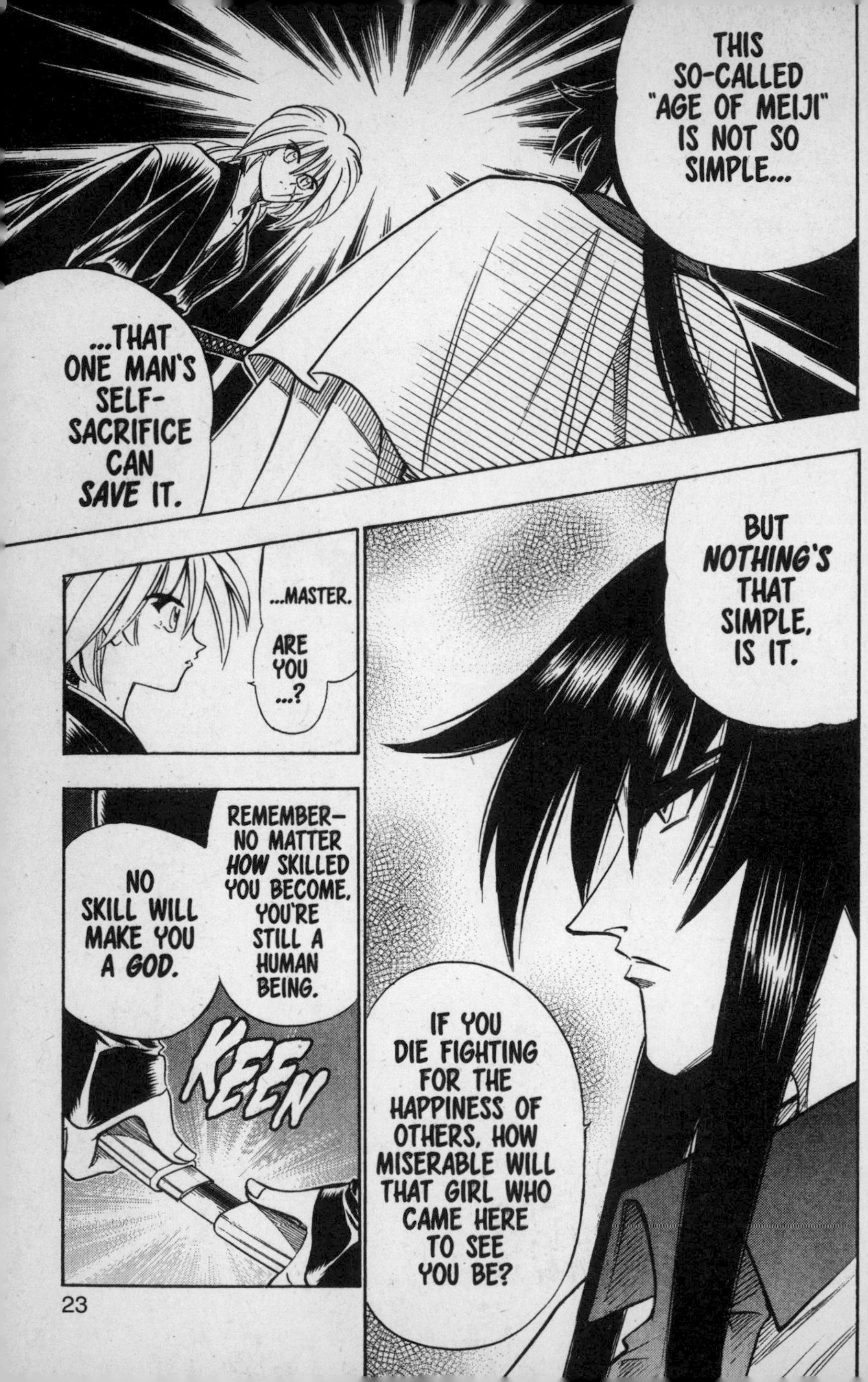
THIS SO-CALLED "AGE OF MEIJI" IS NOT SO SIMPLE...
...THAT ONE MAN'S SELF-SACRIFICE CAN *SAVE* IT.
BUT *NOTHING'S* THAT SIMPLE, IS IT.
IF YOU DIE FIGHTING FOR THE HAPPINESS OF OTHERS, HOW MISERABLE WILL THAT GIRL WHO CAME HERE TO SEE YOU BE?
...MASTER.
ARE YOU ...?
REMEMBER— NO MATTER *HOW* SKILLED YOU BECOME, YOU'RE STILL A HUMAN BEING.
NO SKILL WILL MAKE YOU A *GOD*.
KEEN

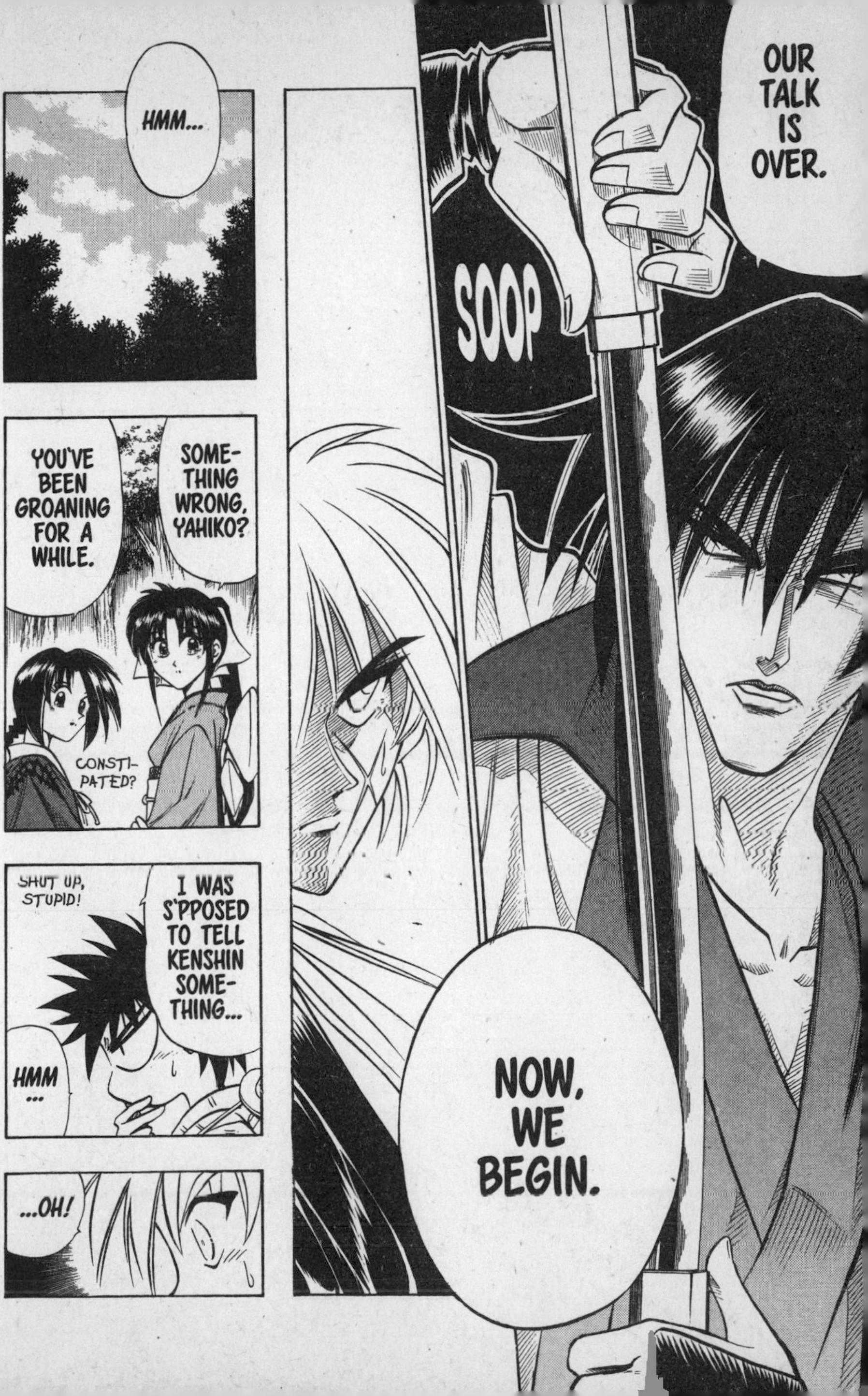
OUR TALK IS OVER.
SOOP
NOW, WE BEGIN.
HMM...
SOME-THING WRONG, YAHIKO?
YOU'VE BEEN GROANING FOR A WHILE.
CONSTI-PATED?
I WAS S'PPOSED TO TELL KENSHIN SOME-THING...
SHUT UP, STUPID!
HMM ...
...OH!

READ THIS WAY

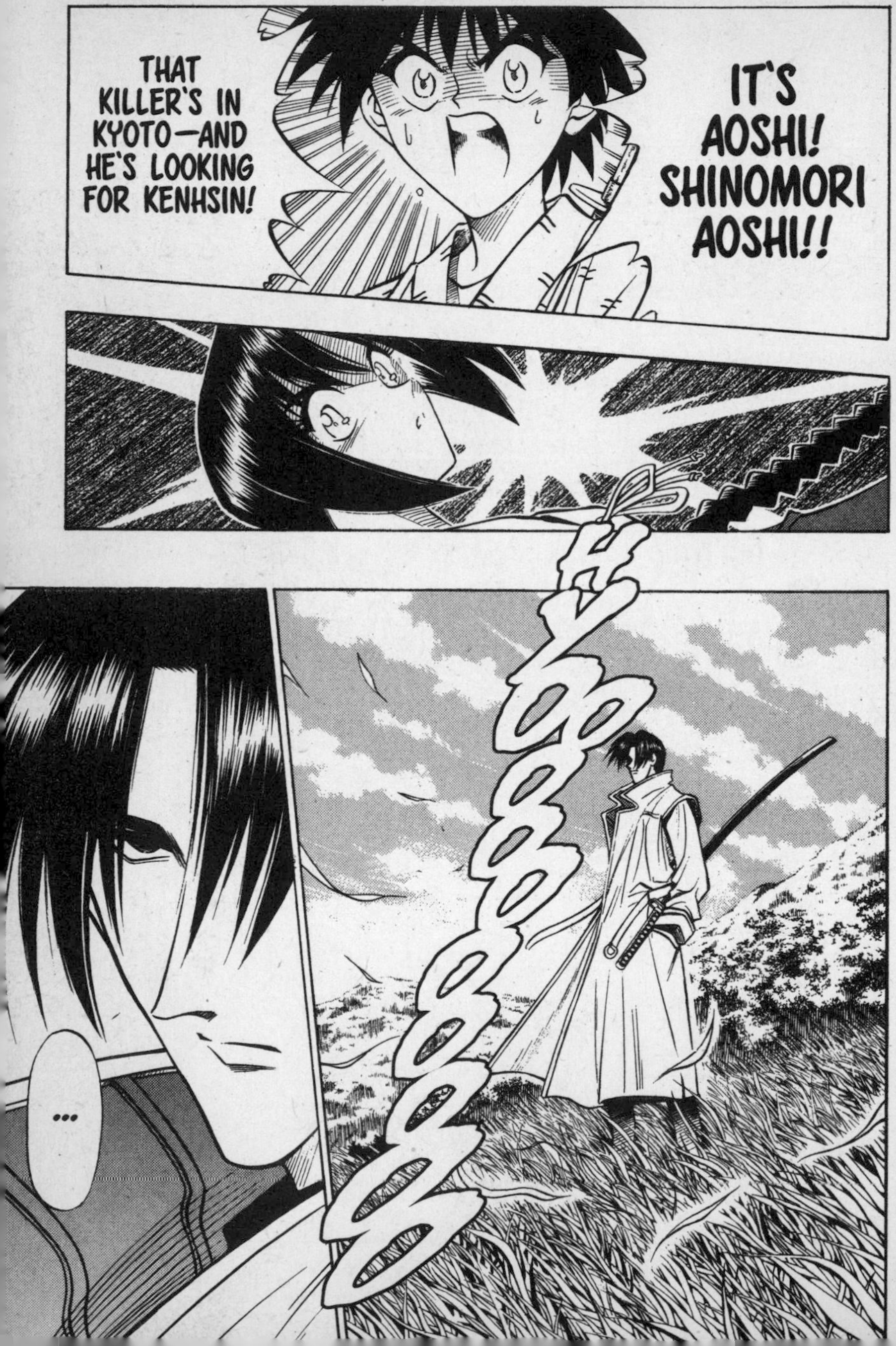

IT'S AOSHI! SHINOMORI AOSHI!!
THAT KILLER'S IN KYOTO—AND HE'S LOOKING FOR KENHSIN!
HYOOOOOOOOOOOSH
...

Rurouni Kenshin

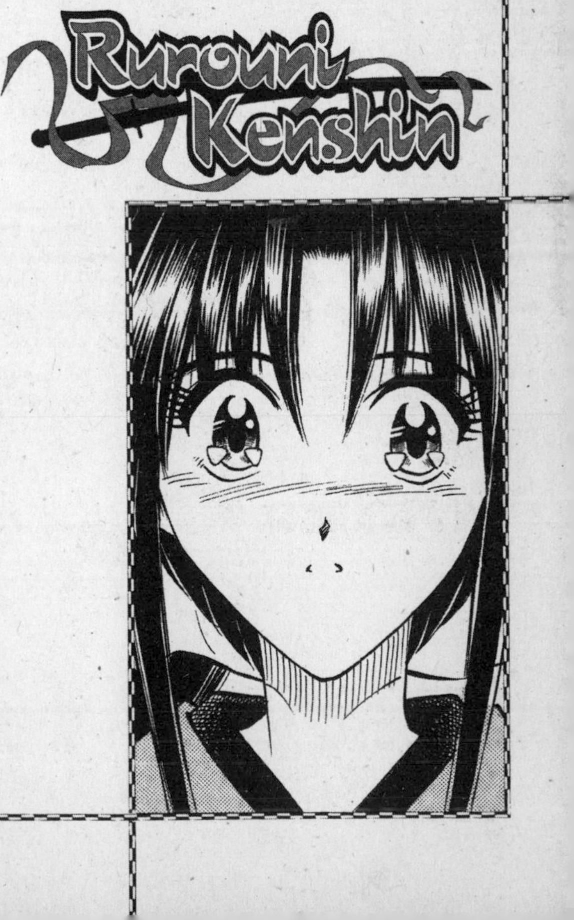

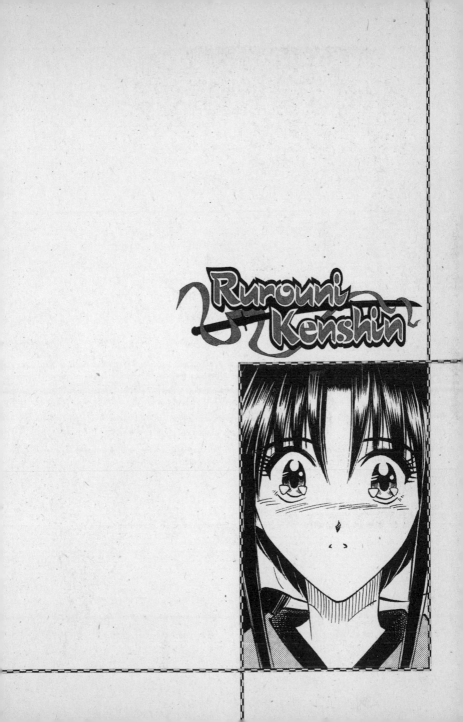

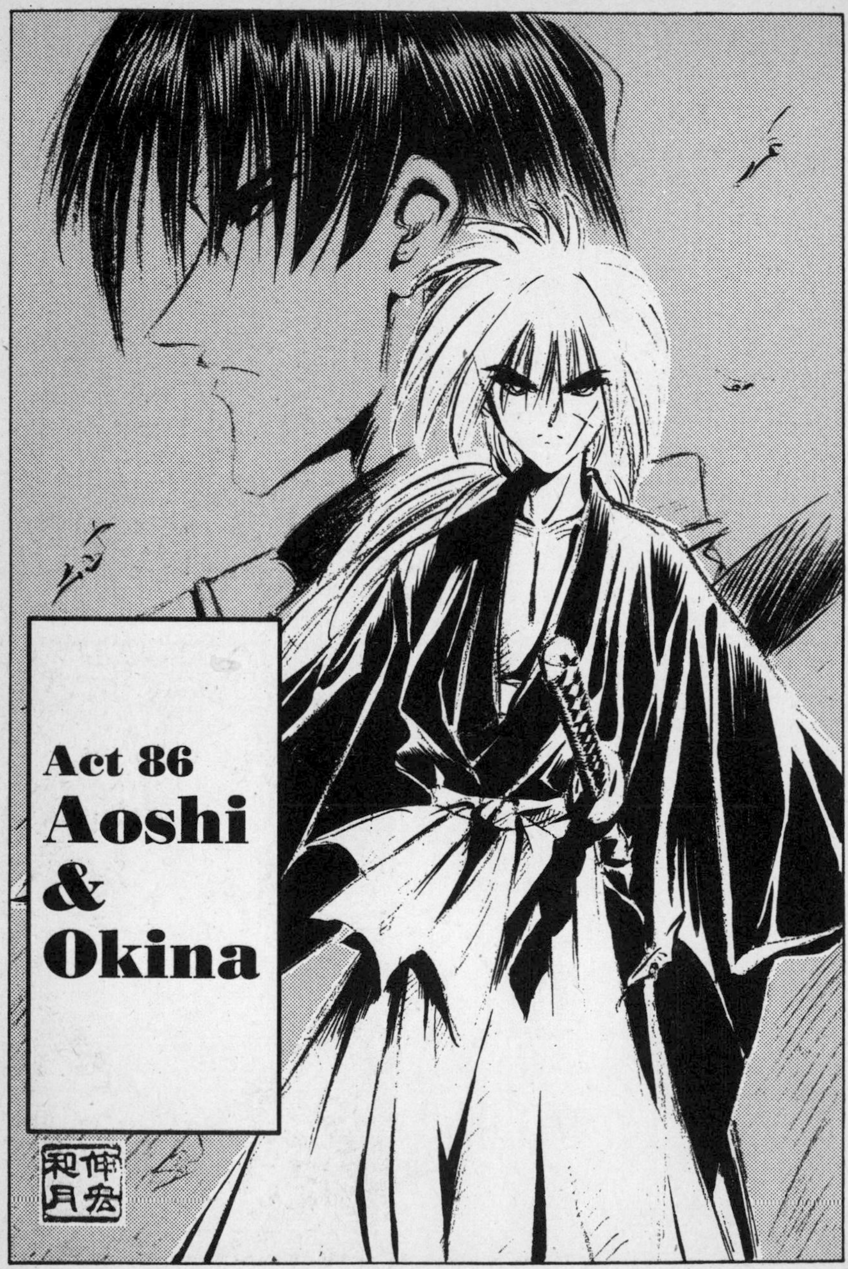
Act 86
Aoshi
&
Okina

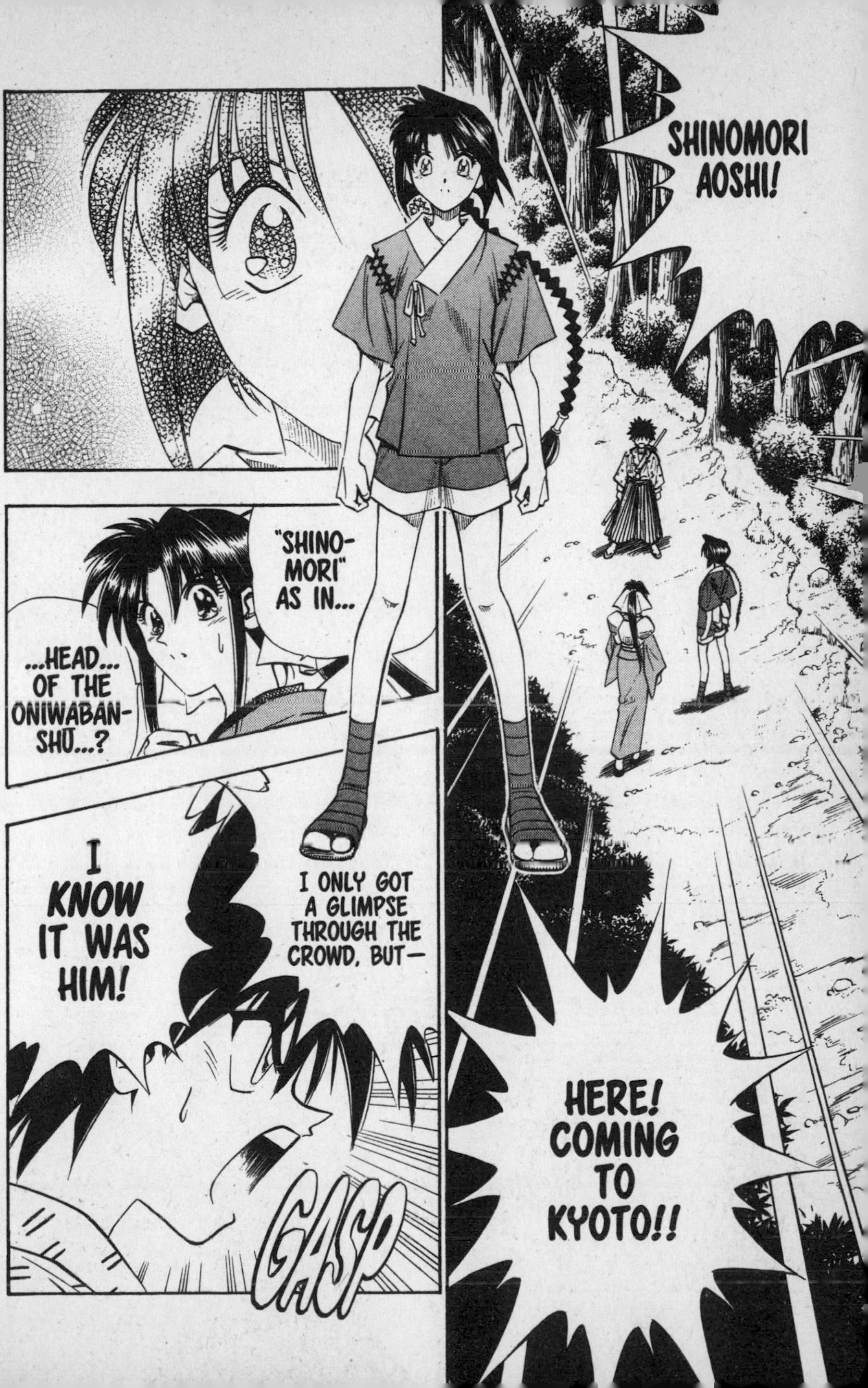
SHINOMORI AOSHI!
HERE! COMING TO KYOTO!!
"SHINOMORI" AS IN...
...HEAD... OF THE ONIWABANSHU...?
I ONLY GOT A GLIMPSE THROUGH THE CROWD, BUT—
I KNOW IT WAS HIM!
GASP

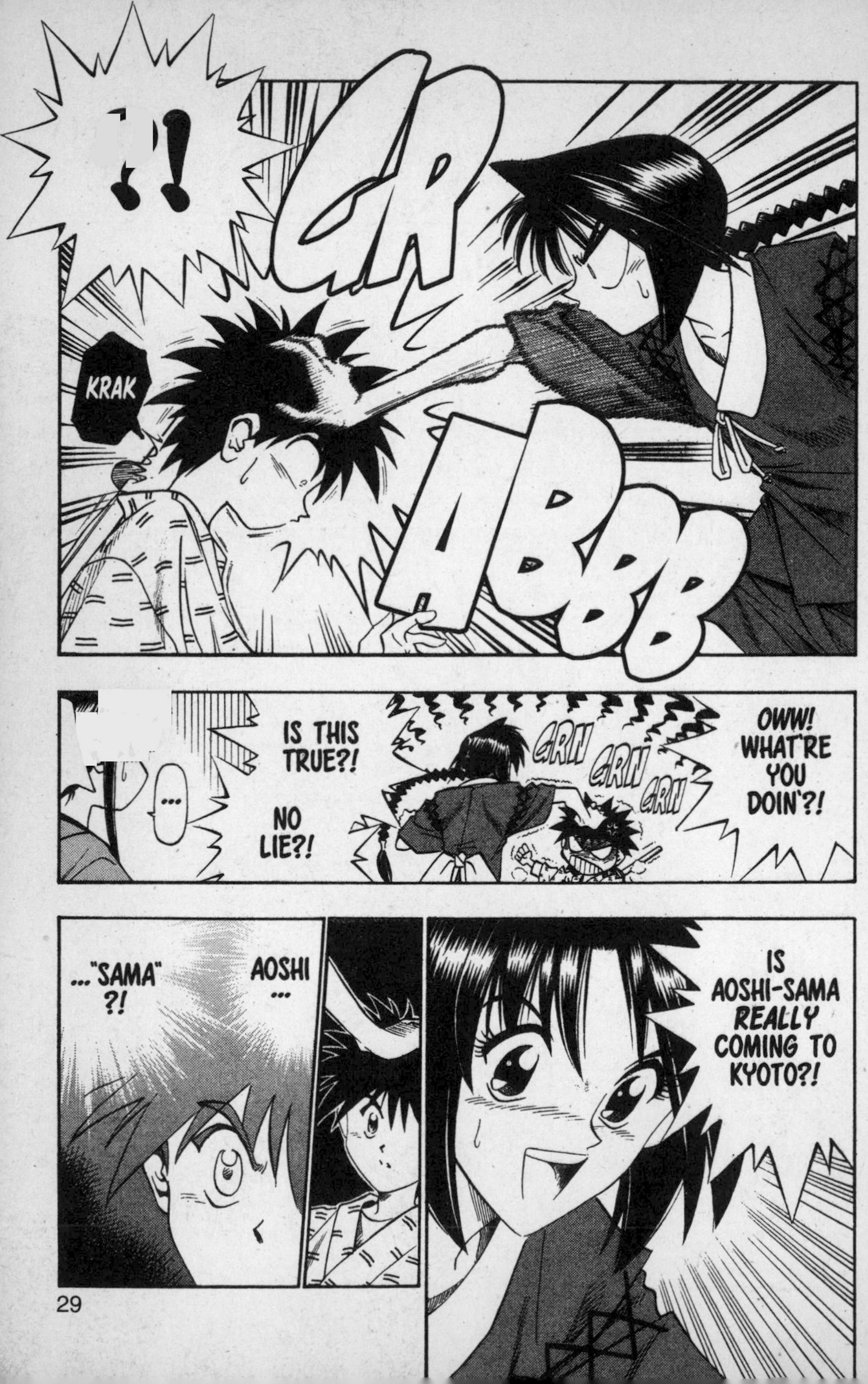
?!
GR
ABBB
KRAK
OWW! WHAT'RE YOU DOIN'?!
GRN
GRN
GRN
IS THIS TRUE?!
NO LIE?!
...
IS AOSHI-SAMA REALLY COMING TO KYOTO?!
AOSHI ...
..."SAMA" ?!

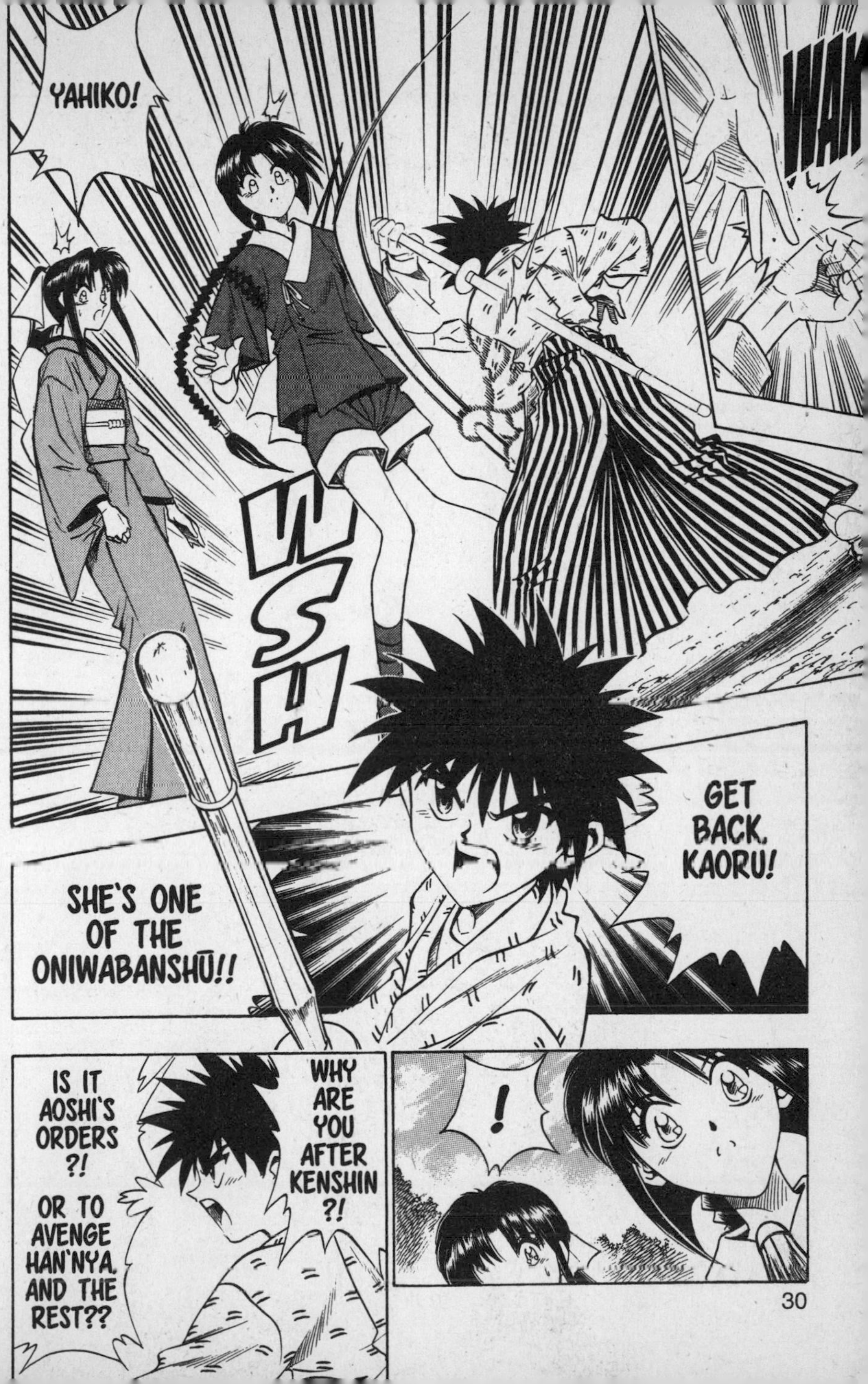
WAK
YAHIKO!
WSSH
GET BACK, KAORU!
SHE'S ONE OF THE ONIWABANSHŪ!!
!
WHY ARE YOU AFTER KENSHIN?!
IS IT AOSHI'S ORDERS?!
OR TO AVENGE HAN'NYA AND THE REST??

READ THIS WAY

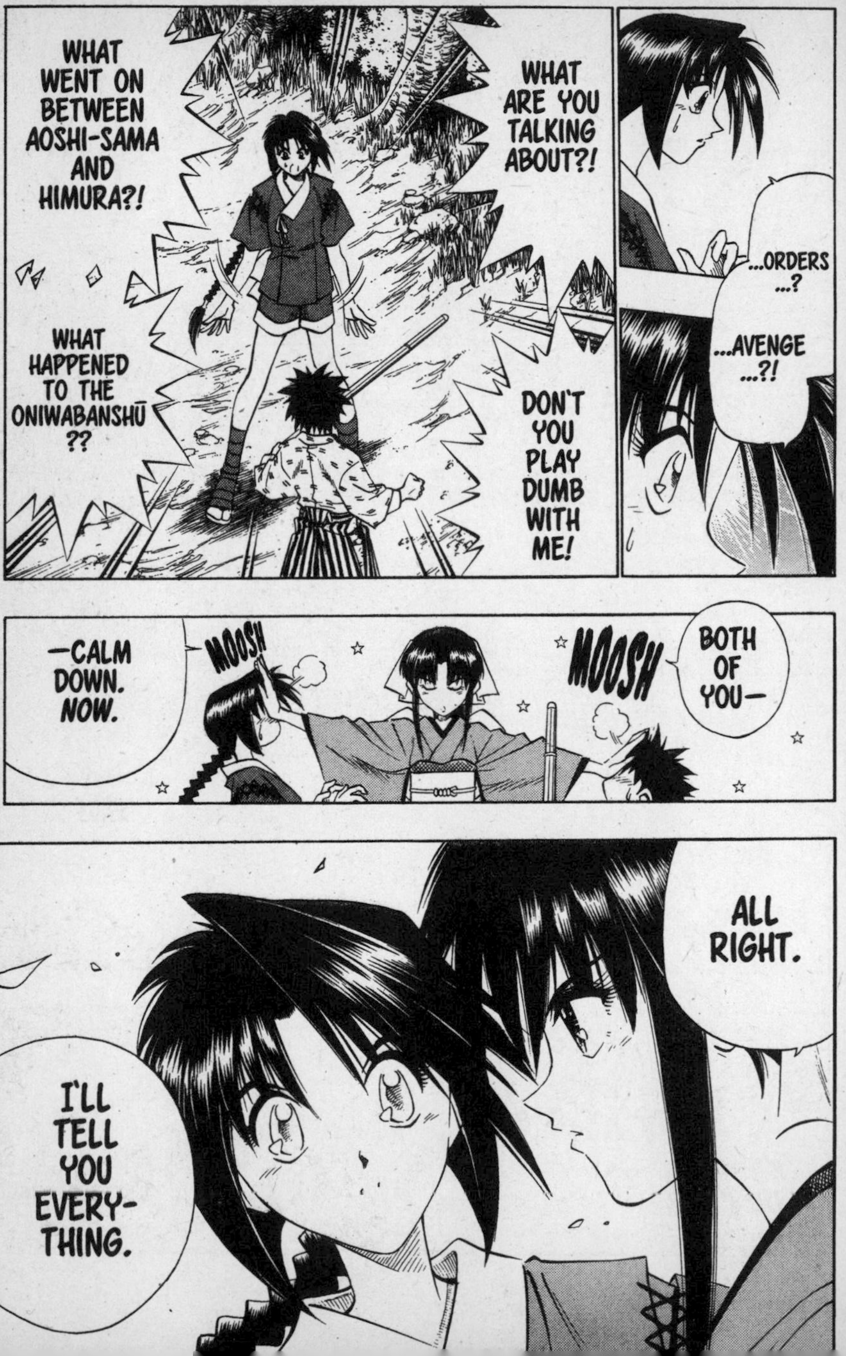
...ORDERS ...?
...AVENGE ...?!
WHAT ARE YOU TALKING ABOUT?!
WHAT WENT ON BETWEEN AOSHI-SAMA AND HIMURA?!
DON'T YOU PLAY DUMB WITH ME!
WHAT HAPPENED TO THE ONIWABANSHŪ??
BOTH OF YOU—
MOOSH
MOOSH
—CALM DOWN. NOW.
ALL RIGHT.
I'LL TELL YOU EVERYTHING.

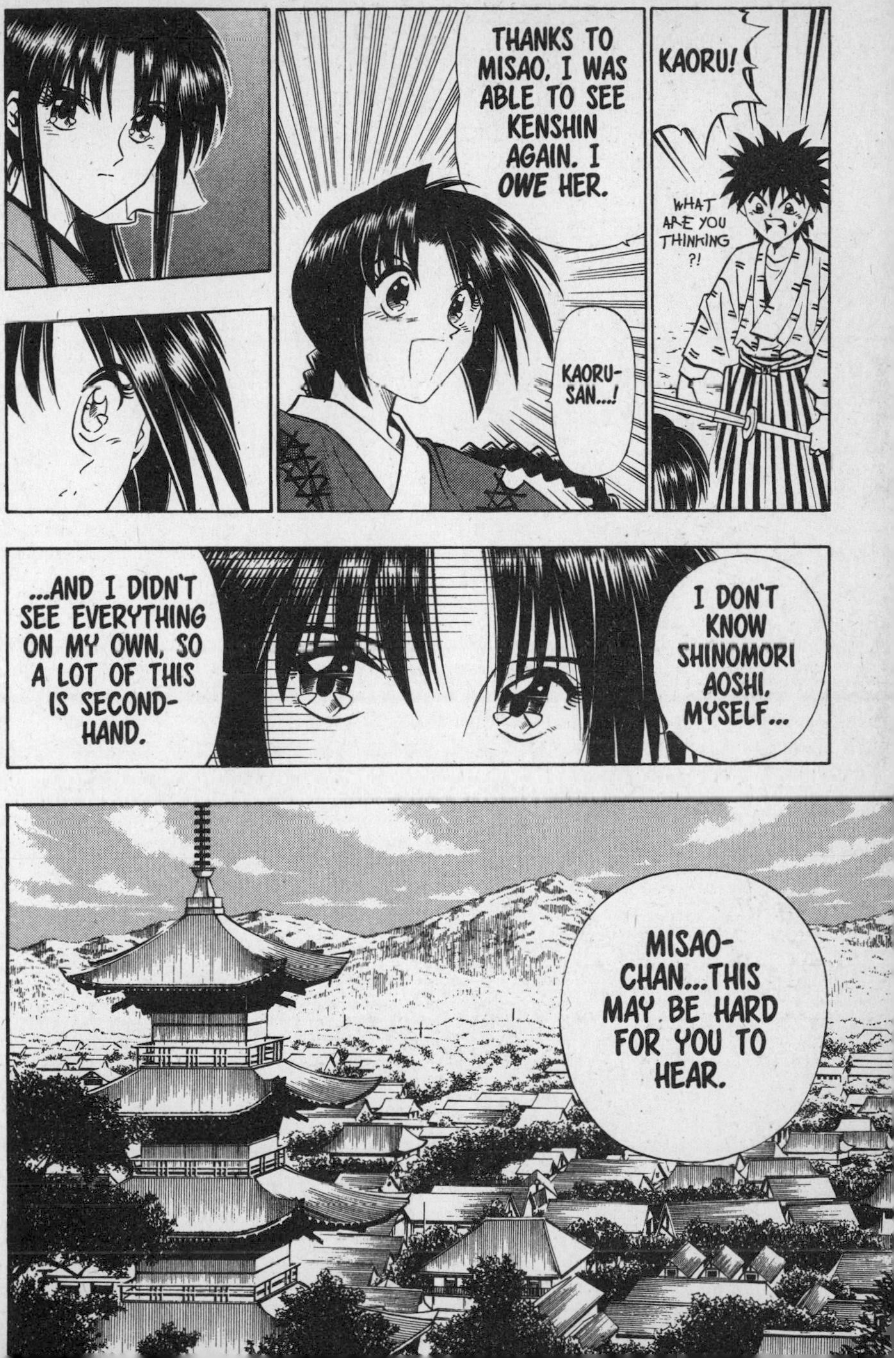
KAORU!
WHAT ARE YOU THINKING ?!
THANKS TO MISAO, I WAS ABLE TO SEE KENSHIN AGAIN. I OWE HER.
KAORU-SAN...!
I DON'T KNOW SHINOMORI AOSHI, MYSELF...
...AND I DIDN'T SEE EVERYTHING ON MY OWN, SO A LOT OF THIS IS SECOND-HAND.
MISAO-CHAN...THIS MAY BE HARD FOR YOU TO HEAR.

READ THIS WAY

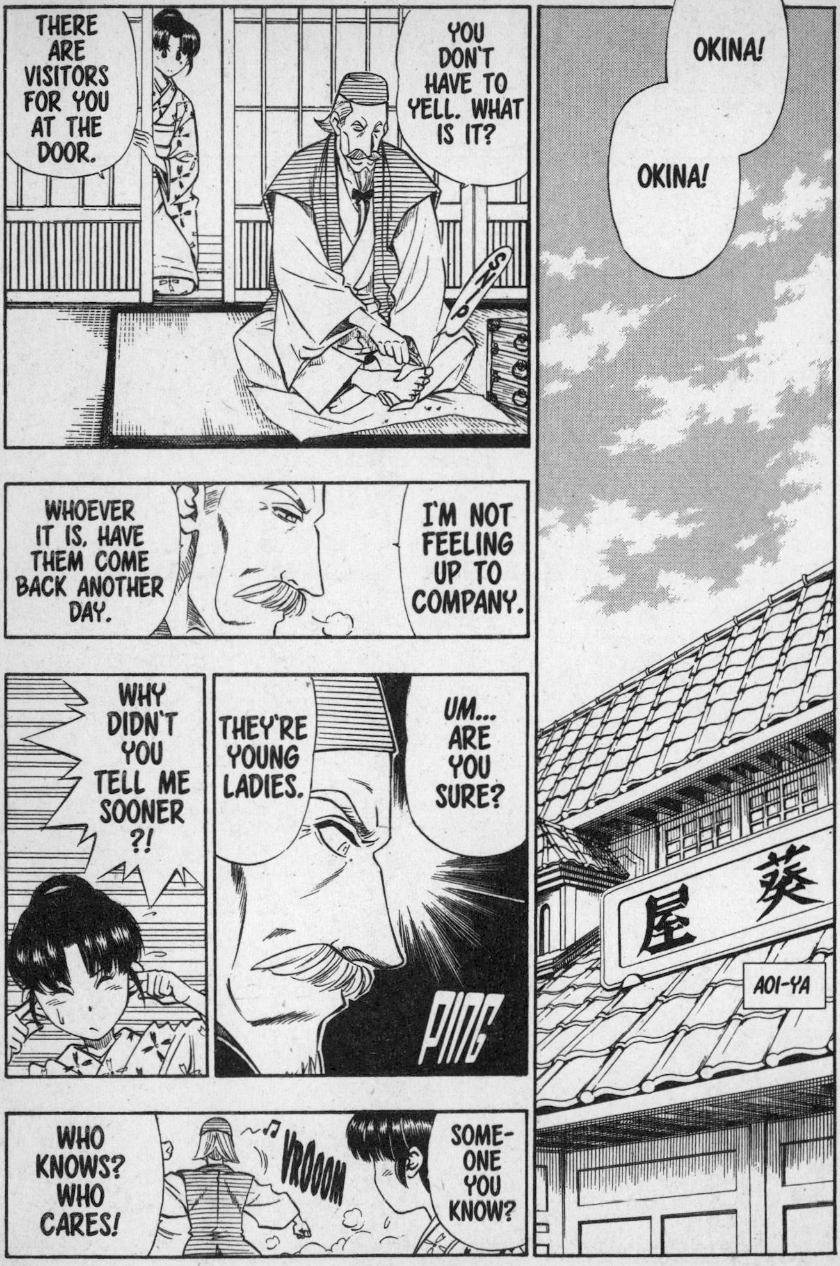

OKINA!
OKINA!
葵屋
AOI-YA
YOU DON'T HAVE TO YELL. WHAT IS IT?
THERE ARE VISITORS FOR YOU AT THE DOOR.
SNIP
I'M NOT FEELING UP TO COMPANY.
WHOEVER IT IS, HAVE THEM COME BACK ANOTHER DAY.
UM... ARE YOU SURE?
THEY'RE YOUNG LADIES.
PING
WHY DIDN'T YOU TELL ME SOONER?!
SOME-ONE YOU KNOW?
VROOOM
WHO KNOWS? WHO CARES!

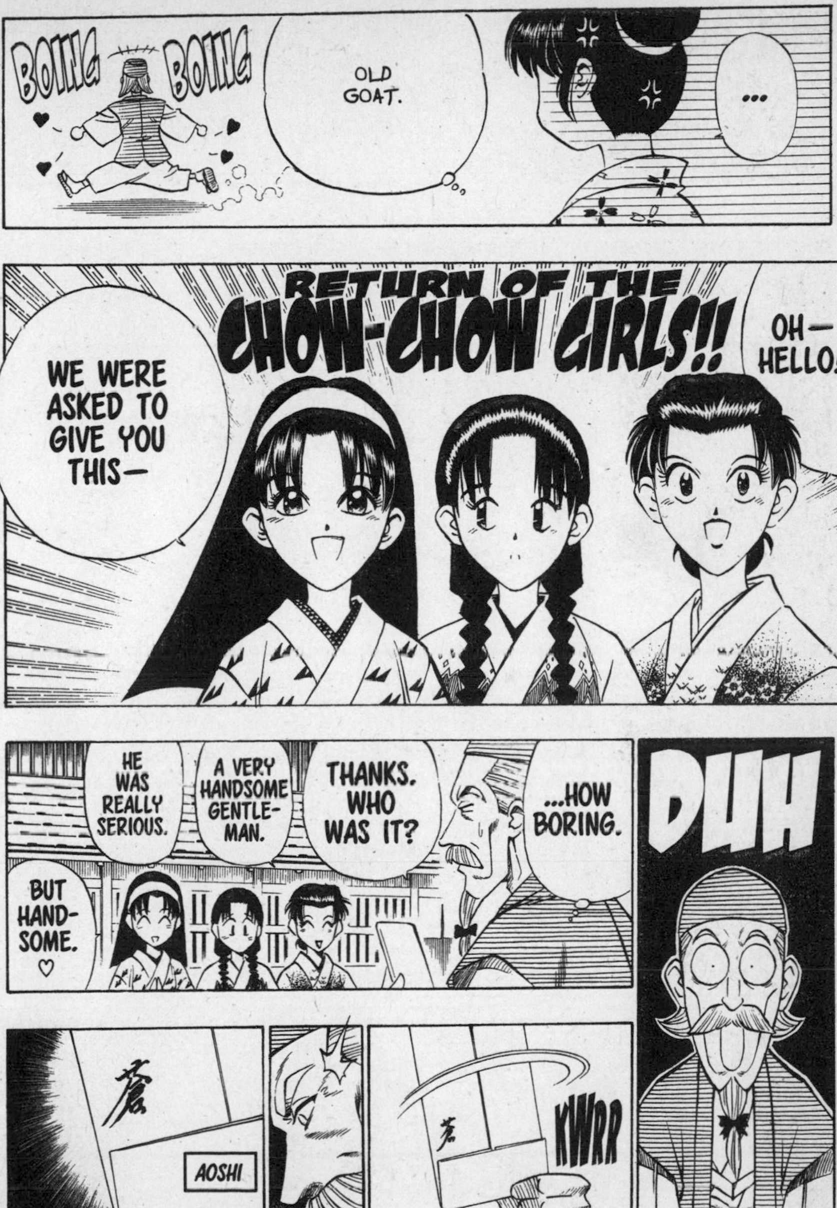
...
OLD GOAT.
BOING BOING
OH— HELLO!
RETURN OF THE CHOW-CHOW GIRLS!!
WE WERE ASKED TO GIVE YOU THIS—
DUH
...HOW BORING.
THANKS. WHO WAS IT?
A VERY HANDSOME GENTLEMAN.
HE WAS REALLY SERIOUS.
BUT HANDSOME. ♡
KWRR
蒼
蒼
AOSHI

READ THIS WAY

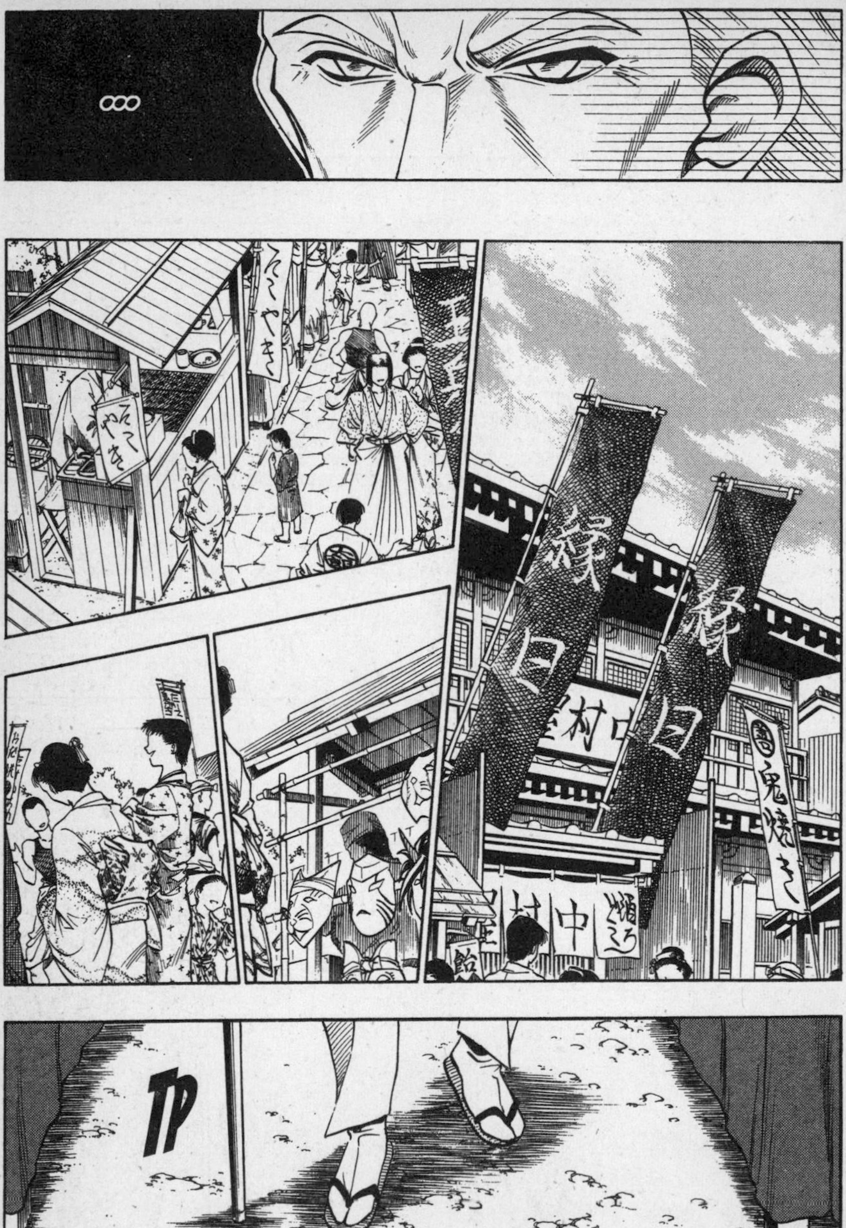
...
縁日
縁日
鬼焼き
TP

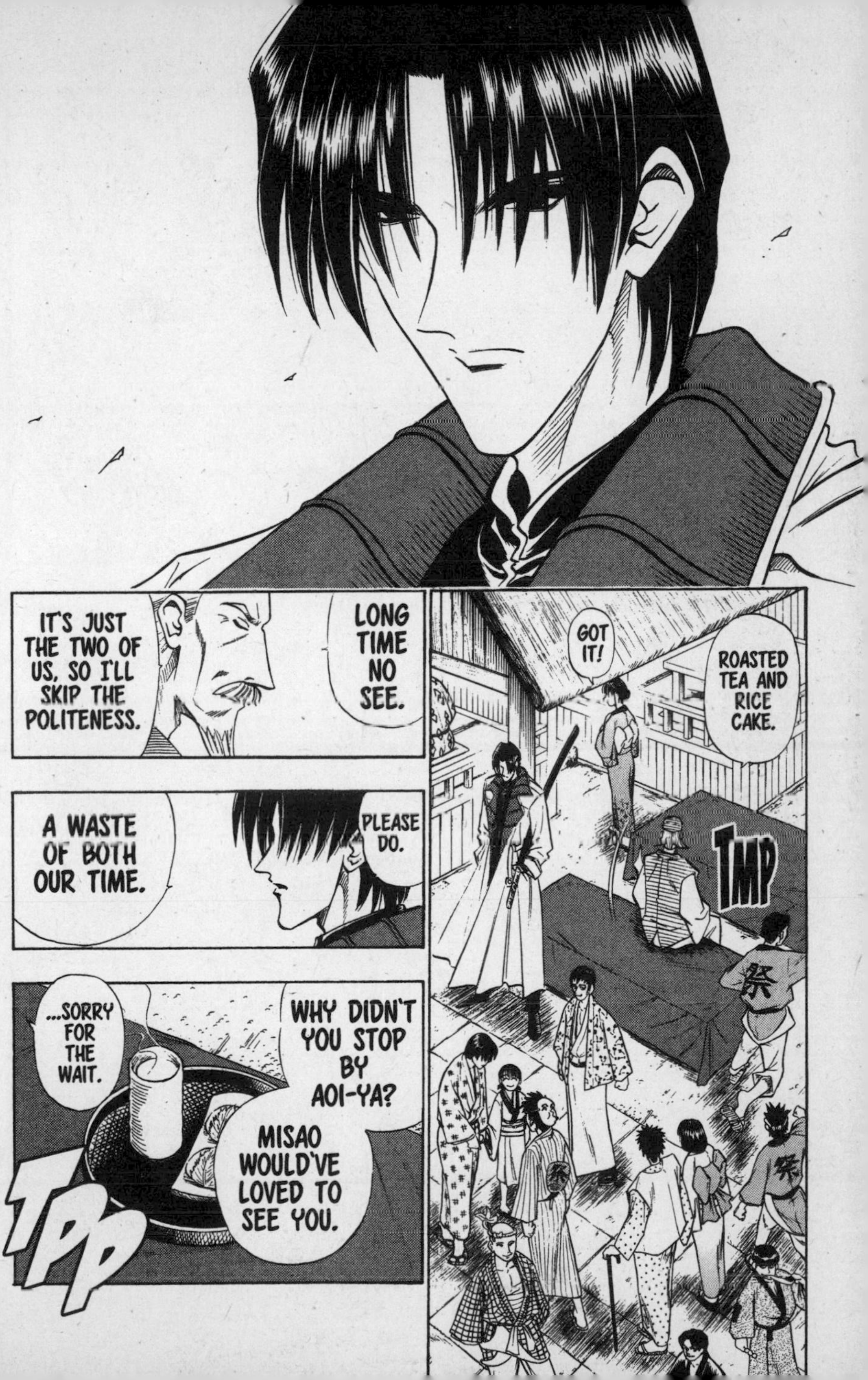
ROASTED TEA AND RICE CAKE.
GOT IT!
TMP
LONG TIME NO SEE.
IT'S JUST THE TWO OF US, SO I'LL SKIP THE POLITENESS.
PLEASE DO.
A WASTE OF BOTH OUR TIME.
WHY DIDN'T YOU STOP BY AOI-YA?
MISAO WOULD'VE LOVED TO SEE YOU.
...SORRY FOR THE WAIT.
TPP

READ THIS WAY

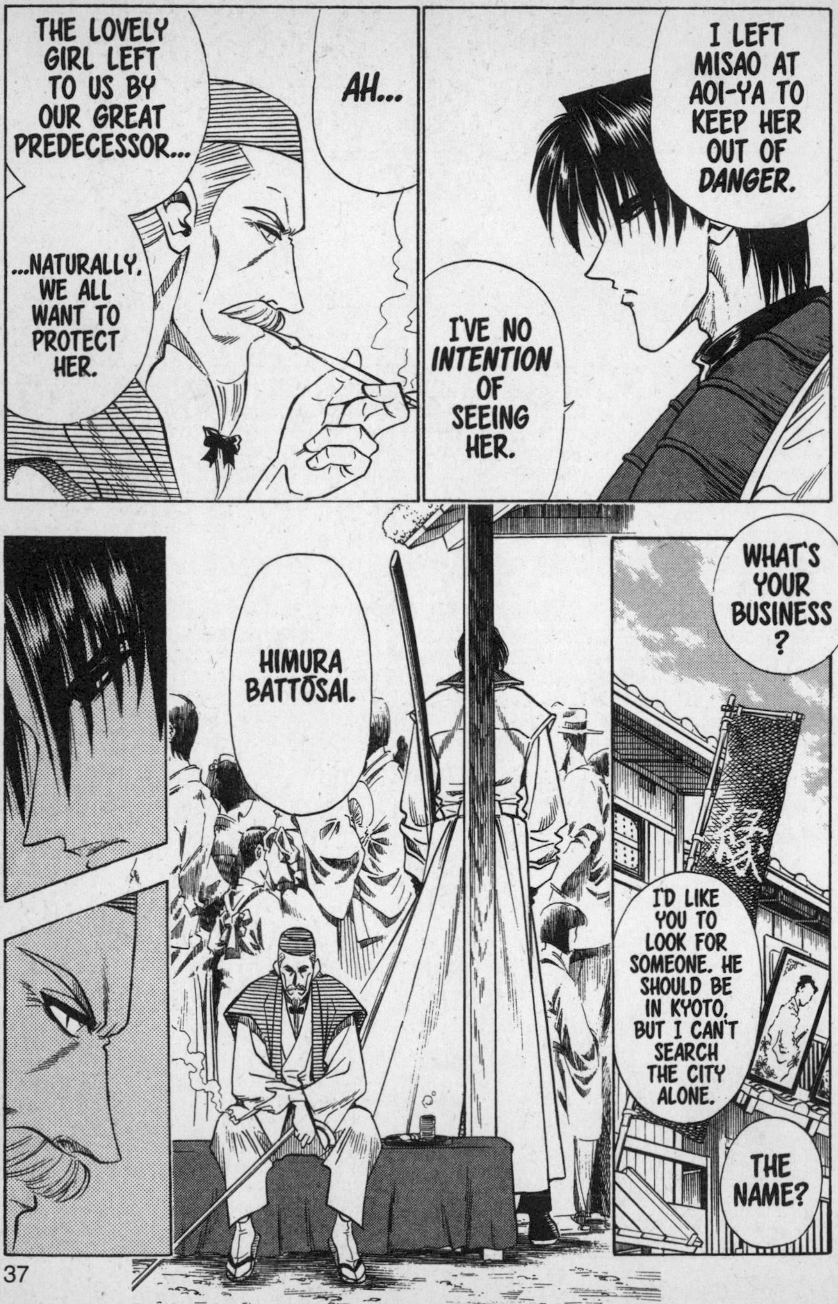

I LEFT MISAO AT AOI-YA TO KEEP HER OUT OF DANGER.
I'VE NO INTENTION OF SEEING HER.
AH...
THE LOVELY GIRL LEFT TO US BY OUR GREAT PREDECESSOR...
...NATURALLY, WE ALL WANT TO PROTECT HER.
WHAT'S YOUR BUSINESS?
I'D LIKE YOU TO LOOK FOR SOMEONE. HE SHOULD BE IN KYOTO, BUT I CAN'T SEARCH THE CITY ALONE.
THE NAME?
HIMURA BATTŌSAI.

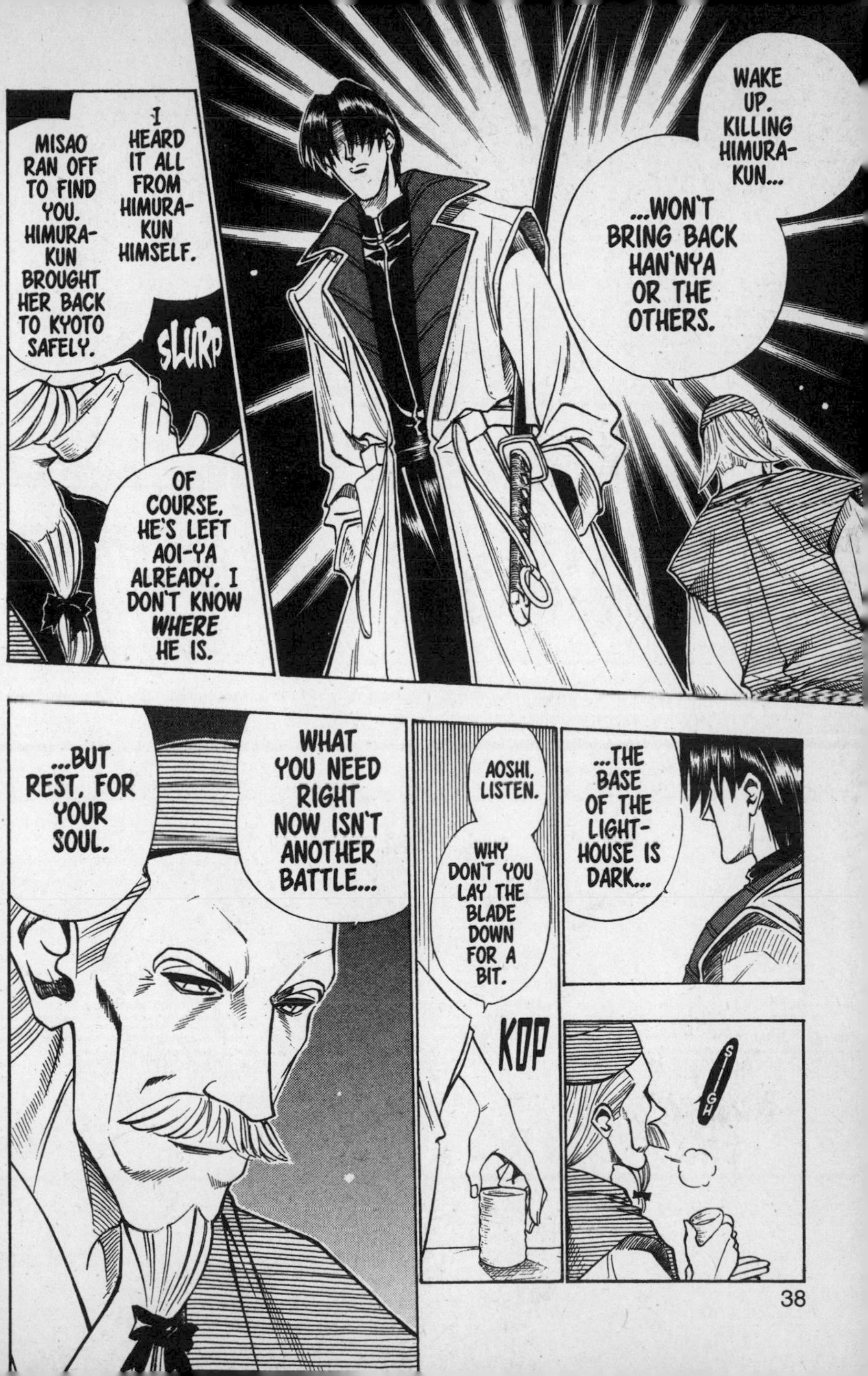
WAKE UP. KILLING HIMURA-KUN...
...WON'T BRING BACK HAN'NYA OR THE OTHERS.
I HEARD IT ALL FROM HIMURA-KUN HIMSELF.
MISAO RAN OFF TO FIND YOU. HIMURA-KUN BROUGHT HER BACK TO KYOTO SAFELY.
SLURP
OF COURSE, HE'S LEFT AOI-YA ALREADY. I DON'T KNOW *WHERE* HE IS.
...THE BASE OF THE LIGHT-HOUSE IS DARK...
SIGH
AOSHI, LISTEN.
WHY DON'T YOU LAY THE BLADE DOWN FOR A BIT.
KOP
WHAT YOU NEED RIGHT NOW ISN'T ANOTHER BATTLE...
...BUT REST, FOR YOUR SOUL.

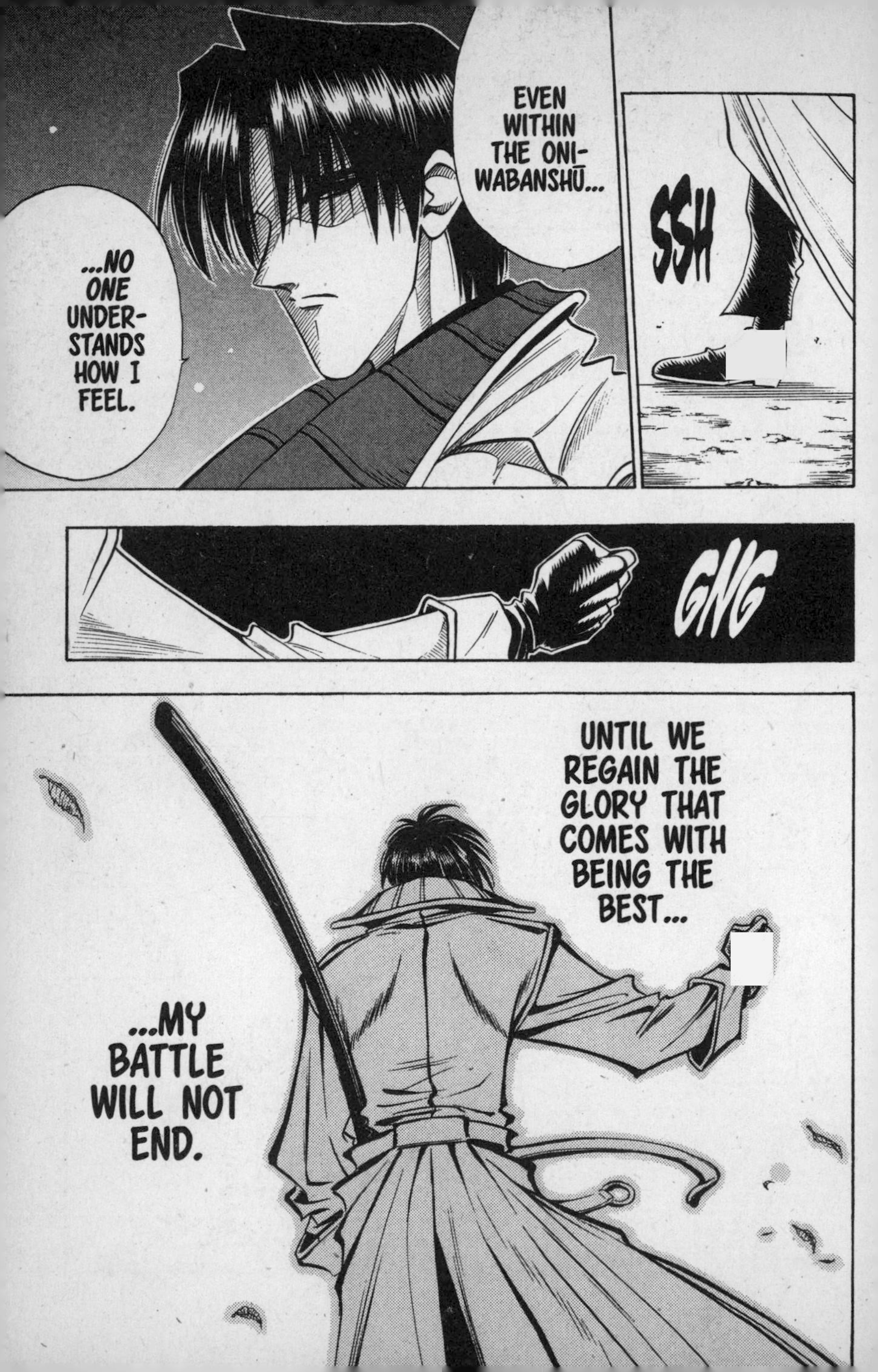
SSH
EVEN WITHIN THE ONI-WABANSHŪ...
...NO ONE UNDER-STANDS HOW I FEEL.
GNG
UNTIL WE REGAIN THE GLORY THAT COMES WITH BEING THE BEST...
...MY BATTLE WILL NOT END.

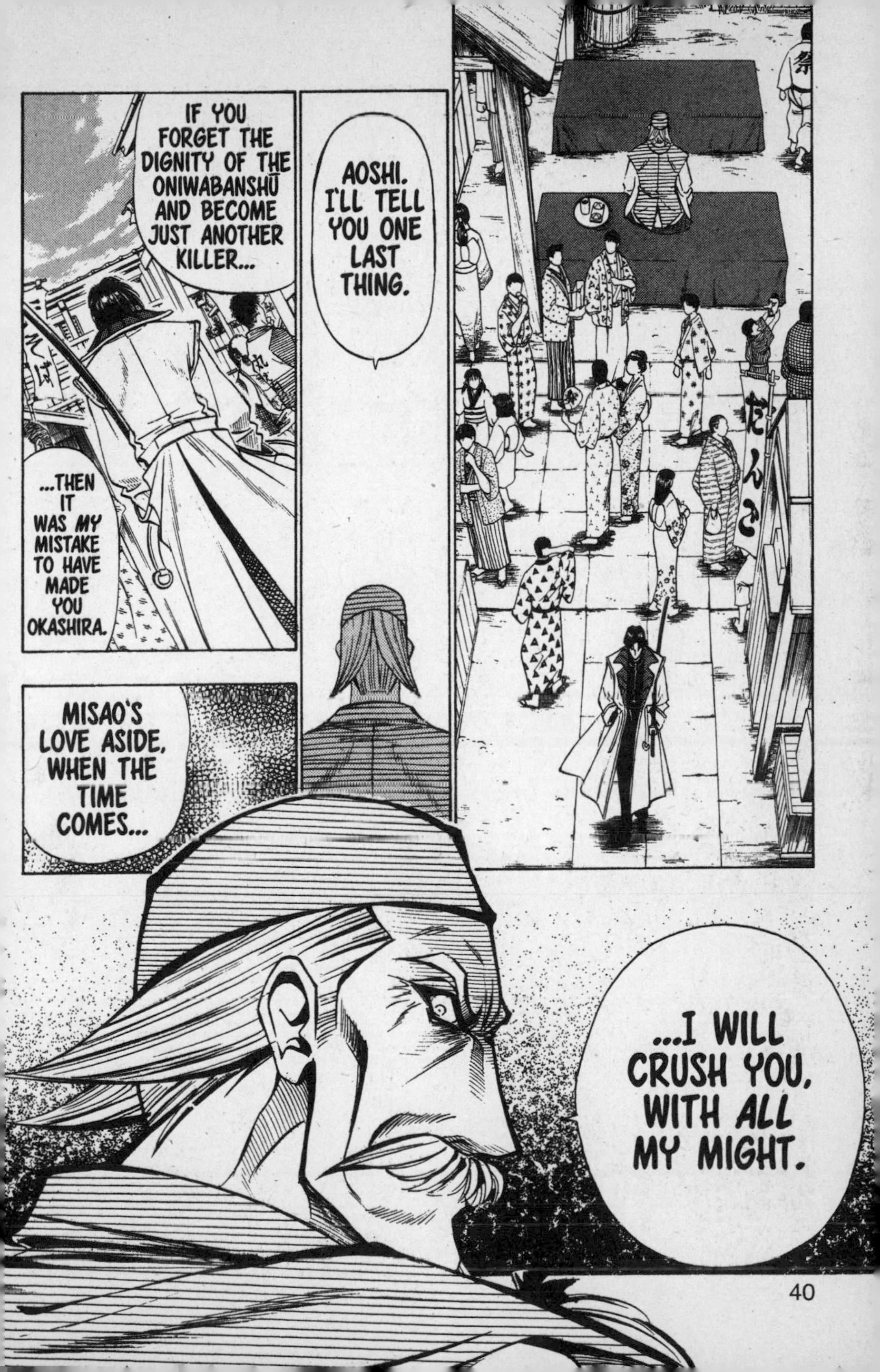
AOSHI. I'LL TELL YOU ONE LAST THING.
IF YOU FORGET THE DIGNITY OF THE ONIWABANSHŪ AND BECOME JUST ANOTHER KILLER...
...THEN IT WAS *MY* MISTAKE TO HAVE MADE YOU OKASHIRA.
MISAO'S LOVE ASIDE, WHEN THE TIME COMES...
...I WILL CRUSH YOU, WITH *ALL* MY MIGHT.

READ THIS WAY

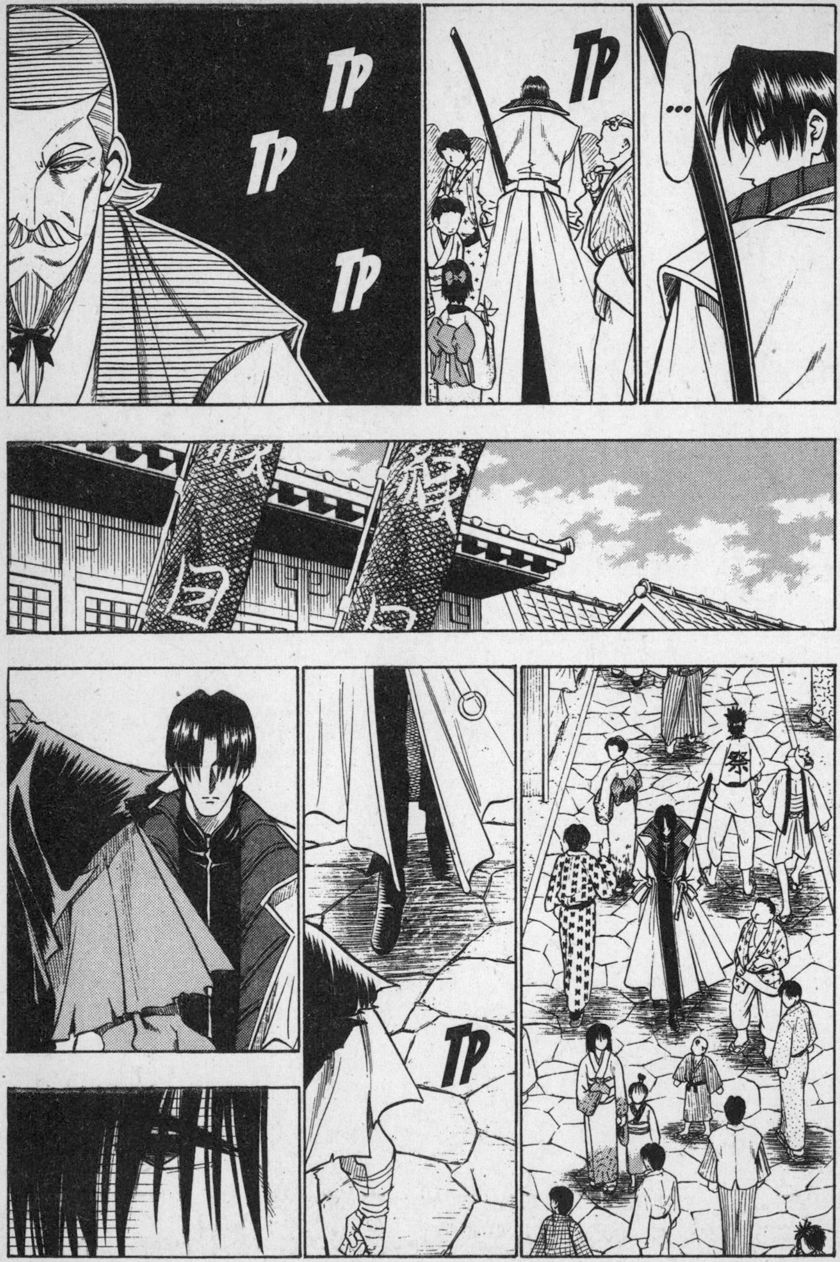
...
TP
TP
TP
TP
TP

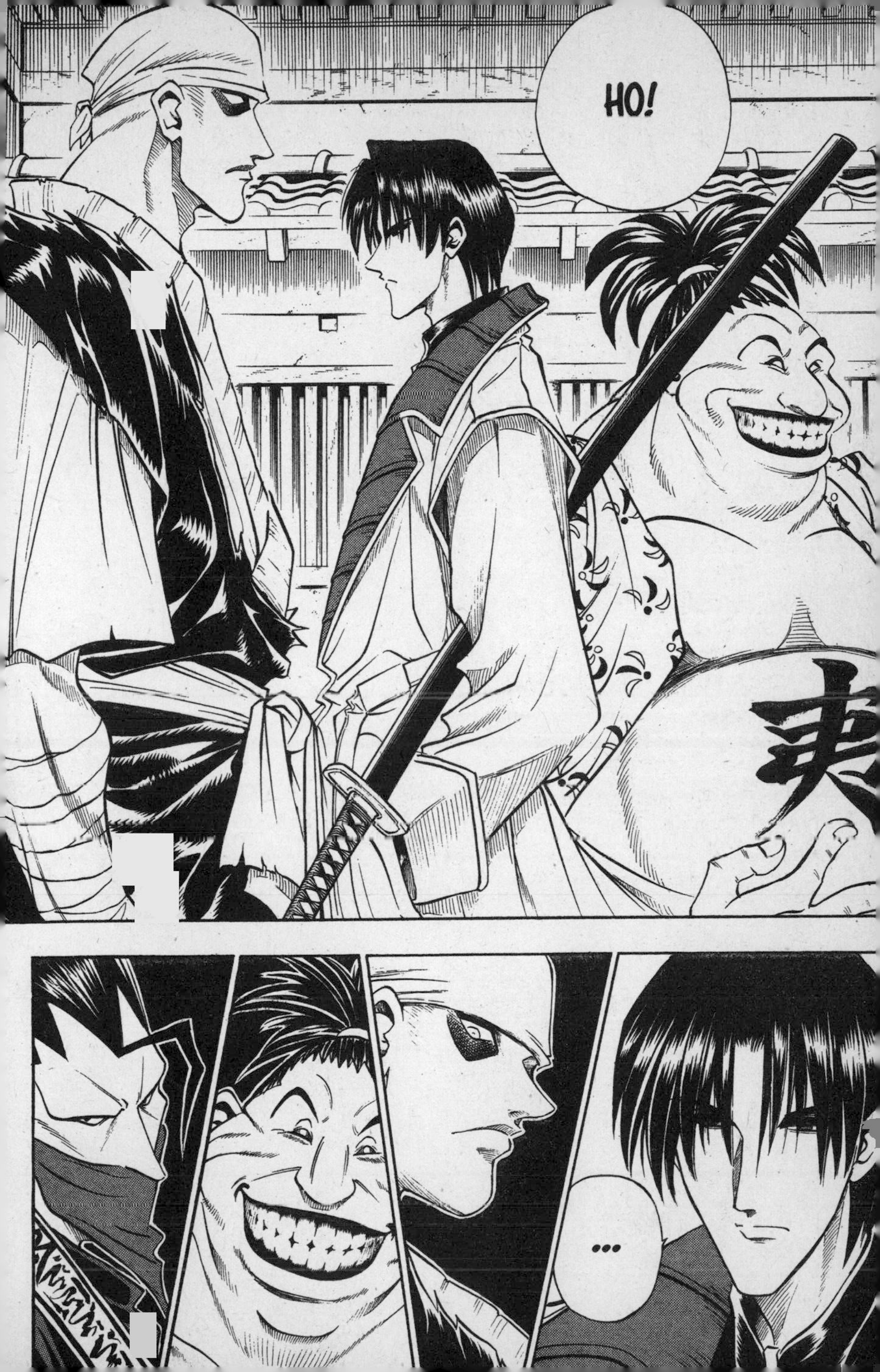
HO!
...

READ THIS WAY

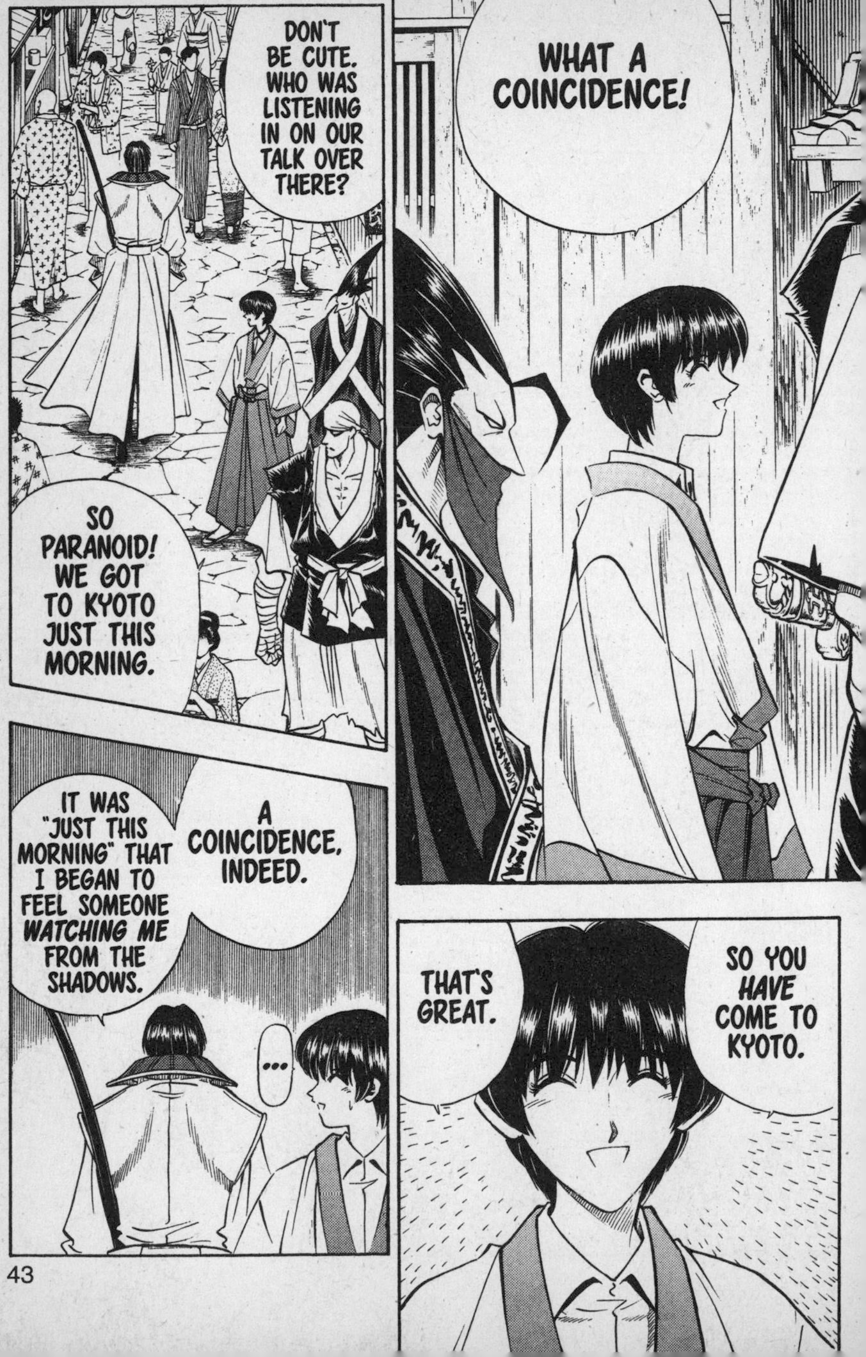
WHAT A COINCIDENCE!
DON'T BE CUTE. WHO WAS LISTENING IN ON OUR TALK OVER THERE?
SO PARANOID! WE GOT TO KYOTO JUST THIS MORNING.
A COINCIDENCE, INDEED.
IT WAS "JUST THIS MORNING" THAT I BEGAN TO FEEL SOMEONE *WATCHING ME* FROM THE SHADOWS.
...
SO YOU *HAVE* COME TO KYOTO.
THAT'S GREAT.

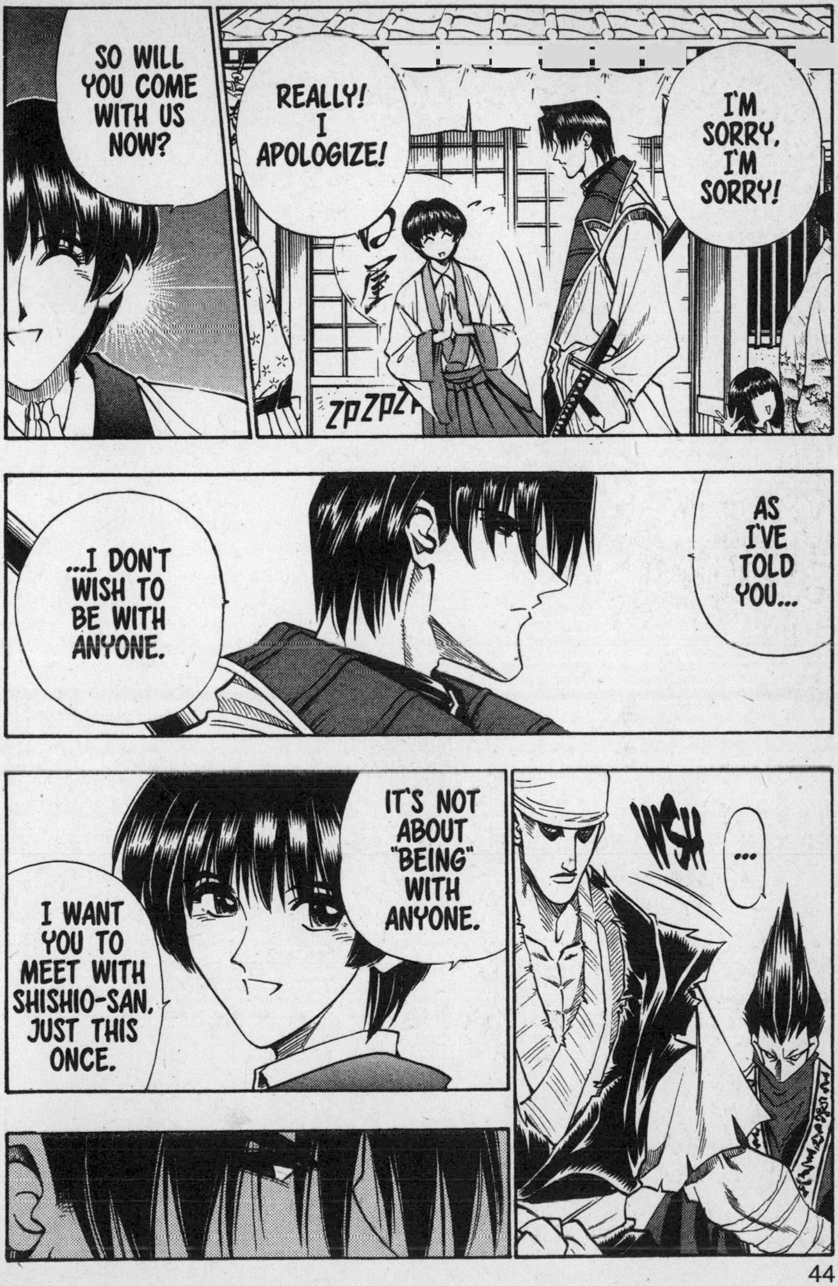
I'M SORRY, I'M SORRY!
REALLY! I APOLOGIZE!
ZPZPZ
SO WILL YOU COME WITH US NOW?
AS I'VE TOLD YOU...
...I DON'T WISH TO BE WITH ANYONE.
...
WSH
IT'S NOT ABOUT "BEING" WITH ANYONE.
I WANT YOU TO MEET WITH SHISHIO-SAN, JUST THIS ONCE.

READ THIS WAY

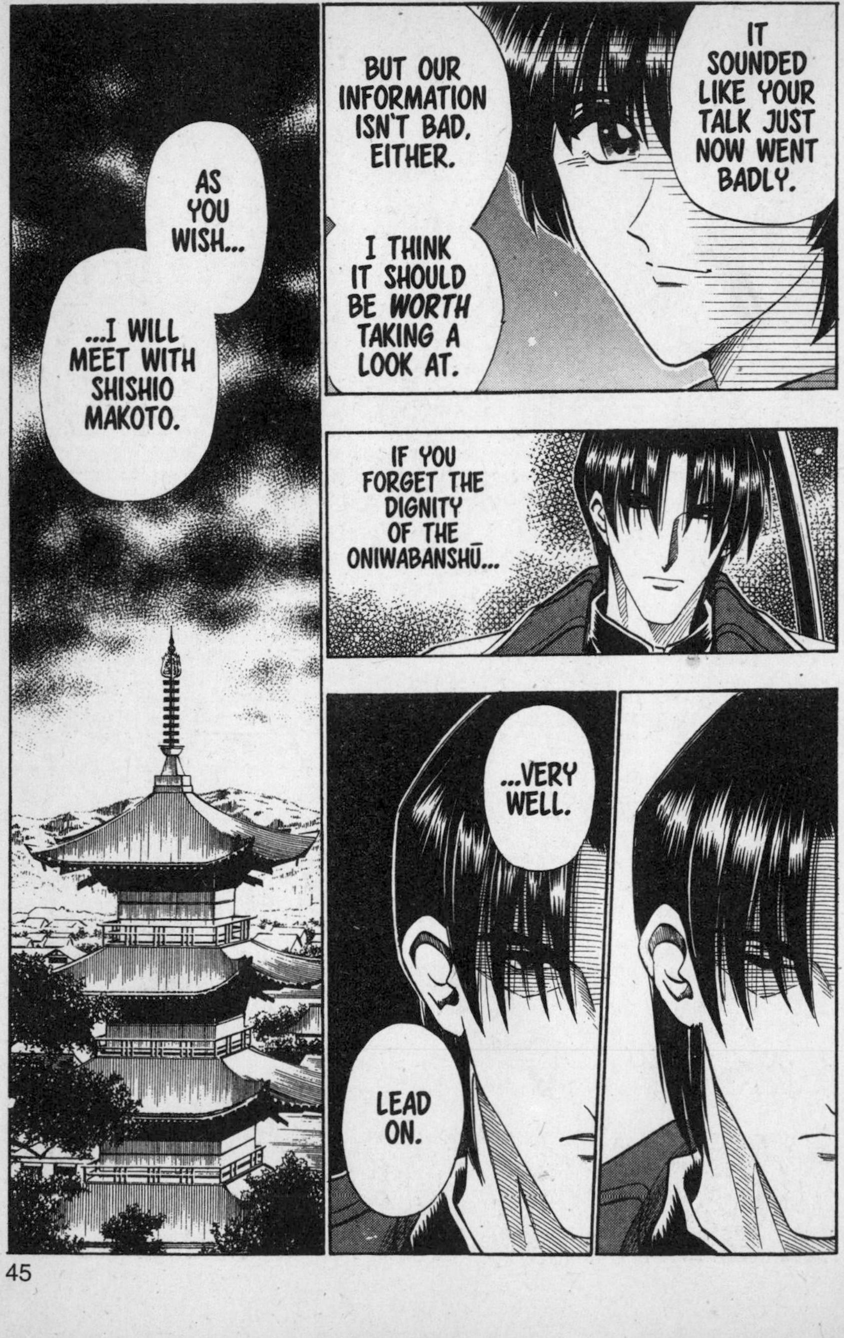
IT SOUNDED LIKE YOUR TALK JUST NOW WENT BADLY.
BUT OUR INFORMATION ISN'T BAD, EITHER.
I THINK IT SHOULD BE *WORTH* TAKING A LOOK AT.
IF YOU FORGET THE DIGNITY OF THE ONIWABANSHŪ...
...VERY WELL.
LEAD ON.
AS YOU WISH...
...I WILL MEET WITH SHISHIO MAKOTO.

Rurouni Kenshin

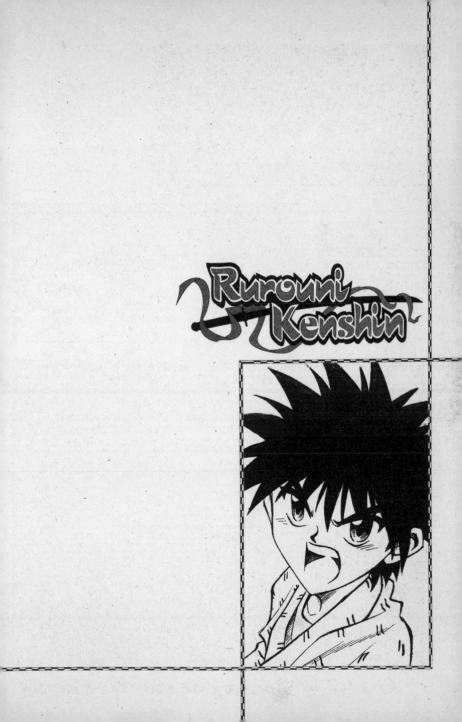

FROM THE CITY OF KYOTO, UNDER THE SKIES TO THE NORTHEAST, PAST THE "DEMON GATE"...

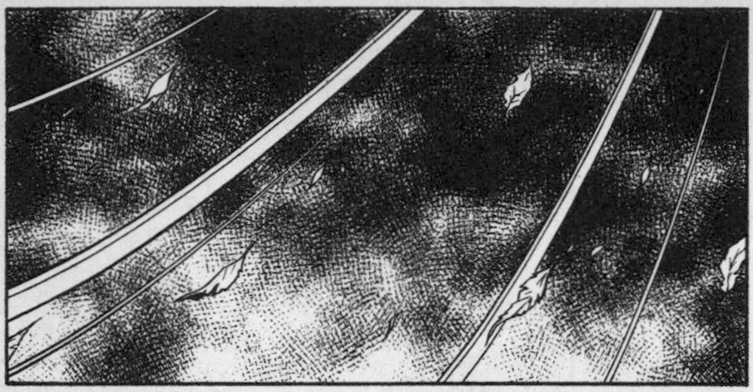

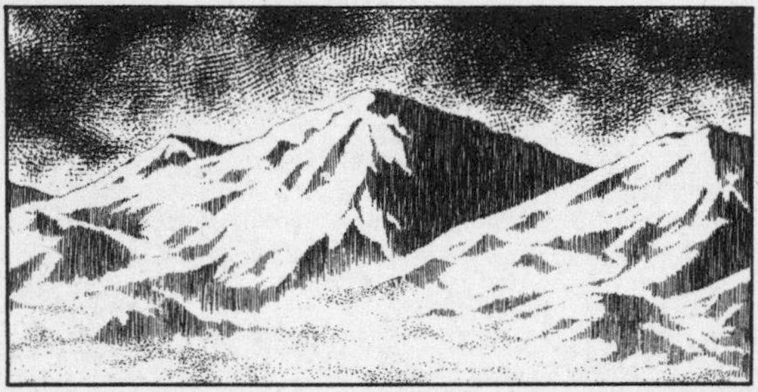

...STANDS MT. HIEI, LEGENDARY AS A SPIRITUAL SITE. AND ON ONE SHOULDER OF IT...

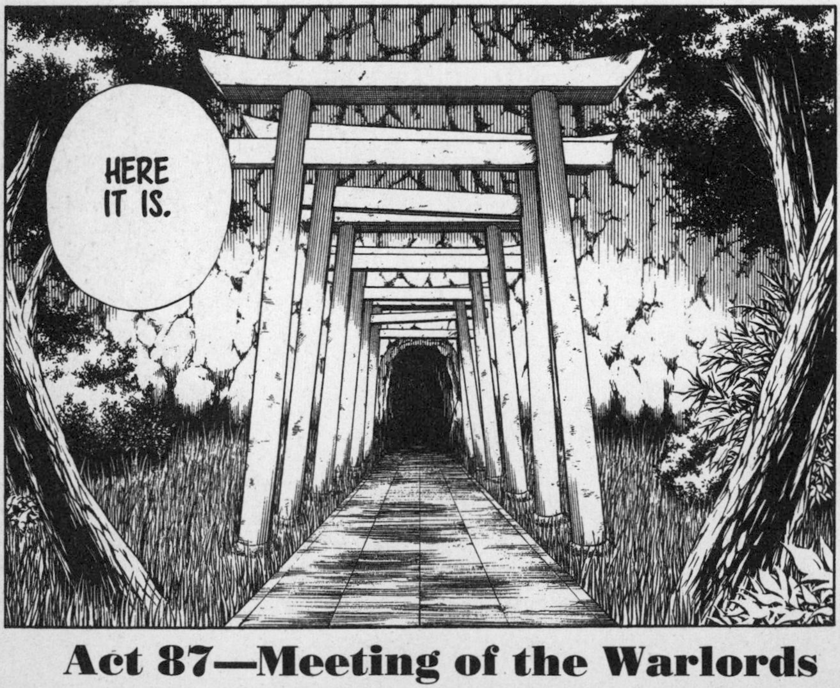
HERE IT IS.

Act 87—Meeting of the Warlords

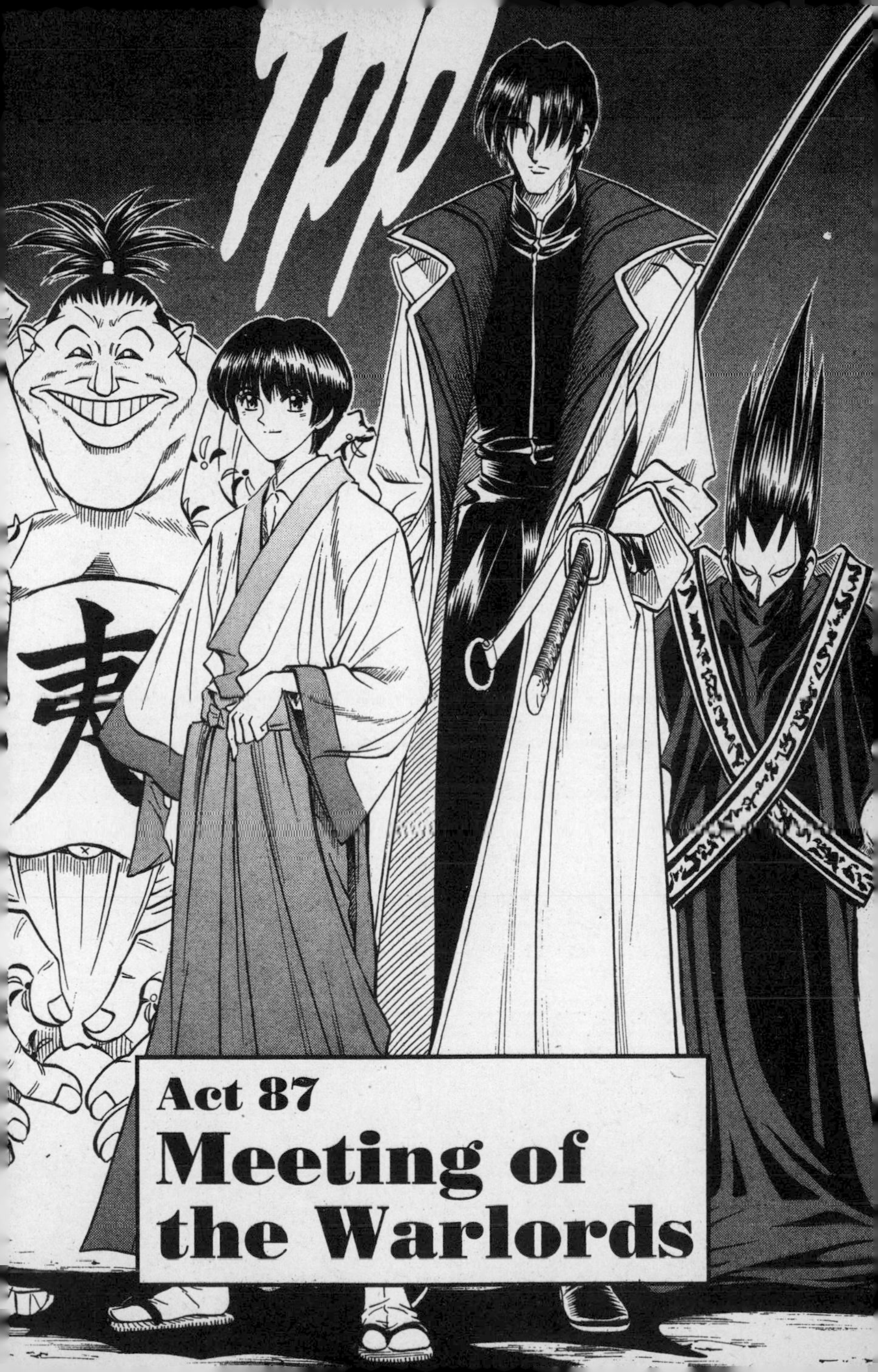
Act 87
Meeting of the Warlords

READ THIS WAY

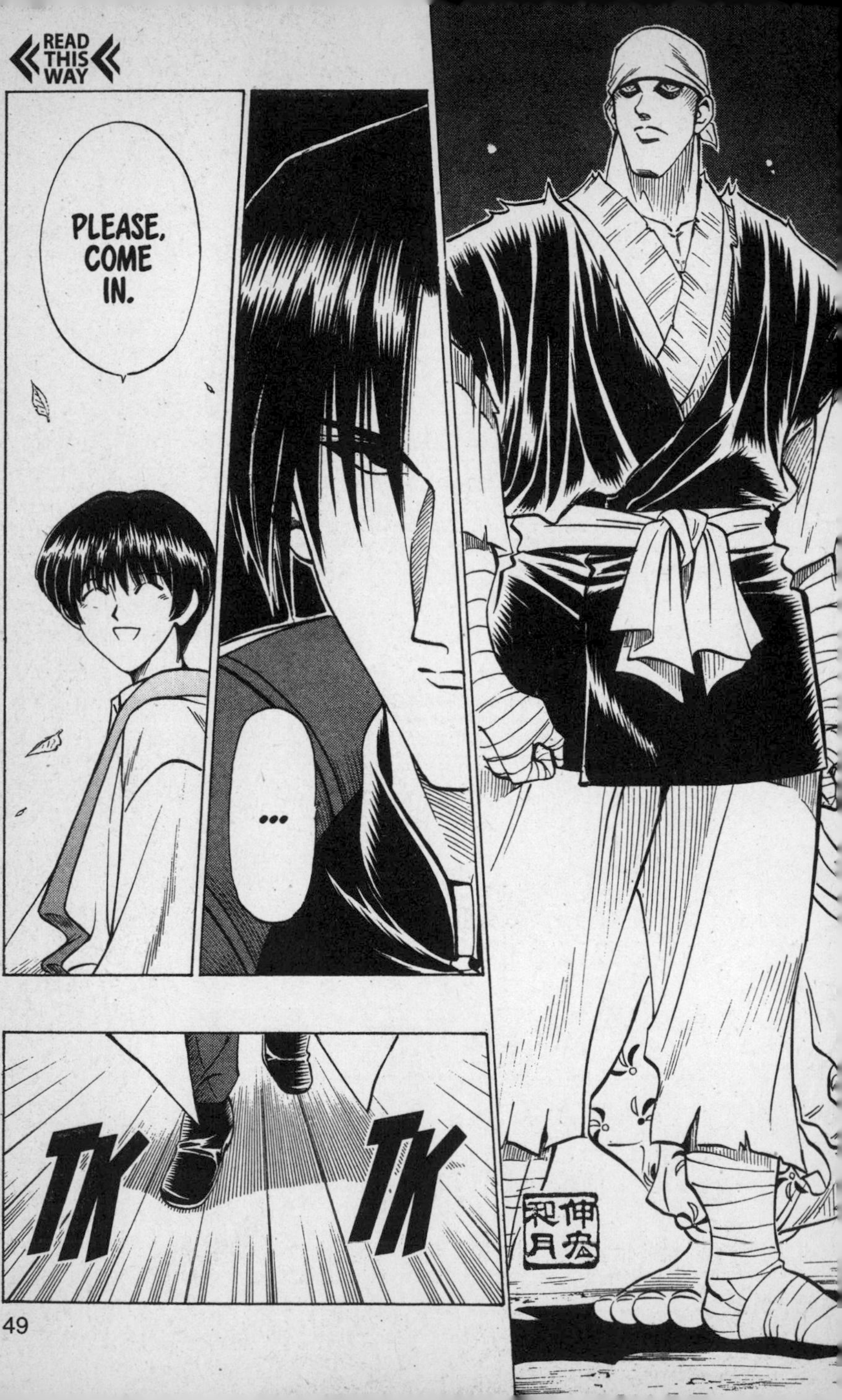

伸宏和月
...
PLEASE, COME IN.
TK
TK

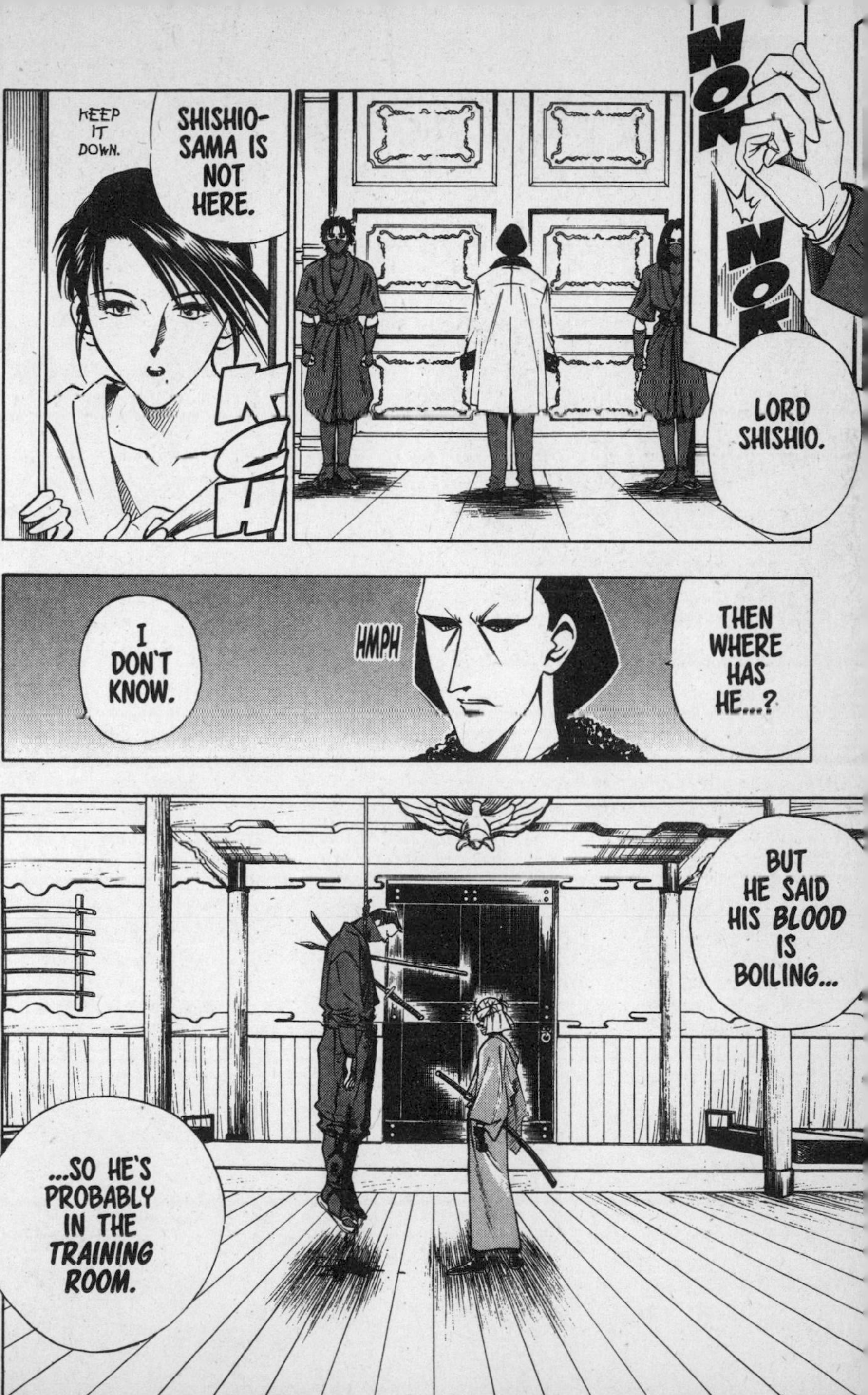
NOK
NOK
LORD SHISHIO.
SHISHIO-SAMA IS NOT HERE.
KEEP IT DOWN.
KCH
THEN WHERE HAS HE...?
HMPH
I DON'T KNOW.
BUT HE SAID HIS BLOOD IS BOILING...
...SO HE'S PROBABLY IN THE TRAINING ROOM.

READ THIS WAY

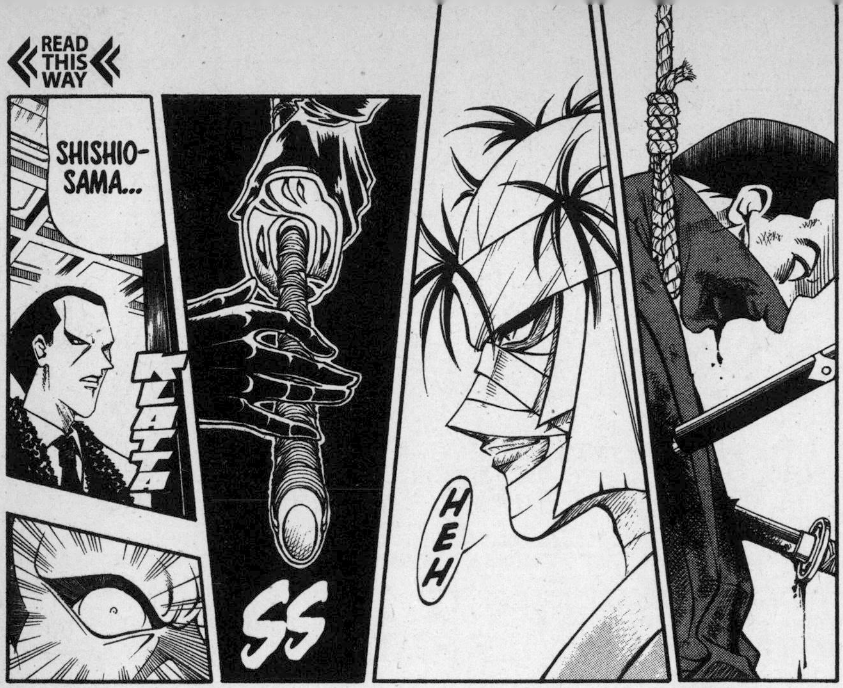
HEH
SS
SHISHIO-SAMA...
KLATTA

Hey again. Watsuki here with another of his dopey sidebars. In "Secret Life of Characters" #20 (Volume 7), I briefly mentioned my collection of American-comics action figures. In my "X-Men" collection, I have only three more to go! Those three have been tough ones—not that they're terribly rare. It's all just for fun. I'm not at the point where I pay big money for any of it. The search is a part of it too, so I've been taking it slow. Recently I've begun to stray a bit and have started collecting "Spawn." The figures are a little more expensive than "X-Men" figures, but the craftsmanship is awesome—basically at "garage kit" level. They're popular, of course, and therefore hard to find, but I figure on tracking them down over the long haul. Speaking of good craftsmanship, there's now a stuffed Kenshin for those arcade "UFO Catcher" things. So far I've seen only a prototype, but it's worth a look (shameless plug). In a time when toys overflow the market, and instead of regretting your purchase 'cause it's this-or-that series, it's better to consult your wallet and buy only the stuff you think is worth it. There's a lot of "RuroKen" merchandise out there, but you'd still be smart to consider quality before shelling out.

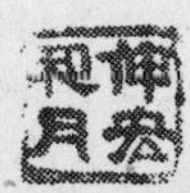

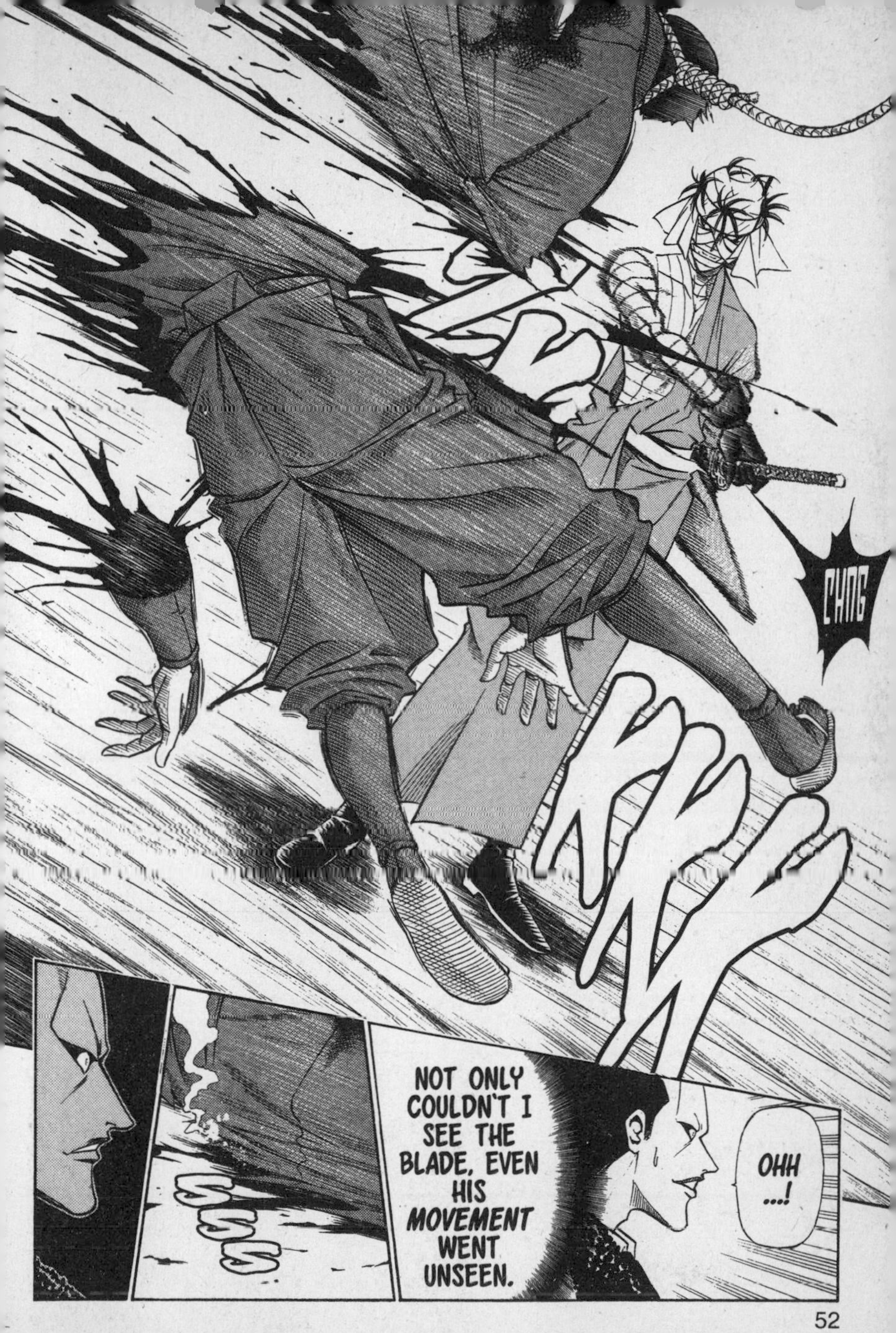
CHNG
OHH ...!
NOT ONLY COULDN'T I SEE THE BLADE, EVEN HIS MOVEMENT WENT UNSEEN.
SSS

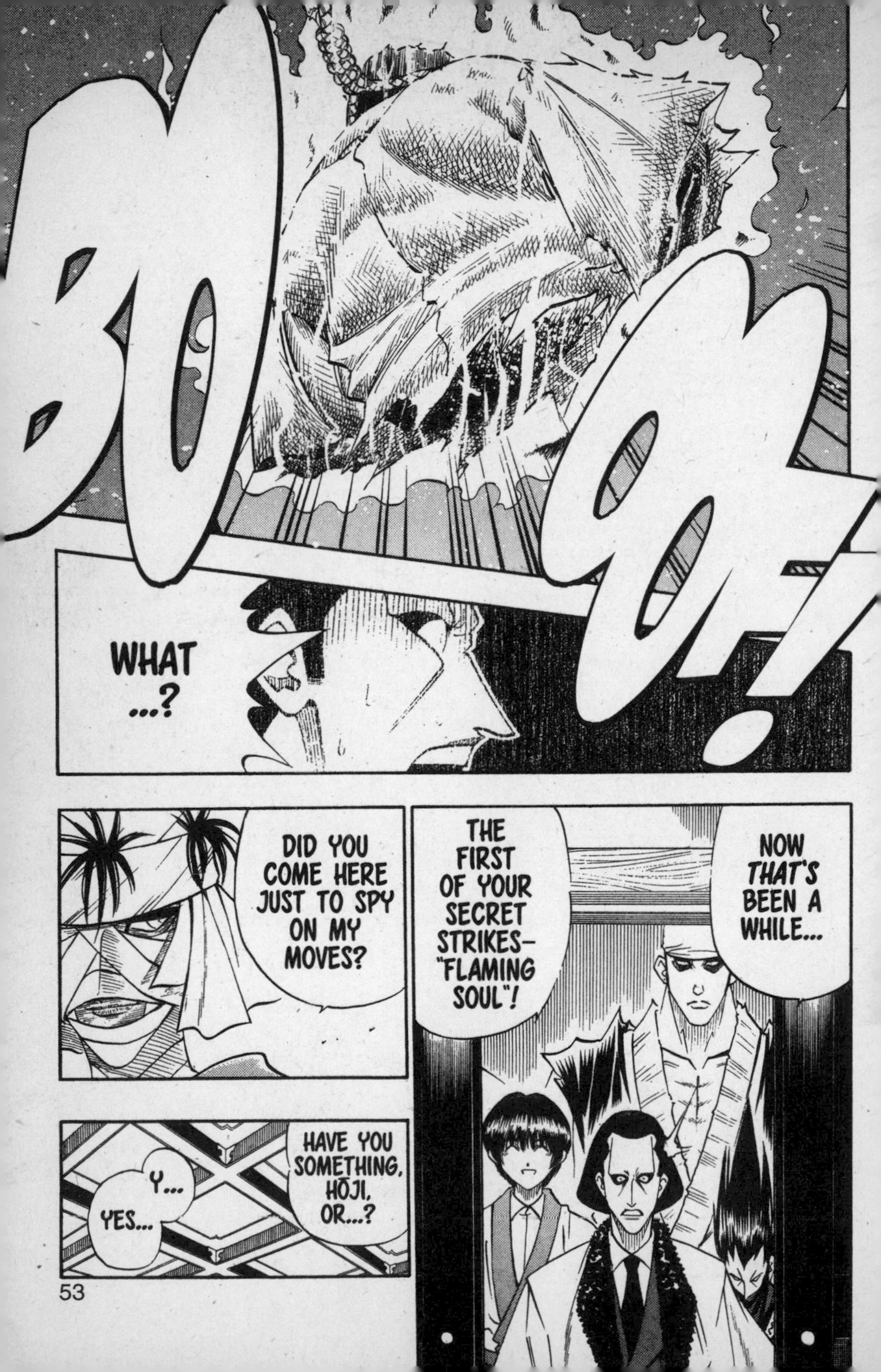
BOOM!
WHAT ...?
NOW *THAT'S* BEEN A WHILE...
THE FIRST OF YOUR SECRET STRIKES— "FLAMING SOUL"!
DID YOU COME HERE JUST TO SPY ON MY MOVES?
HAVE YOU SOMETHING, HŌJI, OR...?
Y... YES...

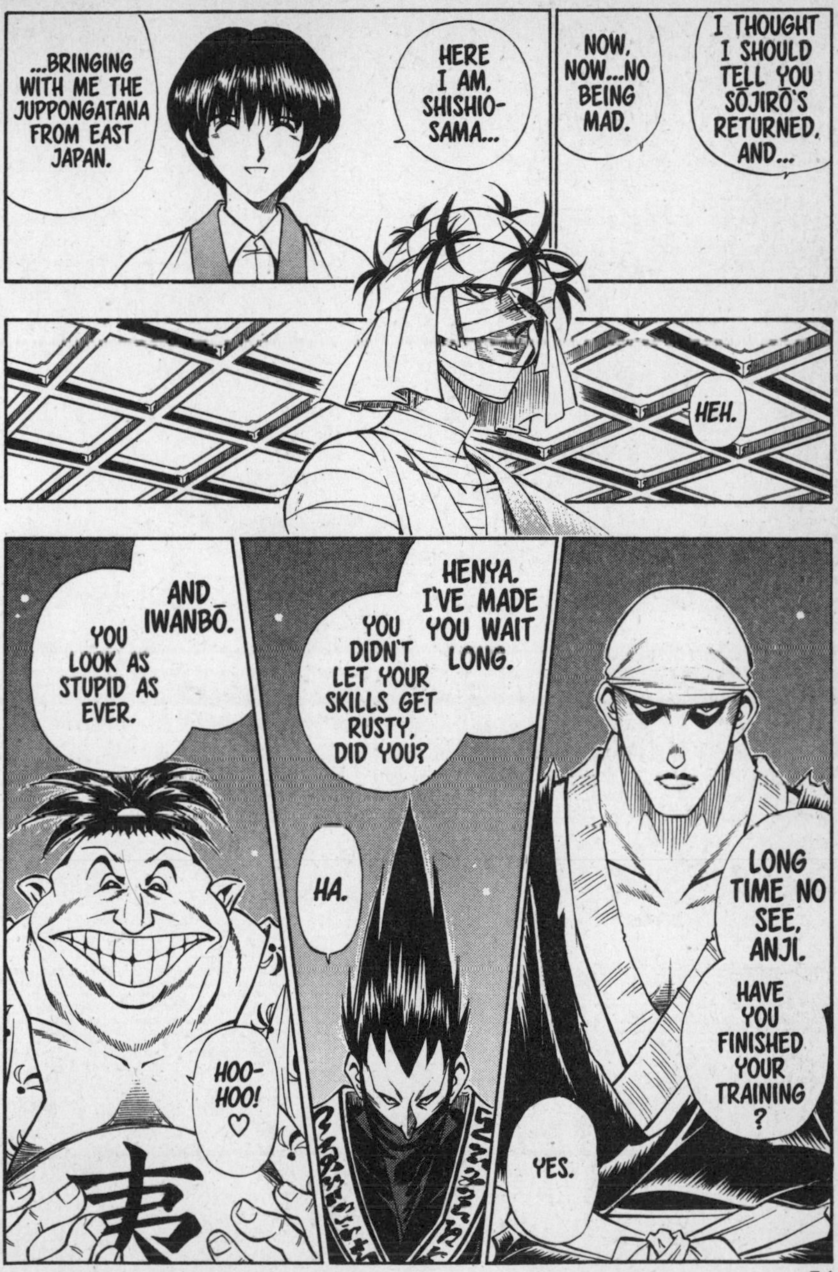
I THOUGHT I SHOULD TELL YOU SŌJIRŌ'S RETURNED, AND...
NOW, NOW...NO BEING MAD.
HERE I AM, SHISHIO-SAMA...
...BRINGING WITH ME THE JUPPONGATANA FROM EAST JAPAN.
HEH.
LONG TIME NO SEE, ANJI.
HAVE YOU FINISHED YOUR TRAINING?
YES.
HENYA. I'VE MADE YOU WAIT LONG.
YOU DIDN'T LET YOUR SKILLS GET RUSTY, DID YOU?
HA.
AND IWANBŌ.
YOU LOOK AS STUPID AS EVER.
HOO-HOO! ♡

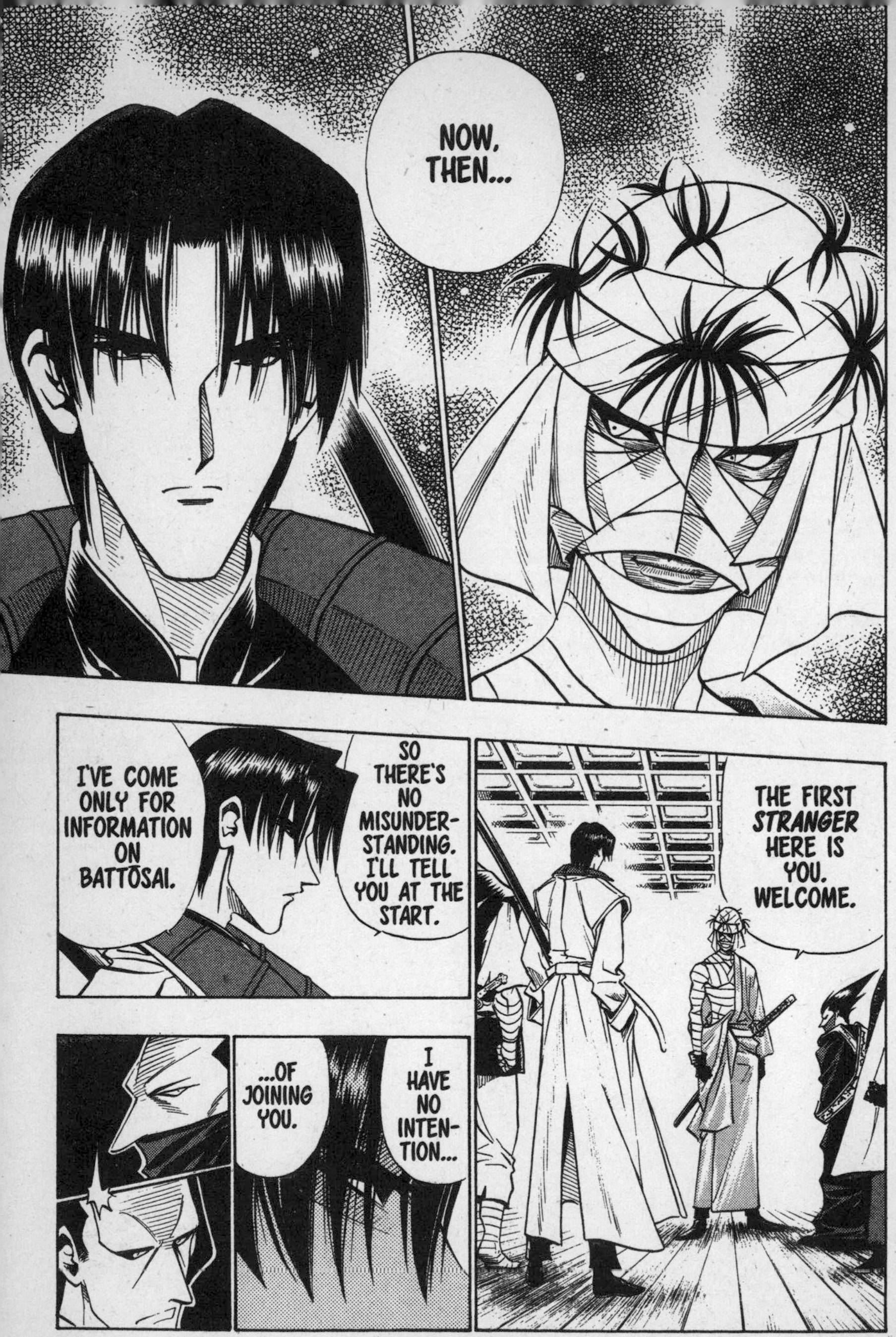
NOW, THEN...
THE FIRST *STRANGER* HERE IS YOU. WELCOME.
SO THERE'S NO MISUNDERSTANDING. I'LL TELL YOU AT THE START.
I'VE COME ONLY FOR INFORMATION ON BATTŌSAI.
I HAVE NO INTENTION...
...OF JOINING YOU.

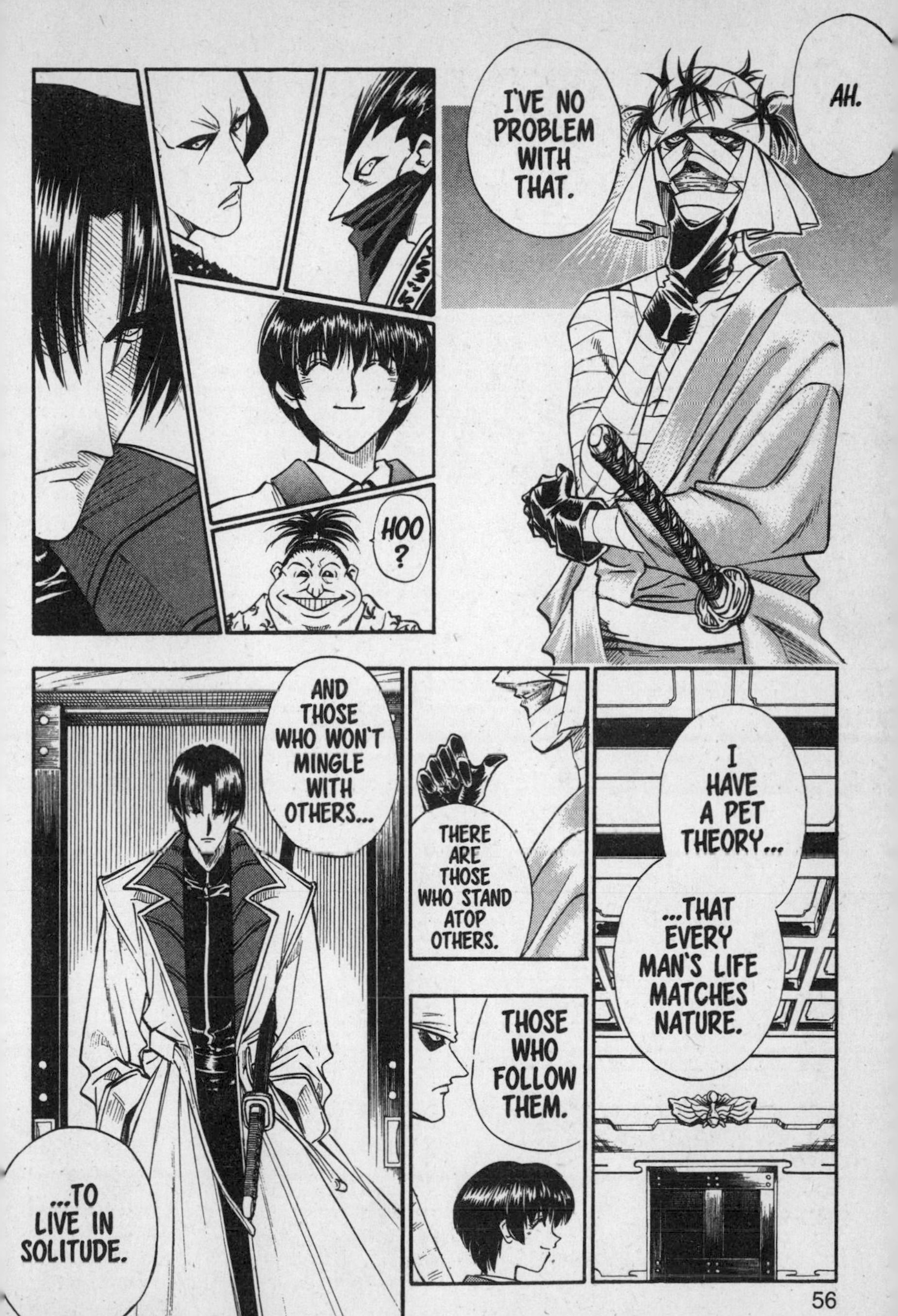
AH.
I'VE NO PROBLEM WITH THAT.
HOO?
I HAVE A PET THEORY...
...THAT EVERY MAN'S LIFE MATCHES NATURE.
THERE ARE THOSE WHO STAND ATOP OTHERS.
THOSE WHO FOLLOW THEM.
AND THOSE WHO WON'T MINGLE WITH OTHERS...
...TO LIVE IN SOLITUDE.

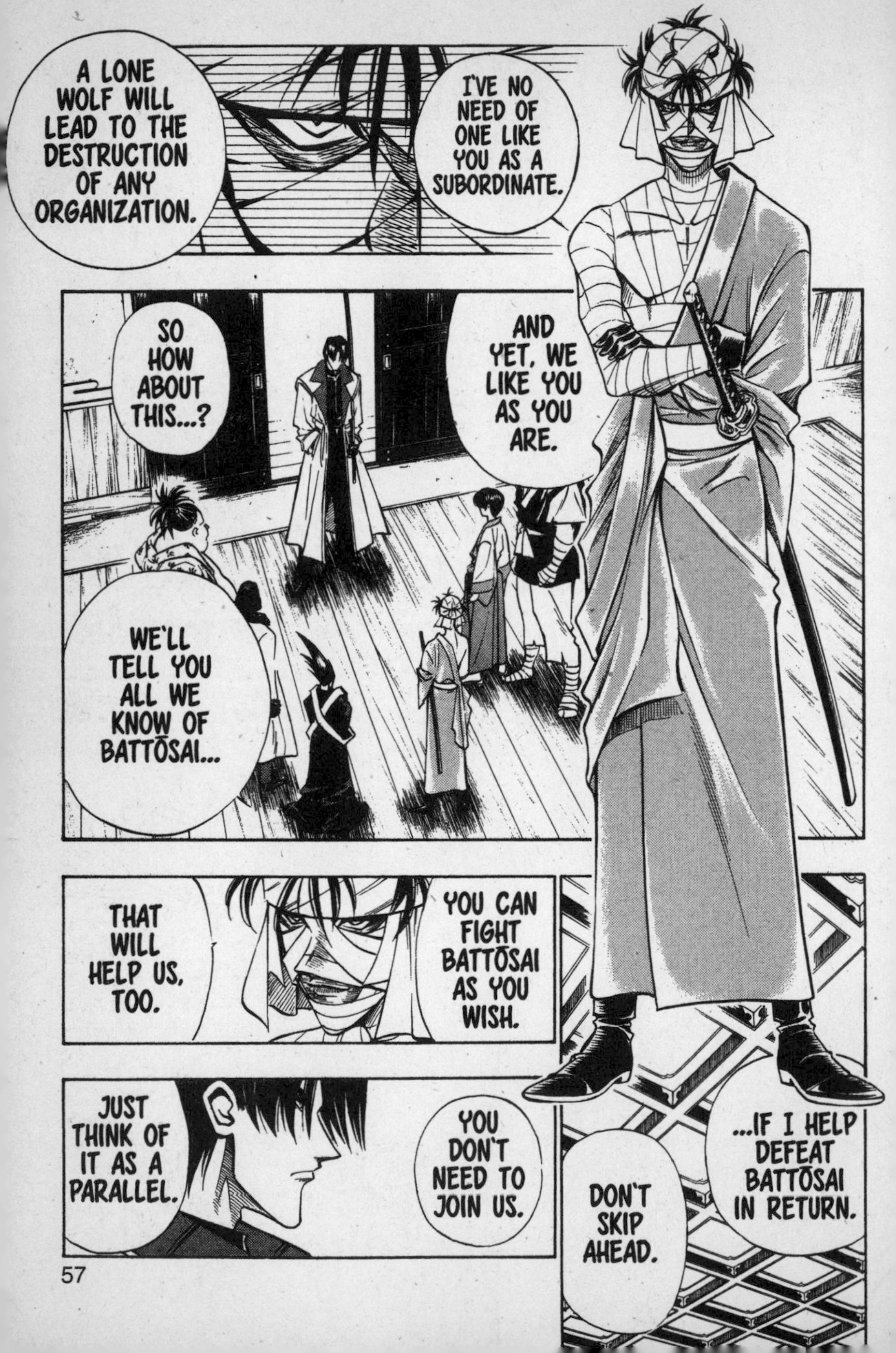
I'VE NO NEED OF ONE LIKE YOU AS A SUBORDINATE.
A LONE WOLF WILL LEAD TO THE DESTRUCTION OF ANY ORGANIZATION.
AND YET, WE LIKE YOU AS YOU ARE.
SO HOW ABOUT THIS...?
WE'LL TELL YOU ALL WE KNOW OF BATTŌSAI...
YOU CAN FIGHT BATTŌSAI AS YOU WISH.
THAT WILL HELP US, TOO.
...IF I HELP DEFEAT BATTŌSAI IN RETURN.
DON'T SKIP AHEAD.
YOU DON'T NEED TO JOIN US.
JUST THINK OF IT AS A PARALLEL.

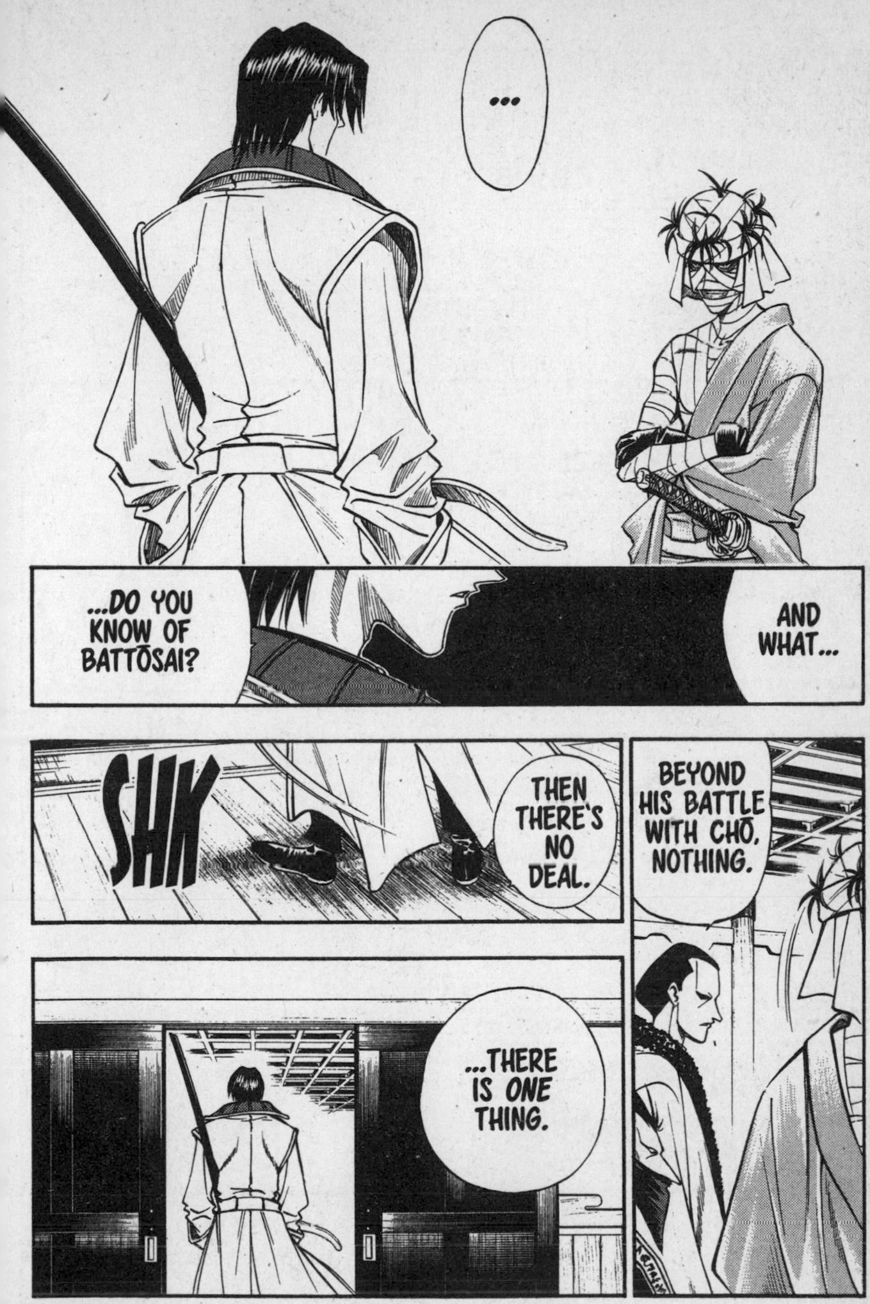
...
AND WHAT...
...DO YOU KNOW OF BATTŌSAI?
BEYOND HIS BATTLE WITH CHŌ, NOTHING.
THEN THERE'S NO DEAL.
SHK
...THERE IS ONE THING.

READ THIS WAY

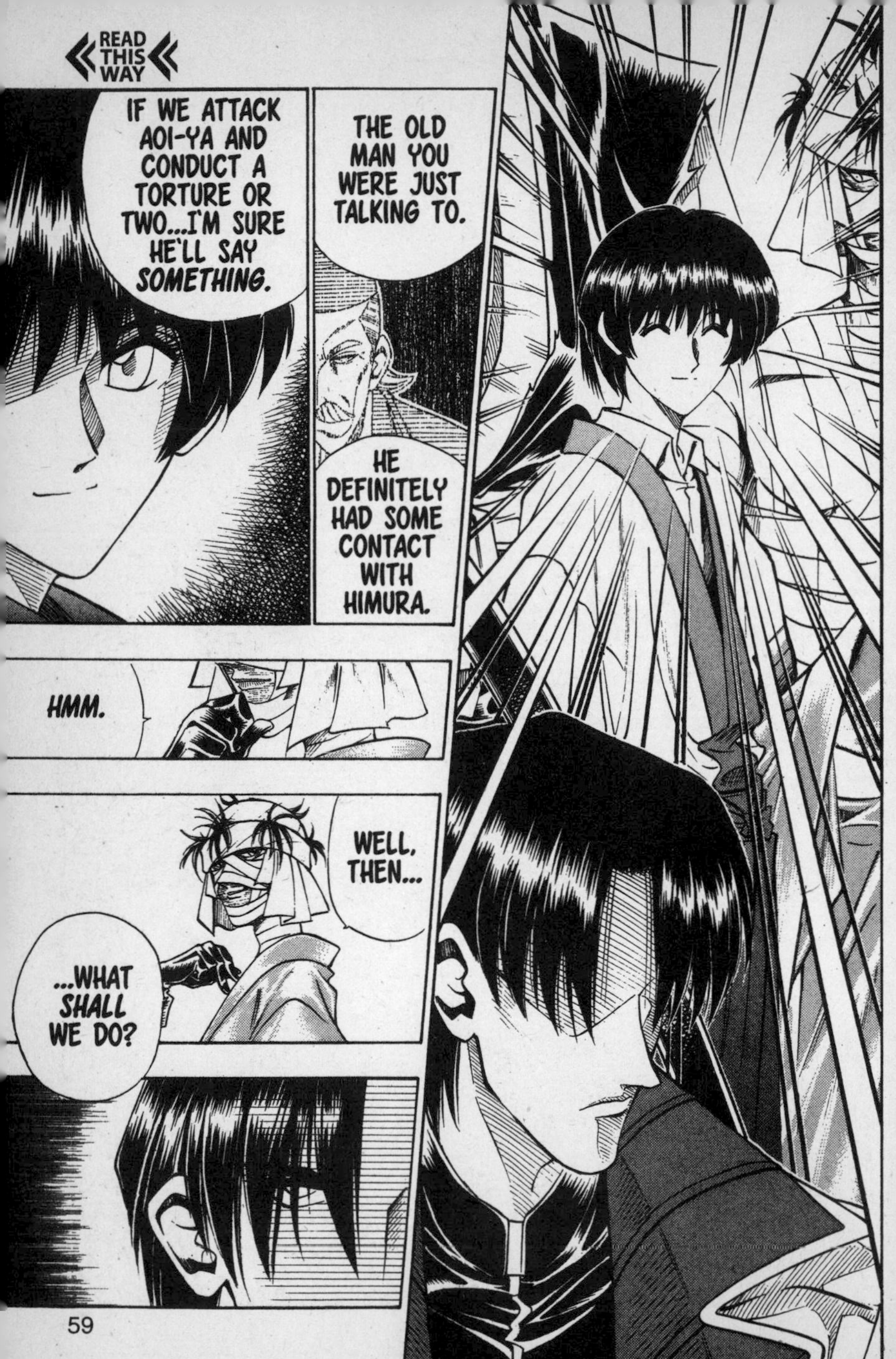
THE OLD MAN YOU WERE JUST TALKING TO.
HE DEFINITELY HAD SOME CONTACT WITH HIMURA.
IF WE ATTACK AOI-YA AND CONDUCT A TORTURE OR TWO...I'M SURE HE'LL SAY SOMETHING.
HMM.
WELL, THEN...
...WHAT SHALL WE DO?

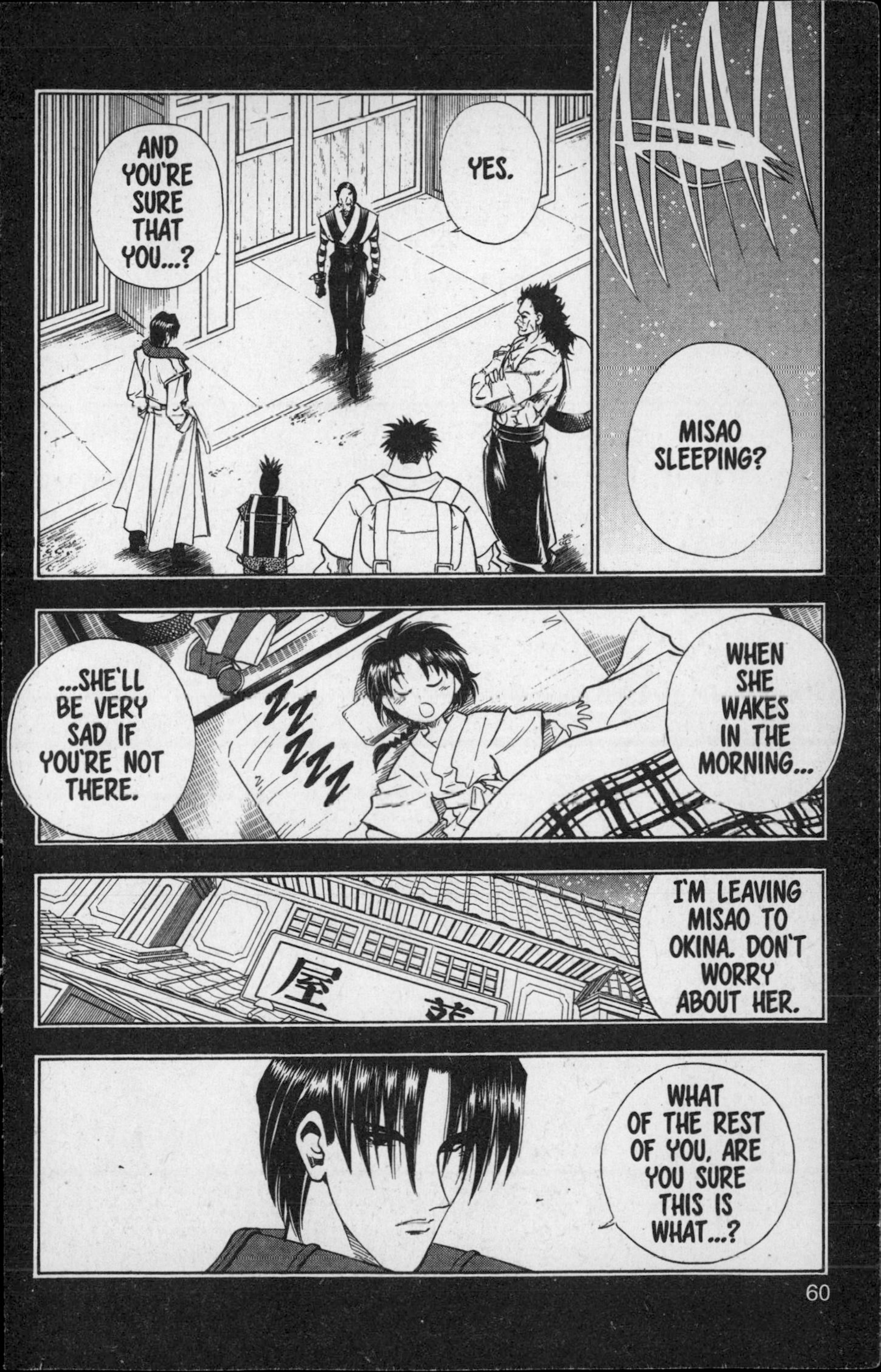
MISAO SLEEPING?
YES.
AND YOU'RE SURE THAT YOU...?
WHEN SHE WAKES IN THE MORNING...
ZZZZZ
...SHE'LL BE VERY SAD IF YOU'RE NOT THERE.
I'M LEAVING MISAO TO OKINA. DON'T WORRY ABOUT HER.
屋
WHAT OF THE REST OF YOU, ARE YOU SURE THIS IS WHAT...?

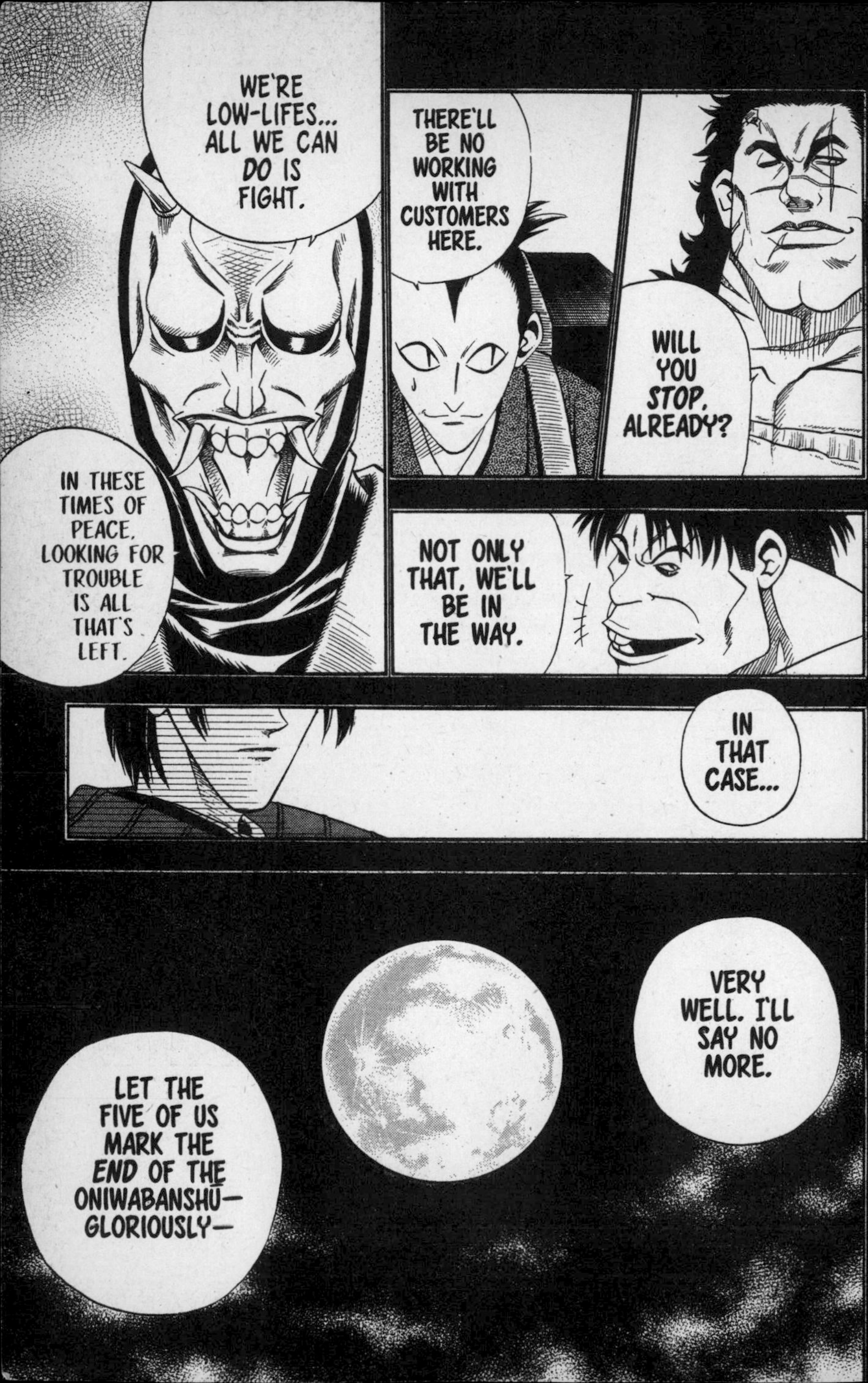
WILL YOU STOP, ALREADY?
THERE'LL BE NO WORKING WITH CUSTOMERS HERE.
NOT ONLY THAT, WE'LL BE IN THE WAY.
WE'RE LOW-LIFES... ALL WE CAN DO IS FIGHT.
IN THESE TIMES OF PEACE, LOOKING FOR TROUBLE IS ALL THAT'S LEFT.
IN THAT CASE...
VERY WELL. I'LL SAY NO MORE.
LET THE FIVE OF US MARK THE END OF THE ONIWABANSHŪ— GLORIOUSLY—

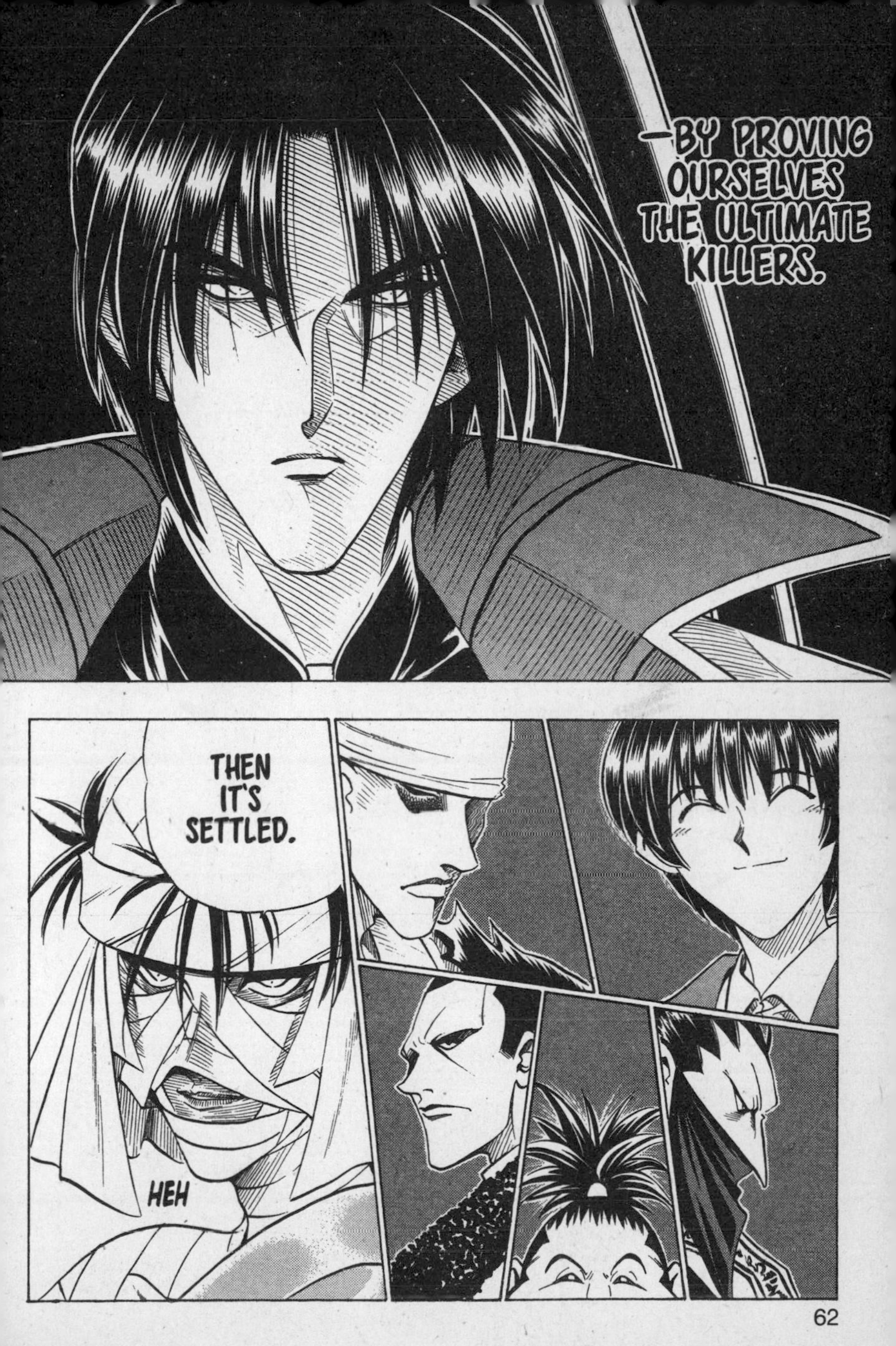
—BY PROVING OURSELVES THE ULTIMATE KILLERS.
THEN IT'S SETTLED.
HEH

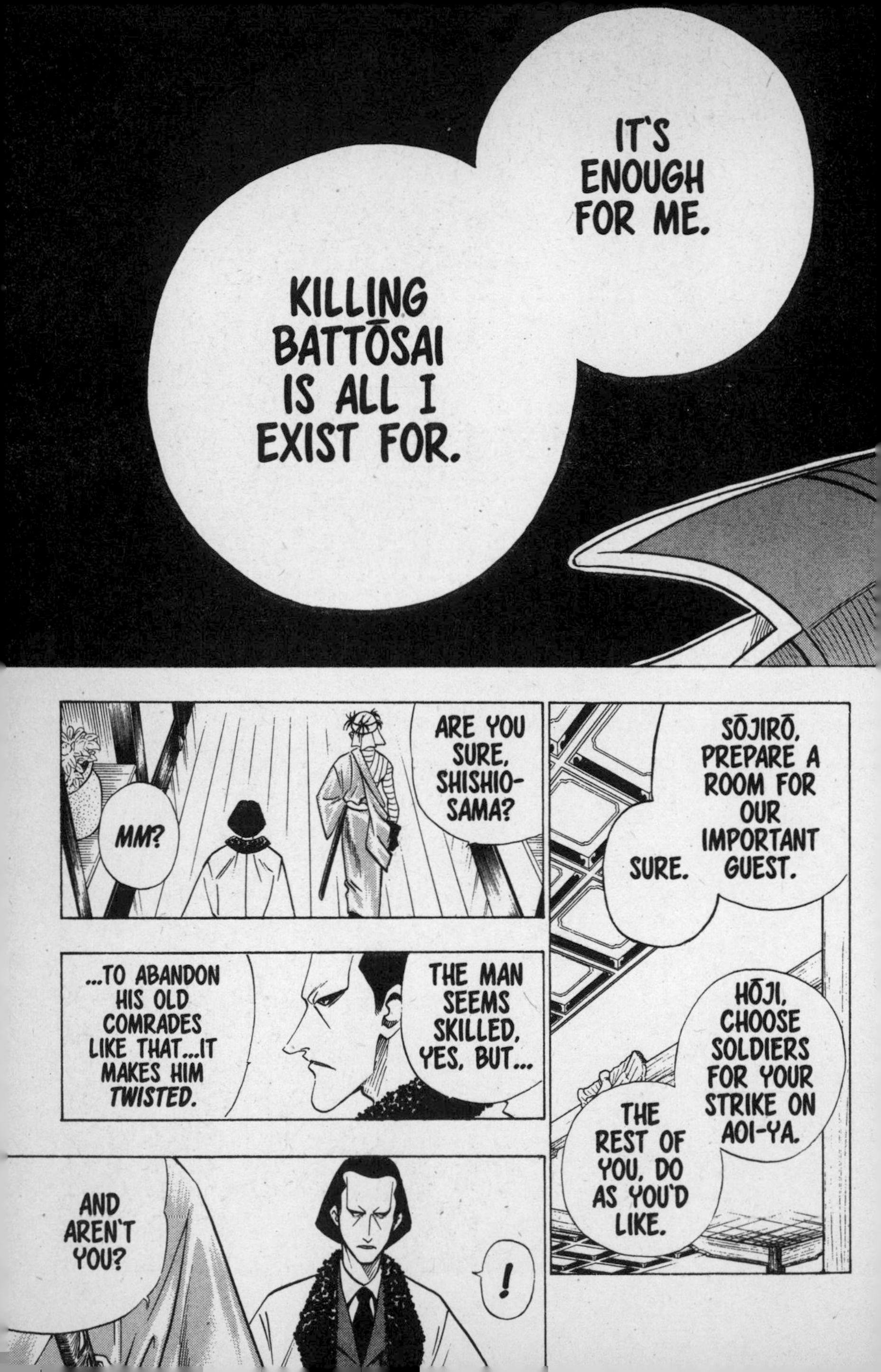
IT'S ENOUGH FOR ME.
KILLING BATTŌSAI IS ALL I EXIST FOR.
SŌJIRŌ, PREPARE A ROOM FOR OUR IMPORTANT GUEST.
SURE.
HŌJI, CHOOSE SOLDIERS FOR YOUR STRIKE ON AOI-YA.
THE REST OF YOU, DO AS YOU'D LIKE.
ARE YOU SURE, SHISHIO-SAMA?
MM?
THE MAN SEEMS SKILLED, YES, BUT...
...TO ABANDON HIS OLD COMRADES LIKE THAT...IT MAKES HIM *TWISTED*.
!
AND AREN'T YOU?

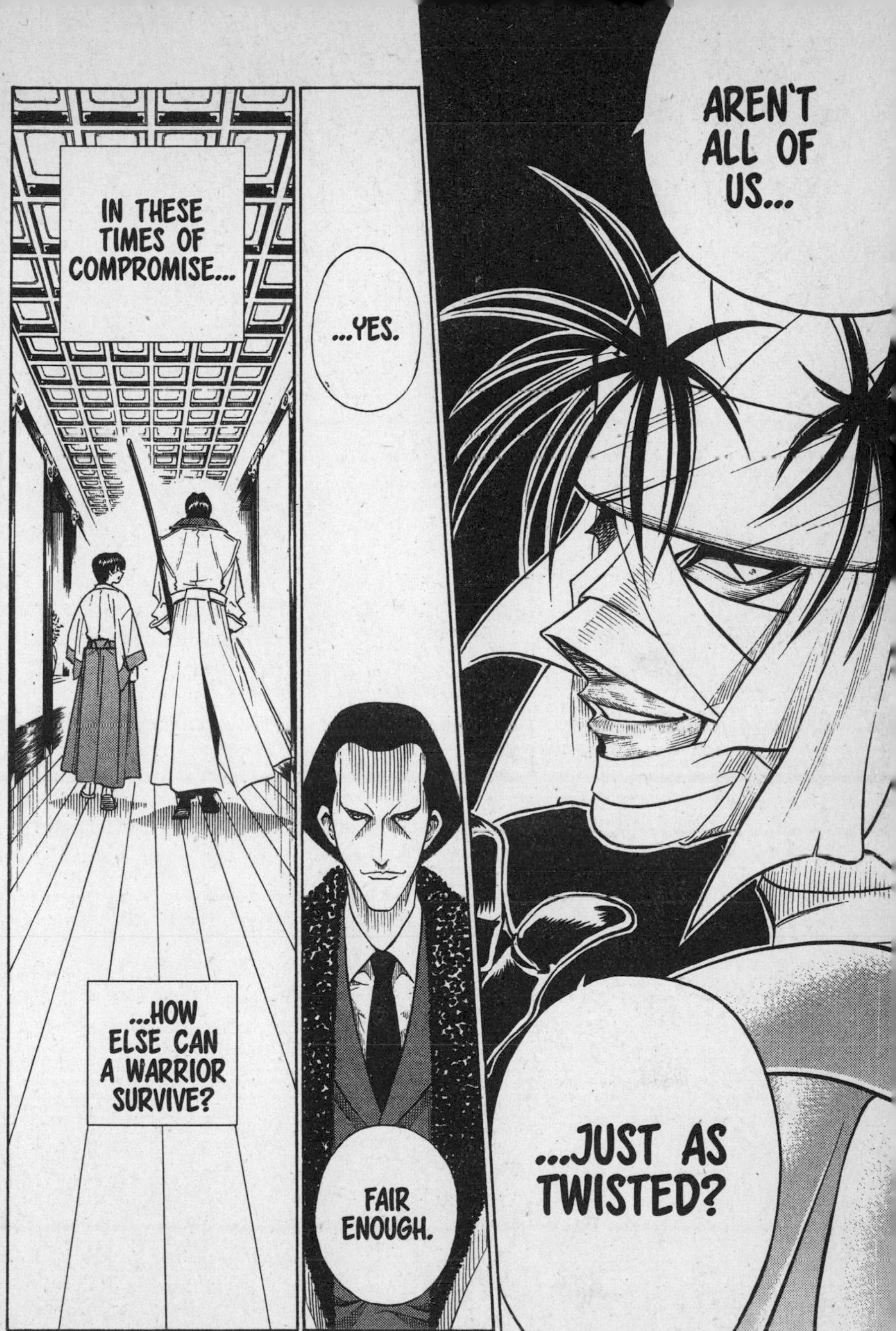
AREN'T ALL OF US...
...JUST AS TWISTED?
...YES.
FAIR ENOUGH.
IN THESE TIMES OF COMPROMISE...
...HOW ELSE CAN A WARRIOR SURVIVE?

READ THIS WAY

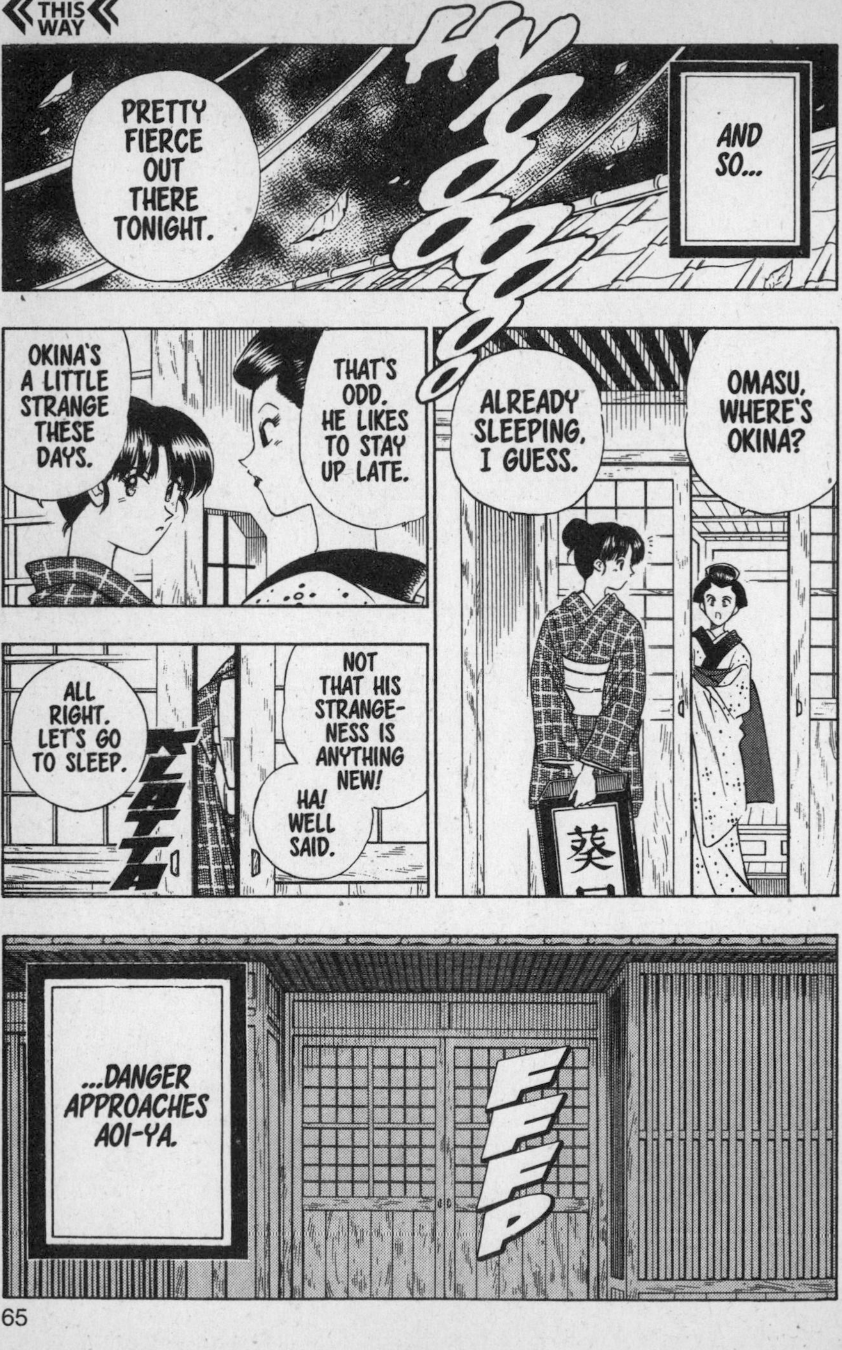
AND SO...
HYOOOOOO
PRETTY FIERCE OUT THERE TONIGHT.
OMASU, WHERE'S OKINA?
ALREADY SLEEPING, I GUESS.
葵
THAT'S ODD. HE LIKES TO STAY UP LATE.
OKINA'S A LITTLE STRANGE THESE DAYS.
NOT THAT HIS STRANGENESS IS ANYTHING NEW!
HA! WELL SAID.
KATTA
ALL RIGHT. LET'S GO TO SLEEP.
FEEP
...DANGER APPROACHES AOI-YA.

Rurouni Kenshin

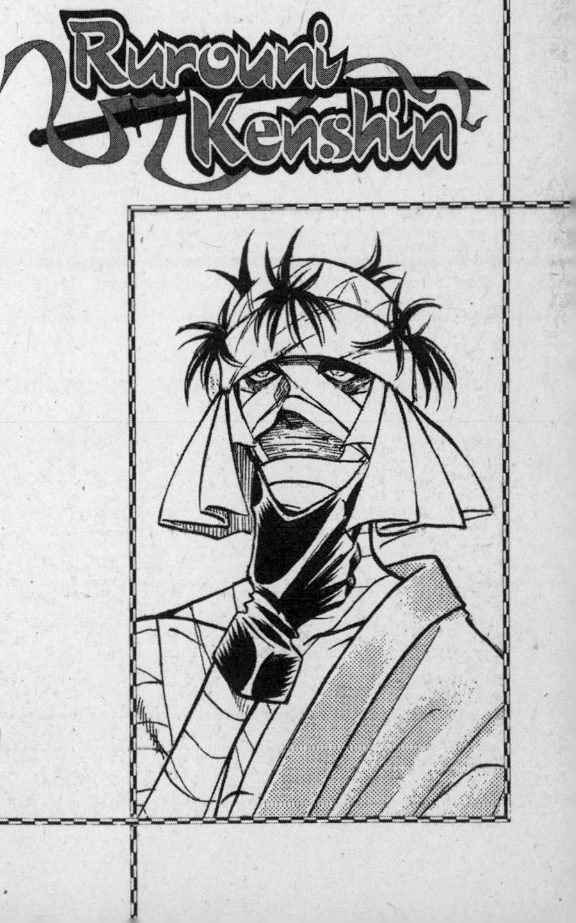

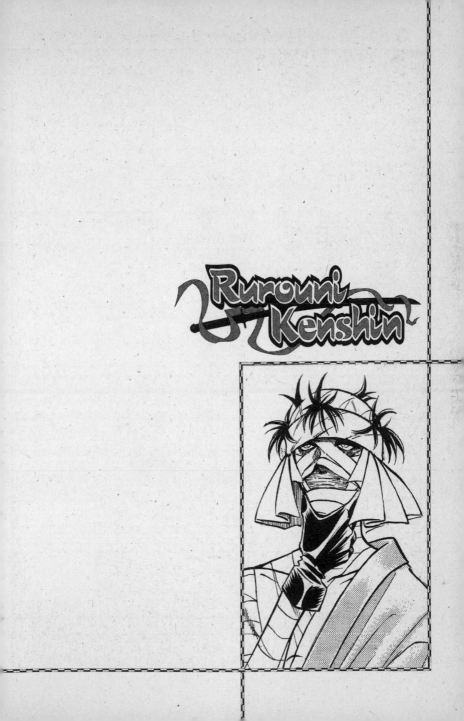

Act 88—Overture to Destruction

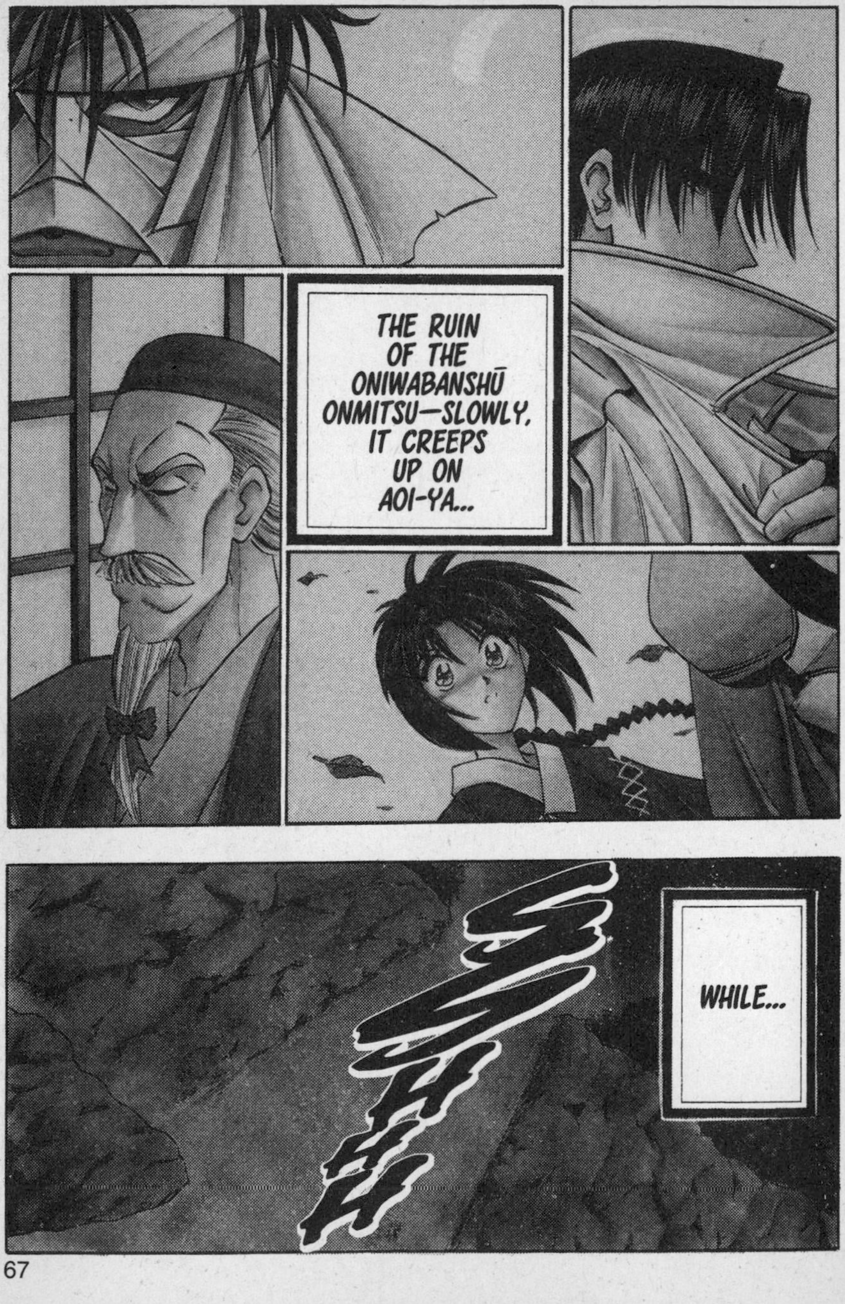
THE RUIN OF THE ONIWABANSHŪ ONMITSU—SLOWLY, IT CREEPS UP ON AOI-YA...
WHILE...

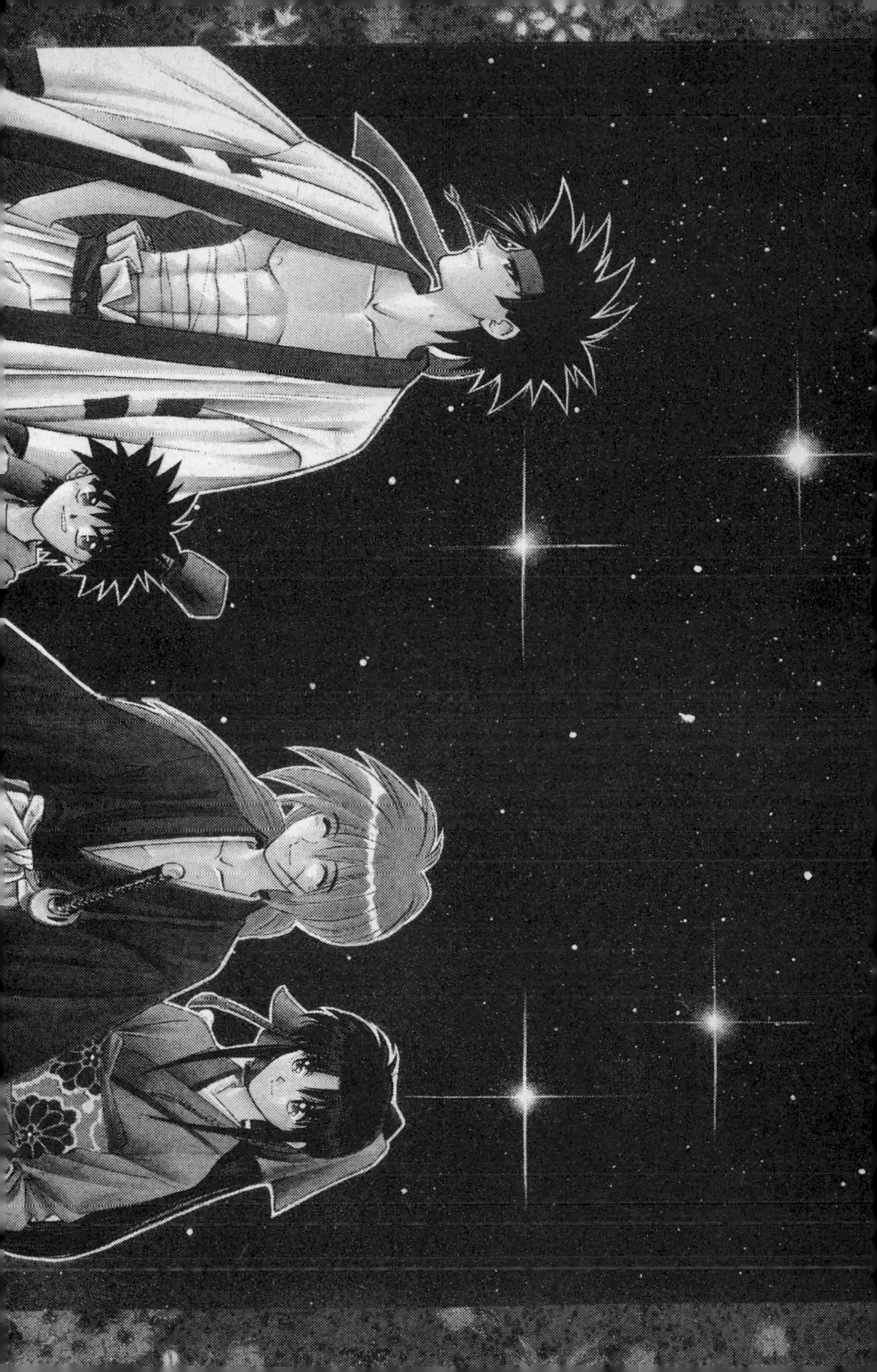

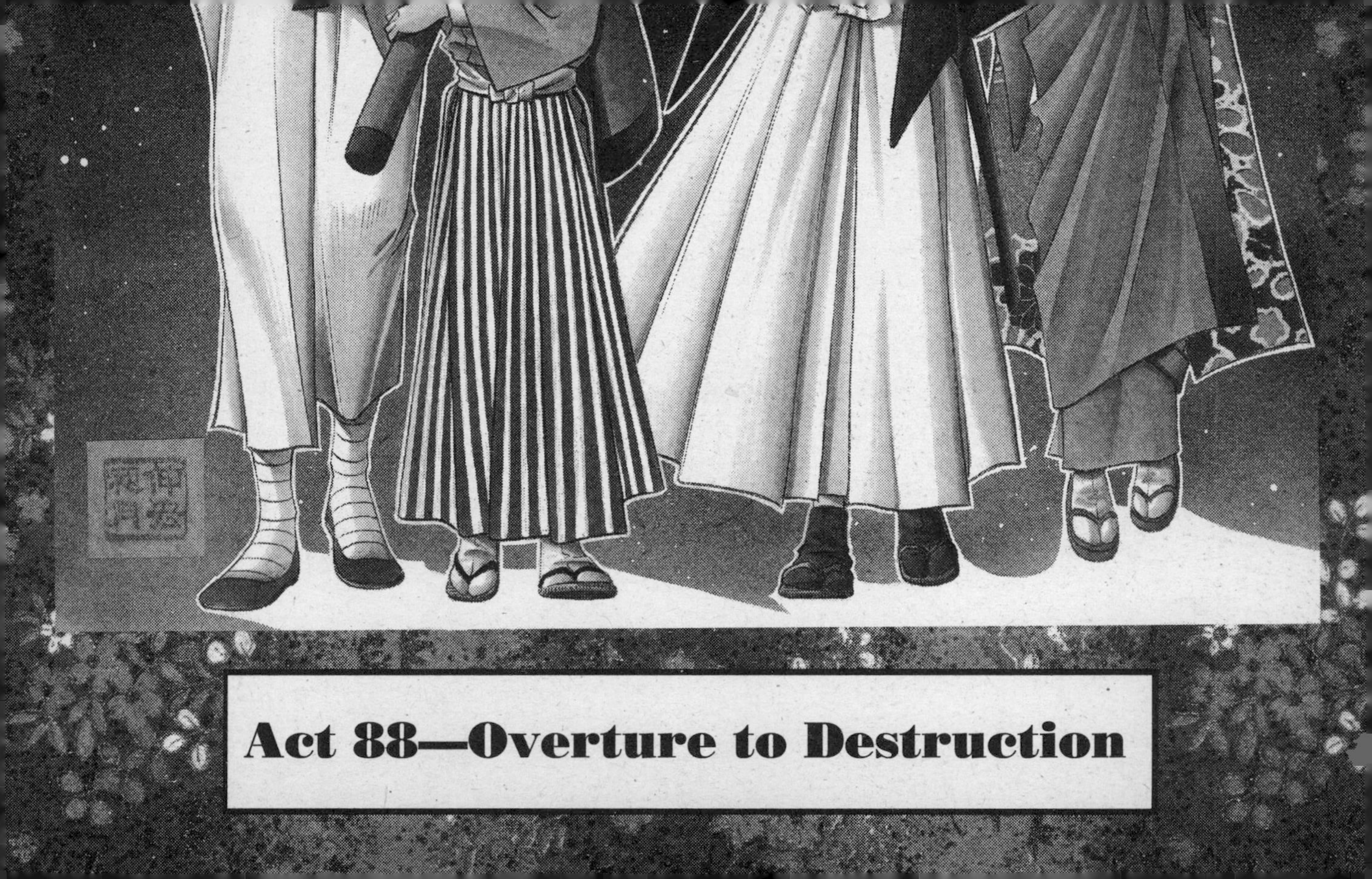

Act 88—Overture to Destruction

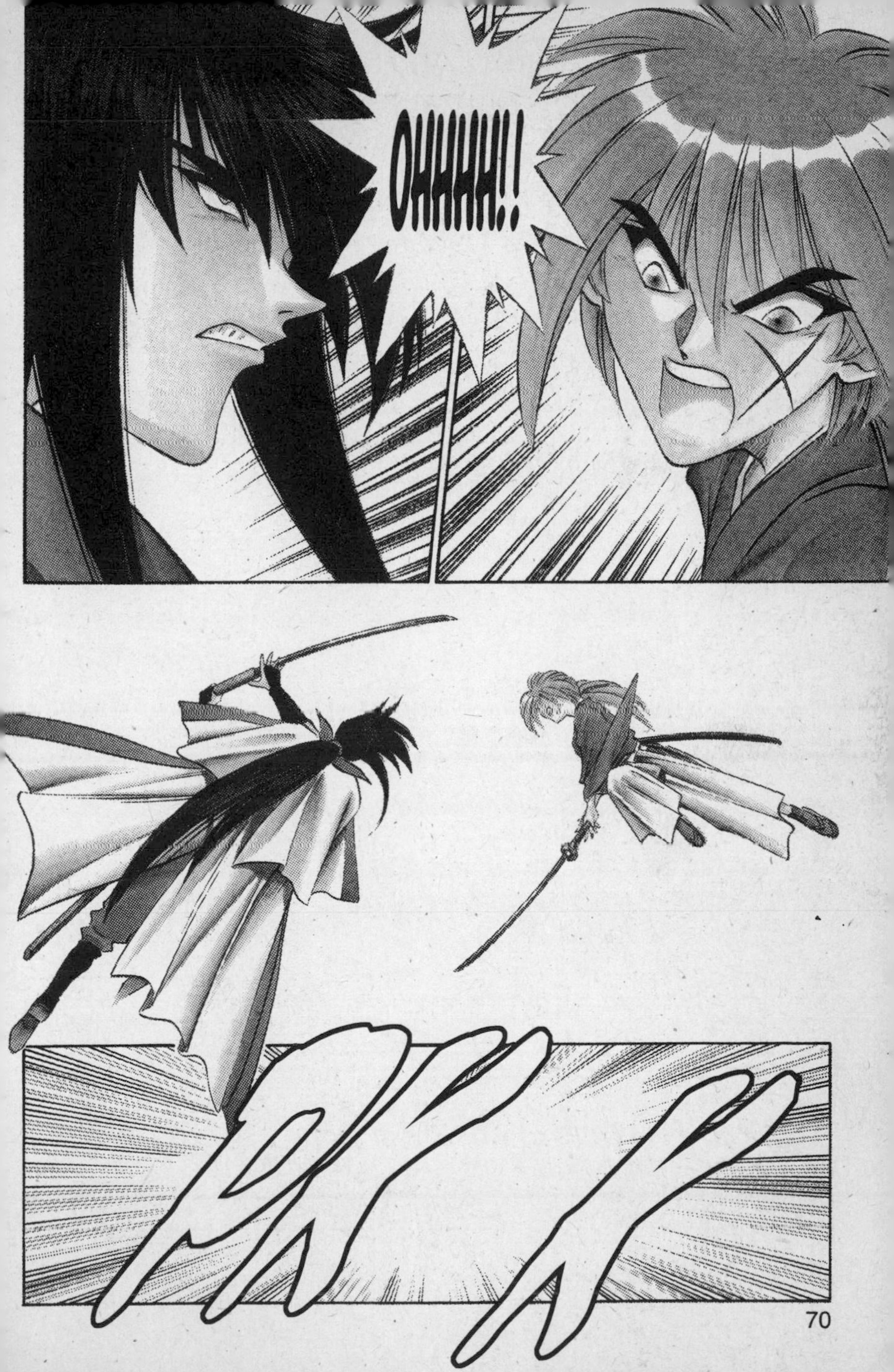
OHHHH!!

READ THIS WAY

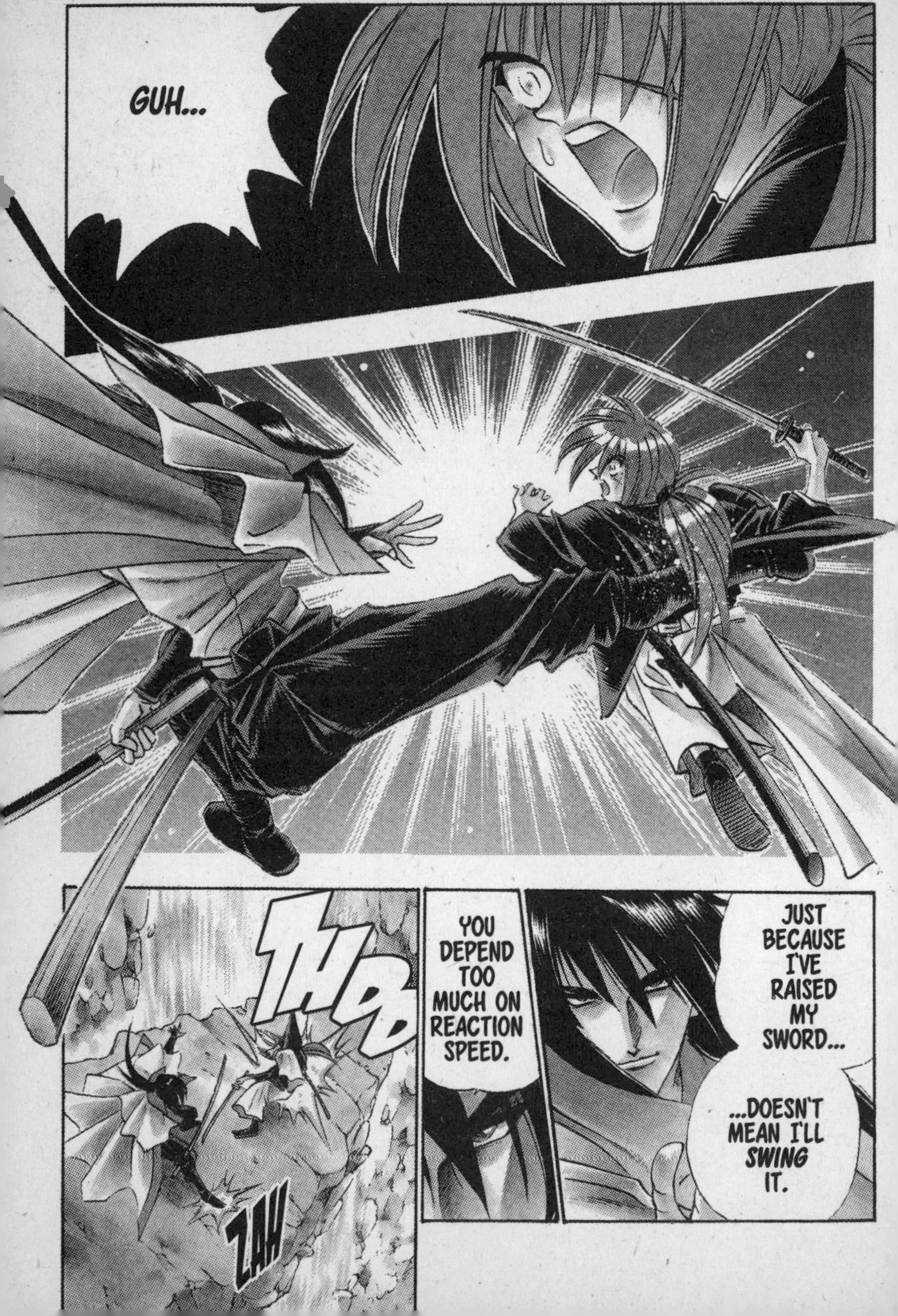
GUH...
JUST BECAUSE I'VE RAISED MY SWORD...
...DOESN'T MEAN I'LL SWING IT.
YOU DEPEND TOO MUCH ON REACTION SPEED.
THD
ZAH

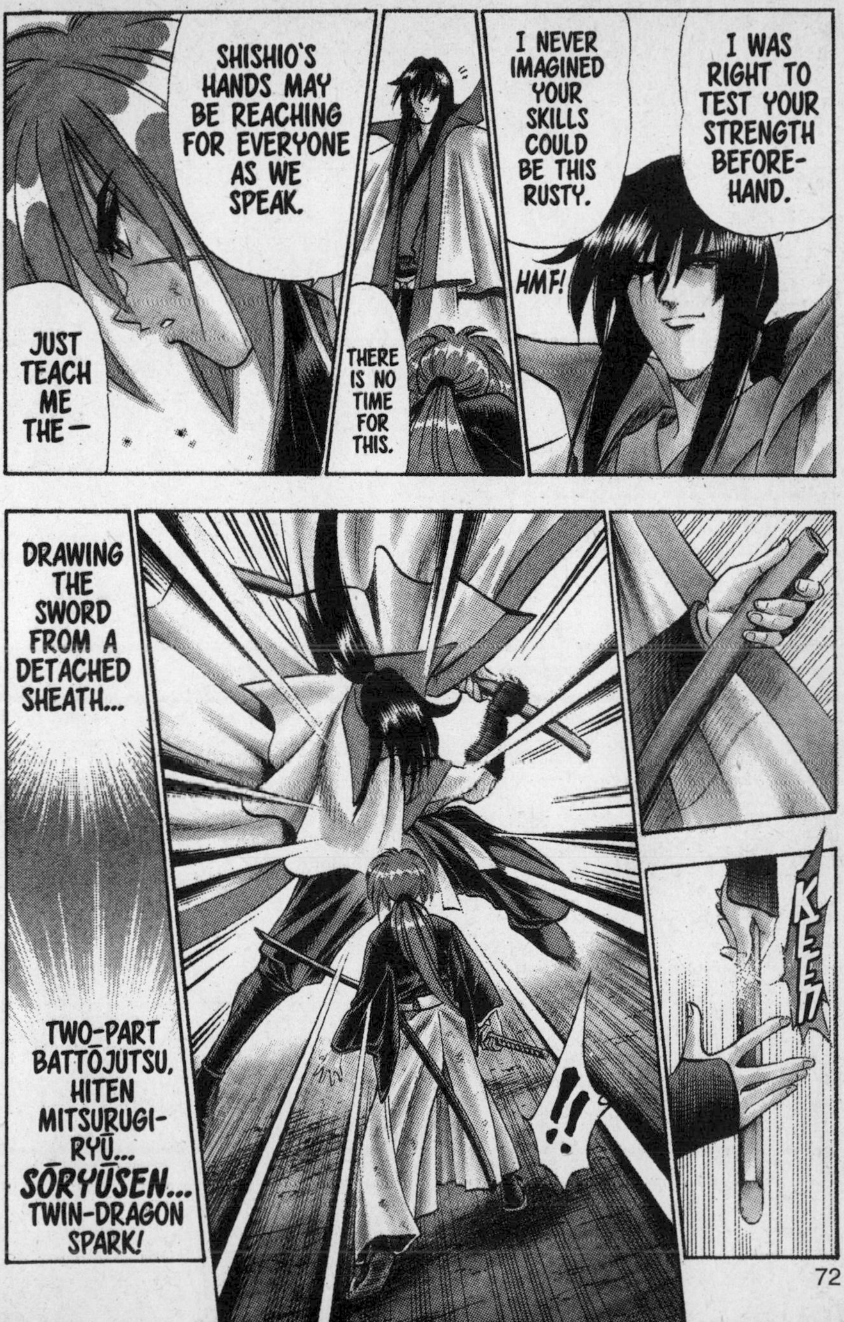
I WAS RIGHT TO TEST YOUR STRENGTH BEFORE-HAND.
I NEVER IMAGINED YOUR SKILLS COULD BE THIS RUSTY.
HMF!
THERE IS NO TIME FOR THIS.
SHISHIO'S HANDS MAY BE REACHING FOR EVERYONE AS WE SPEAK.
JUST TEACH ME THE—
KEEN
DRAWING THE SWORD FROM A DETACHED SHEATH...
!!
TWO-PART BATTŌJUTSU, HITEN MITSURUGI-RYŪ...
SŌRYŪSEN...
TWIN-DRAGON SPARK!

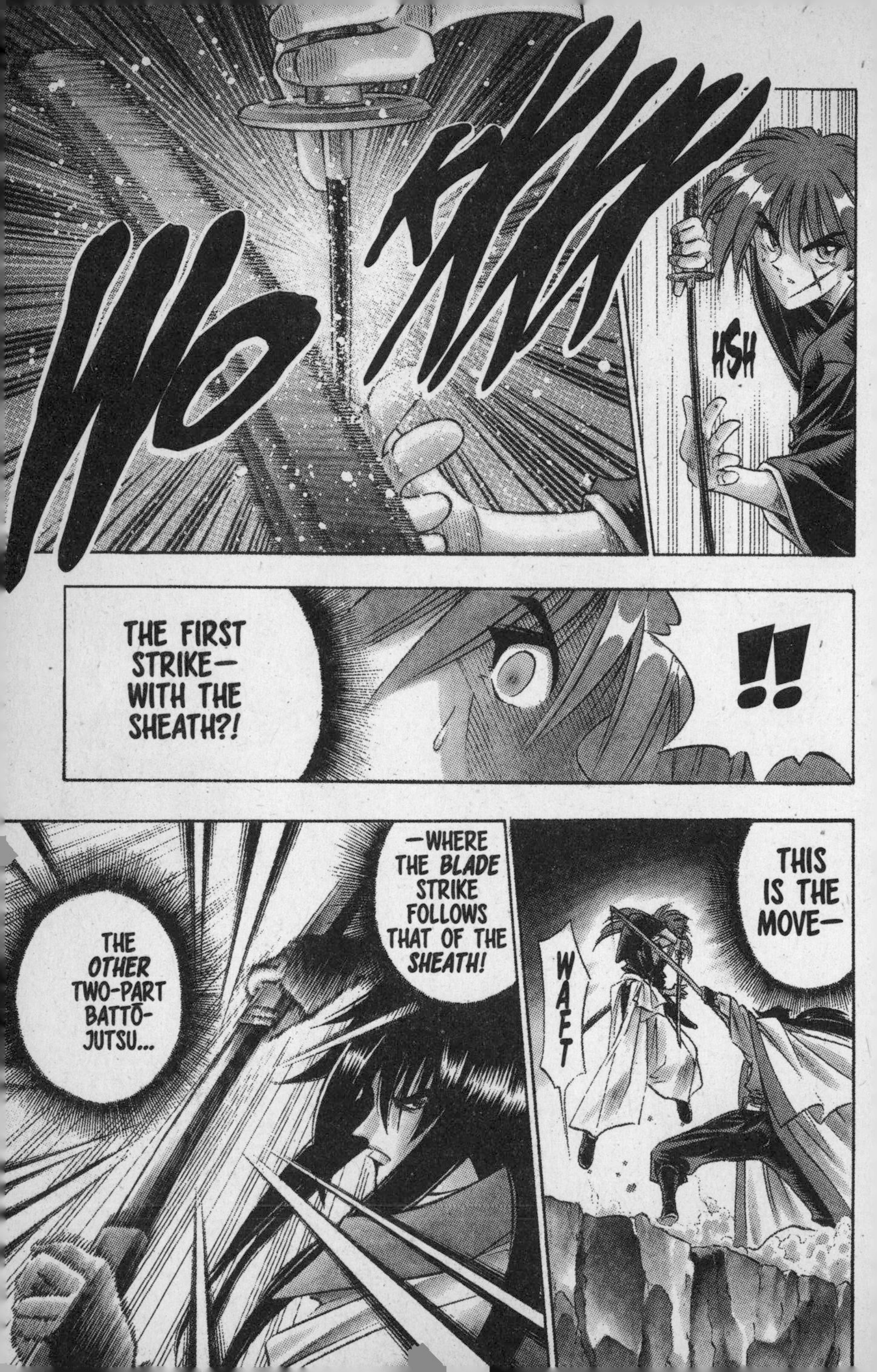

HSH
!!
THE FIRST STRIKE— WITH THE SHEATH?!
THIS IS THE MOVE—
WAFT
—WHERE THE *BLADE* STRIKE FOLLOWS THAT OF THE *SHEATH*!
THE *OTHER* TWO-PART BATTŌ-JUTSU...

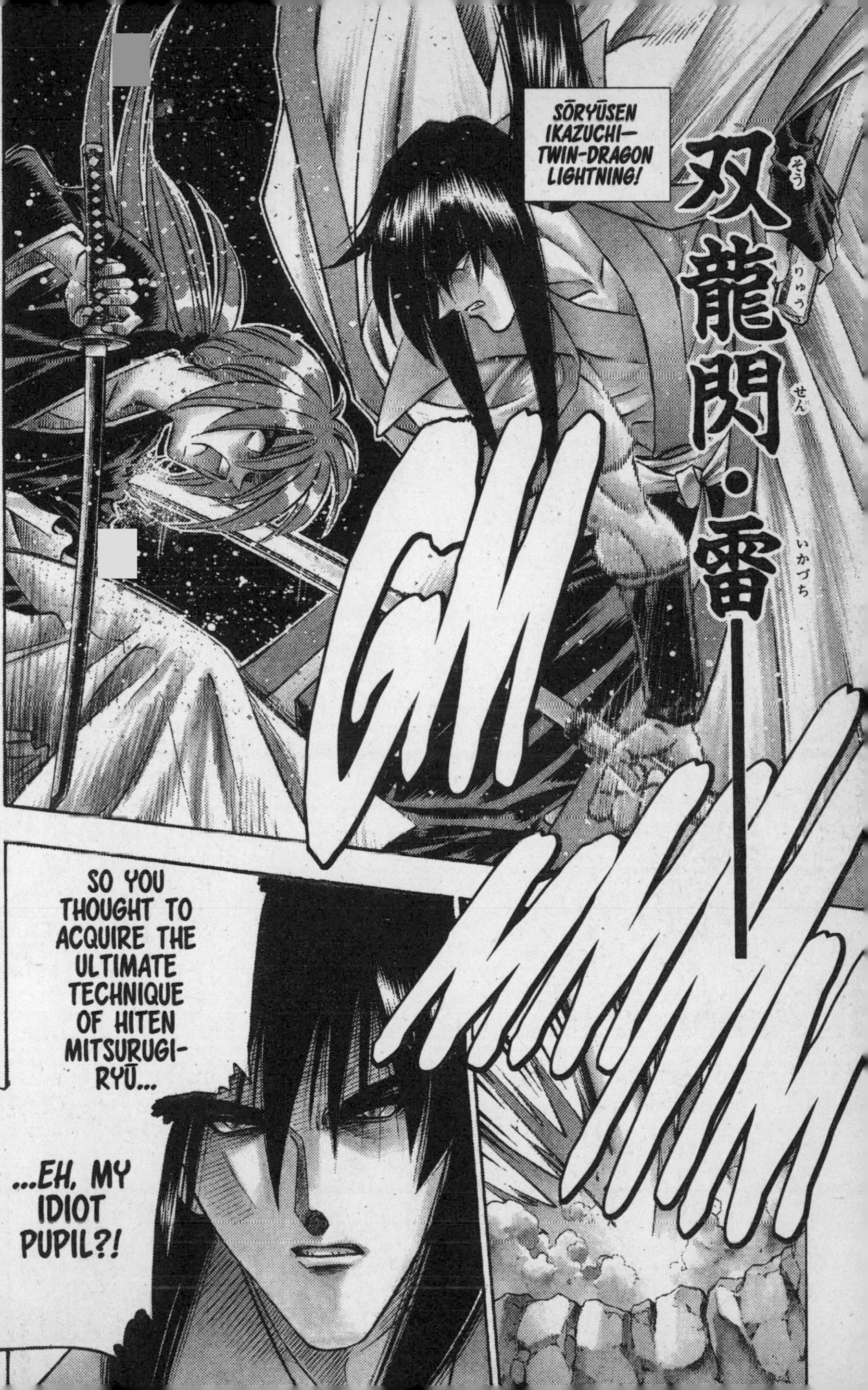

双龍閃・雷—
SŌRYŪSEN IKAZUCHI—TWIN-DRAGON LIGHTNING!
SO YOU THOUGHT TO ACQUIRE THE ULTIMATE TECHNIQUE OF HITEN MITSURUGI-RYŪ...
...EH, MY IDIOT PUPIL?!

READ THIS WAY

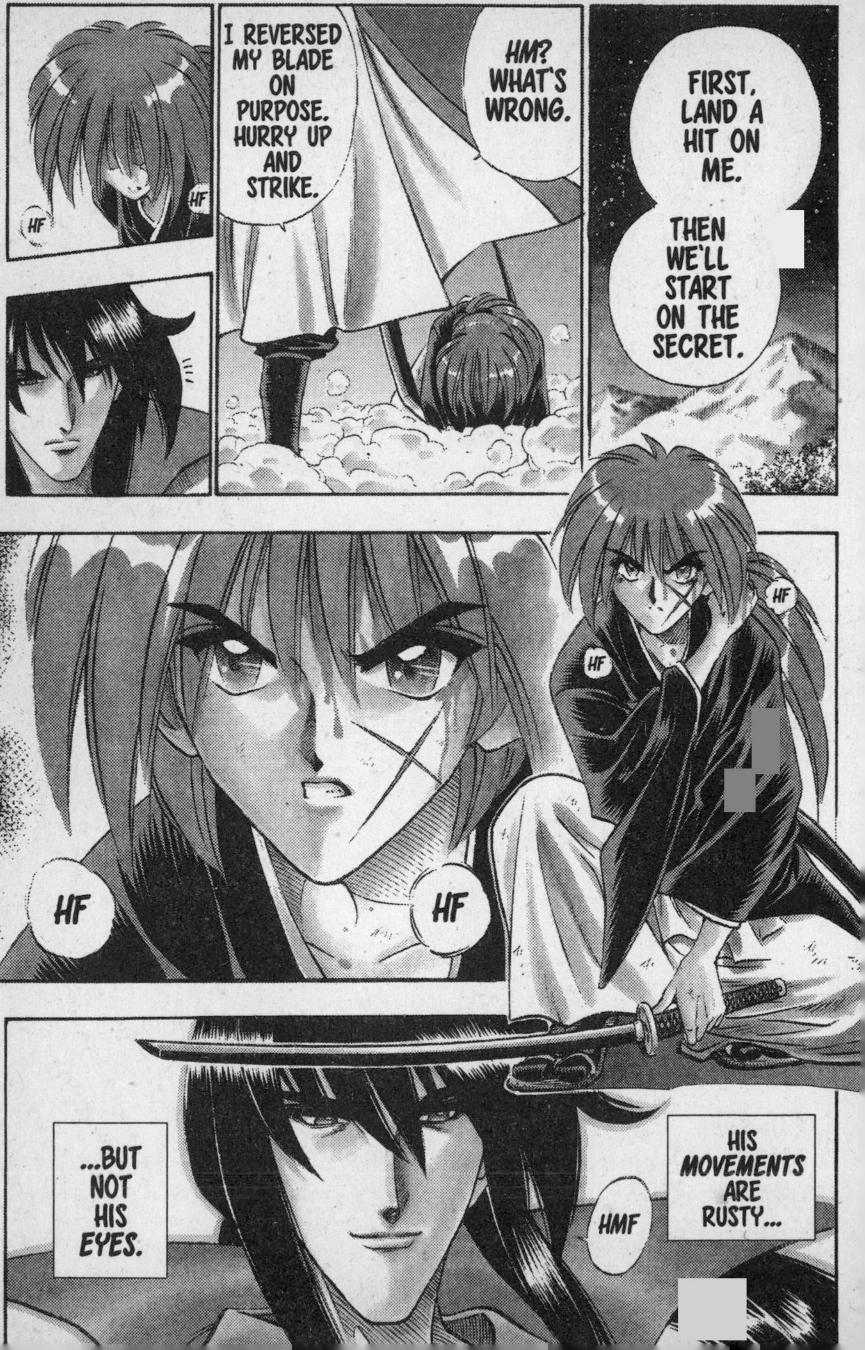
FIRST, LAND A HIT ON ME.
THEN WE'LL START ON THE SECRET.
HM? WHAT'S WRONG.
I REVERSED MY BLADE ON PURPOSE. HURRY UP AND STRIKE.
HF
HF
HF
HF
HF
HF
HIS MOVEMENTS ARE RUSTY...
HMF
...BUT NOT HIS EYES.

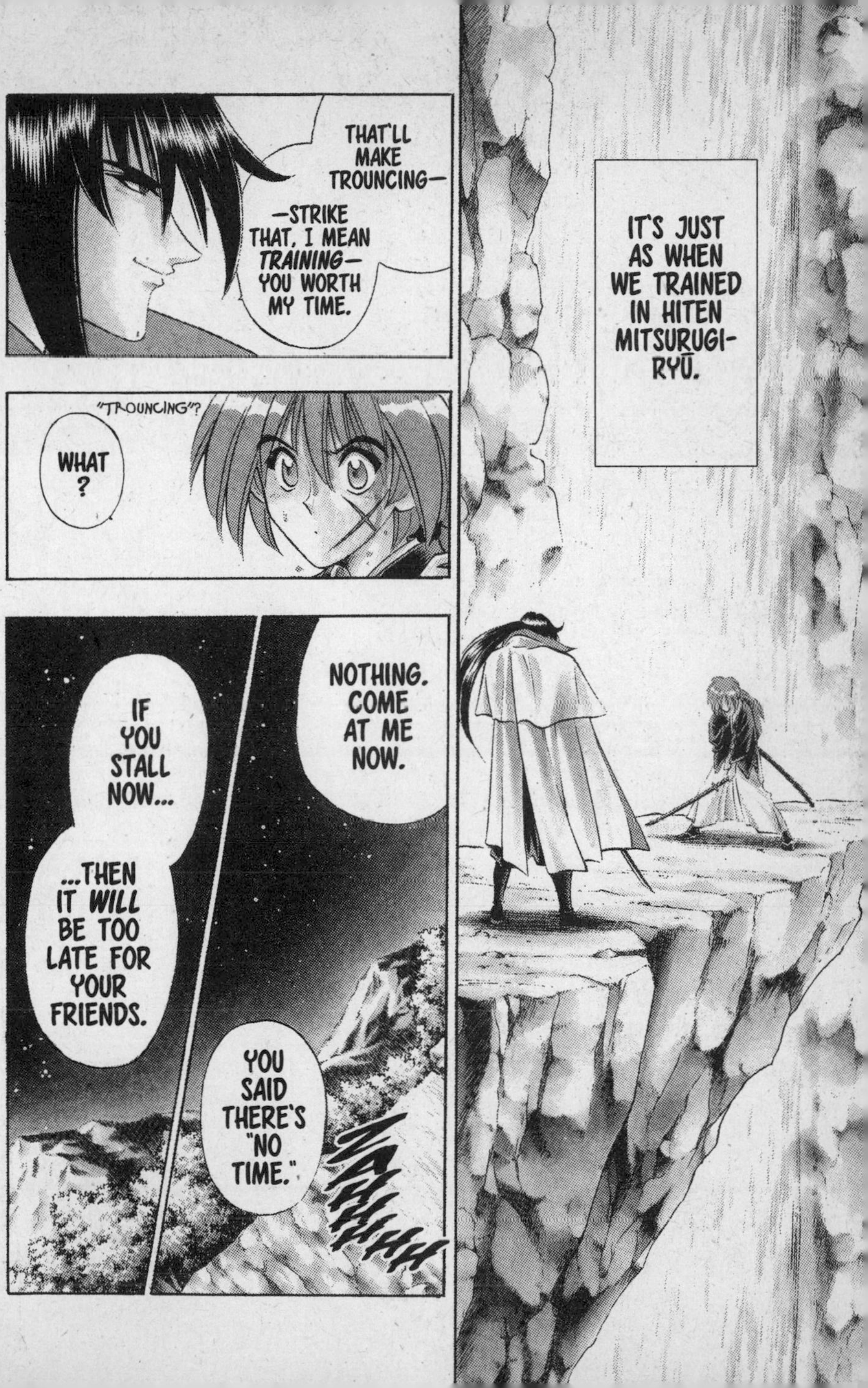
IT'S JUST AS WHEN WE TRAINED IN HITEN MITSURUGI-RYŪ.
THAT'LL MAKE TROUNCING—
—STRIKE THAT, I MEAN *TRAINING*— YOU WORTH MY TIME.
"TROUNCING"?
WHAT ?
NOTHING. COME AT ME NOW.
YOU SAID THERE'S "NO TIME."
IF YOU STALL NOW...
...THEN IT *WILL* BE TOO LATE FOR YOUR FRIENDS.

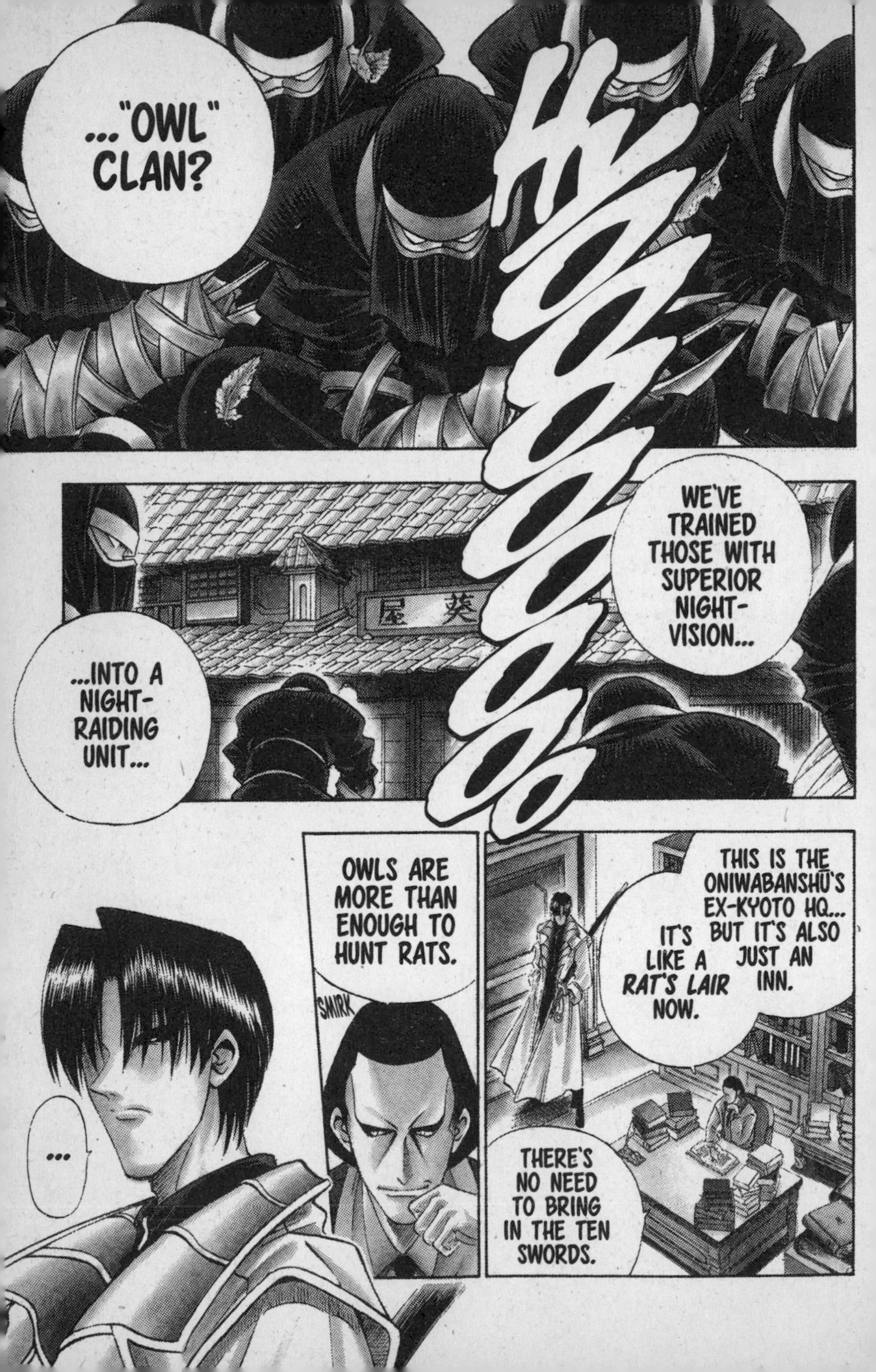
..."OWL" CLAN?
WE'VE TRAINED THOSE WITH SUPERIOR NIGHT-VISION...
葵屋
...INTO A NIGHT-RAIDING UNIT...
THIS IS THE ONIWABANSHŪ'S EX-KYOTO HQ... BUT IT'S ALSO JUST AN INN.
IT'S LIKE A *RAT'S LAIR* NOW.
THERE'S NO NEED TO BRING IN THE TEN SWORDS.
OWLS ARE MORE THAN ENOUGH TO HUNT RATS.
SMIRK
...

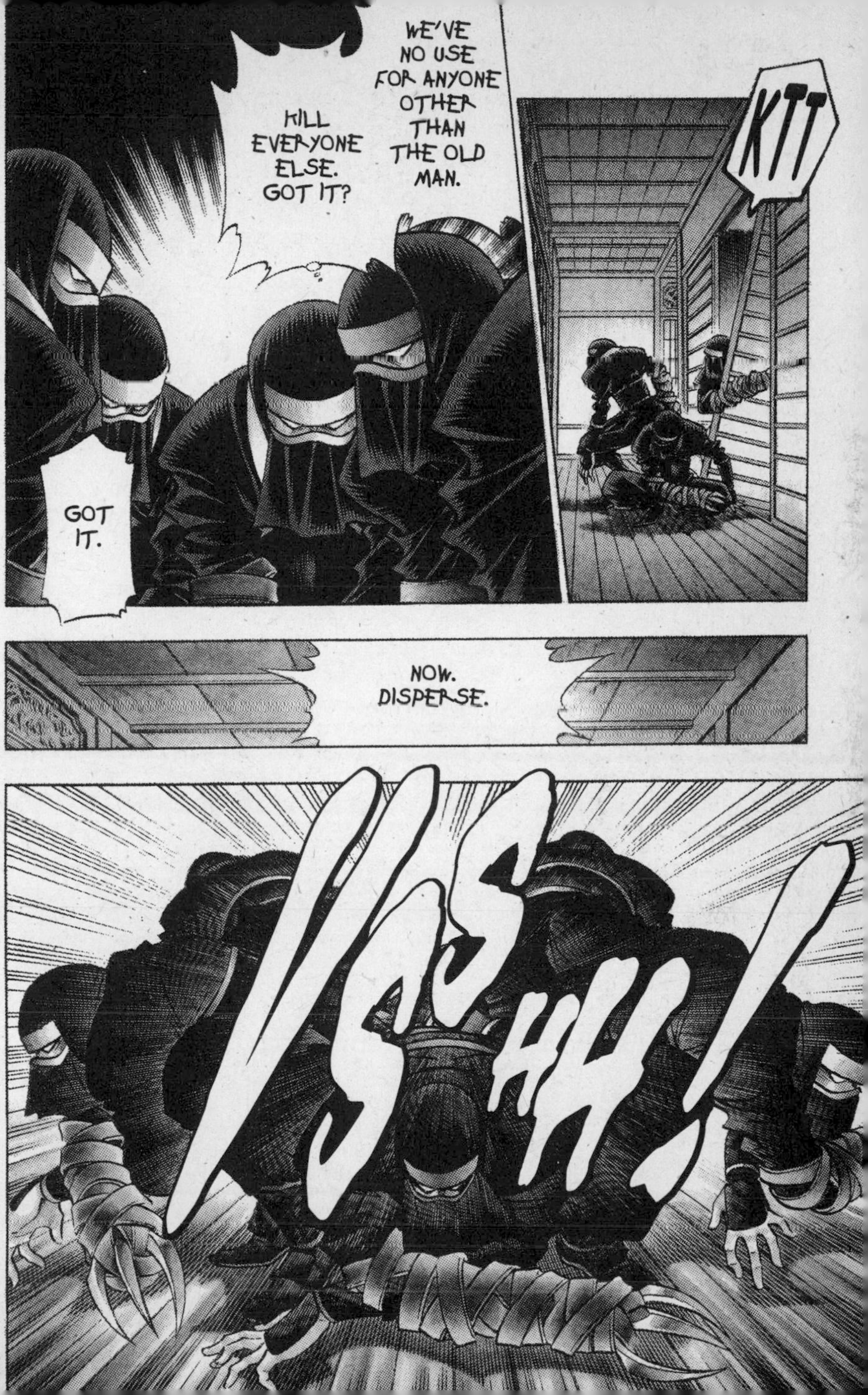
KTT
WE'VE NO USE FOR ANYONE OTHER THAN THE OLD MAN.
KILL EVERYONE ELSE. GOT IT?
GOT IT.
NOW. DISPERSE.
VSHH!

READ THIS WAY

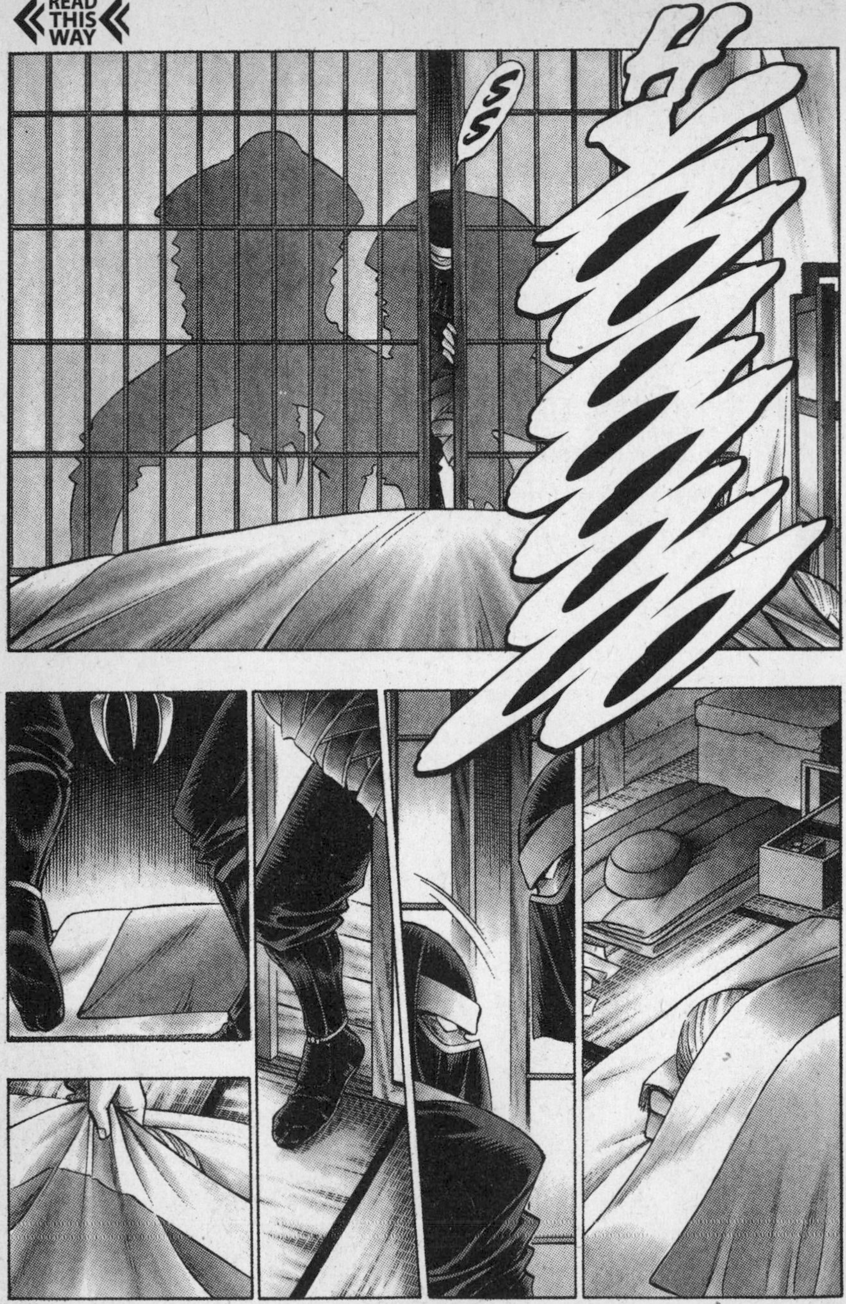
SS

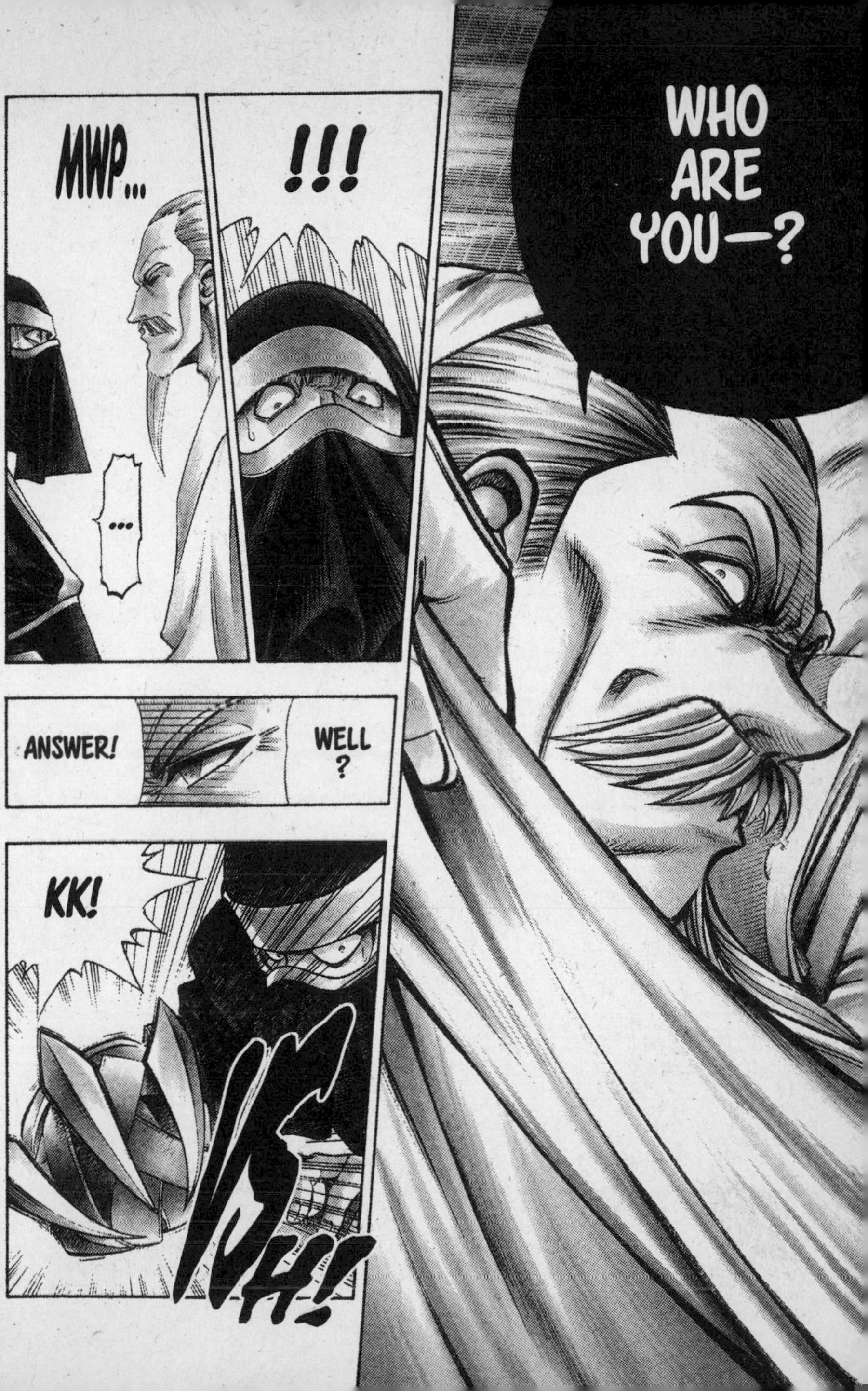
WHO ARE YOU—?
!!!
MWP...
...
WELL ?
ANSWER!
KK!
VCH!!

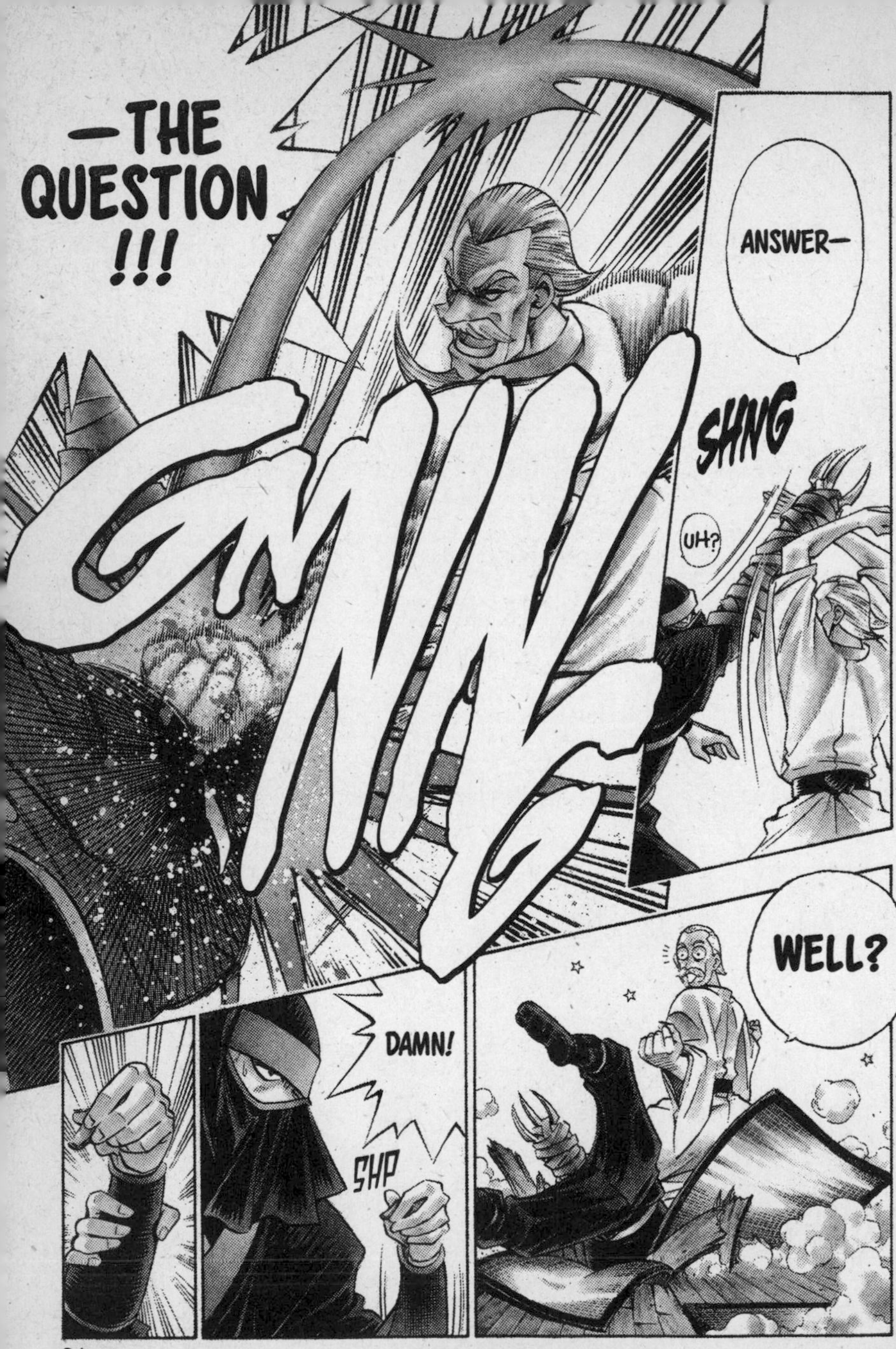
ANSWER—
SHNG
UH?
—THE QUESTION !!!
WELL?
DAMN!
SHP

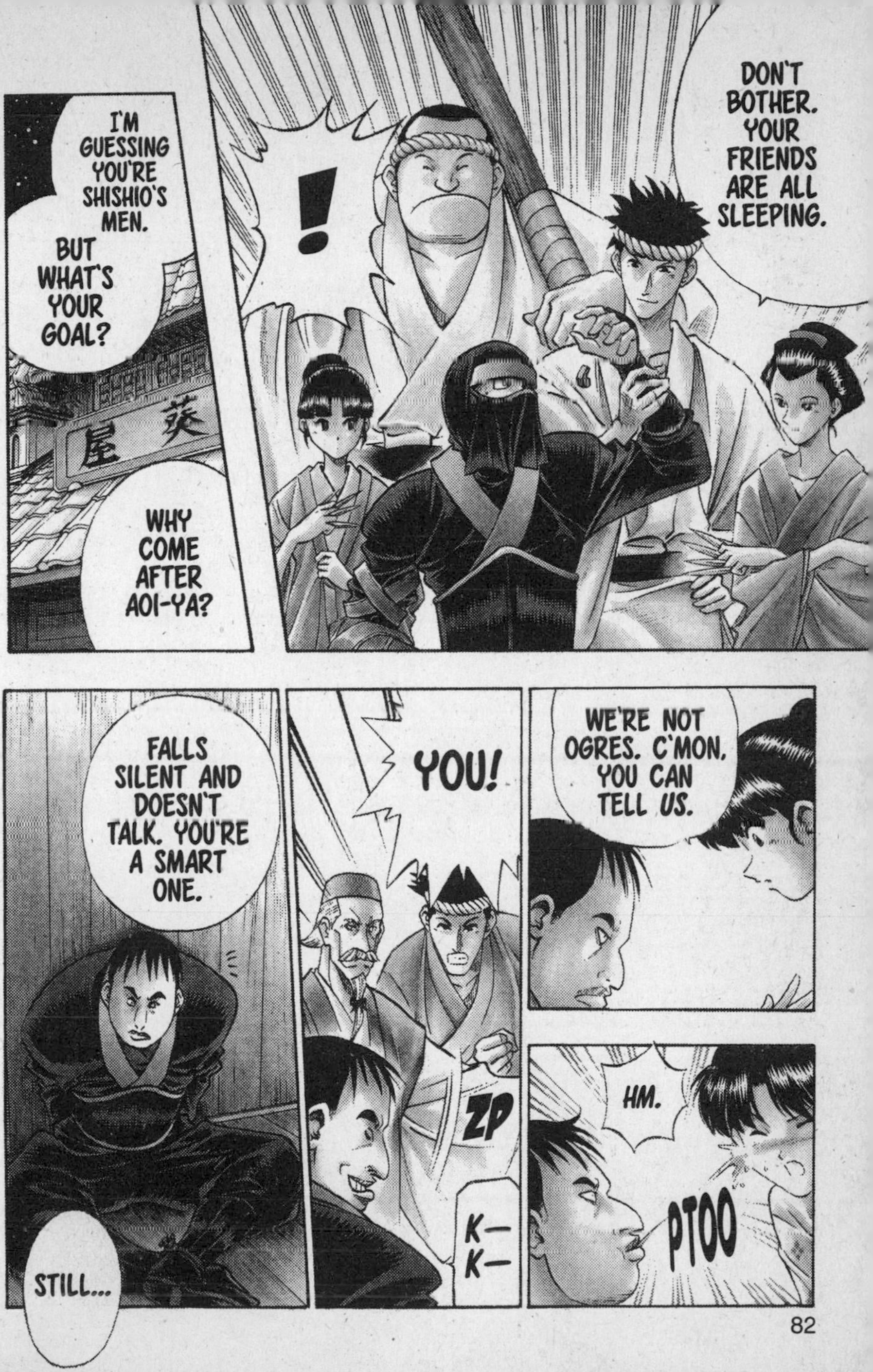
DON'T BOTHER. YOUR FRIENDS ARE ALL SLEEPING.
!
I'M GUESSING YOU'RE SHISHIO'S MEN.
BUT WHAT'S YOUR GOAL?
葵屋
WHY COME AFTER AOI-YA?
WE'RE NOT OGRES. C'MON, YOU CAN TELL US.
HM.
PTOO
YOU!
ZP
K— K—
FALLS SILENT AND DOESN'T TALK. YOU'RE A SMART ONE.
STILL...

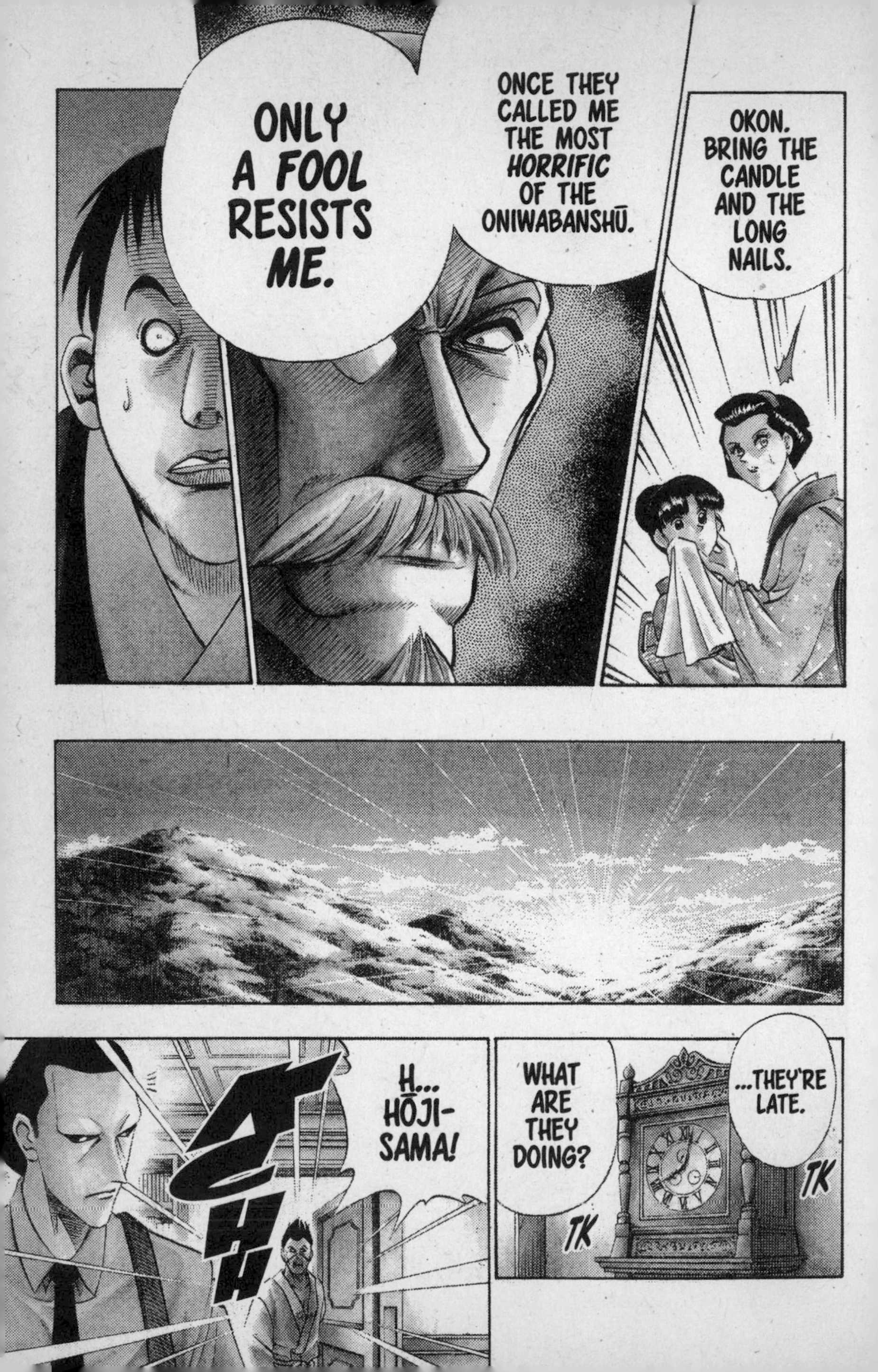
OKON. BRING THE CANDLE AND THE LONG NAILS.
ONCE THEY CALLED ME THE MOST *HORRIFIC* OF THE ONIWABANSHŪ.
ONLY A *FOOL* RESISTS *ME.*
...THEY'RE LATE.
TK
WHAT ARE THEY DOING?
TK
H... HŌJI-SAMA!

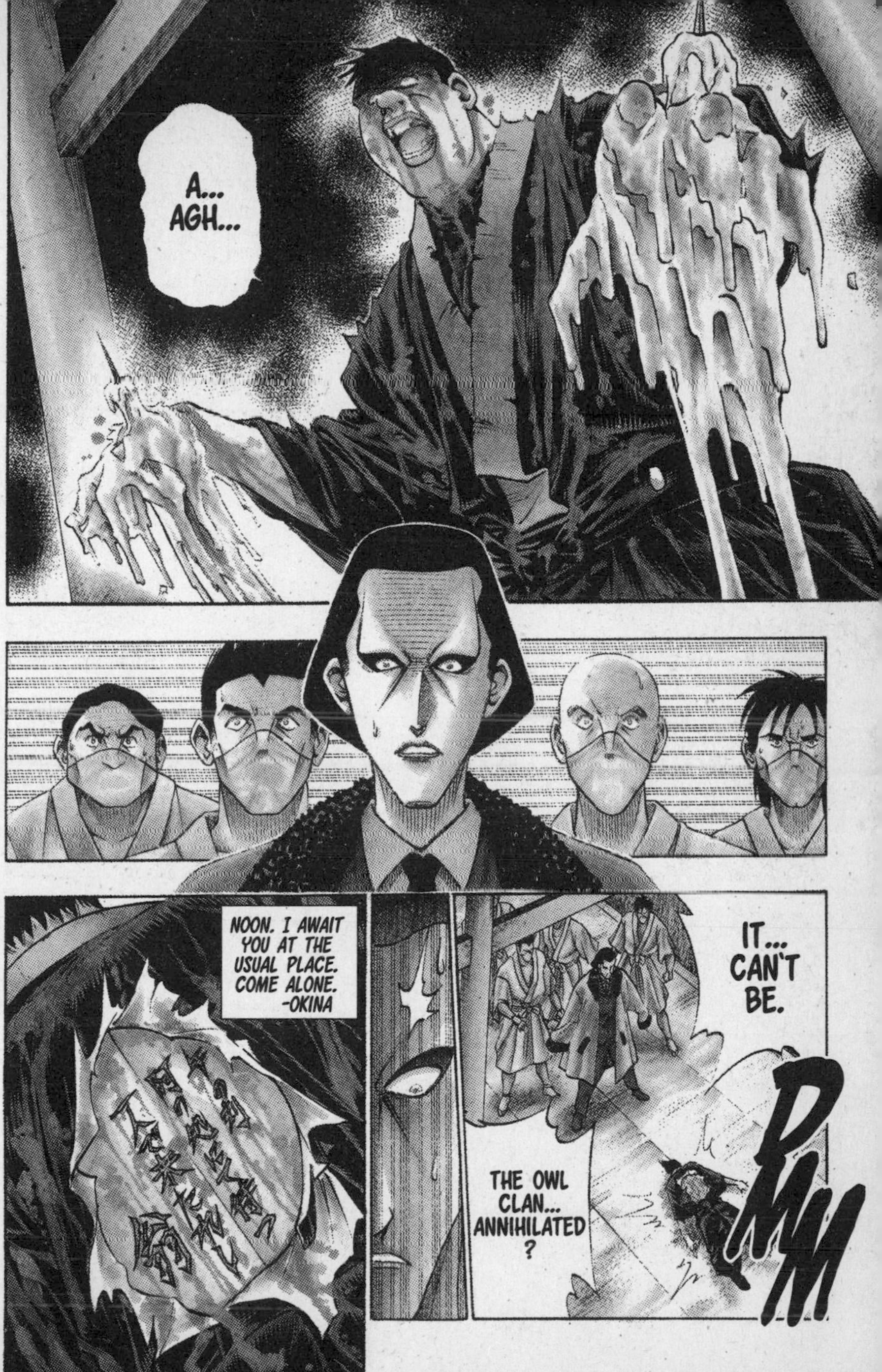
A... AGH...
IT... CAN'T BE.
THE OWL CLAN... ANNIHILATED?
PMM
NOON. I AWAIT YOU AT THE USUAL PLACE. COME ALONE. -OKINA

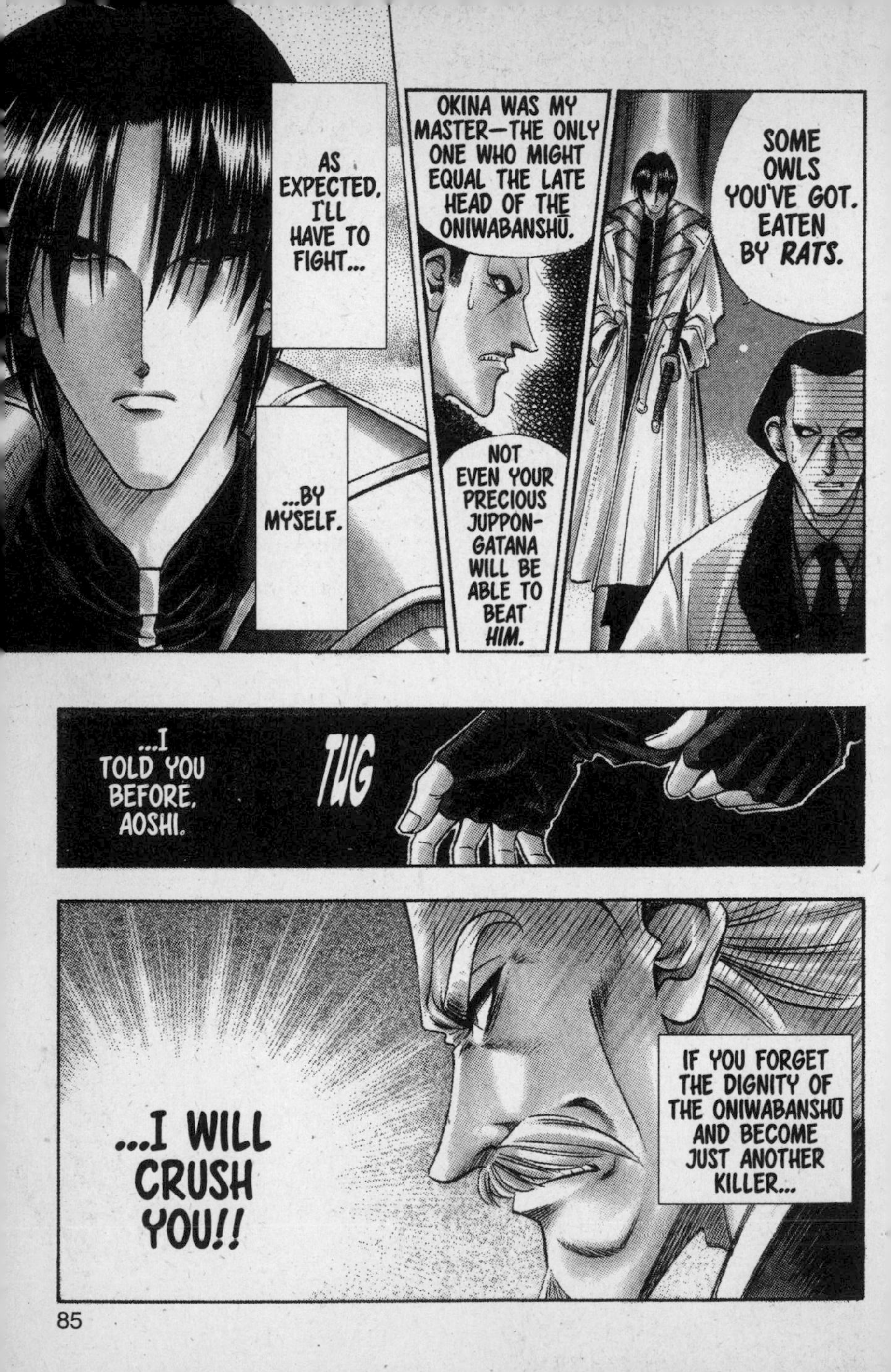
SOME OWLS YOU'VE GOT. EATEN BY RATS.
OKINA WAS MY MASTER—THE ONLY ONE WHO MIGHT EQUAL THE LATE HEAD OF THE ONIWABANSHŪ.
NOT EVEN YOUR PRECIOUS JUPPON-GATANA WILL BE ABLE TO BEAT HIM.
AS EXPECTED, I'LL HAVE TO FIGHT...
...BY MYSELF.
TUG
...I TOLD YOU BEFORE, AOSHI.
IF YOU FORGET THE DIGNITY OF THE ONIWABANSHŪ AND BECOME JUST ANOTHER KILLER...
...I WILL CRUSH YOU!!

Rurouni Kenshin

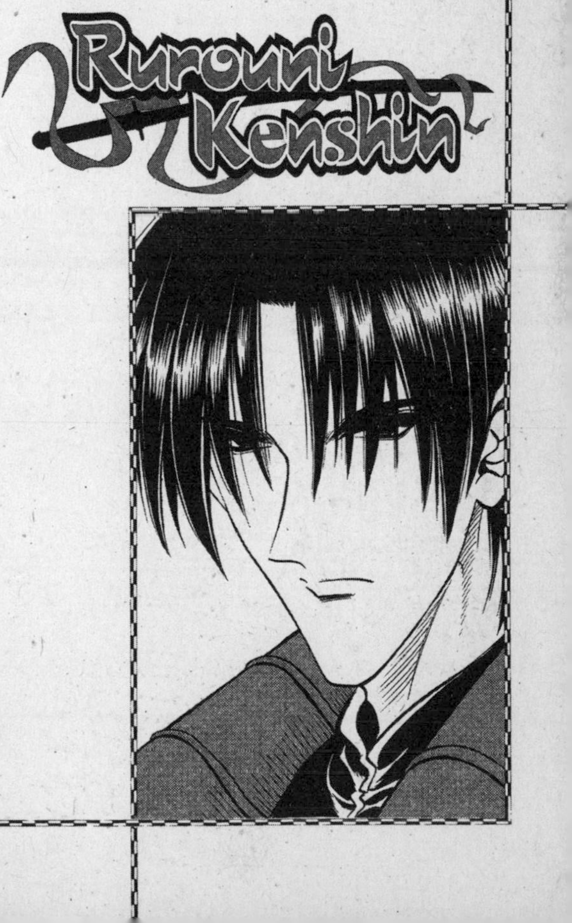

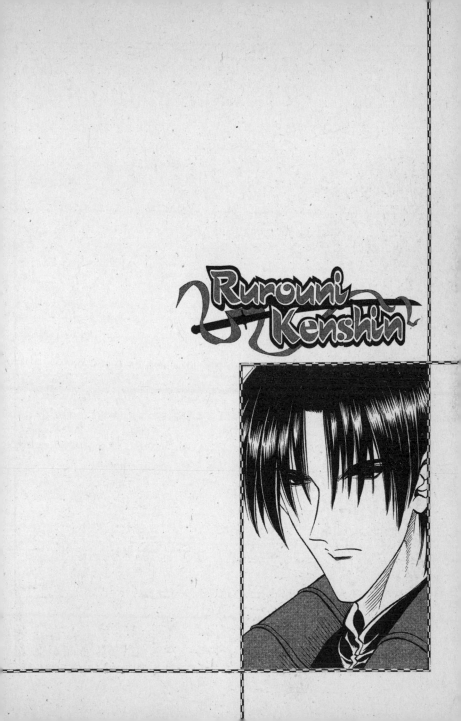

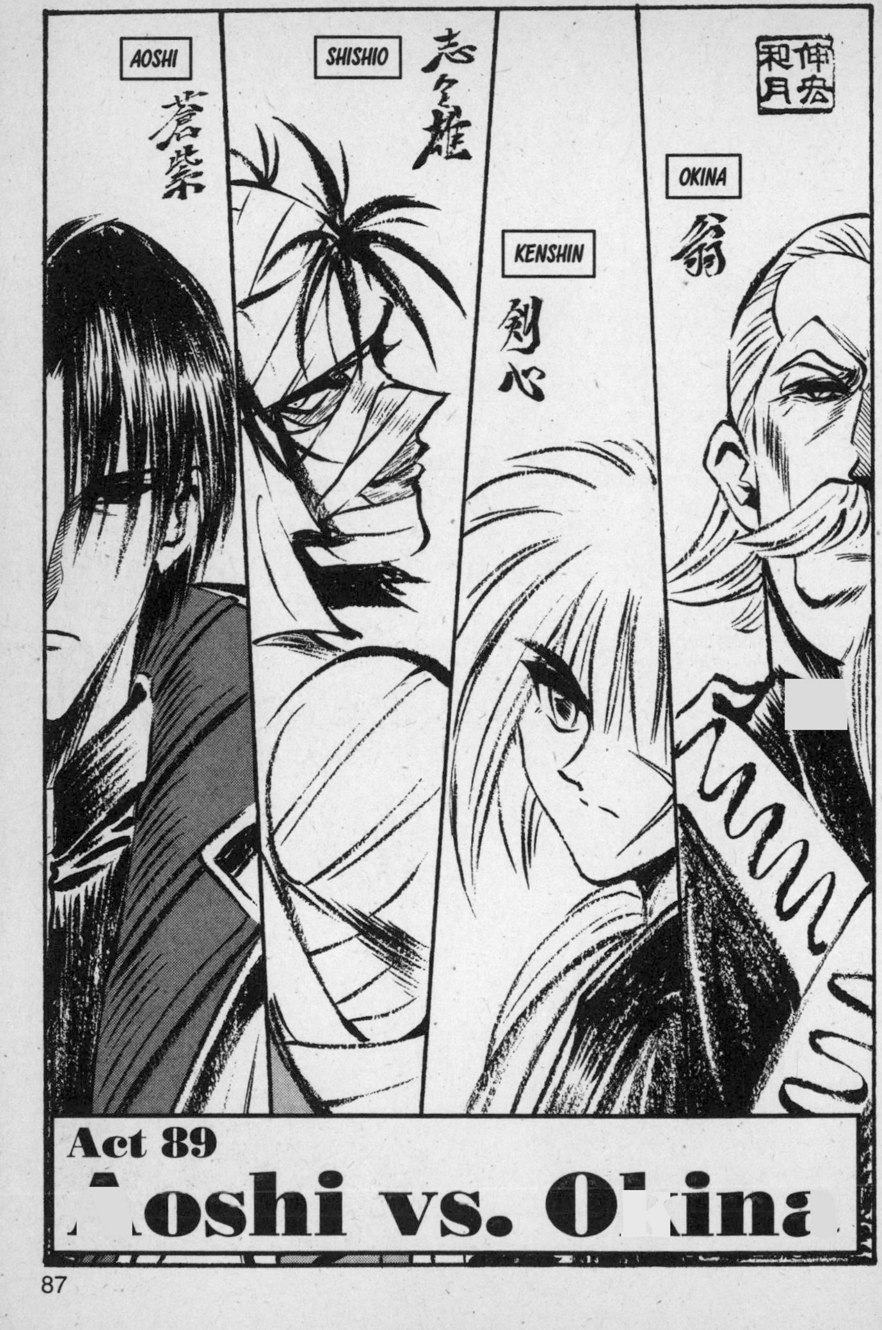
伸宏和月
OKINA
翁
KENSHIN
剣心
SHISHIO
志々雄
AOSHI
蒼紫

Act 89
Aoshi vs. Okina

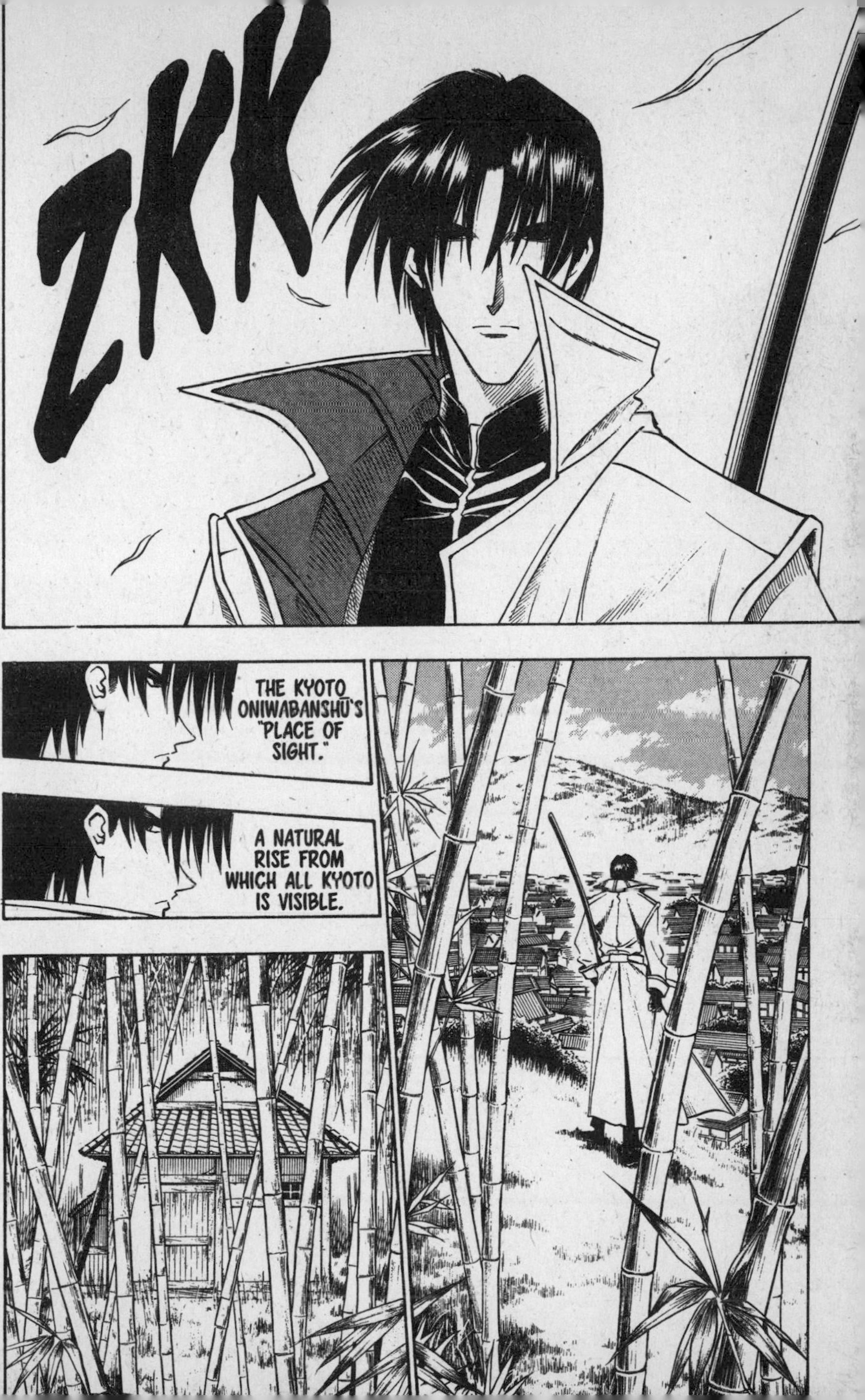
ZKK
THE KYOTO ONIWABANSHŪ'S "PLACE OF SIGHT."
A NATURAL RISE FROM WHICH ALL KYOTO IS VISIBLE.

READ THIS WAY

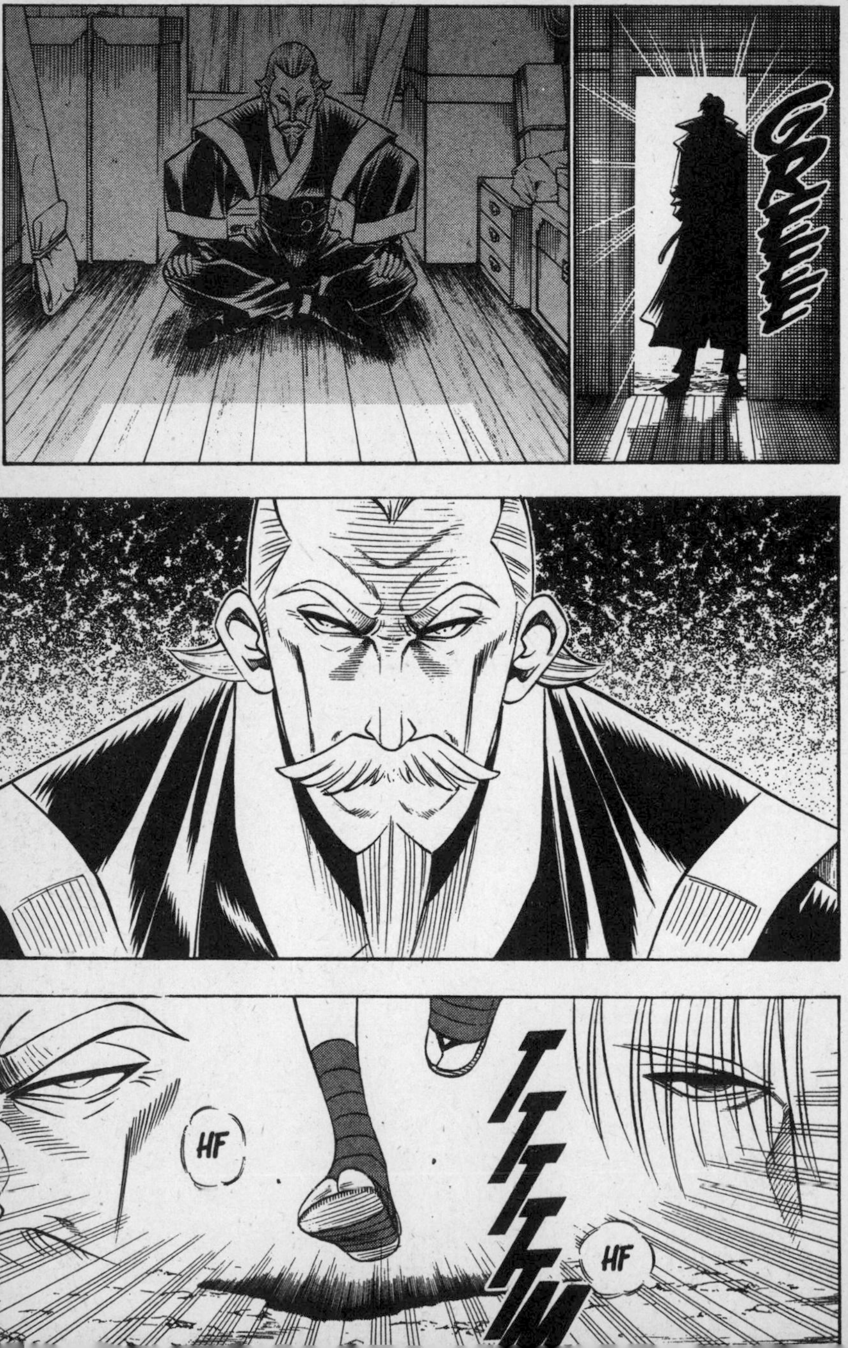
HF
HF

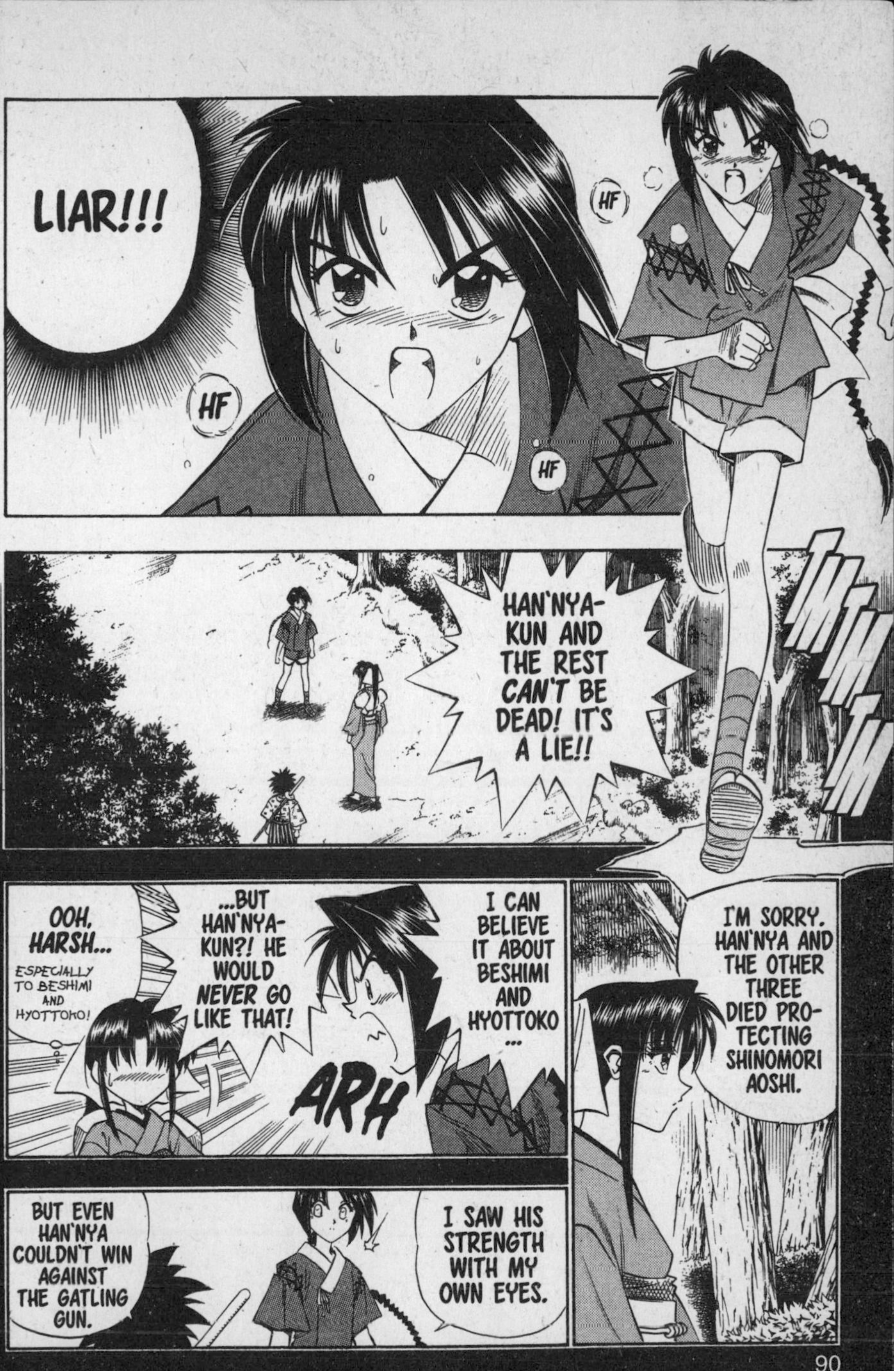
HF
LIAR!!!
HF
HF
HAN'NYA-KUN AND THE REST CAN'T BE DEAD! IT'S A LIE!!
I'M SORRY. HAN'NYA AND THE OTHER THREE DIED PRO-TECTING SHINOMORI AOSHI.
I CAN BELIEVE IT ABOUT BESHIMI AND HYOTTOKO ...
...BUT HAN'NYA-KUN?! HE WOULD NEVER GO LIKE THAT!
ARH
OOH, HARSH...
ESPECIALLY TO BESHIMI AND HYOTTOKO!
I SAW HIS STRENGTH WITH MY OWN EYES.
BUT EVEN HAN'NYA COULDN'T WIN AGAINST THE GATLING GUN.

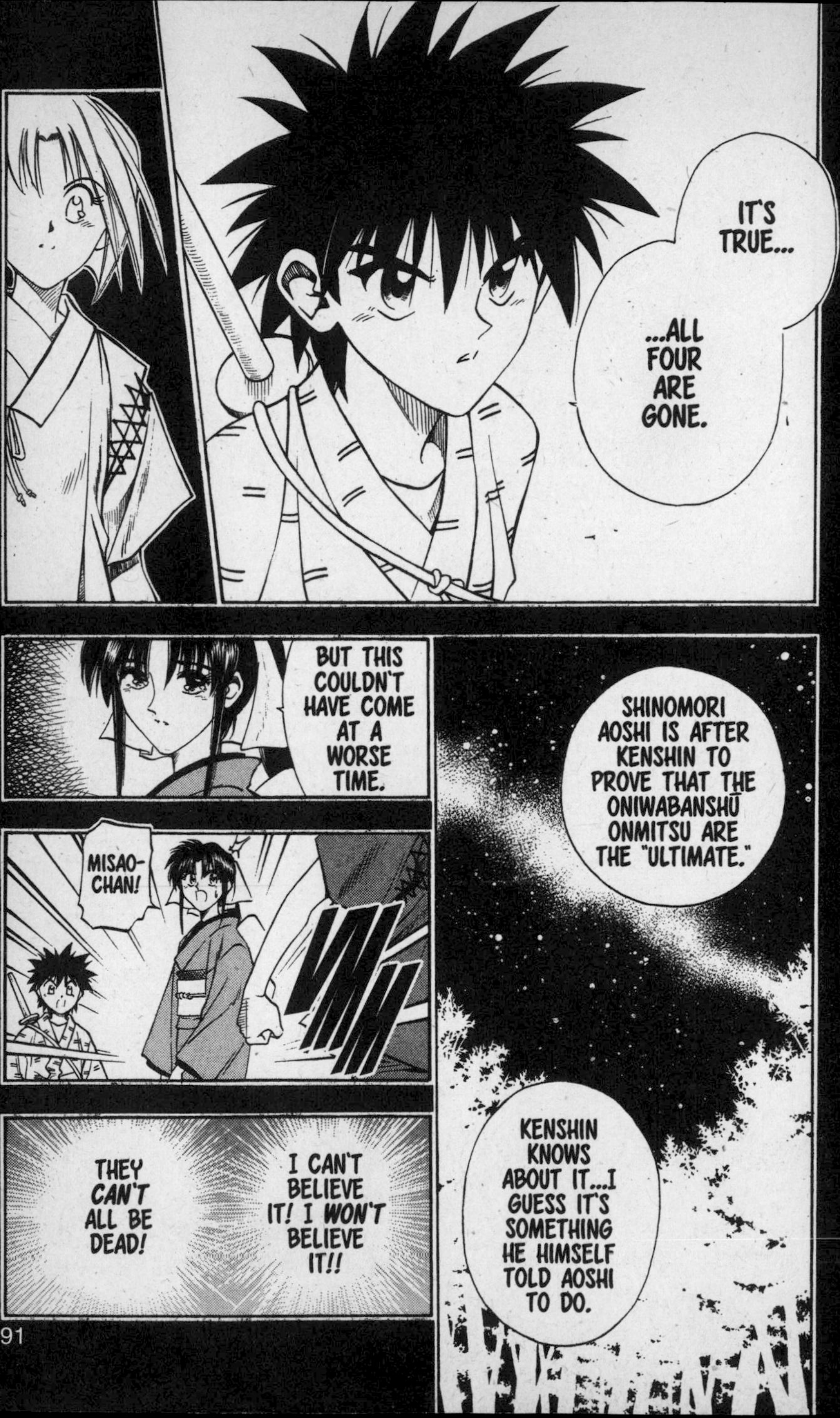
IT'S TRUE...
...ALL FOUR ARE GONE.
SHINOMORI AOSHI IS AFTER KENSHIN TO PROVE THAT THE ONIWABANSHŪ ONMITSU ARE THE "ULTIMATE."
KENSHIN KNOWS ABOUT IT...I GUESS IT'S SOMETHING HE HIMSELF TOLD AOSHI TO DO.
BUT THIS COULDN'T HAVE COME AT A WORSE TIME.
MISAO-CHAN!
I CAN'T BELIEVE IT! I *WON'T* BELIEVE IT!!
THEY *CAN'T* ALL BE DEAD!

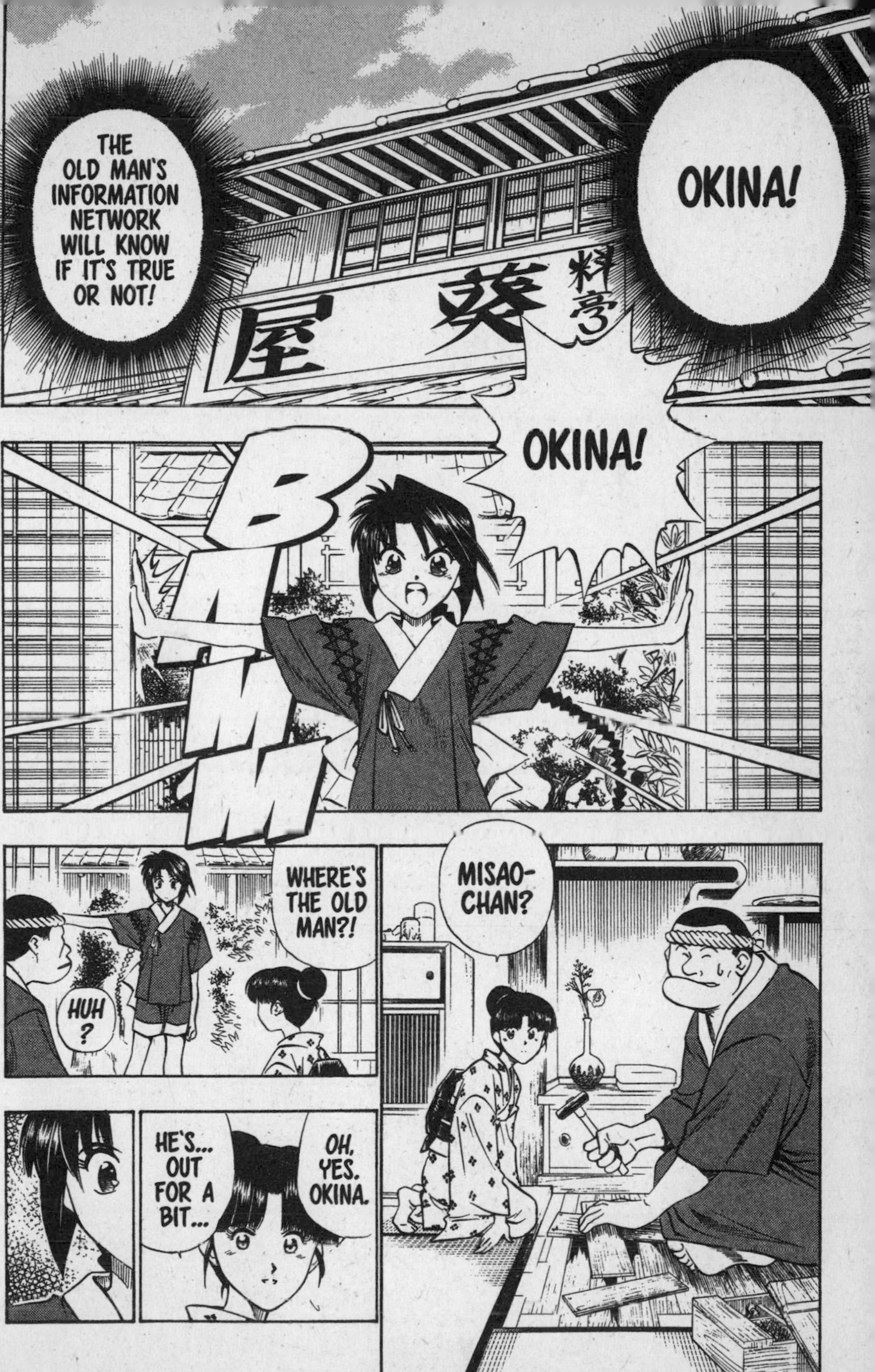

OKINA!
THE OLD MAN'S INFORMATION NETWORK WILL KNOW IF IT'S TRUE OR NOT!
料亭
葵屋
OKINA!
BAMM
MISAO-CHAN?
WHERE'S THE OLD MAN?!
HUH?
OH, YES. OKINA.
HE'S... OUT FOR A BIT...

READ THIS WAY

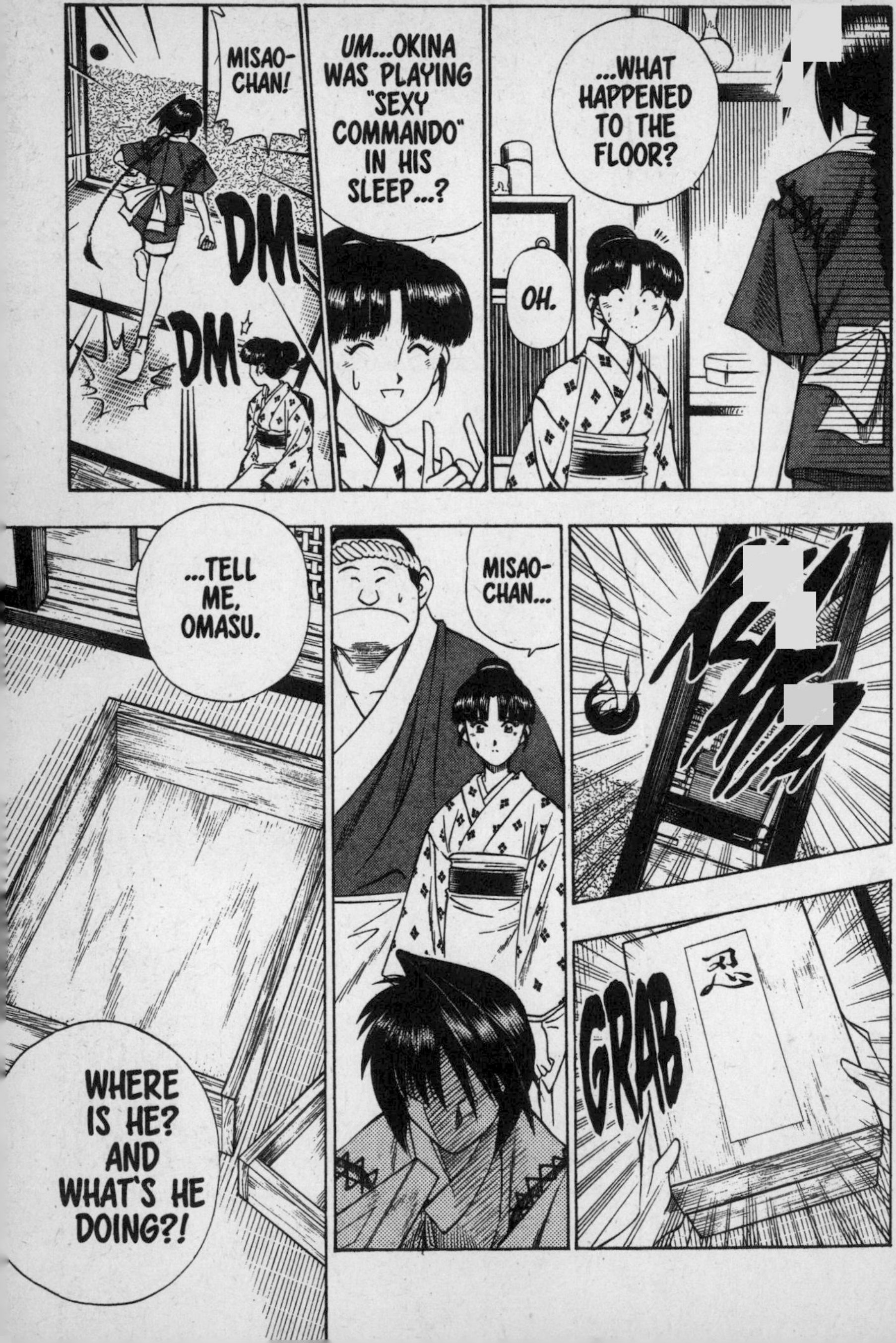
...WHAT HAPPENED TO THE FLOOR?
OH.
UM...OKINA WAS PLAYING "SEXY COMMANDO" IN HIS SLEEP...?
MISAO-CHAN!
DM
DM
GRAB
MISAO-CHAN...
...TELL ME, OMASU.
WHERE IS HE? AND WHAT'S HE DOING?!

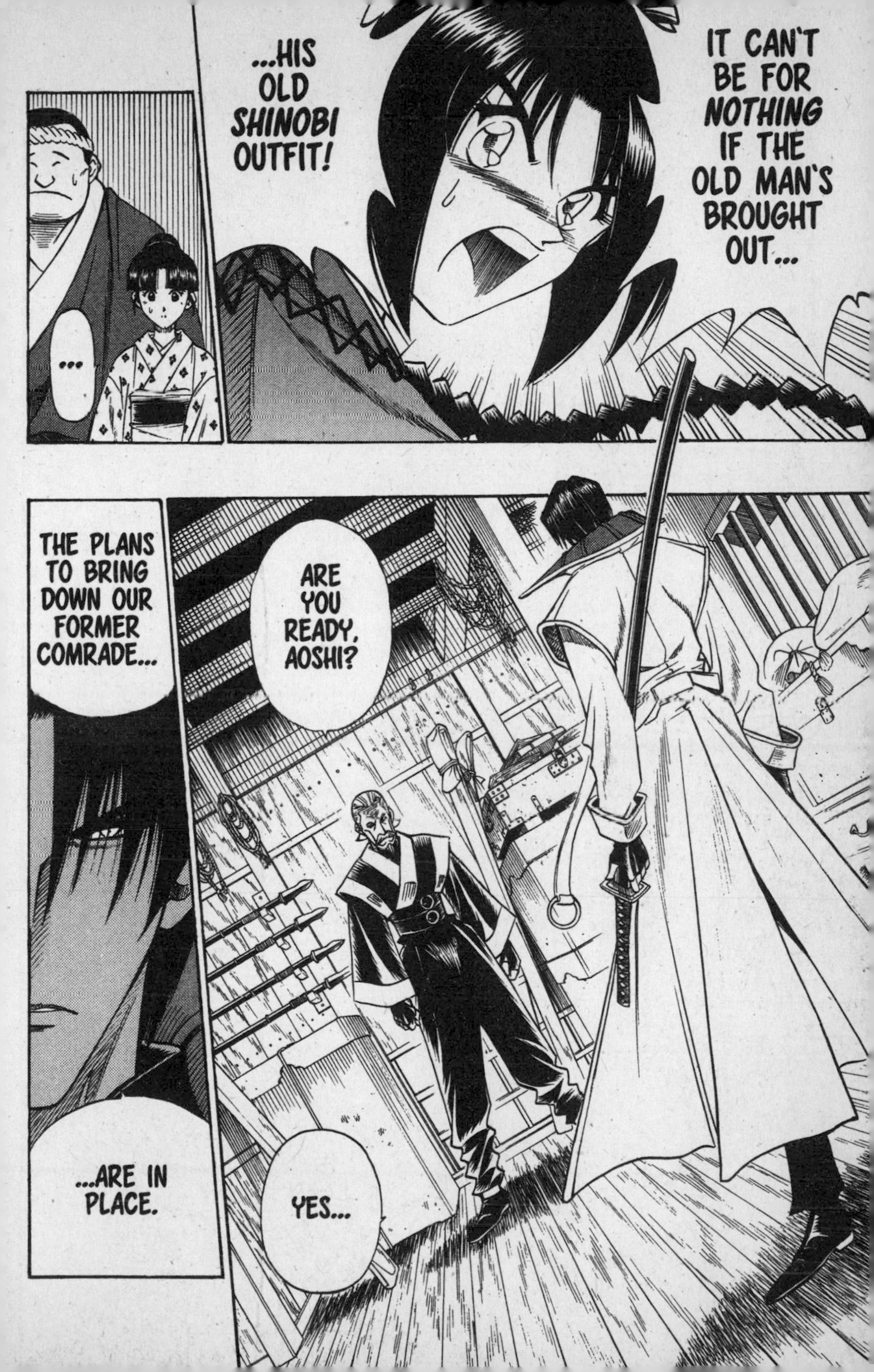
IT CAN'T BE FOR NOTHING IF THE OLD MAN'S BROUGHT OUT...
...HIS OLD SHINOBI OUTFIT!
...
ARE YOU READY, AOSHI?
YES...
THE PLANS TO BRING DOWN OUR FORMER COMRADE...
...ARE IN PLACE.

READ THIS WAY

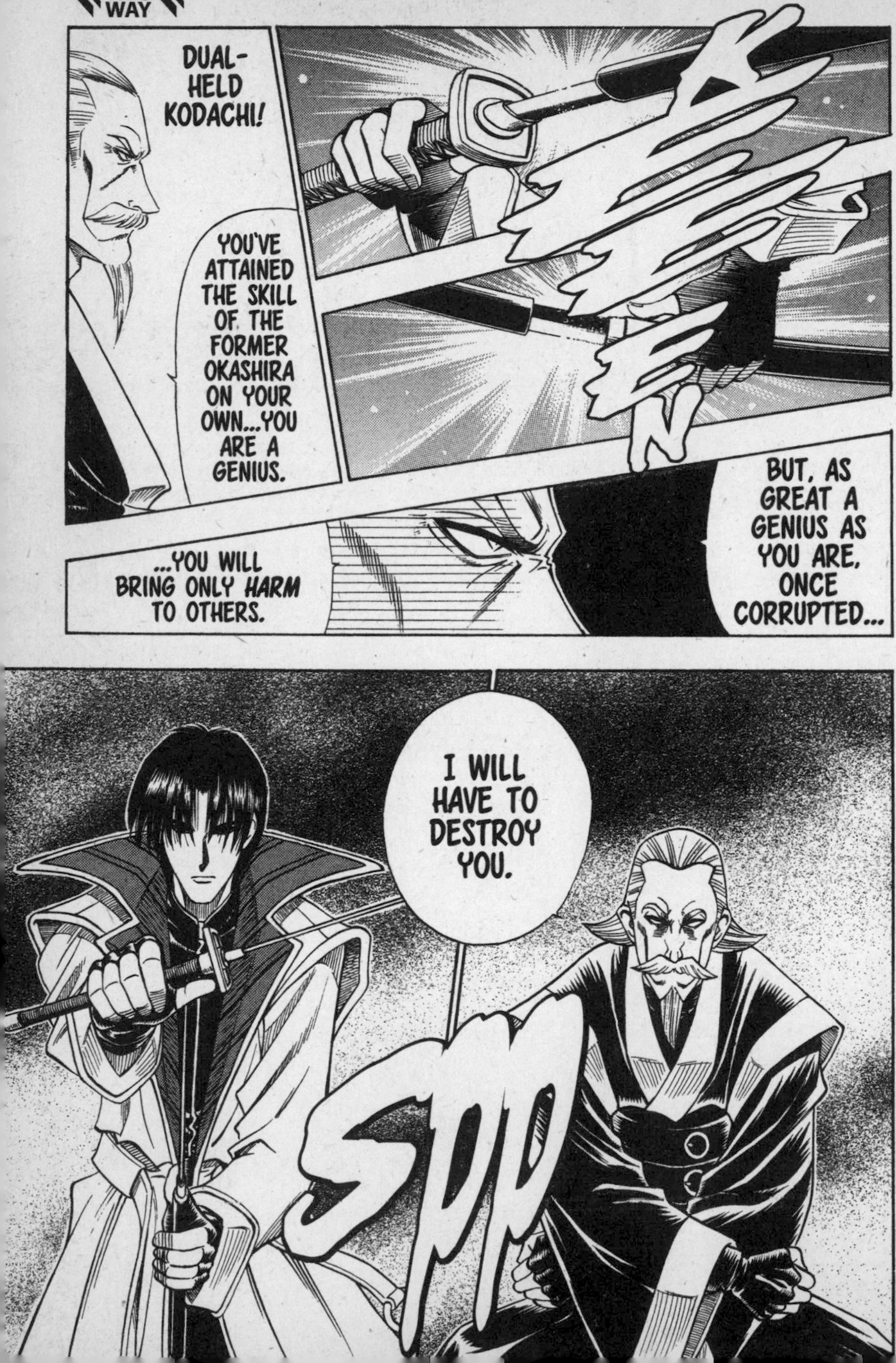
DUAL-HELD KODACHI!
YOU'VE ATTAINED THE SKILL OF THE FORMER OKASHIRA ON YOUR OWN...YOU ARE A GENIUS.
BUT, AS GREAT A GENIUS AS YOU ARE, ONCE CORRUPTED...
...YOU WILL BRING ONLY HARM TO OTHERS.
I WILL HAVE TO DESTROY YOU.
SPP

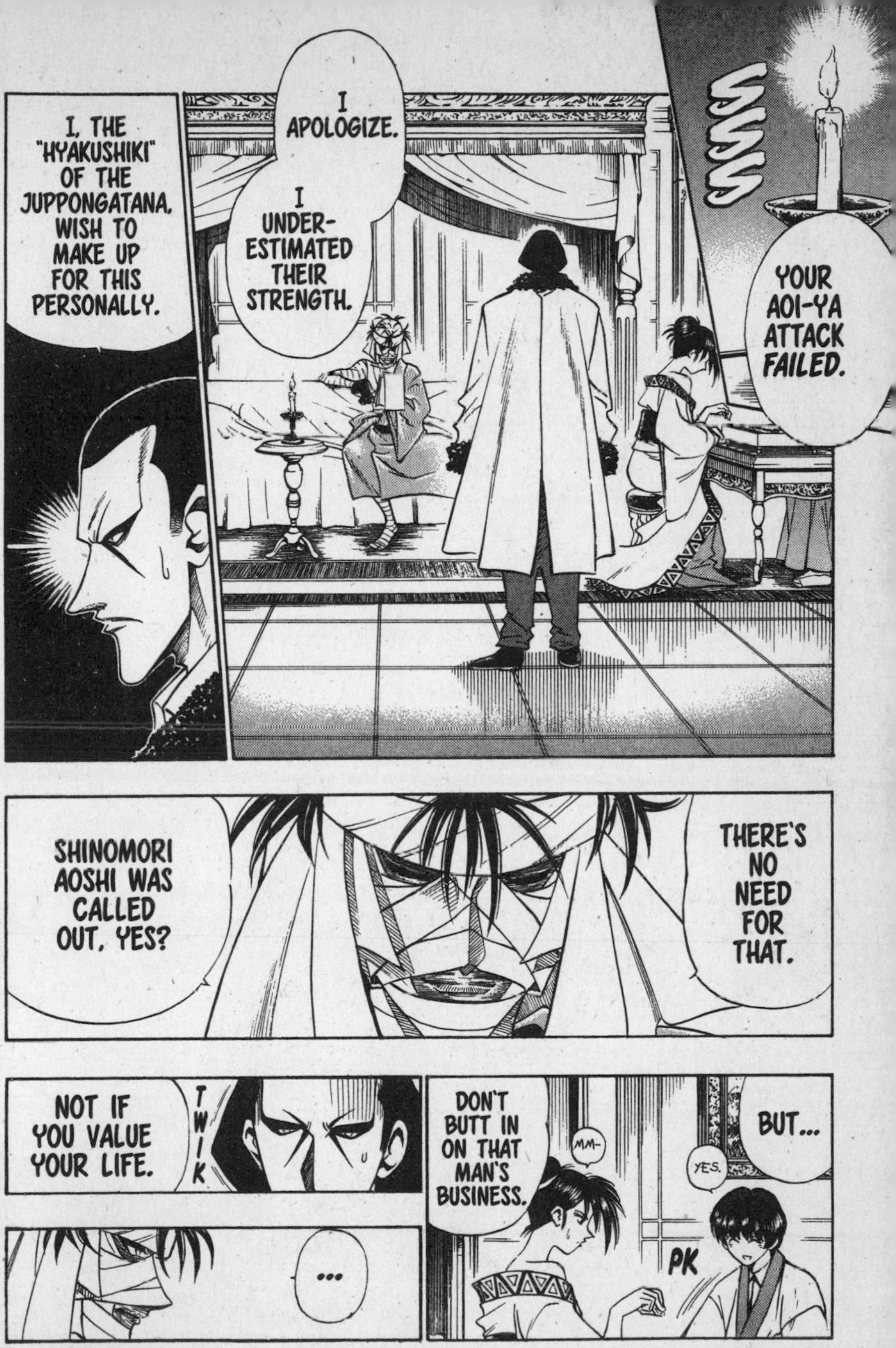
SSS
YOUR AOI-YA ATTACK FAILED.
I APOLOGIZE.
I UNDER-ESTIMATED THEIR STRENGTH.
I, THE "HYAKUSHIKI" OF THE JUPPONGATANA, WISH TO MAKE UP FOR THIS PERSONALLY.
THERE'S NO NEED FOR THAT.
SHINOMORI AOSHI WAS CALLED OUT, YES?
BUT...
YES.
DON'T BUTT IN ON THAT MAN'S BUSINESS.
MM-
PK
TWIK
NOT IF YOU VALUE YOUR LIFE.
...

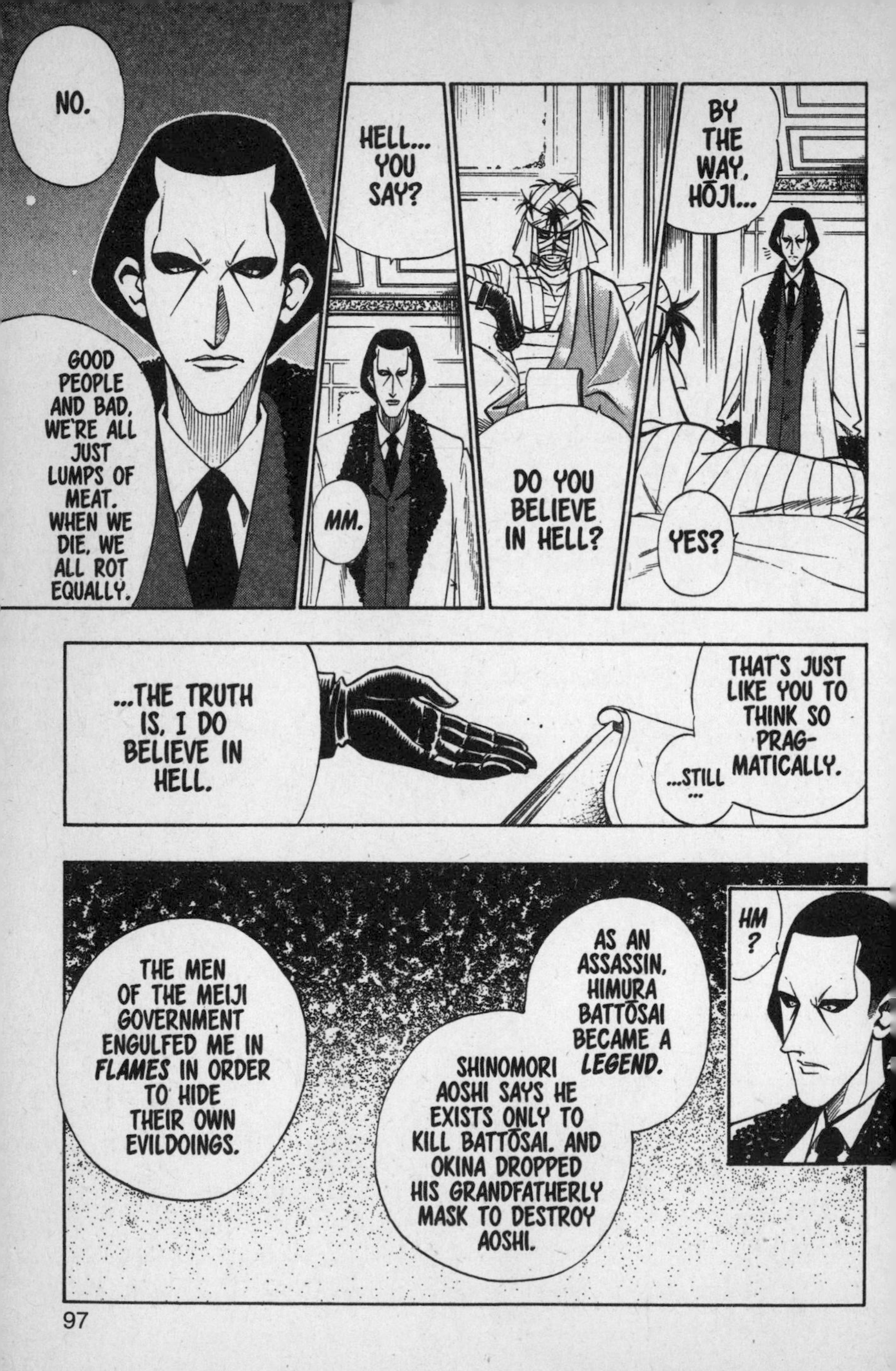
BY THE WAY, HŌJI...
YES?
DO YOU BELIEVE IN HELL?
HELL... YOU SAY?
MM.
NO.
GOOD PEOPLE AND BAD, WE'RE ALL JUST LUMPS OF MEAT. WHEN WE DIE, WE ALL ROT EQUALLY.
THAT'S JUST LIKE YOU TO THINK SO PRAG-MATICALLY.
...STILL...
...THE TRUTH IS, I DO BELIEVE IN HELL.
HM?
AS AN ASSASSIN, HIMURA BATTŌSAI BECAME A LEGEND.
SHINOMORI AOSHI SAYS HE EXISTS ONLY TO KILL BATTŌSAI. AND OKINA DROPPED HIS GRANDFATHERLY MASK TO DESTROY AOSHI.
THE MEN OF THE MEIJI GOVERNMENT ENGULFED ME IN FLAMES IN ORDER TO HIDE THEIR OWN EVILDOINGS.

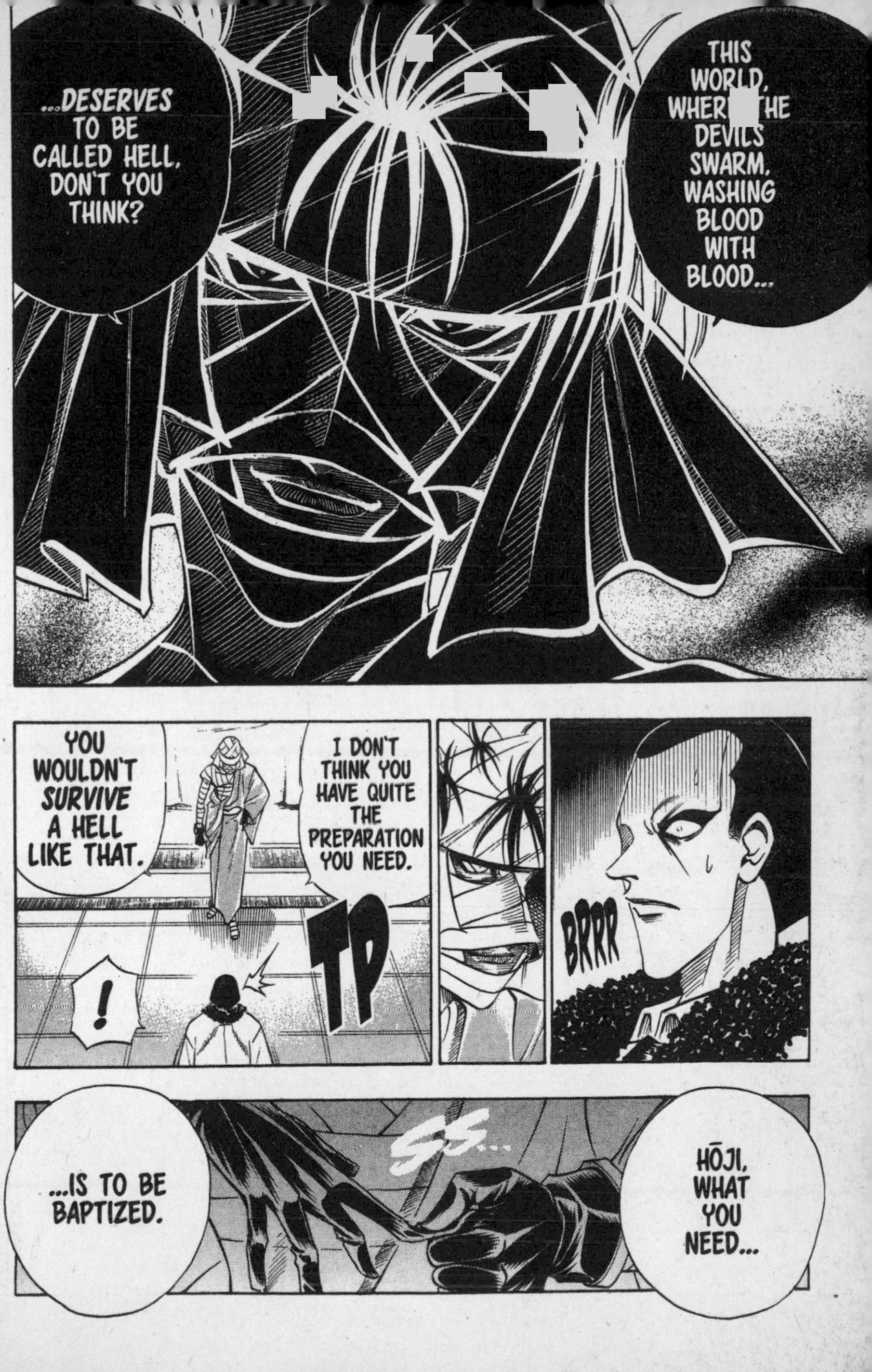
THIS WORLD, WHERE THE DEVILS SWARM, WASHING BLOOD WITH BLOOD...
...DESERVES TO BE CALLED HELL, DON'T YOU THINK?
BRRR
I DON'T THINK YOU HAVE QUITE THE PREPARATION YOU NEED.
YOU WOULDN'T *SURVIVE* A HELL LIKE THAT.
TP
!
HŌJI, WHAT YOU NEED...
SS...
...IS TO BE BAPTIZED.

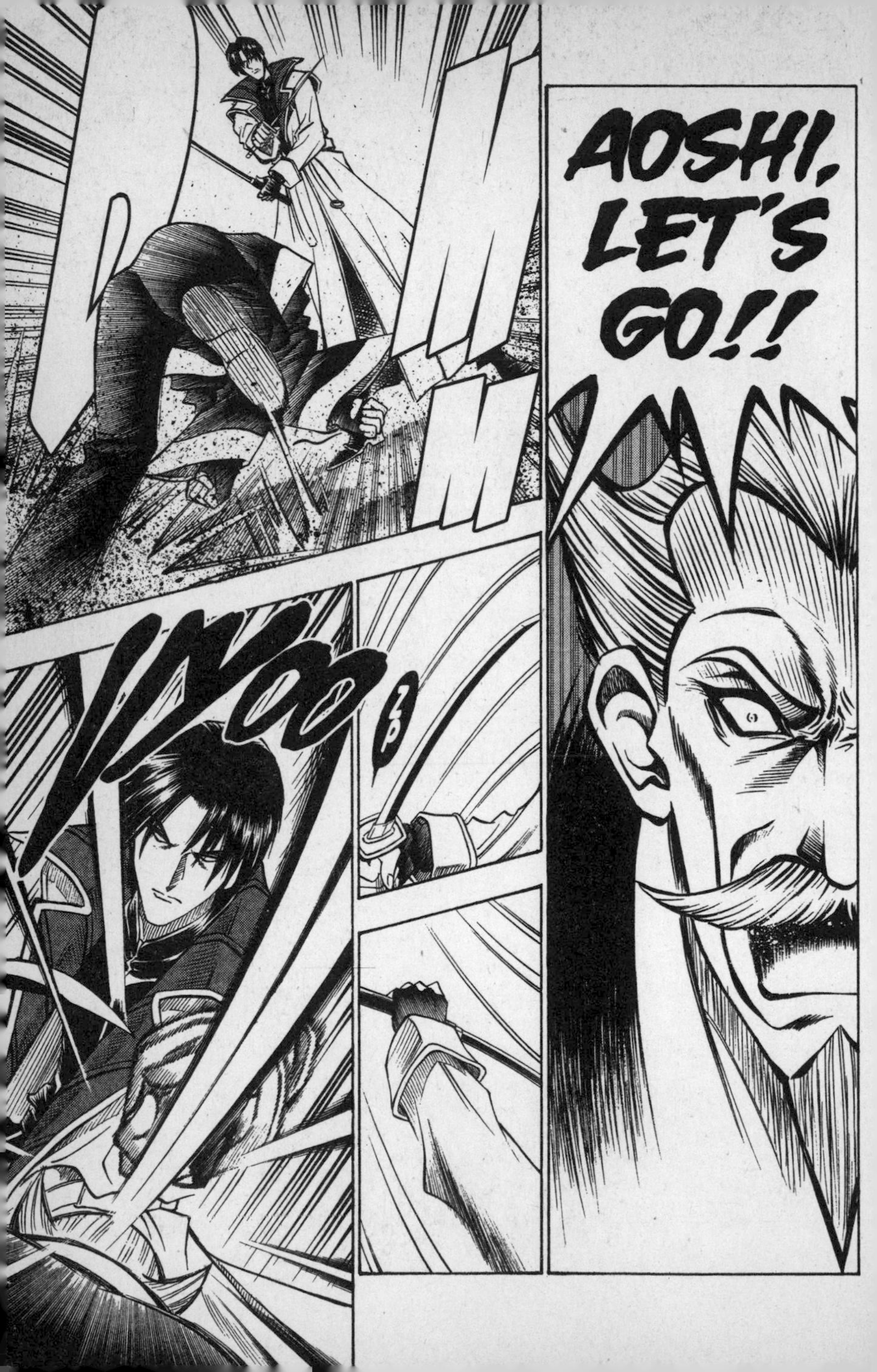
AOSHI, LET'S GO!!
ZIP
VWOO

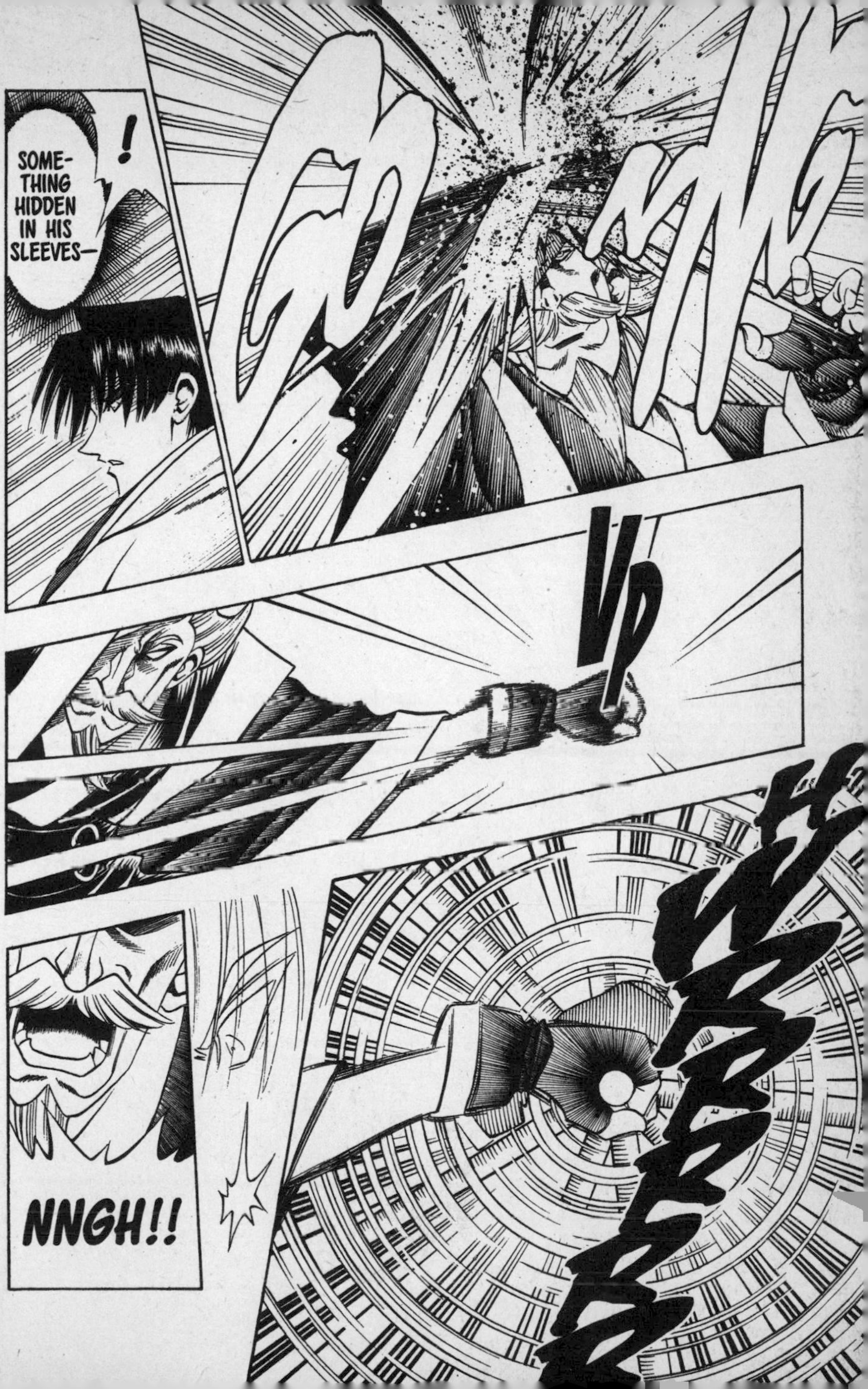
!
SOME-THING HIDDEN IN HIS SLEEVES—
NNGH!!

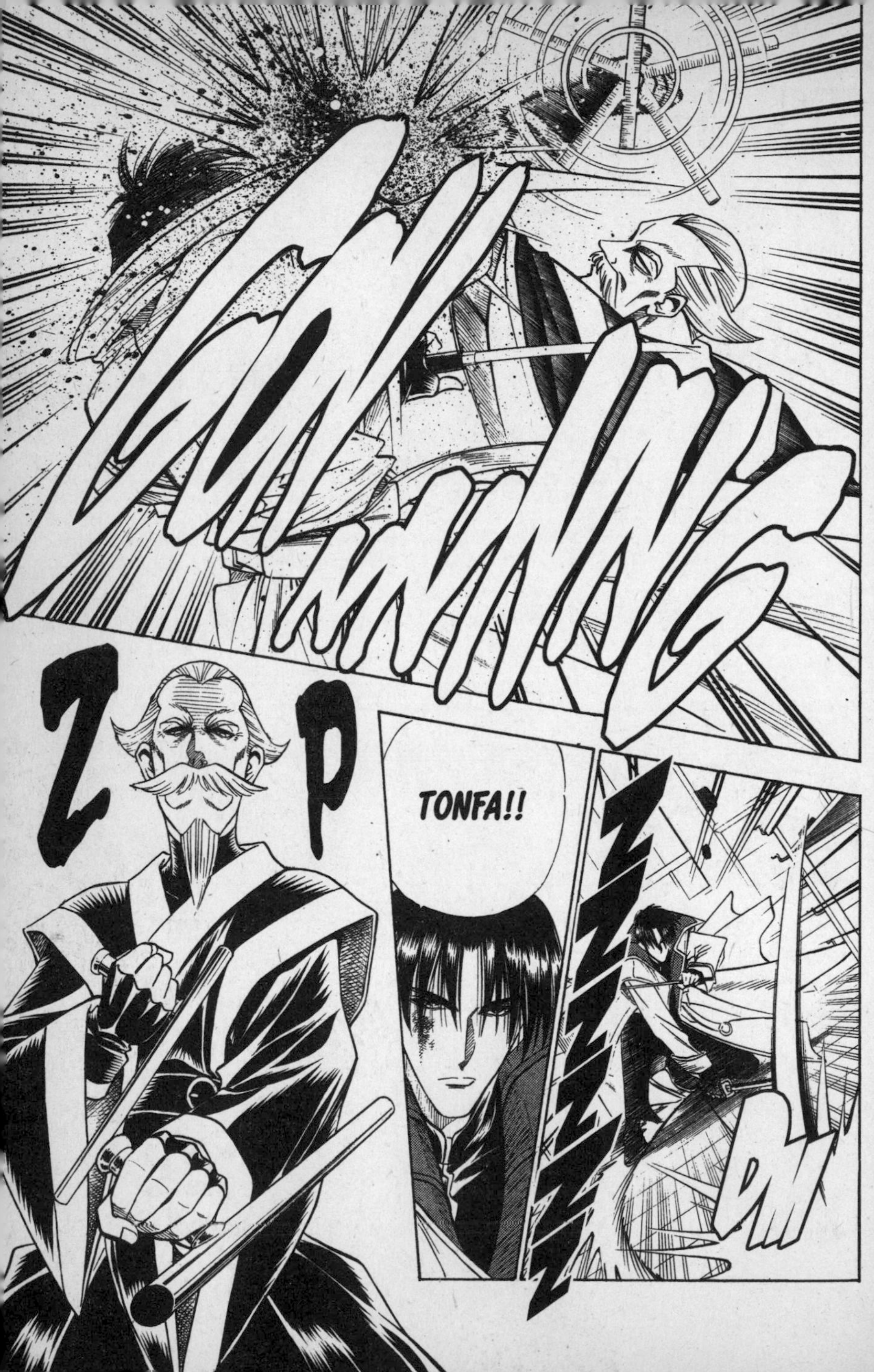
TONFA!!

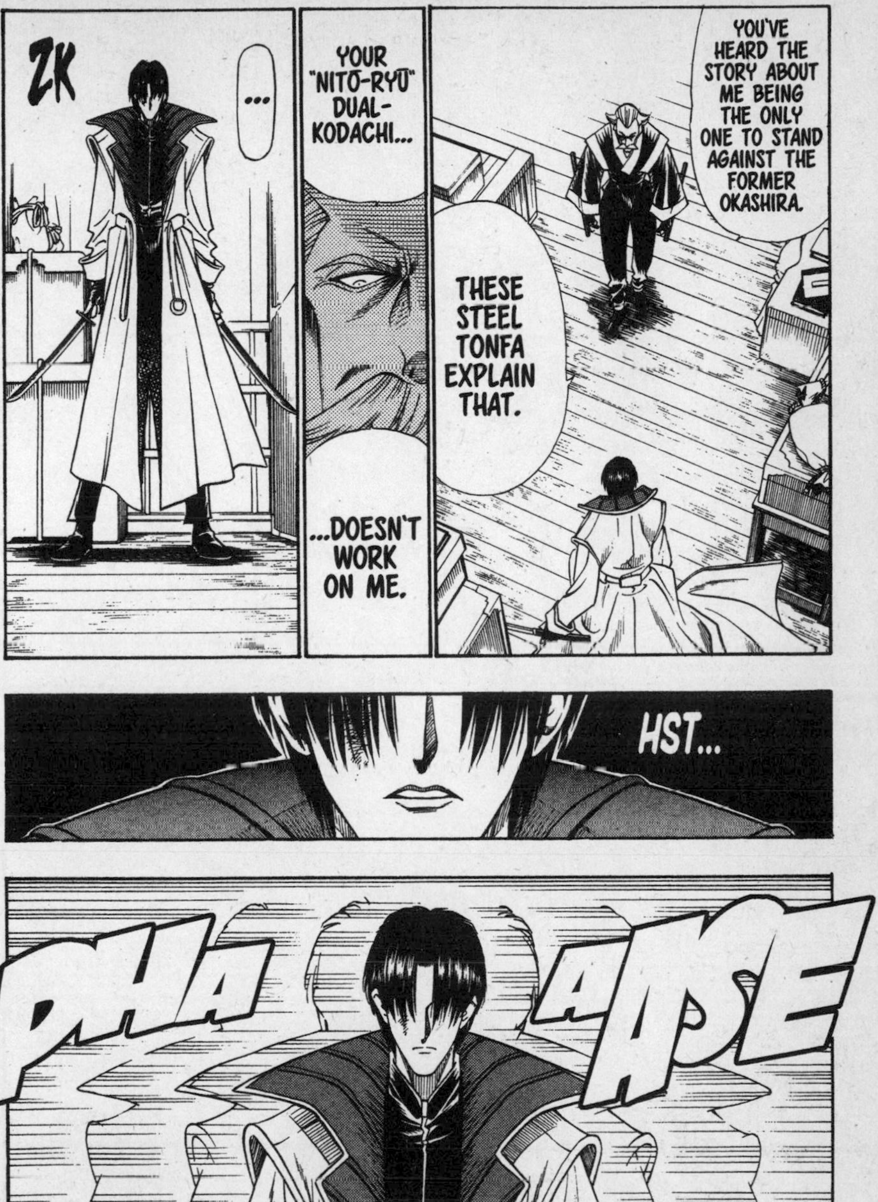
YOU'VE HEARD THE STORY ABOUT ME BEING THE ONLY ONE TO STAND AGAINST THE FORMER OKASHIRA.
THESE STEEL TONFA EXPLAIN THAT.
YOUR "NITŌ-RYŪ" DUAL-KODACHI...
...DOESN'T WORK ON ME.
ZK
...
HST...
DHA
AASE

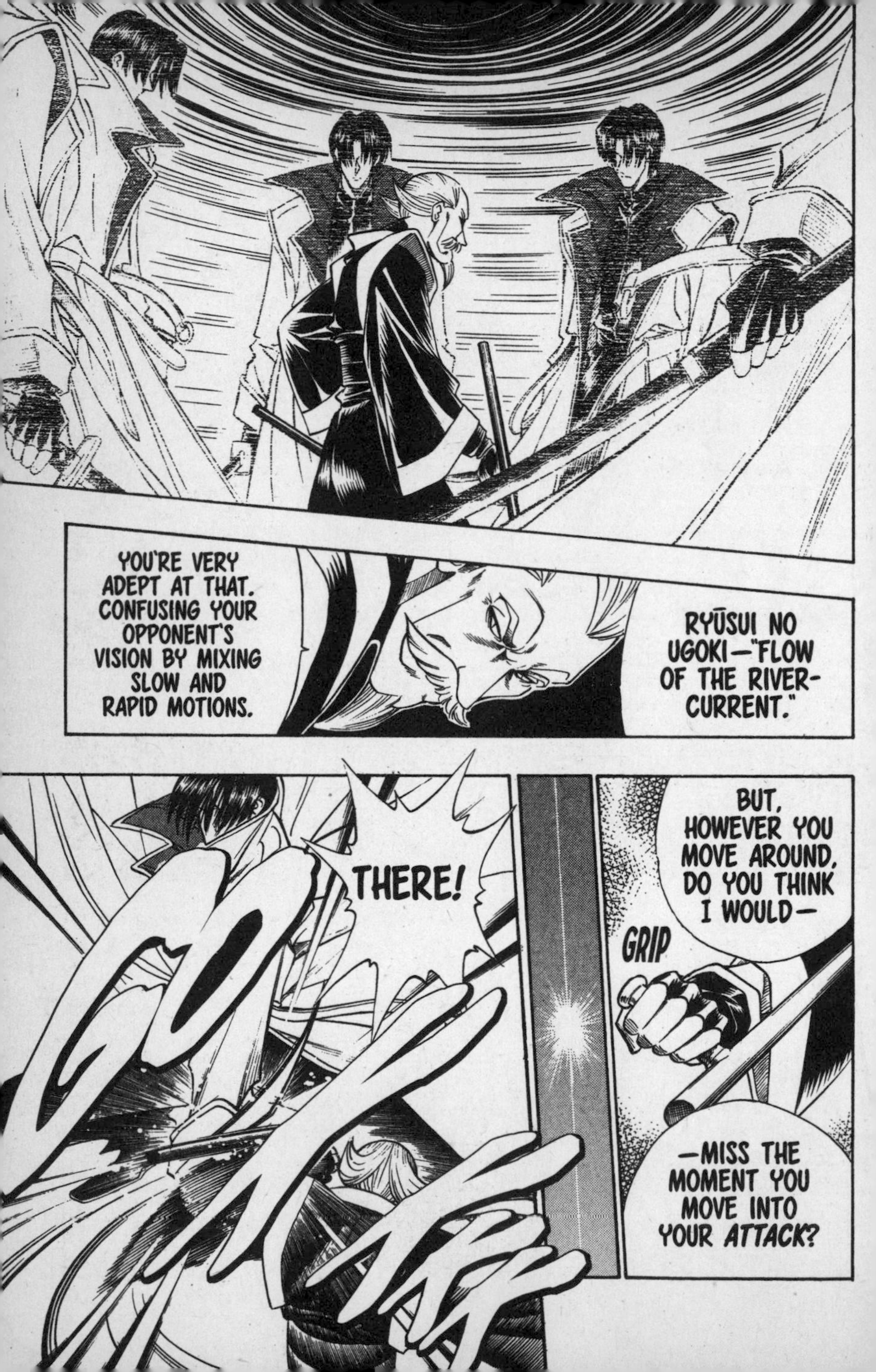
RYŪSUI NO UGOKI—"FLOW OF THE RIVER-CURRENT."
YOU'RE VERY ADEPT AT THAT. CONFUSING YOUR OPPONENT'S VISION BY MIXING SLOW AND RAPID MOTIONS.
BUT, HOWEVER YOU MOVE AROUND, DO YOU THINK I WOULD—
GRIP
—MISS THE MOMENT YOU MOVE INTO YOUR ATTACK?
THERE!

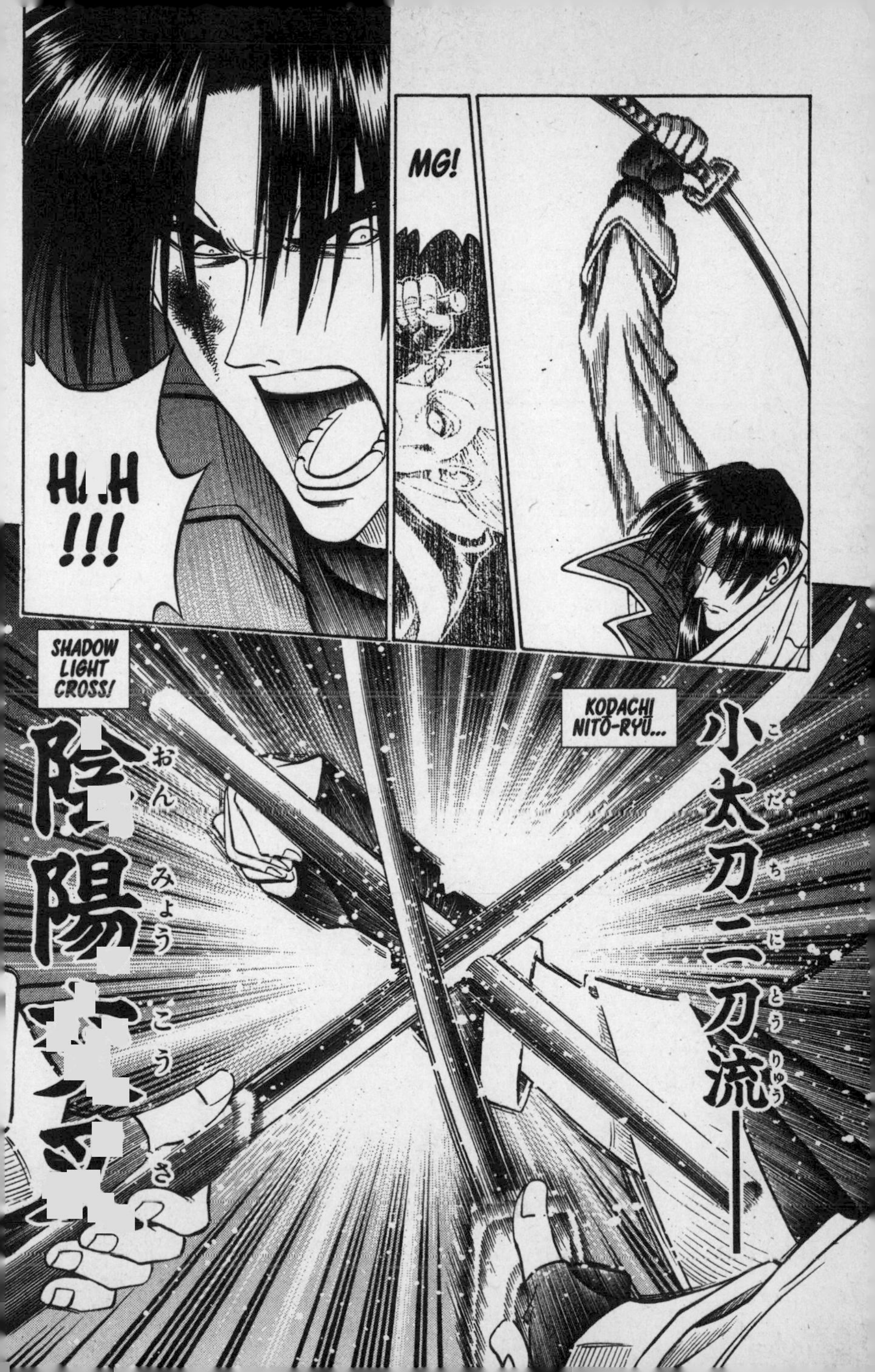
MG!
!!!
KODACHI NITŌ-RYŪ...
小太刀二刀流ー
SHADOW LIGHT CROSS!

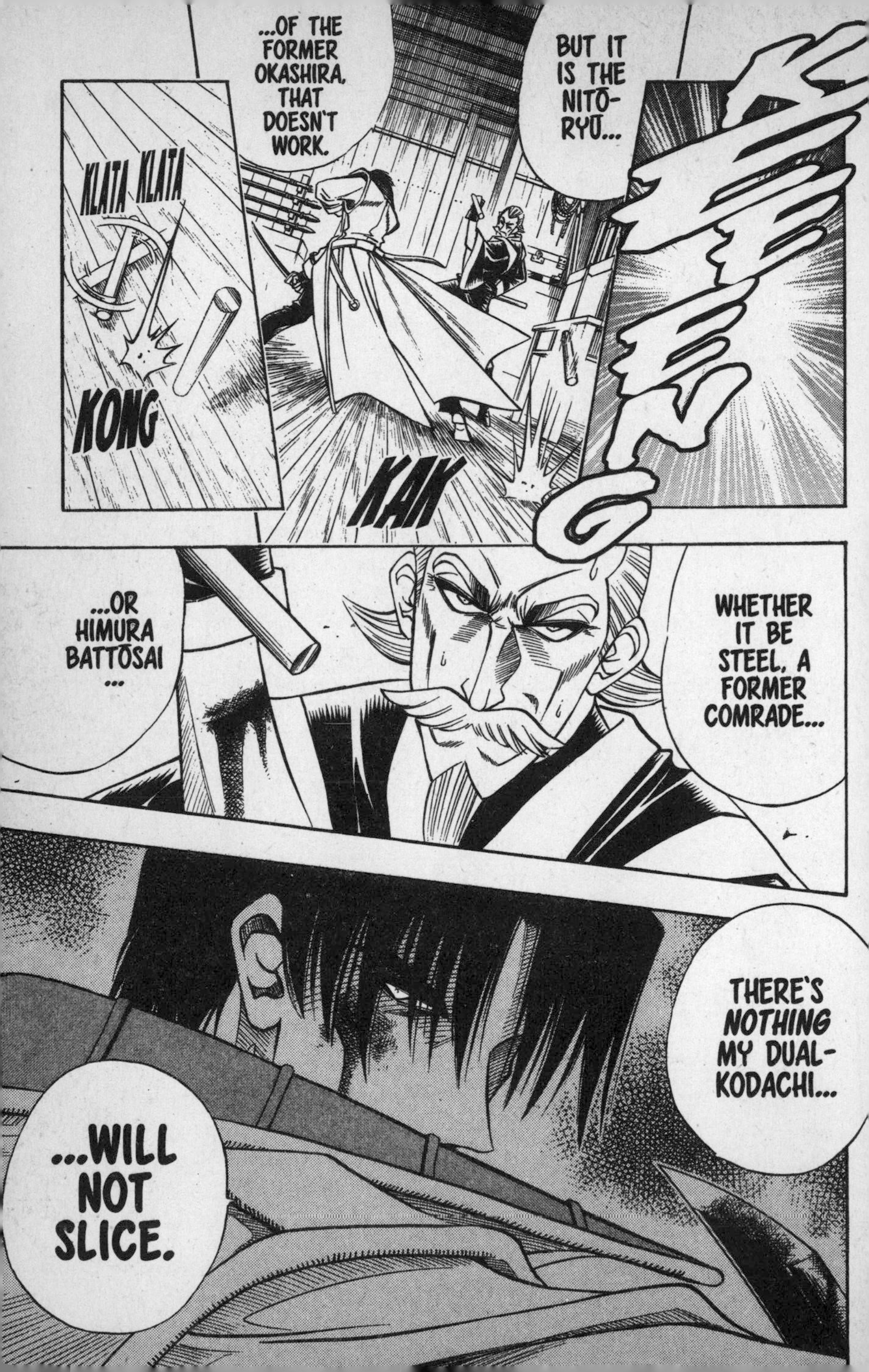
BUT IT IS THE NITŌ-RYŪ...
...OF THE FORMER OKASHIRA, THAT DOESN'T WORK.
KAK
KLATA KLATA
KONG
WHETHER IT BE STEEL, A FORMER COMRADE...
...OR HIMURA BATTŌSAI...
THERE'S *NOTHING* MY DUAL-KODACHI...
...WILL NOT SLICE.

Rurouni Kenshin

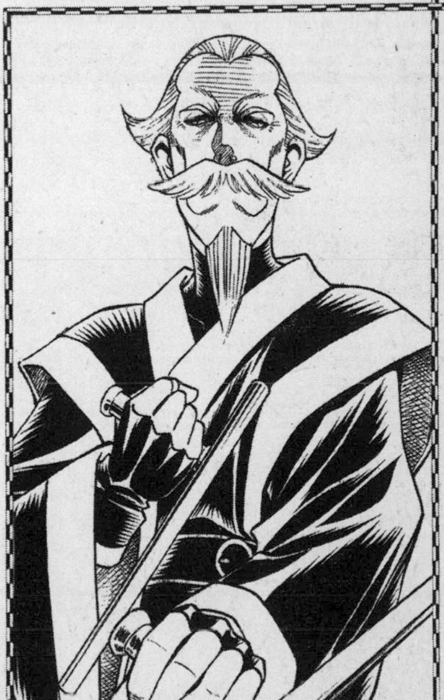

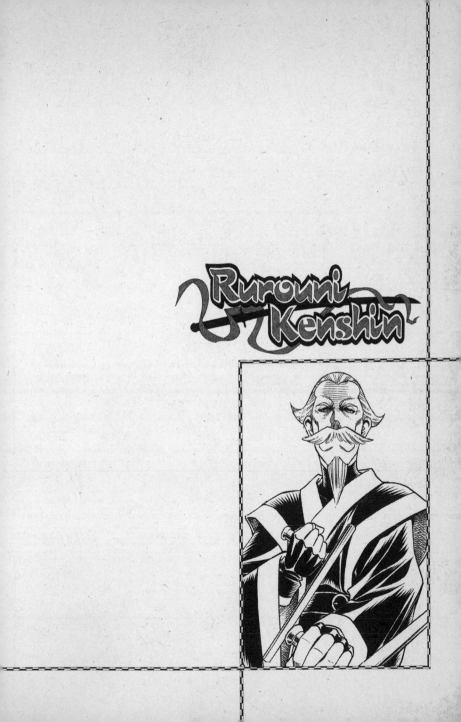

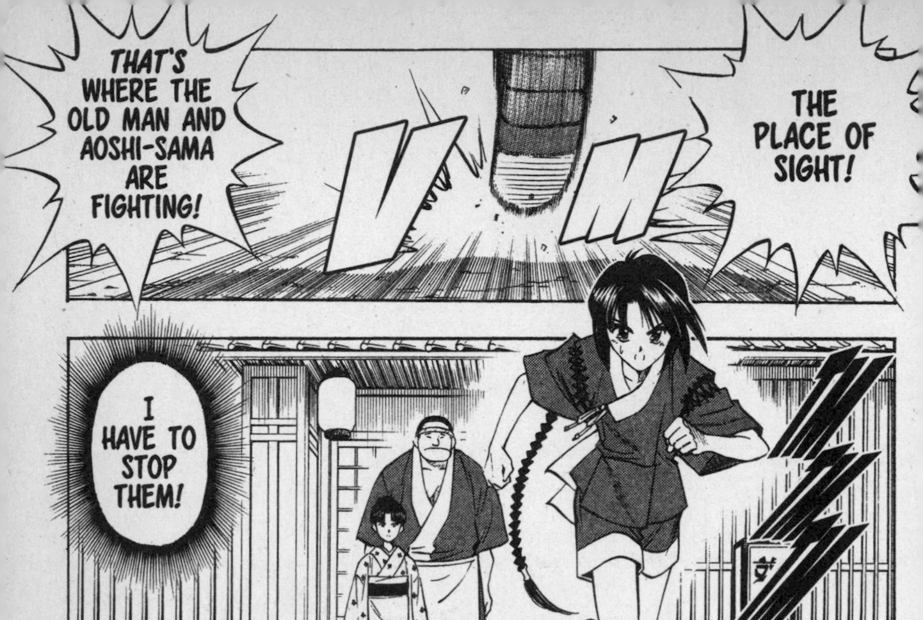
THE PLACE OF SIGHT!
THAT'S WHERE THE OLD MAN AND AOSHI-SAMA ARE FIGHTING!
I HAVE TO STOP THEM!
IF THEY FIGHT FOR REAL, THEY'RE BOTH GOING TO DIE!
I HAVE TO STOP THEM, NO MATTER WHAT!

Act 90—Finale of Fresh Blood

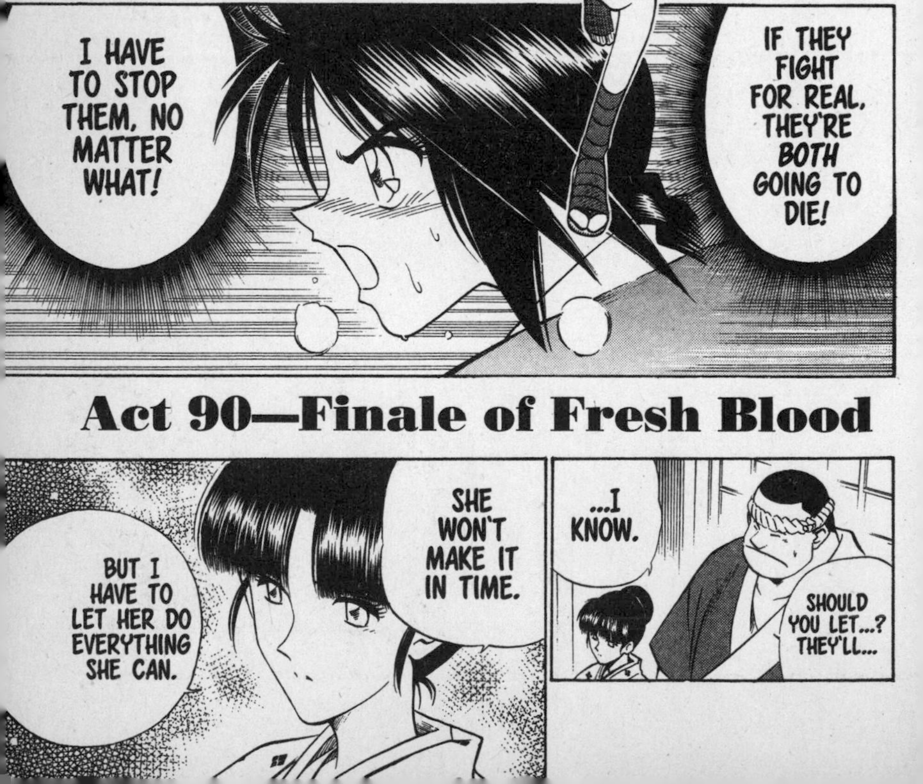
SHOULD YOU LET...? THEY'LL...
...I KNOW.
SHE WON'T MAKE IT IN TIME.
BUT I HAVE TO LET HER DO EVERYTHING SHE CAN.

Act 90
Finale of Fresh Blood

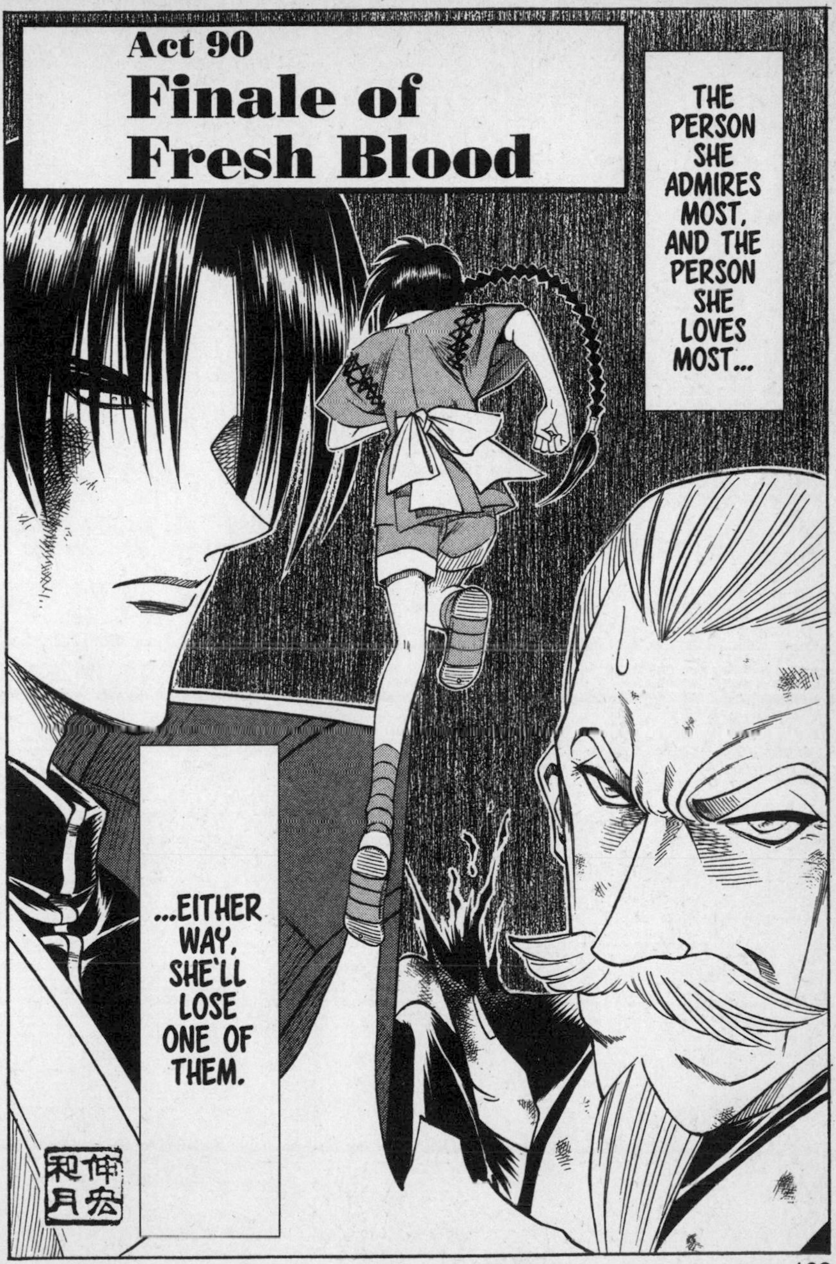
THE PERSON SHE ADMIRES MOST, AND THE PERSON SHE LOVES MOST...
...EITHER WAY, SHE'LL LOSE ONE OF THEM.
和月伸宏

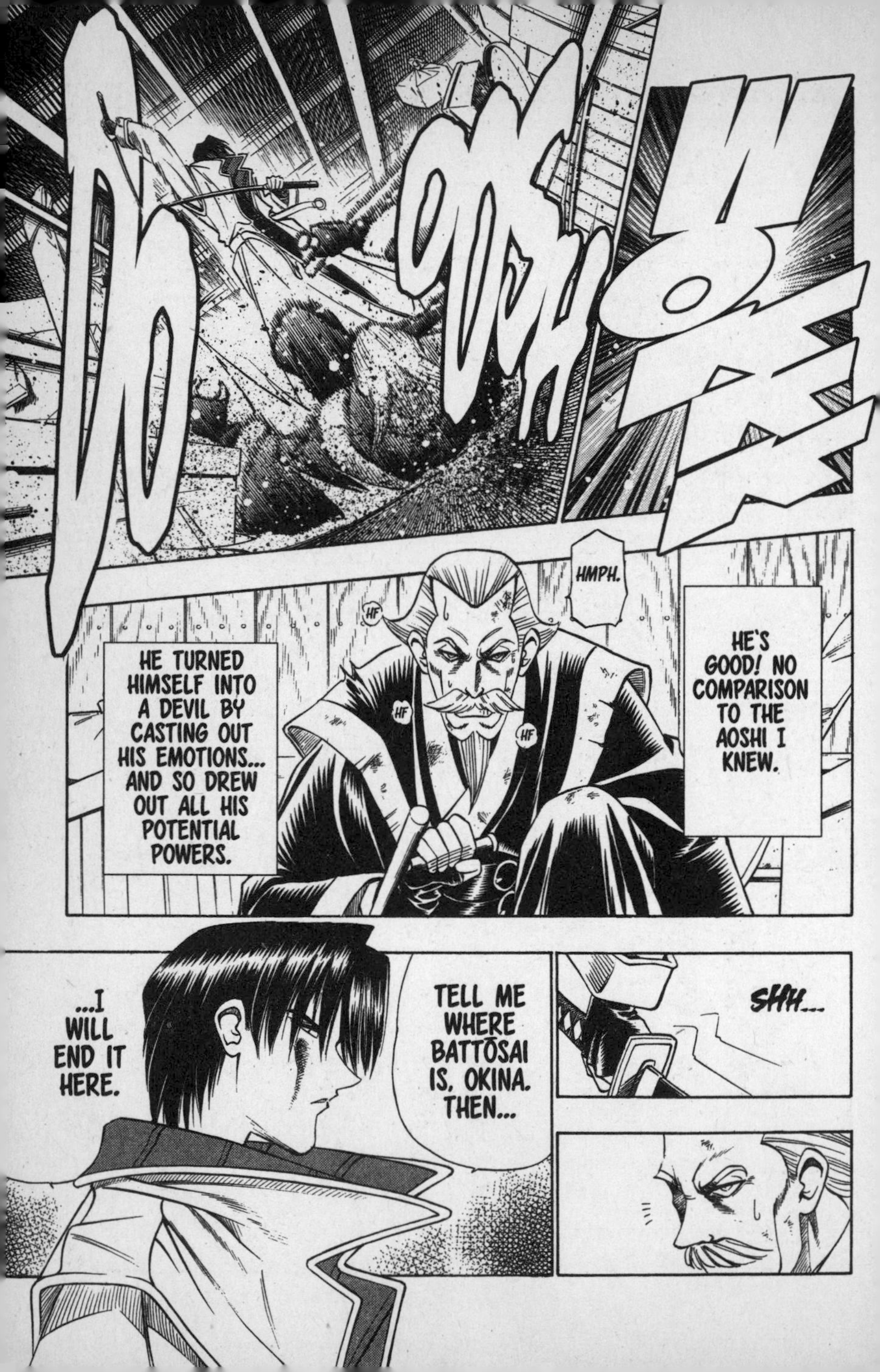
HMPH.
HE'S GOOD! NO COMPARISON TO THE AOSHI I KNEW.
HF
HF
HF
HE TURNED HIMSELF INTO A DEVIL BY CASTING OUT HIS EMOTIONS... AND SO DREW OUT ALL HIS POTENTIAL POWERS.
SHH...
TELL ME WHERE BATTŌSAI IS, OKINA. THEN...
...I WILL END IT HERE.

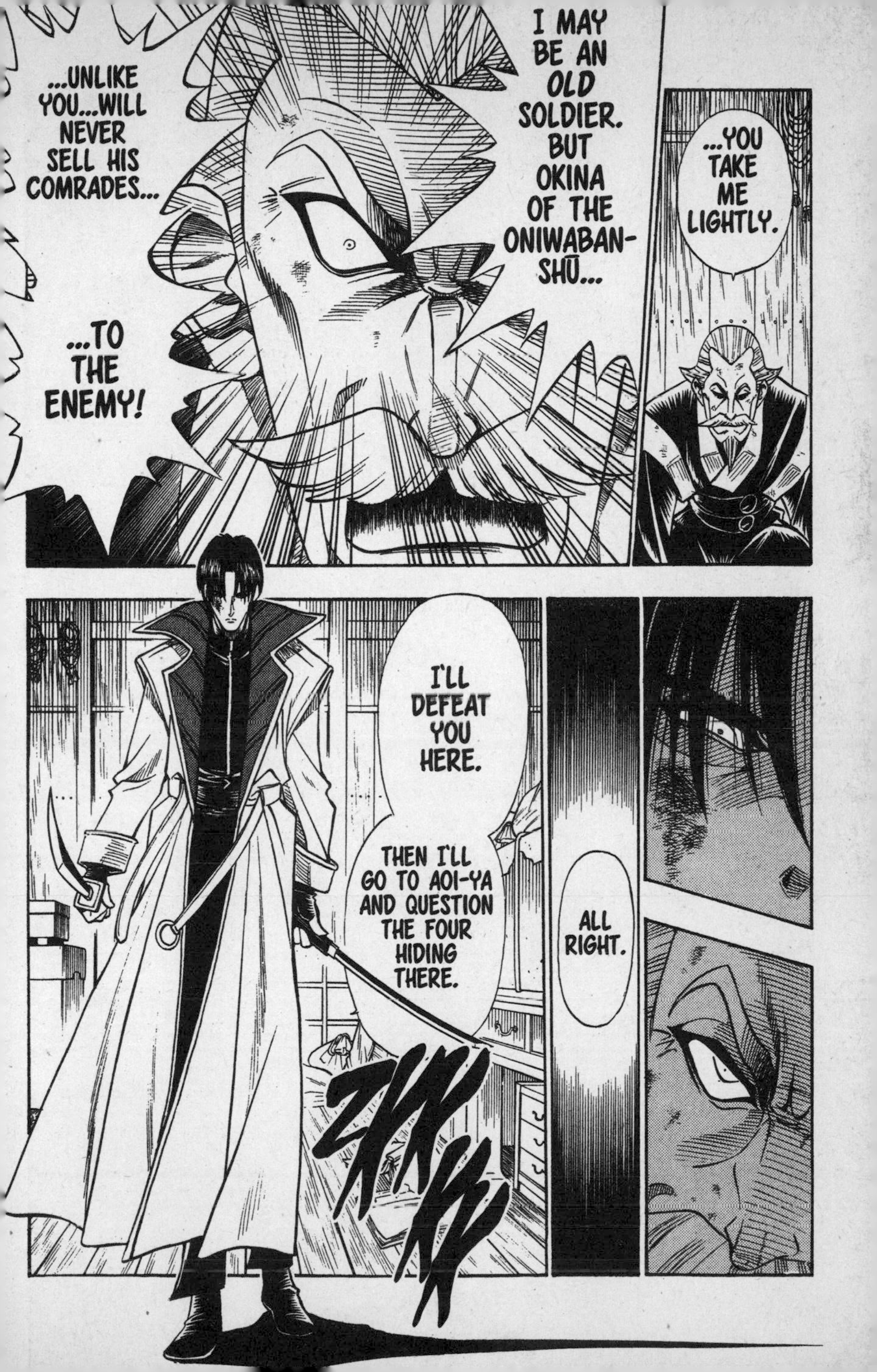
...YOU TAKE ME LIGHTLY.
I MAY BE AN OLD SOLDIER. BUT OKINA OF THE ONIWABANSHŪ...
...UNLIKE YOU...WILL NEVER SELL HIS COMRADES...
...TO THE ENEMY!
ALL RIGHT.
I'LL DEFEAT YOU HERE.
THEN I'LL GO TO AOI-YA AND QUESTION THE FOUR HIDING THERE.

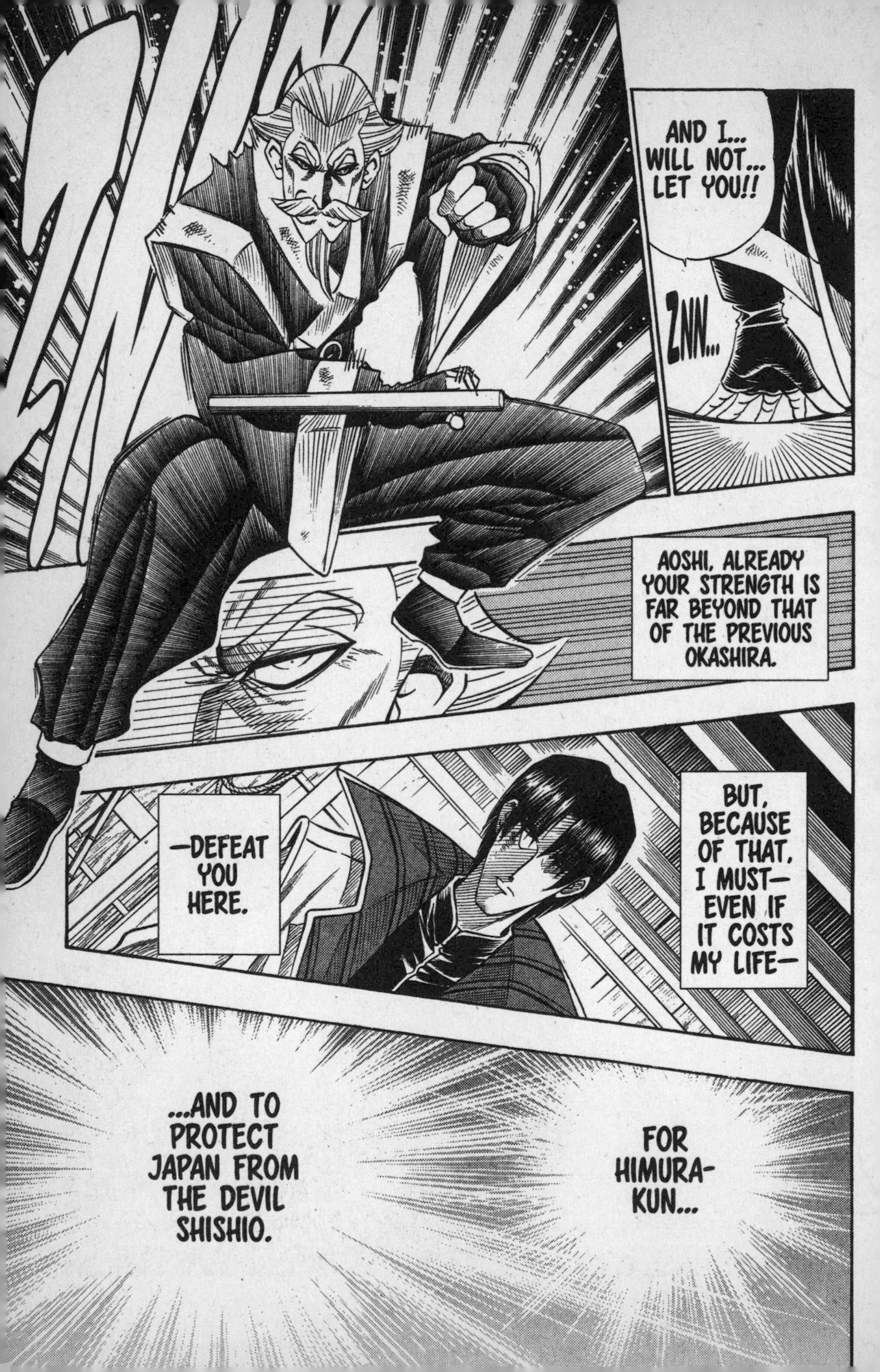
AND I... WILL NOT... LET YOU!!
ZNN...
AOSHI, ALREADY YOUR STRENGTH IS FAR BEYOND THAT OF THE PREVIOUS OKASHIRA.
BUT, BECAUSE OF THAT, I MUST— EVEN IF IT COSTS MY LIFE—
—DEFEAT YOU HERE.
FOR HIMURA-KUN...
...AND TO PROTECT JAPAN FROM THE DEVIL SHISHIO.

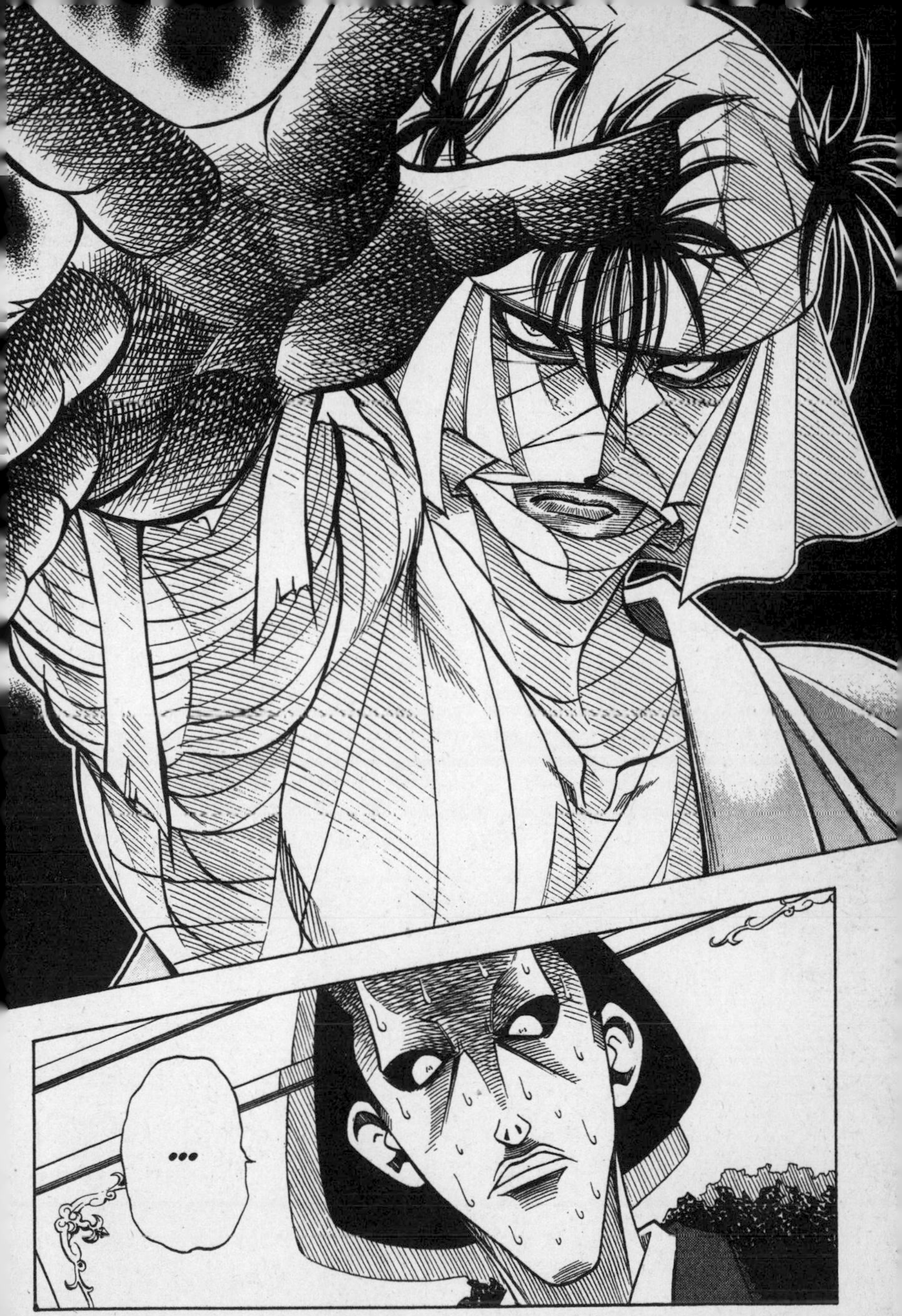
...

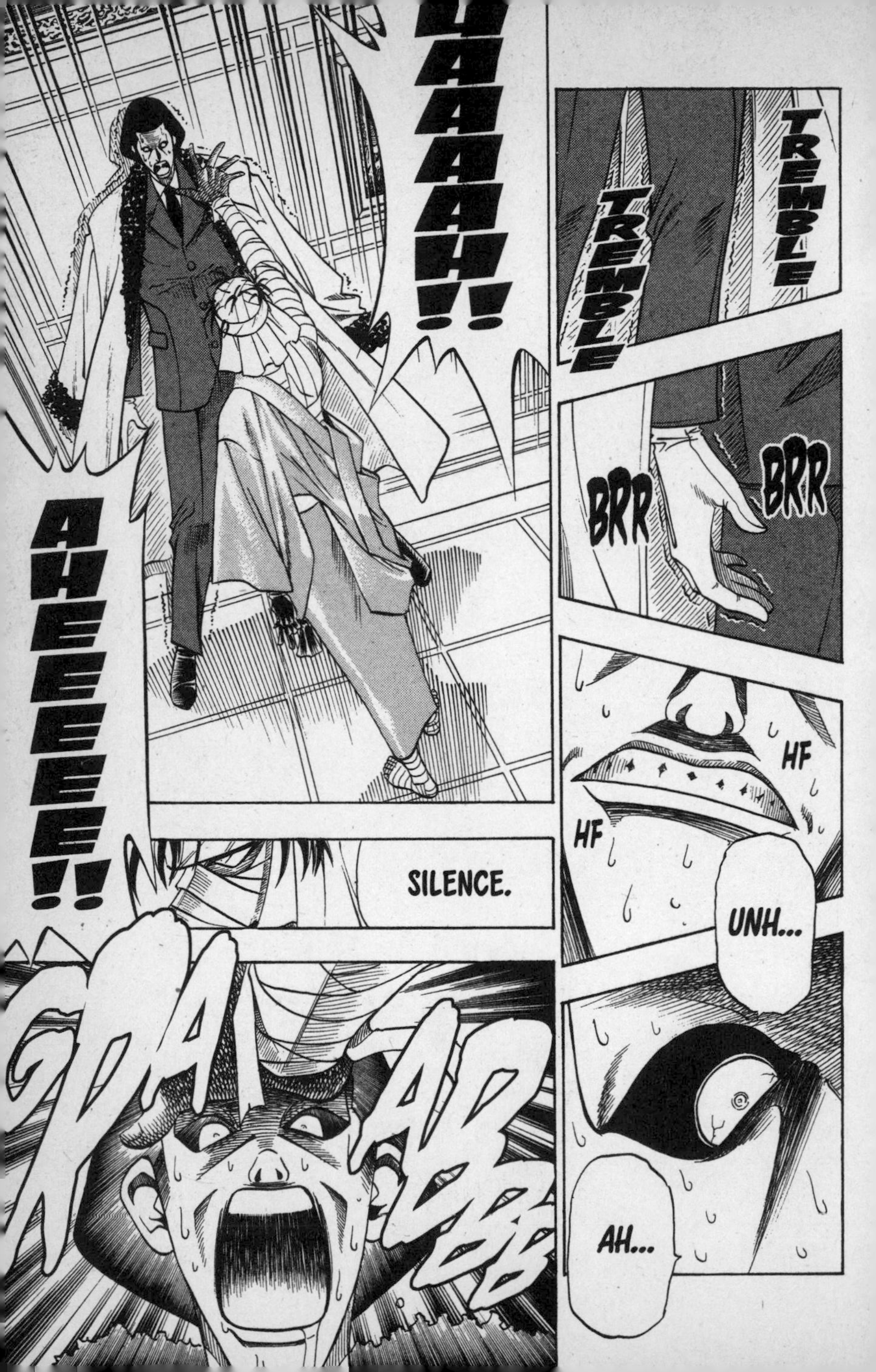
TREMBLE
TREMBLE
BRR
BRR
HF
HF
UNH...
AH...
UAAAAH!!
AHEEEEEEE!!
SILENCE.

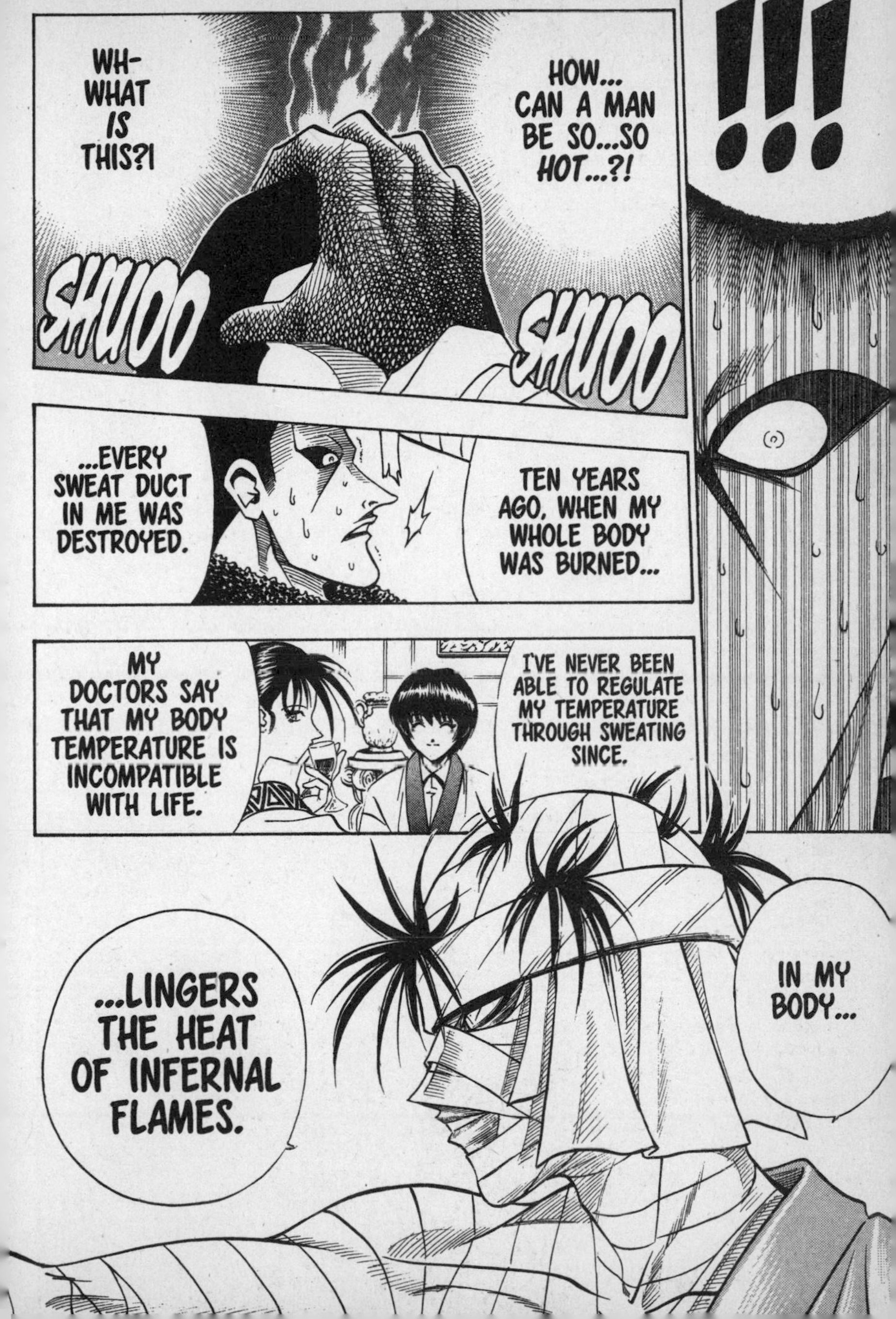
!!!
HOW... CAN A MAN BE SO...SO HOT...?!
WH- WHAT IS THIS?!
SHUOO
SHUOO
TEN YEARS AGO, WHEN MY WHOLE BODY WAS BURNED...
...EVERY SWEAT DUCT IN ME WAS DESTROYED.
I'VE NEVER BEEN ABLE TO REGULATE MY TEMPERATURE THROUGH SWEATING SINCE.
MY DOCTORS SAY THAT MY BODY TEMPERATURE IS INCOMPATIBLE WITH LIFE.
IN MY BODY...
...LINGERS THE HEAT OF INFERNAL FLAMES.

The other day, after work, I had some time before my train, so I went to a karaoke bar with the assistants. Watsuki's not much good at karaoke, but he does like to sing (and hum songs in the bath... badly). So I was pretty excited...but then it turned out the assistants were really, really good.

There were guys who could sing the current hits exactly right, and guys who sang with such sweet voices, women were swooning. And my senpai—he was like a pro! Not many can sing Yashiki Takajin like him (not many can sing Yashiki Takajin, period).

Most amazing was the youngest on the staff, my 2nd senior assistant. Okay, so, his actual singing sucked...but the way he sang, *that* was hilarious. He was like a manga character. It was fun to see another side of the assistants, a side none of them show at work. "I have a great staff," I thought, and realized that listening to them was more of a stress-reliever and more enjoyable than singing myself would have been. I'm definitely up for karaoke again.

伸宏和月

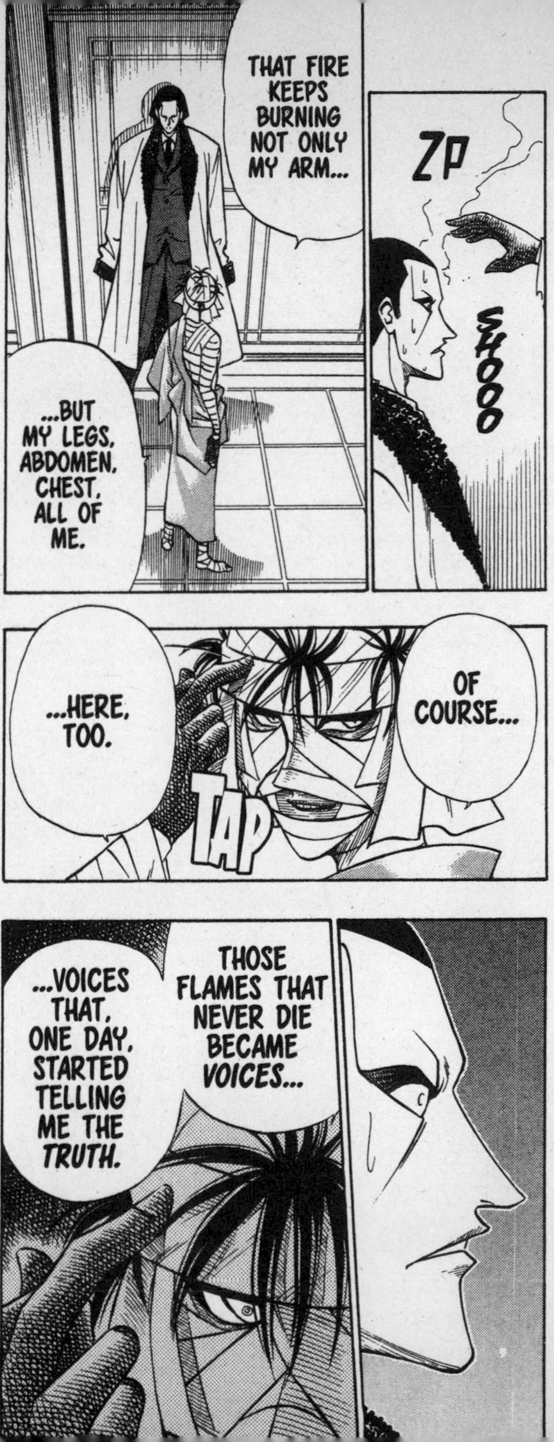
ZP
SHOOO
THAT FIRE KEEPS BURNING NOT ONLY MY ARM...
...BUT MY LEGS, ABDOMEN, CHEST, ALL OF ME.
OF COURSE...
TAP
...HERE, TOO.
THOSE FLAMES THAT NEVER DIE BECAME VOICES...
...VOICES THAT, ONE DAY, STARTED TELLING ME THE *TRUTH.*

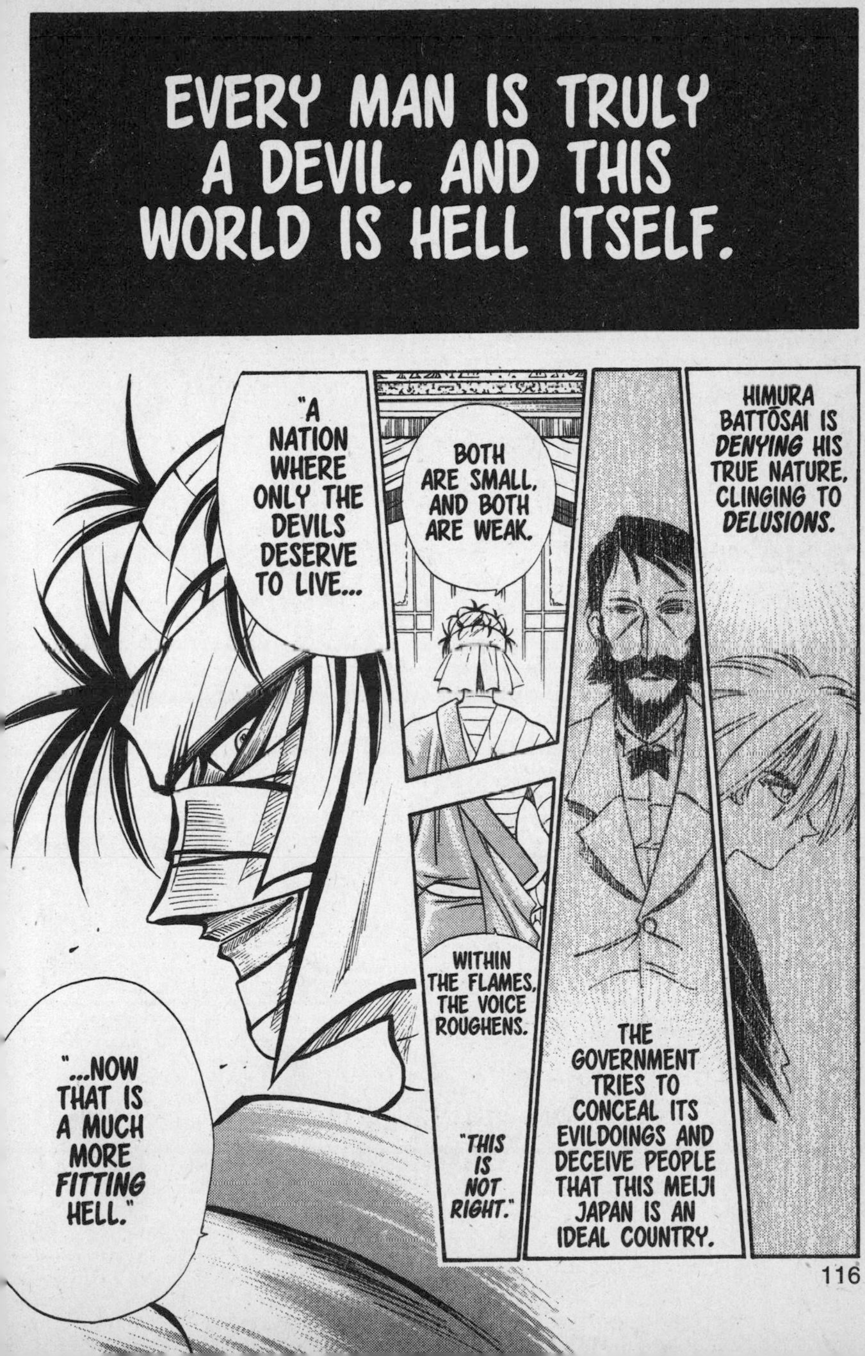
EVERY MAN IS TRULY A DEVIL. AND THIS WORLD IS HELL ITSELF.
HIMURA BATTŌSAI IS *DENYING* HIS TRUE NATURE, CLINGING TO *DELUSIONS.*
THE GOVERNMENT TRIES TO CONCEAL ITS EVILDOINGS AND DECEIVE PEOPLE THAT THIS MEIJI JAPAN IS AN IDEAL COUNTRY.
BOTH ARE SMALL, AND BOTH ARE WEAK.
WITHIN THE FLAMES, THE VOICE ROUGHENS.
"THIS IS NOT RIGHT."
"A NATION WHERE ONLY THE DEVILS DESERVE TO LIVE...
"...NOW THAT IS A MUCH MORE *FITTING* HELL."

READ THIS WAY

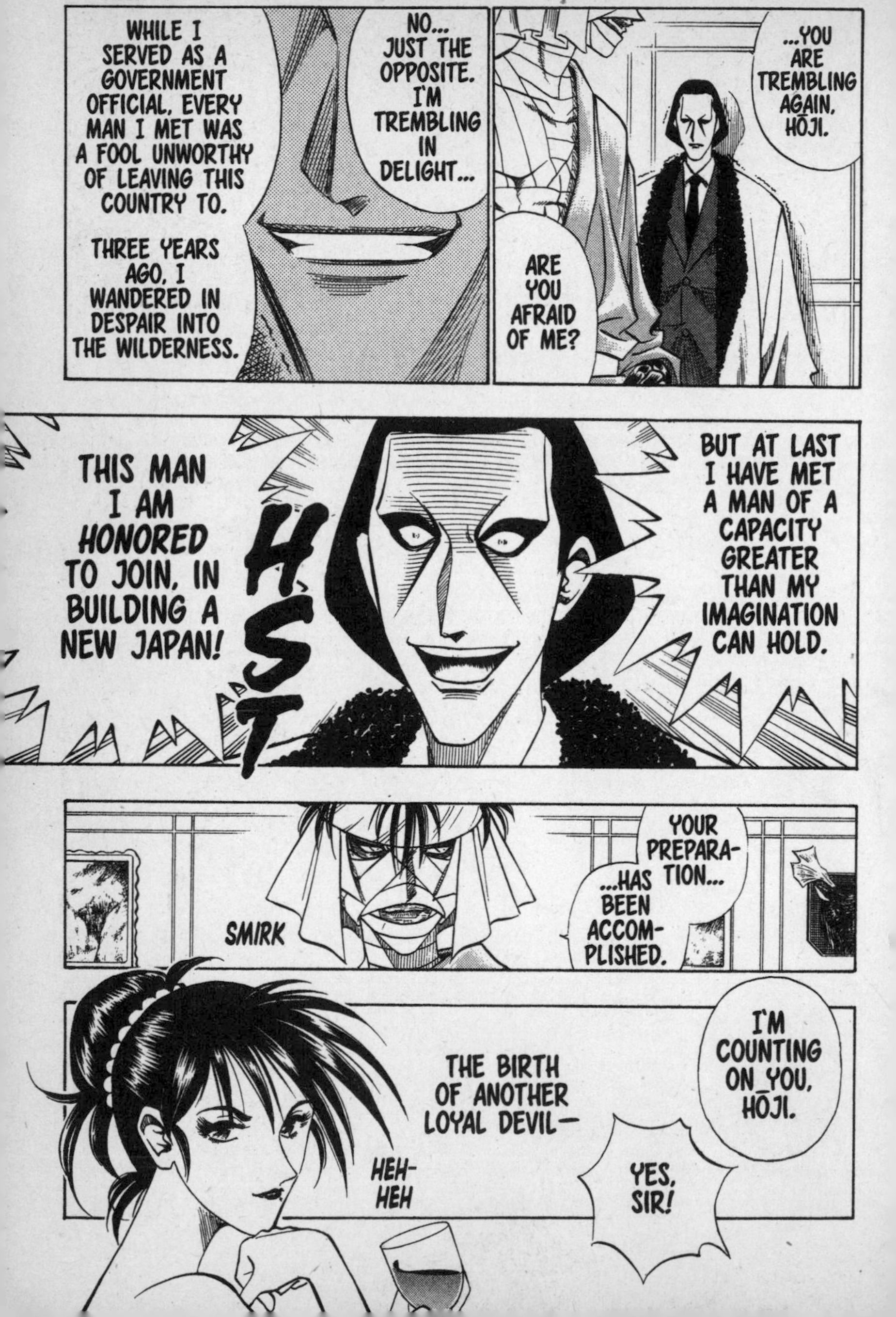
...YOU ARE TREMBLING AGAIN, HŌJI.
ARE YOU AFRAID OF ME?
NO... JUST THE OPPOSITE. I'M TREMBLING IN DELIGHT...
WHILE I SERVED AS A GOVERNMENT OFFICIAL, EVERY MAN I MET WAS A FOOL UNWORTHY OF LEAVING THIS COUNTRY TO.
THREE YEARS AGO, I WANDERED IN DESPAIR INTO THE WILDERNESS.
BUT AT LAST I HAVE MET A MAN OF A CAPACITY GREATER THAN MY IMAGINATION CAN HOLD.
HST
THIS MAN I AM *HONORED* TO JOIN, IN BUILDING A NEW JAPAN!
YOUR PREPARATION...
...HAS BEEN ACCOMPLISHED.
SMIRK
I'M COUNTING ON YOU, HŌJI.
YES, SIR!
THE BIRTH OF ANOTHER LOYAL DEVIL—
HEH-HEH

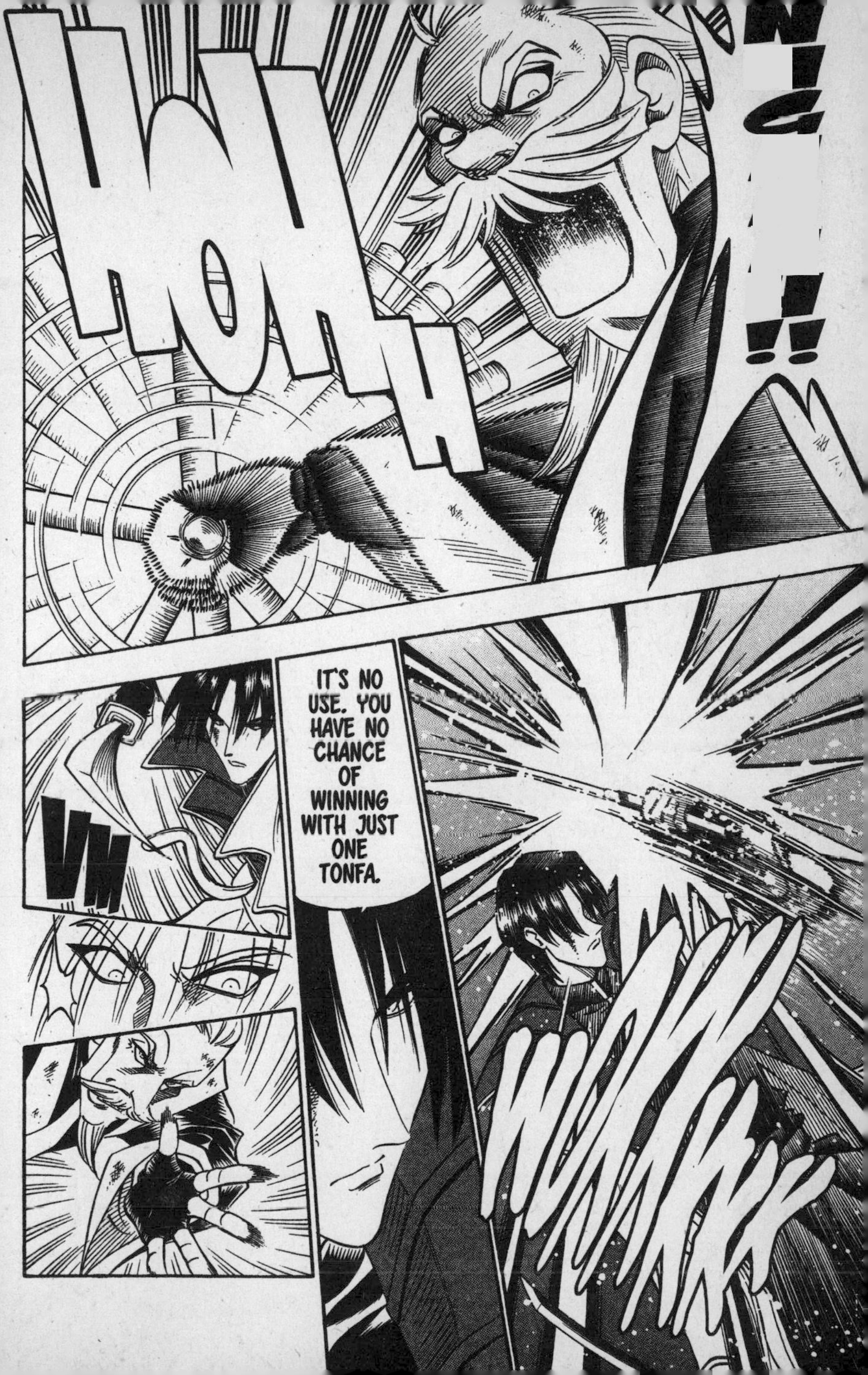

IT'S NO USE. YOU HAVE NO CHANCE OF WINNING WITH JUST ONE TONFA.
VM

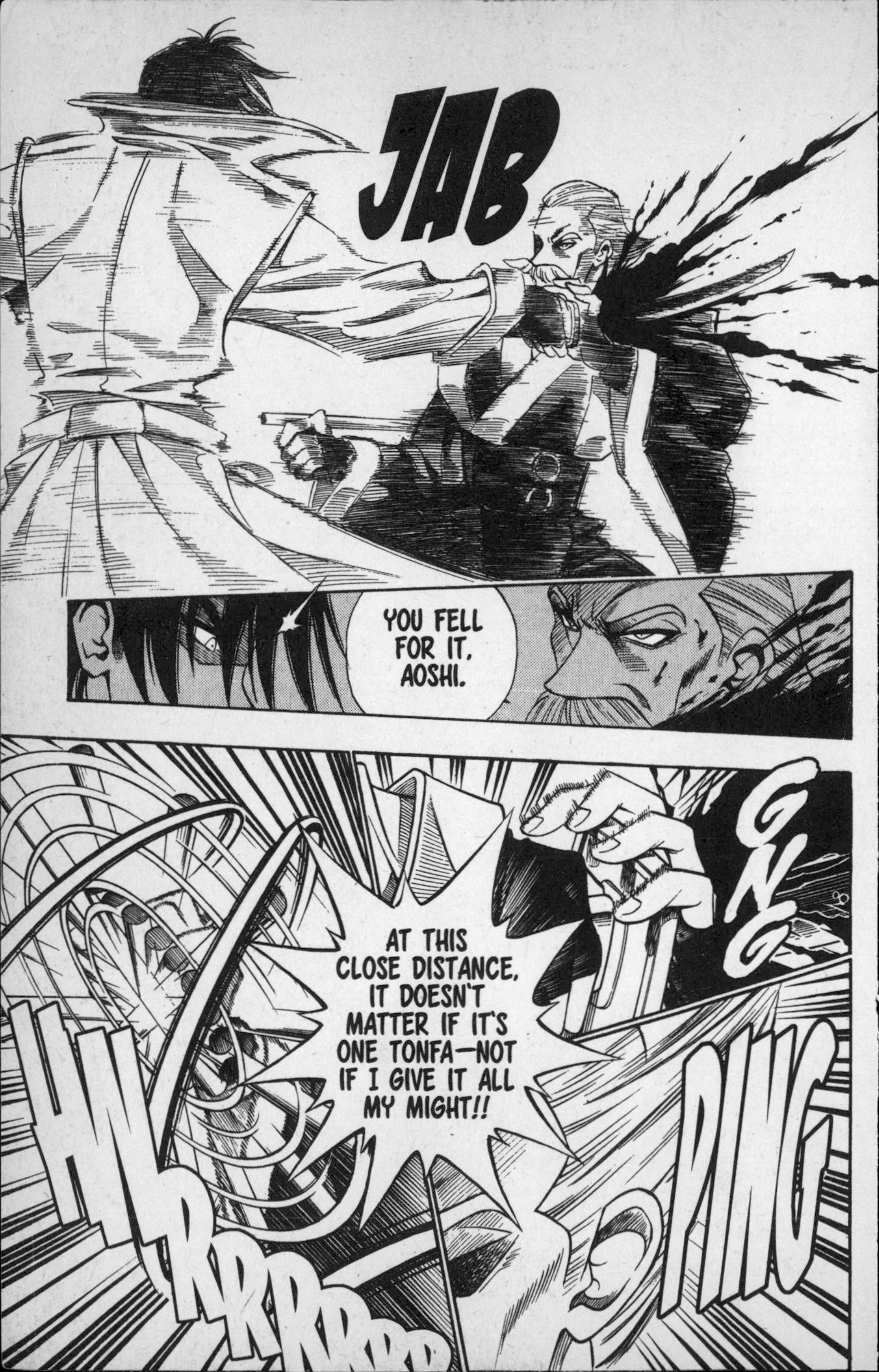
JAB
YOU FELL FOR IT, AOSHI.
AT THIS CLOSE DISTANCE, IT DOESN'T MATTER IF IT'S ONE TONFA—NOT IF I GIVE IT ALL MY MIGHT!!

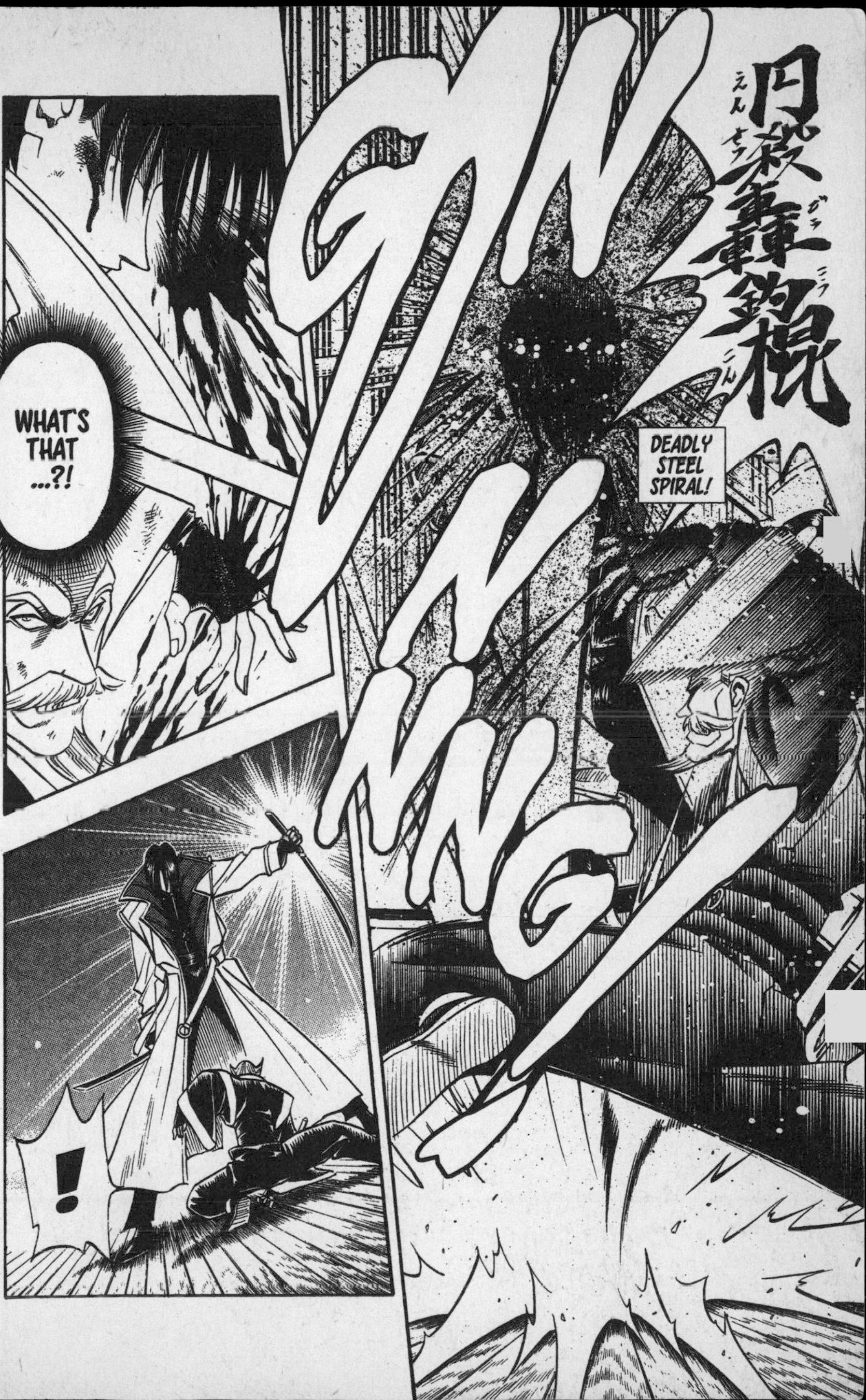

円殺轟鈎棍
DEADLY STEEL SPIRAL!
WHAT'S THAT ...?!
!

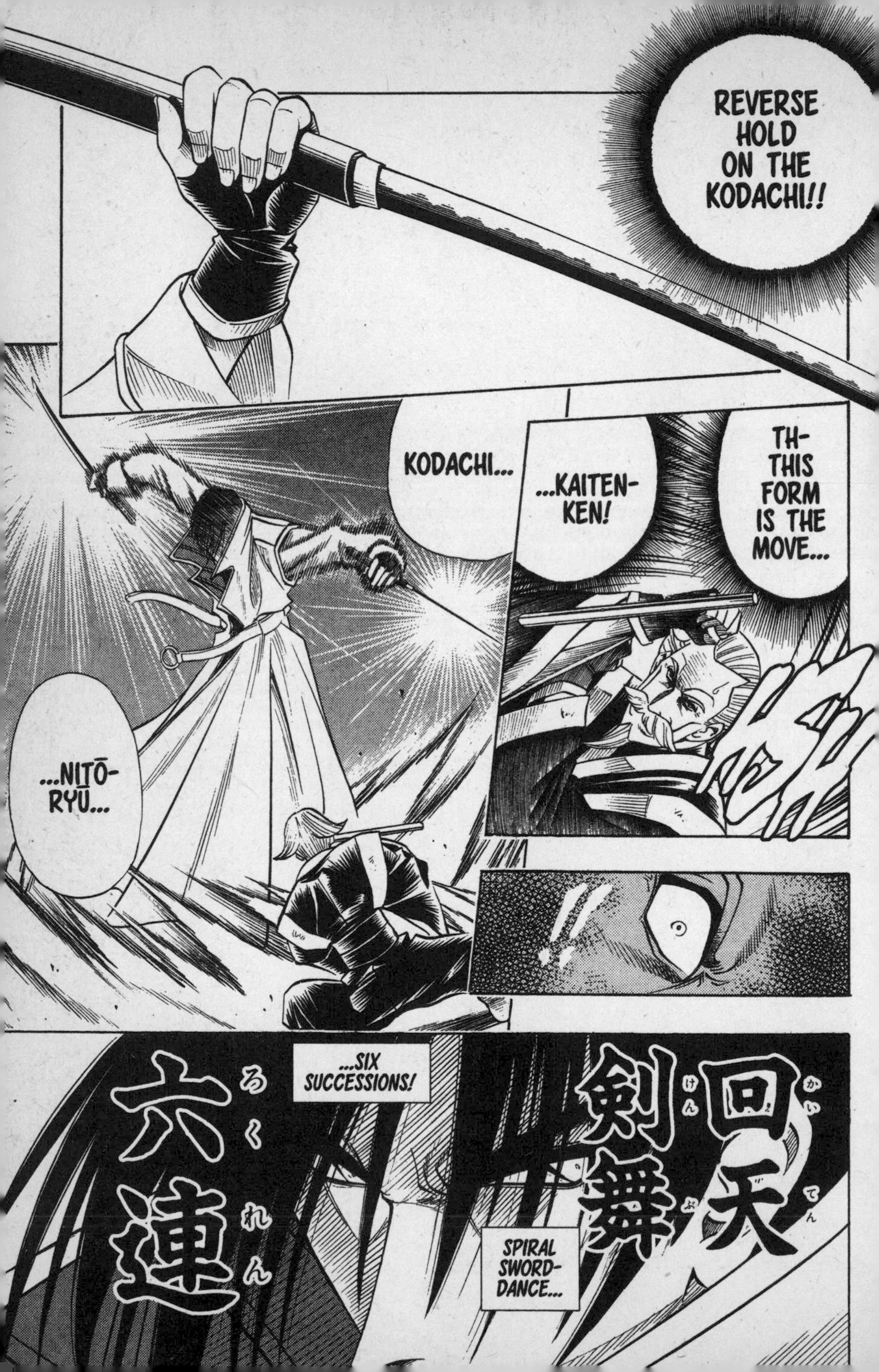
REVERSE HOLD ON THE KODACHI!!
TH-THIS FORM IS THE MOVE...
...KAITEN-KEN!
KODACHI...
...NITŌ-RYŪ...
!!
回天剣舞六連
SPIRAL SWORD-DANCE...
...SIX SUCCESSIONS!

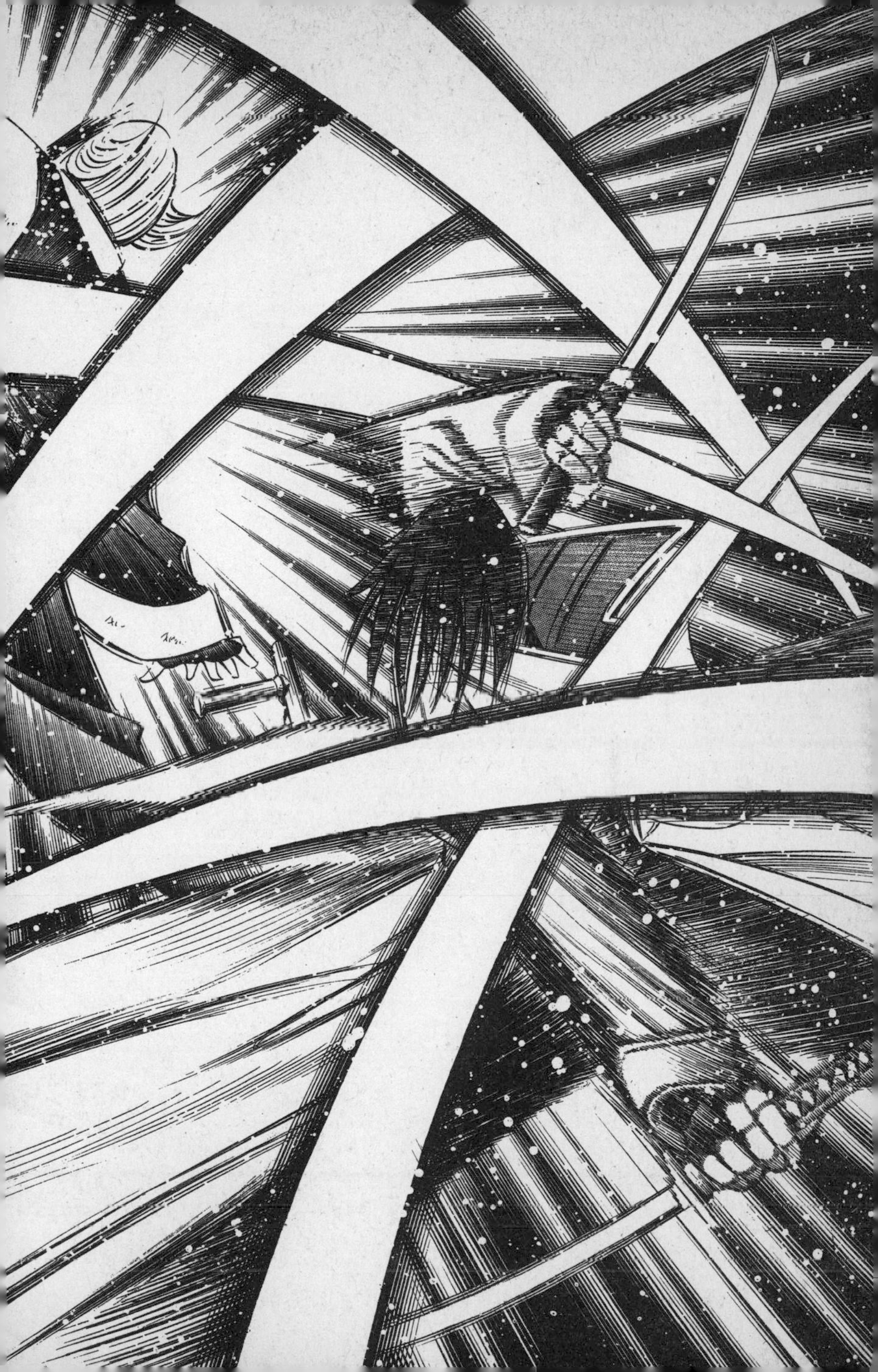

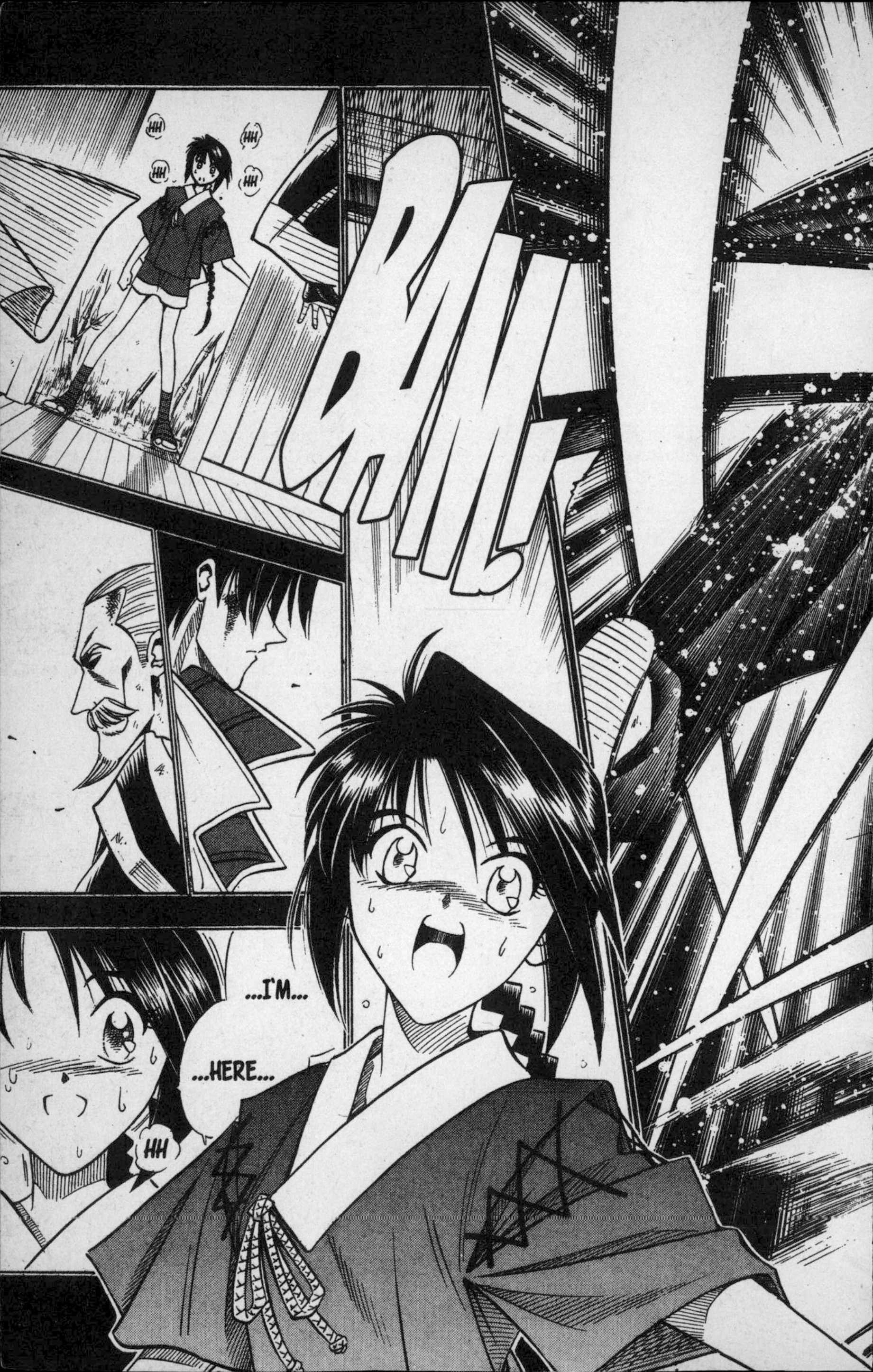
BAM!
HH
HH
HH
HH
...I'M...
...HERE...
HH

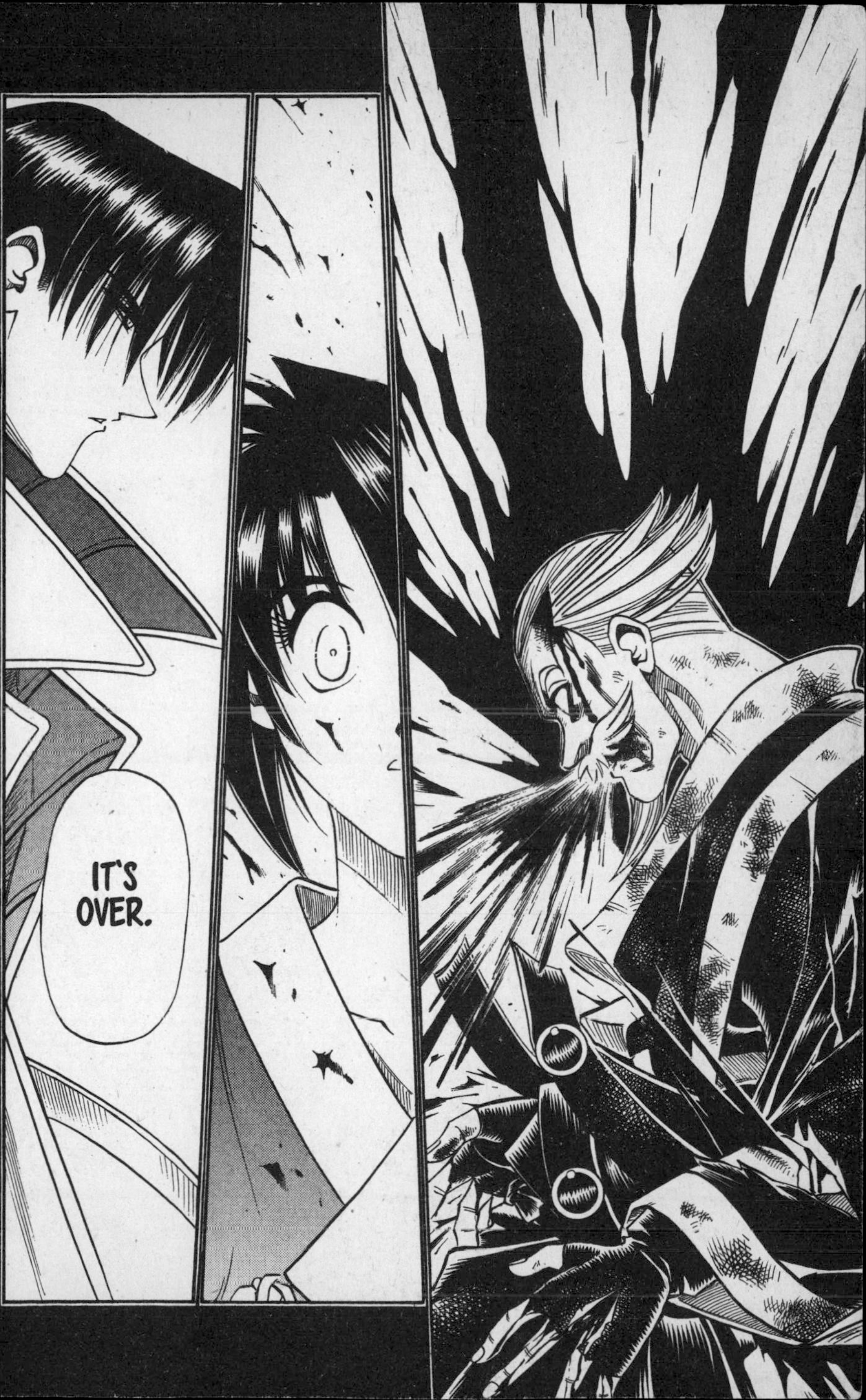
IT'S OVER.

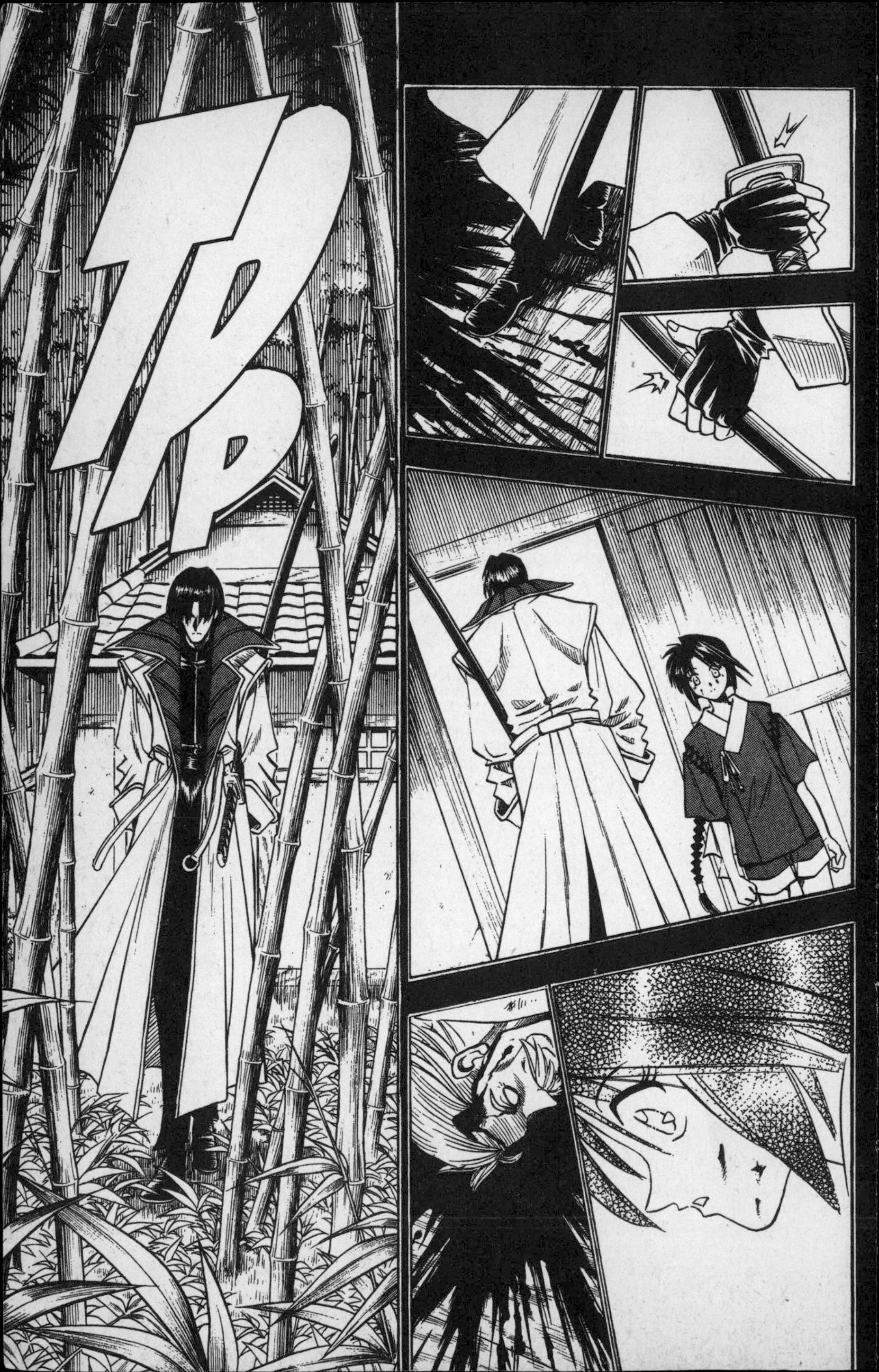

The Secret Life of Characters (31)
—Okina (Kashiwazaki Nenji)—

There's no specific model in terms of personality—he's simply Watsuki's image of what an "old soldier" would be.

By nature a gentle, run-down-at-the-seams old man, when the younger generation gets confused, or does something wrong, Okina summons up his powers and sets those young'uns straight. Maybe that's the typical old man of a generation ago in Japan...? When I think about it now, I suppose there's a bit of "Kohei" from Ikenami Shōtarō's "*Kenkyaku Shōbai (The Sword Trade)*" in him.

This "Aoshi vs. Okina" story arc and the alliance between Aoshi and Shishio may have come as a surprise to many readers. The plot twist was actually sparked by a comment in a letter I received, saying, "I'll bet Aoshi is gonna be another of those characters who *just* happens to be around to help Kenshin in times of need." When I read that, it kind of got to me, and I said to myself, "Fine, then, I'll make him a bad guy." As a result, the already-long Kyoto Saga became even longer, so now I'm regretting it a bit....

As for Okina, I like him a lot since he's a character who's been able to tie up loose ends. Design-wise, his model is "Kaizō Tokijirō" in my master Obata Takeshi's "*Cyborg Ji'I-chan 'G' (Cyborg Grandpa 'G')*." Learning from his past misdeeds, Watsuki has been very careful to make certain his design doesn't resemble it too much, but still the assistants guessed right away (but then, they're all too clever for their own good).

One thing I'm not satisfied with is Okina's hair. It was supposed to stand up when he's really angry—making him resemble Sally's dad from the anime—but, because of a lack of available pages, this hasn't ended up coming across too well.

Act 91
Misao's Decision

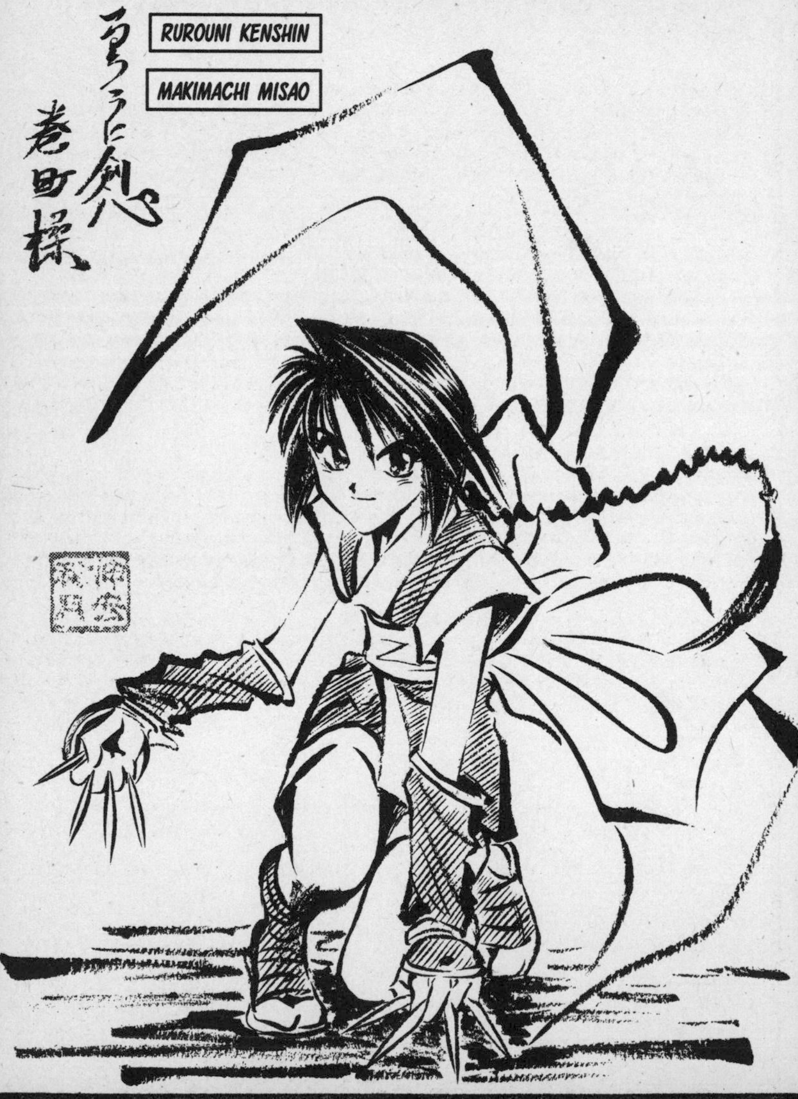
RUROUNI KENSHIN
MAKIMACHI MISAO

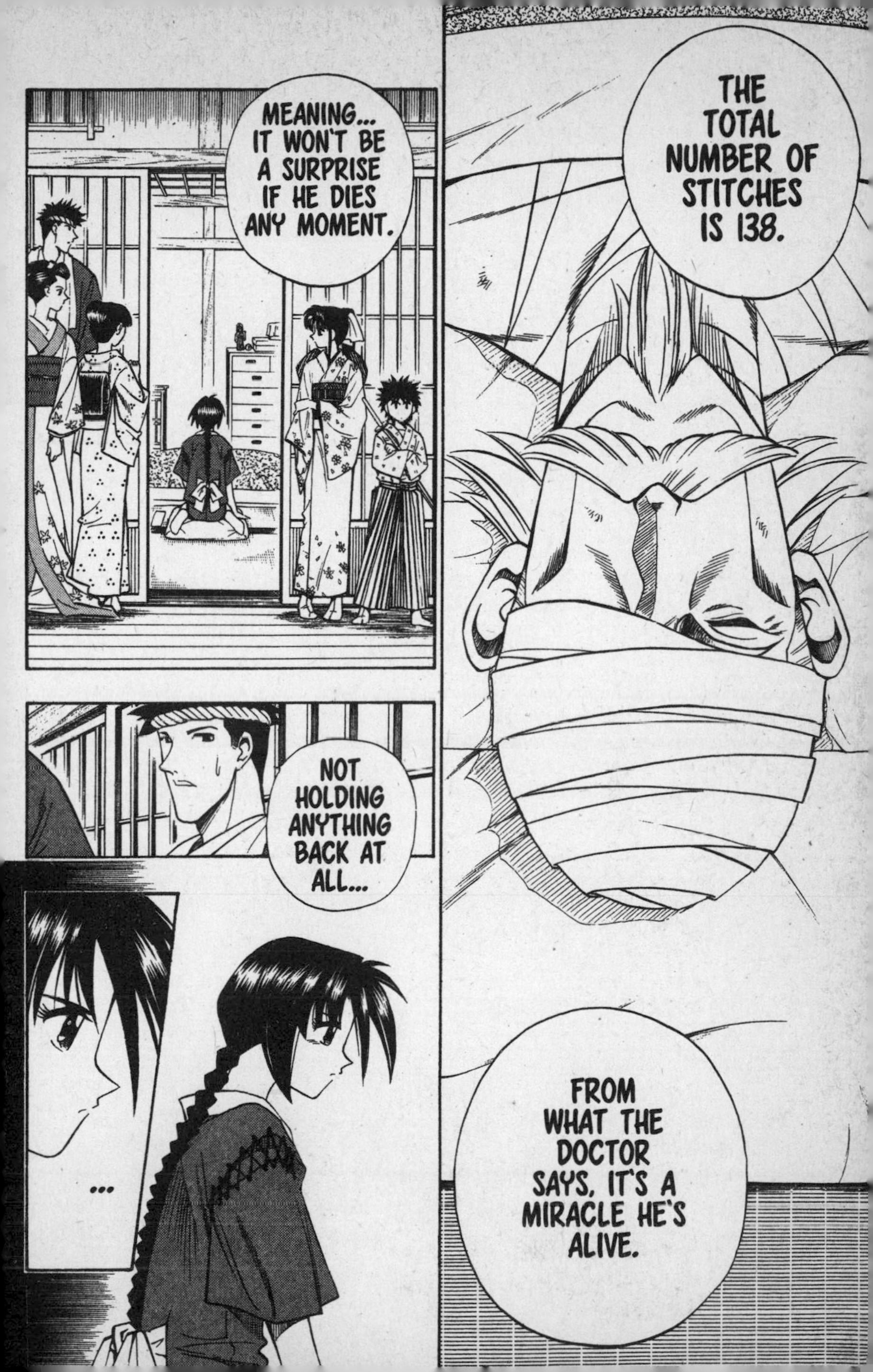
THE TOTAL NUMBER OF STITCHES IS 138.
FROM WHAT THE DOCTOR SAYS, IT'S A MIRACLE HE'S ALIVE.
MEANING... IT WON'T BE A SURPRISE IF HE DIES ANY MOMENT.
NOT HOLDING ANYTHING BACK AT ALL...
...

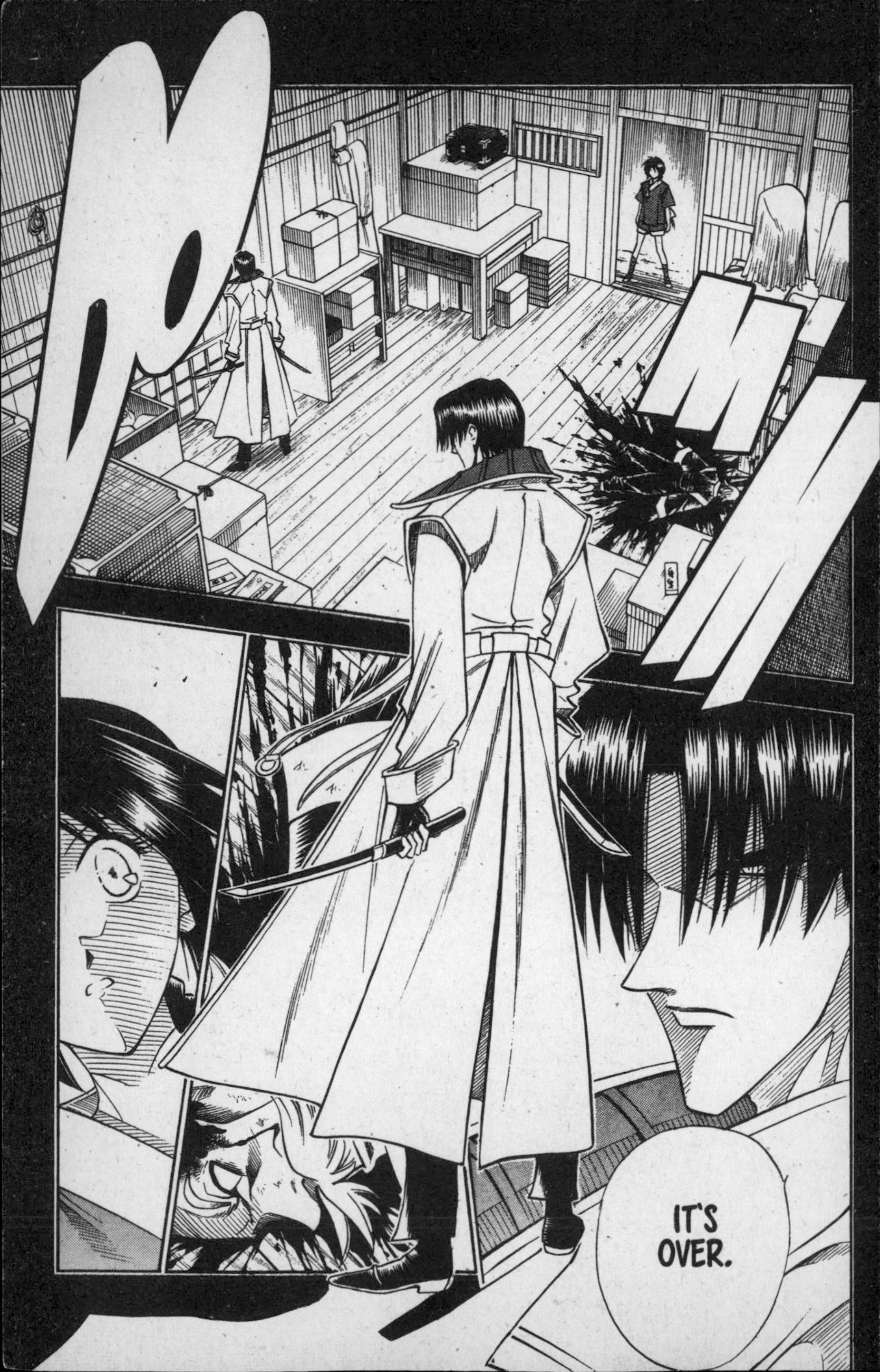
IT'S OVER.

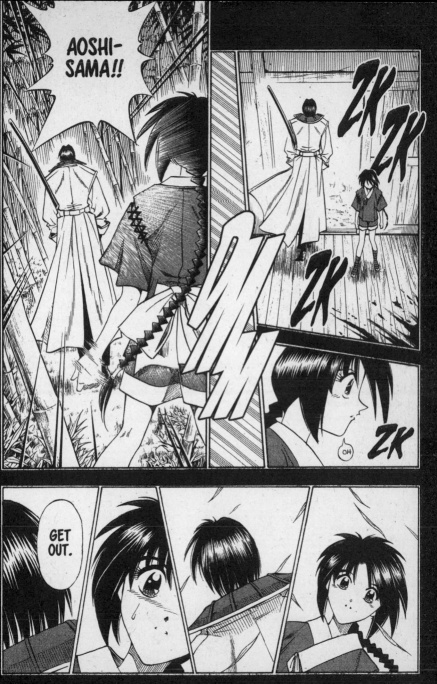

AOSHI-SAMA!!

ZK

ZK

ZK

ZK

OH

GET OUT.

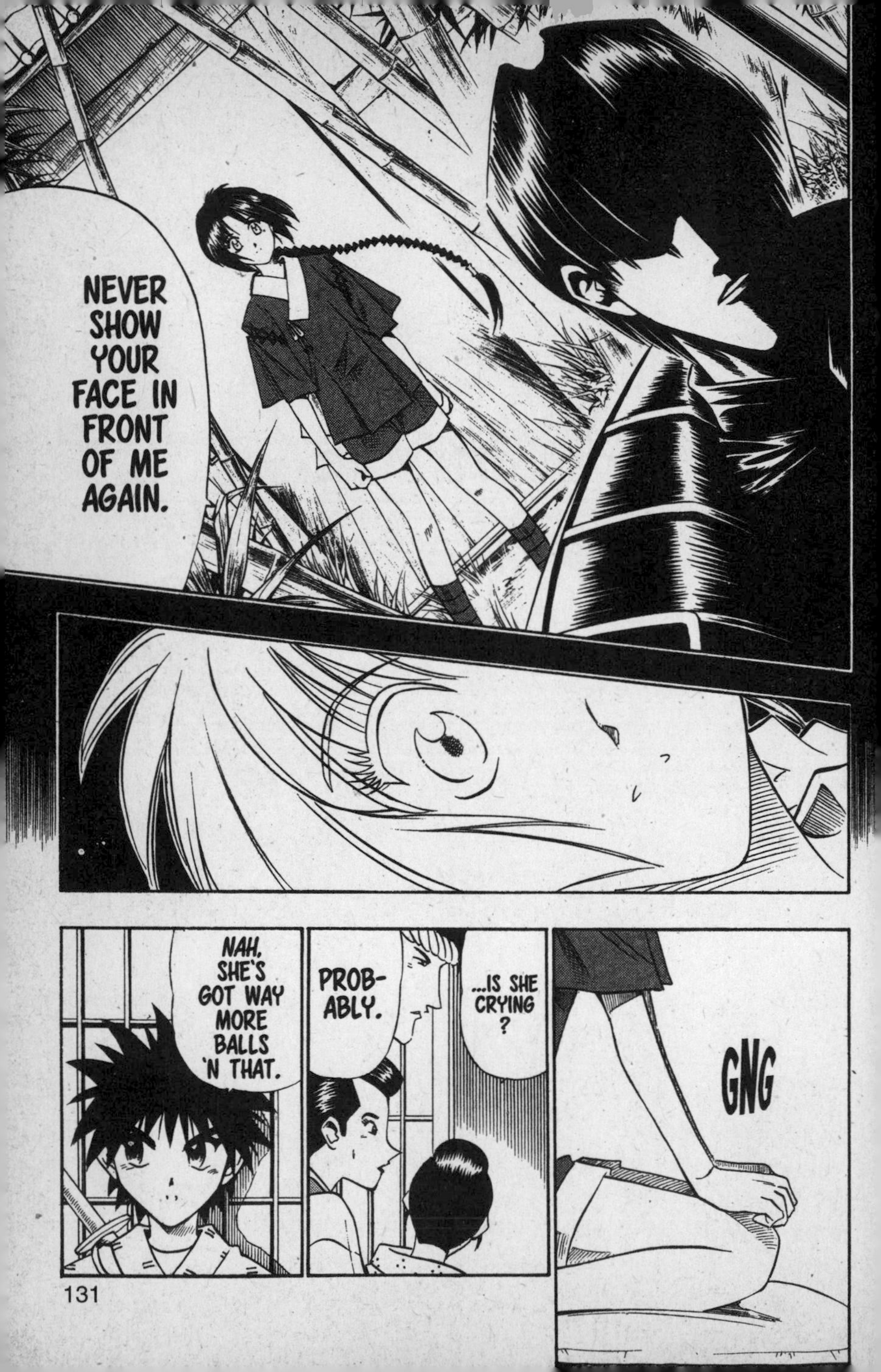
NEVER SHOW YOUR FACE IN FRONT OF ME AGAIN.
GNG
...IS SHE CRYING?
PROB-ABLY.
NAH, SHE'S GOT WAY MORE BALLS 'N THAT.

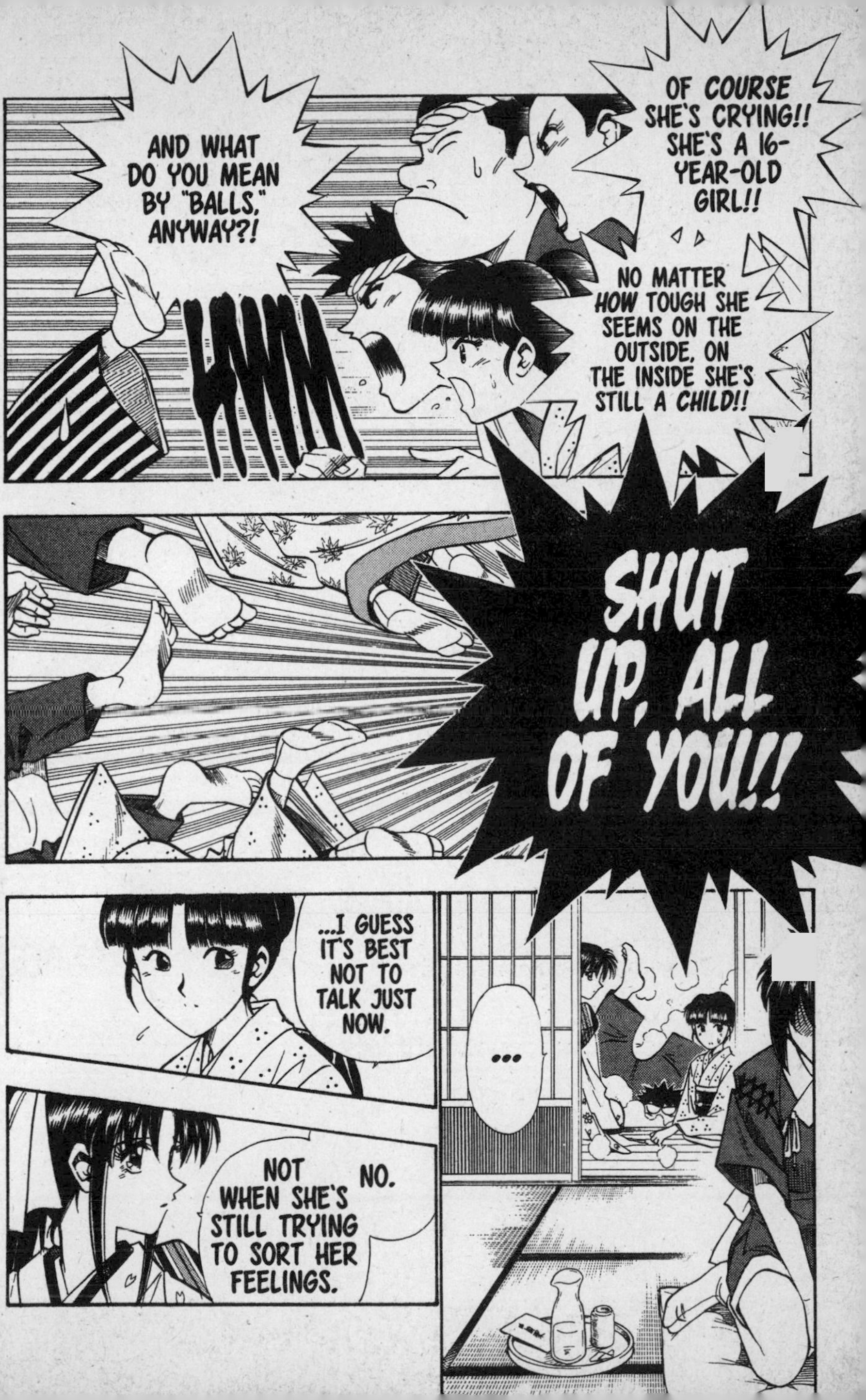
OF COURSE SHE'S CRYING!! SHE'S A 16-YEAR-OLD GIRL!!
NO MATTER HOW TOUGH SHE SEEMS ON THE OUTSIDE, ON THE INSIDE SHE'S STILL A CHILD!!
AND WHAT DO YOU MEAN BY "BALLS," ANYWAY?!
SHUT UP, ALL OF YOU!!
...
...I GUESS IT'S BEST NOT TO TALK JUST NOW.
NO.
NOT WHEN SHE'S STILL TRYING TO SORT HER FEELINGS.

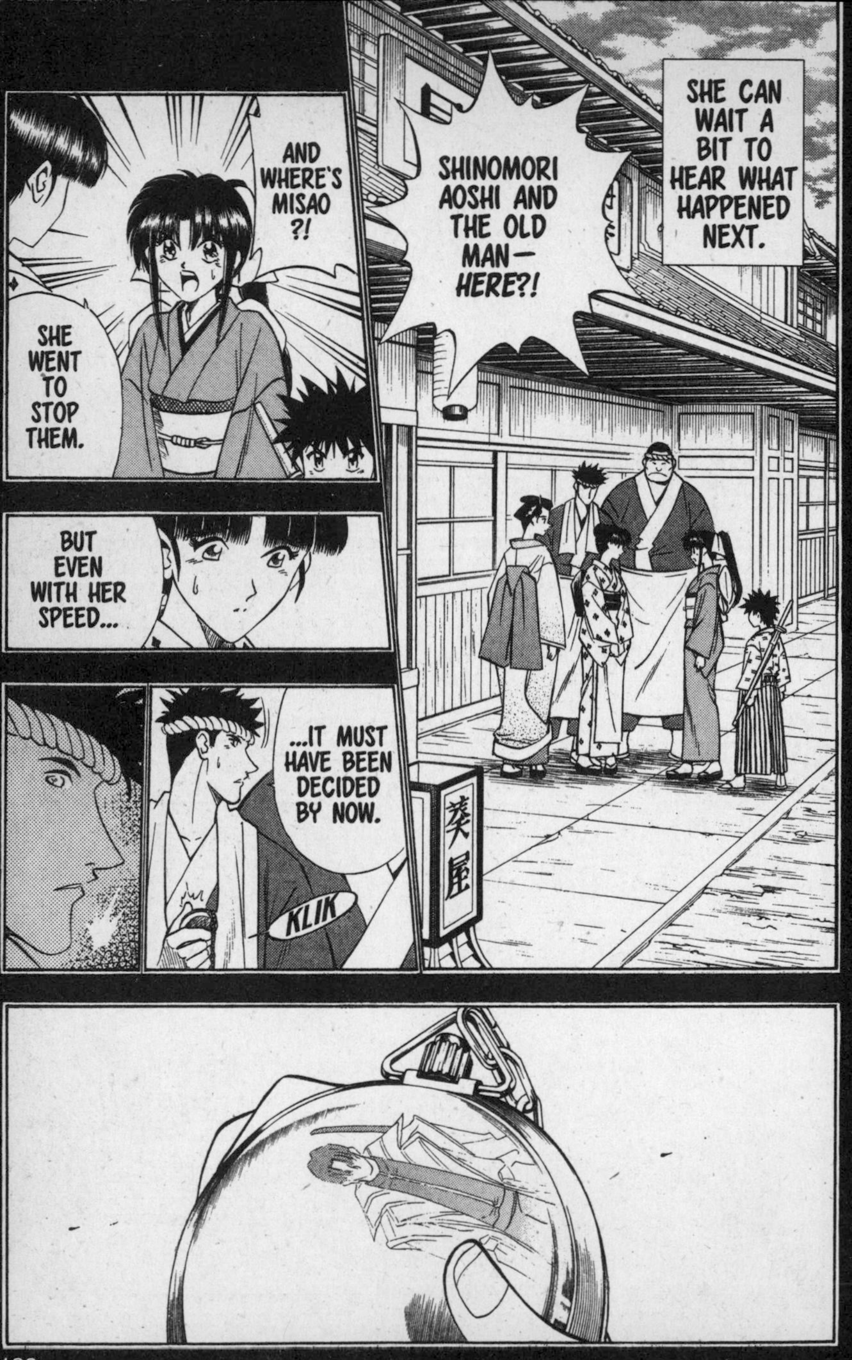
SHE CAN WAIT A BIT TO HEAR WHAT HAPPENED NEXT.
SHINOMORI AOSHI AND THE OLD MAN— HERE?!
葵屋
AND WHERE'S MISAO ?!
SHE WENT TO STOP THEM.
BUT EVEN WITH HER SPEED...
...IT MUST HAVE BEEN DECIDED BY NOW.
KLIK

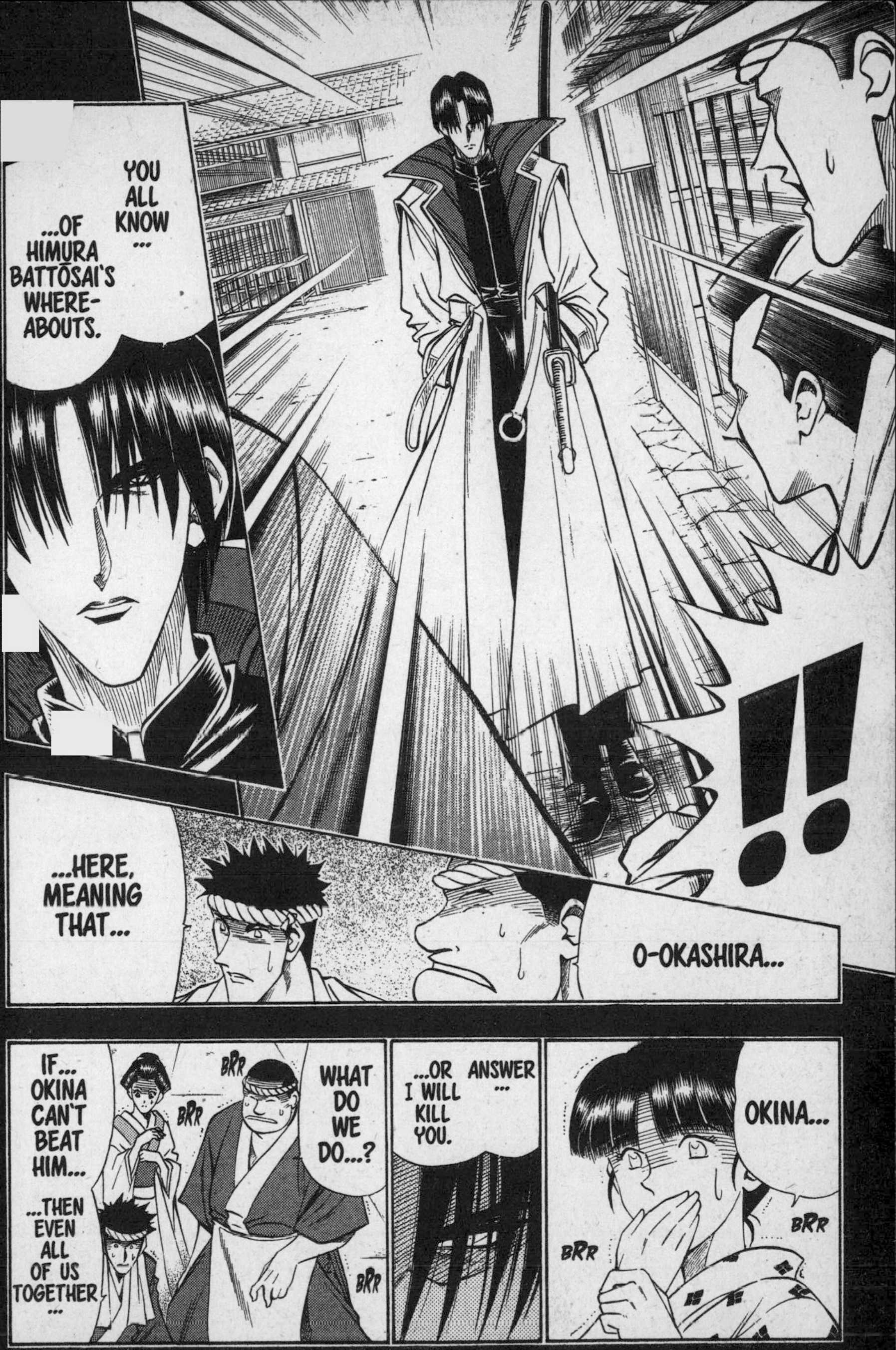
YOU ALL KNOW ...
...OF HIMURA BATTŌSAI'S WHEREABOUTS.
!!
O-OKASHIRA...
...HERE, MEANING THAT...
OKINA...
BRR
BRR
ANSWER ...
...OR I WILL KILL YOU.
WHAT DO WE DO...?
BRR
BRR
BRR
IF... OKINA CAN'T BEAT HIM...
...THEN EVEN ALL OF US TOGETHER ...

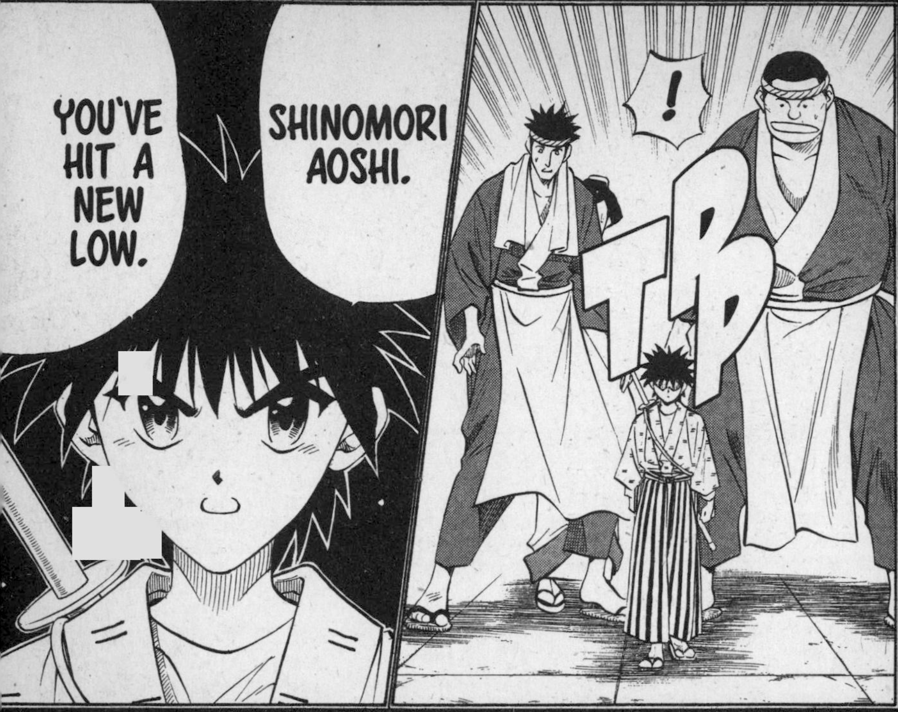

!
TB
SHINOMORI AOSHI.
YOU'VE HIT A NEW LOW.

In the [redacted] come back to video games—what else? Mainly, for me it's combat games[redacted]d last time, I'm now on "*Vampire Hunter*" and "*Samurai Spirits: Zankurō Musōken.*" In "*Vampire Hunter,*" I recently played Gallon. I used the beast cannon over and [redacted]—it feels pretty good when it works. My main character's Morrigan, though, [redacted]ourse. For "*Samurai Spirits,*" I'm Shura-mode Genjūrō, all the way. I finished [redacted] 1 the other day, so now I'm trying to beat Level 2 in "Swordsman" mode. At first, it didn't go so well, but once I got the hang of the special move "*Reiha,*" the rest was pretty easy. I still think the balance is a bit off (setting aside the fact that I probably just suck), and I do try not to depend on "*Reiha*" too much.

I'm wo[redacted] hard on getting triple-kills, or five kills in a row, and before anyone points out t[redacted] have time for video games even though I'm always complaining about not having time to write, keep in mind that, for me, being able to play 2–3 hours a week is still a pretty good week. Some weeks, I can't even play at all. I haven't gotten to "Tekken 2," for example, even though I've already bought it. And since a 3-D game is different from a 2-D game, it'll be a while before I can enjoy it—and then I'll be back to "*Vampir[redacted]Hunter*" and "*Samurai Spirits*" again. The assistants have played "Tekken 2," at leas[redacted]so I've been able to see all the endings (sure, maybe that's not how you're **supposed** to do it, but the opposing lives of "King" and "Armor King" are to die for—those two are so cool!). I know that, to those who haven't played the game, this is all complete nonsense, so I guess I'd better sign off. See you next volume.

和月伸宏

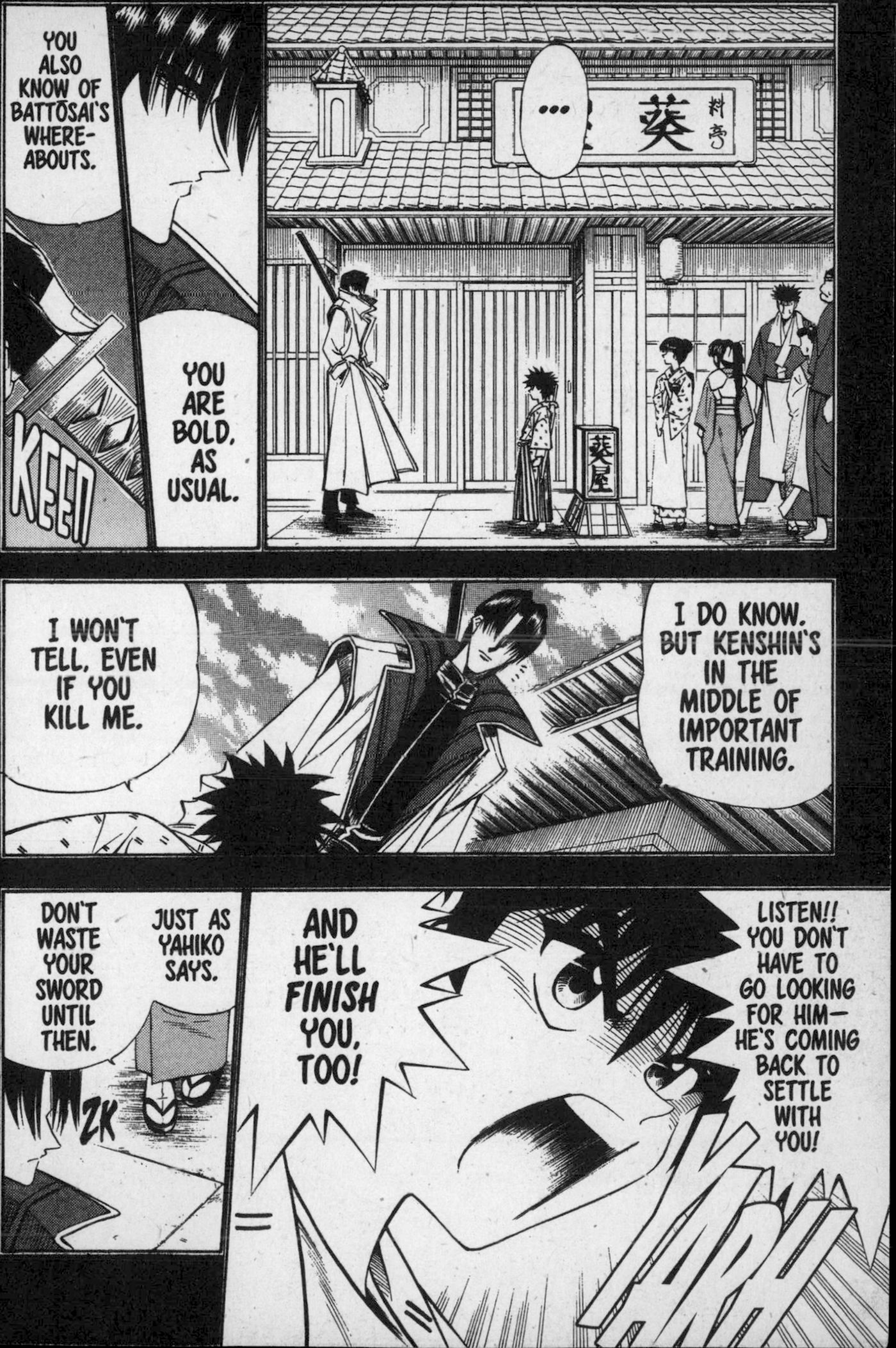
...
YOU ARE BOLD, AS USUAL.
YOU ALSO KNOW OF BATTŌSAI'S WHEREABOUTS.
KEEN
I DO KNOW. BUT KENSHIN'S IN THE MIDDLE OF IMPORTANT TRAINING.
I WON'T TELL, EVEN IF YOU KILL ME.
LISTEN!! YOU DON'T HAVE TO GO LOOKING FOR HIM—HE'S COMING BACK TO SETTLE WITH YOU!
AND HE'LL FINISH YOU, TOO!
JUST AS YAHIKO SAYS.
DON'T WASTE YOUR SWORD UNTIL THEN.
ZK

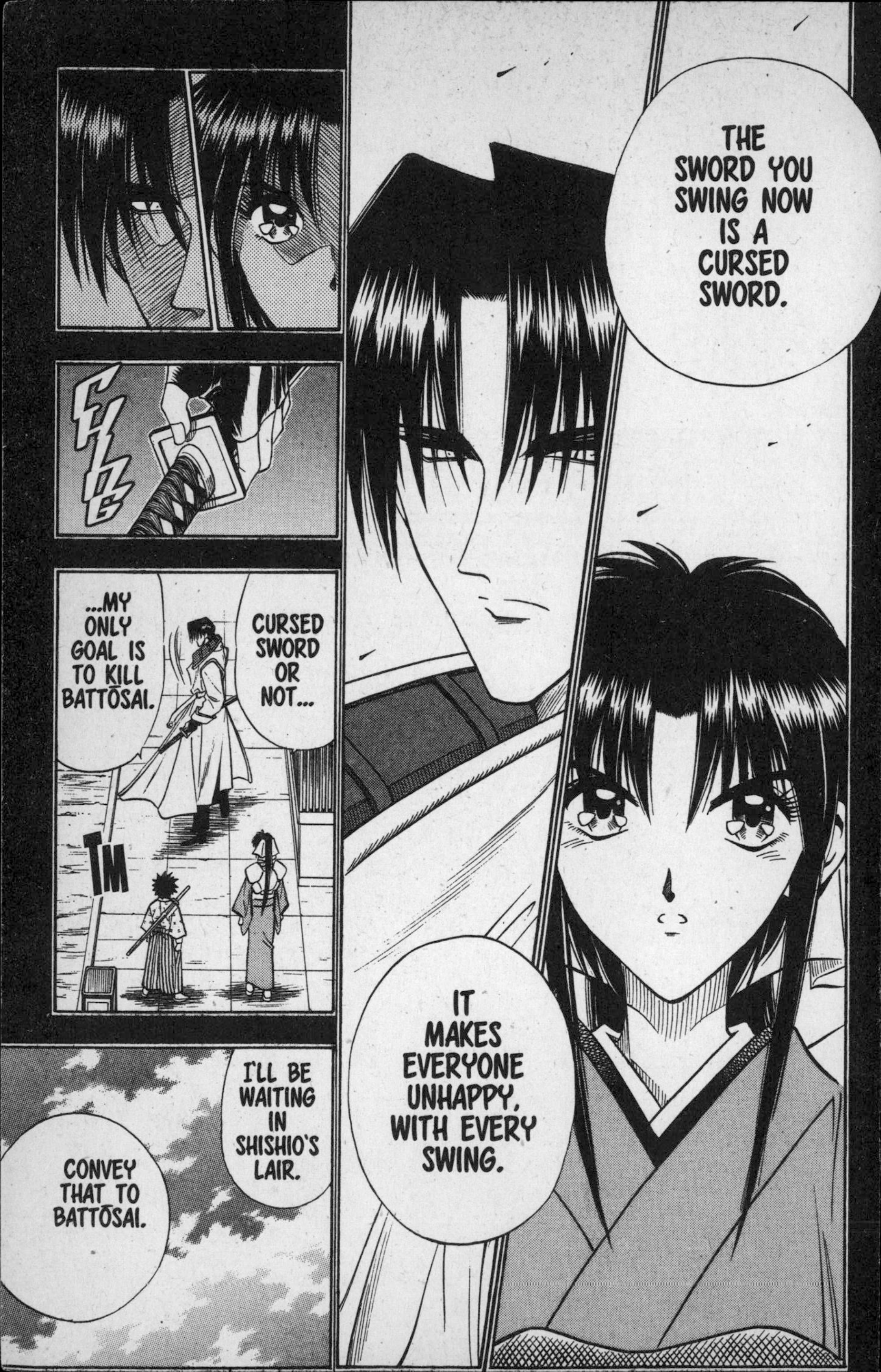
THE SWORD YOU SWING NOW IS A CURSED SWORD.
IT MAKES EVERYONE UNHAPPY, WITH EVERY SWING.
CURSED SWORD OR NOT...
...MY ONLY GOAL IS TO KILL BATTŌSAI.
TM
I'LL BE WAITING IN SHISHIO'S LAIR.
CONVEY THAT TO BATTŌSAI.

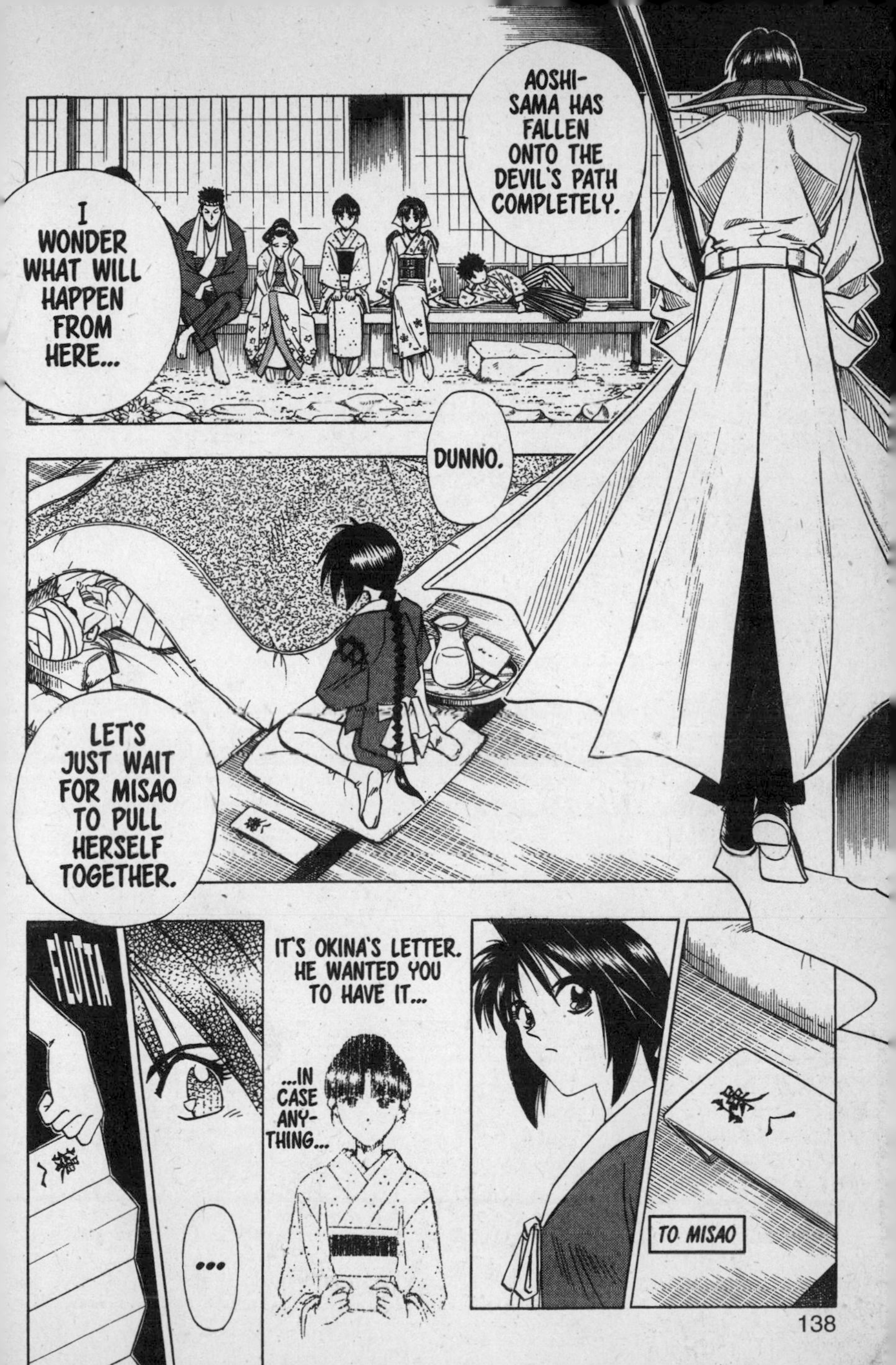
AOSHI-SAMA HAS FALLEN ONTO THE DEVIL'S PATH COMPLETELY.
I WONDER WHAT WILL HAPPEN FROM HERE...
DUNNO.
LET'S JUST WAIT FOR MISAO TO PULL HERSELF TOGETHER.
TO MISAO
IT'S OKINA'S LETTER. HE WANTED YOU TO HAVE IT...
...IN CASE ANYTHING...
FLUTTA
...

READ THIS WAY

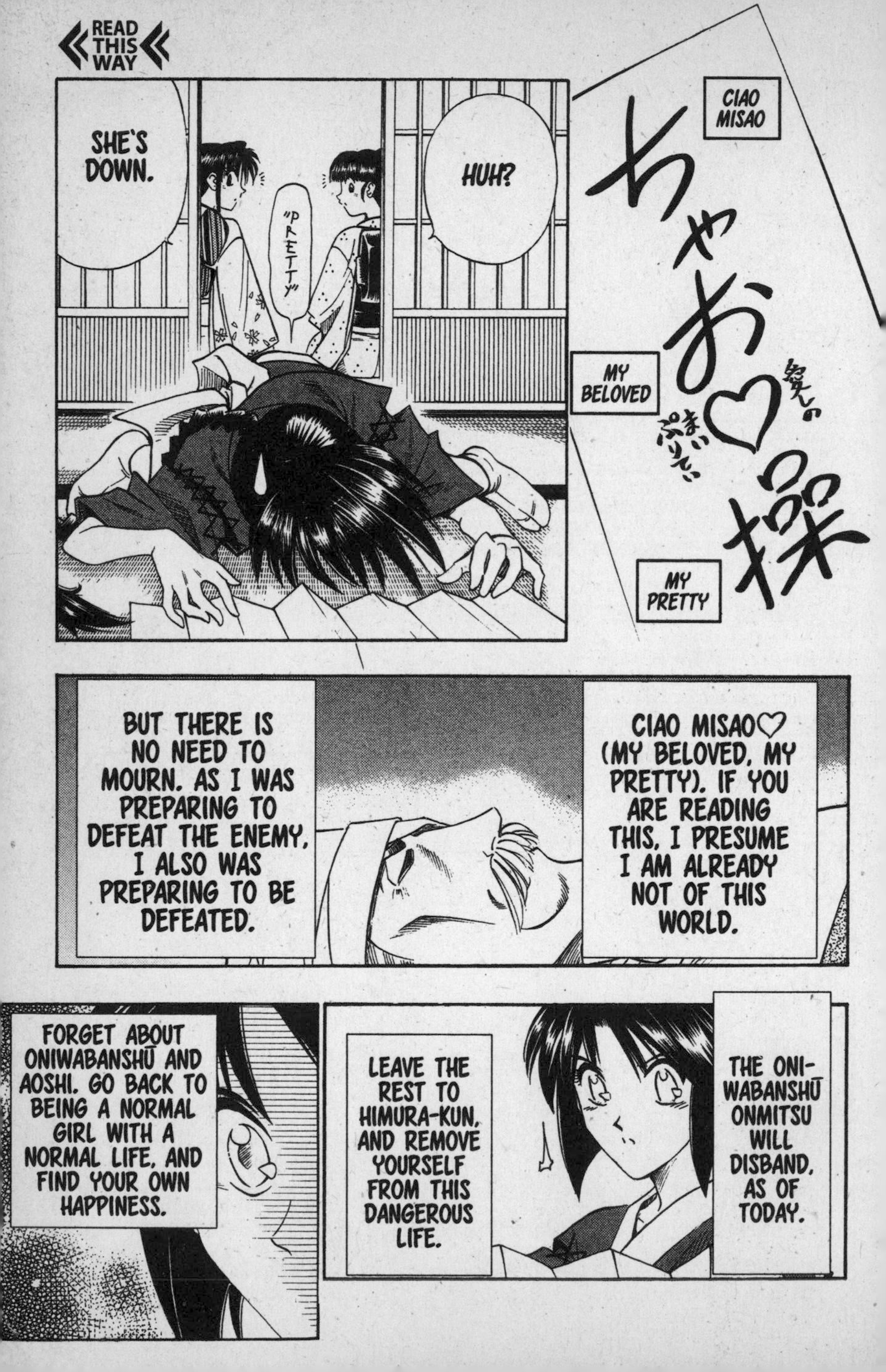
CIAO MISAO
ちゃお♡操
MY BELOVED
MY PRETTY
HUH?
"PRETTY"
SHE'S DOWN.
CIAO MISAO♡ (MY BELOVED, MY PRETTY). IF YOU ARE READING THIS, I PRESUME I AM ALREADY NOT OF THIS WORLD.
BUT THERE IS NO NEED TO MOURN. AS I WAS PREPARING TO DEFEAT THE ENEMY, I ALSO WAS PREPARING TO BE DEFEATED.
THE ONI-WABANSHŪ ONMITSU WILL DISBAND, AS OF TODAY.
LEAVE THE REST TO HIMURA-KUN, AND REMOVE YOURSELF FROM THIS DANGEROUS LIFE.
FORGET ABOUT ONIWABANSHŪ AND AOSHI. GO BACK TO BEING A NORMAL GIRL WITH A NORMAL LIFE, AND FIND YOUR OWN HAPPINESS.

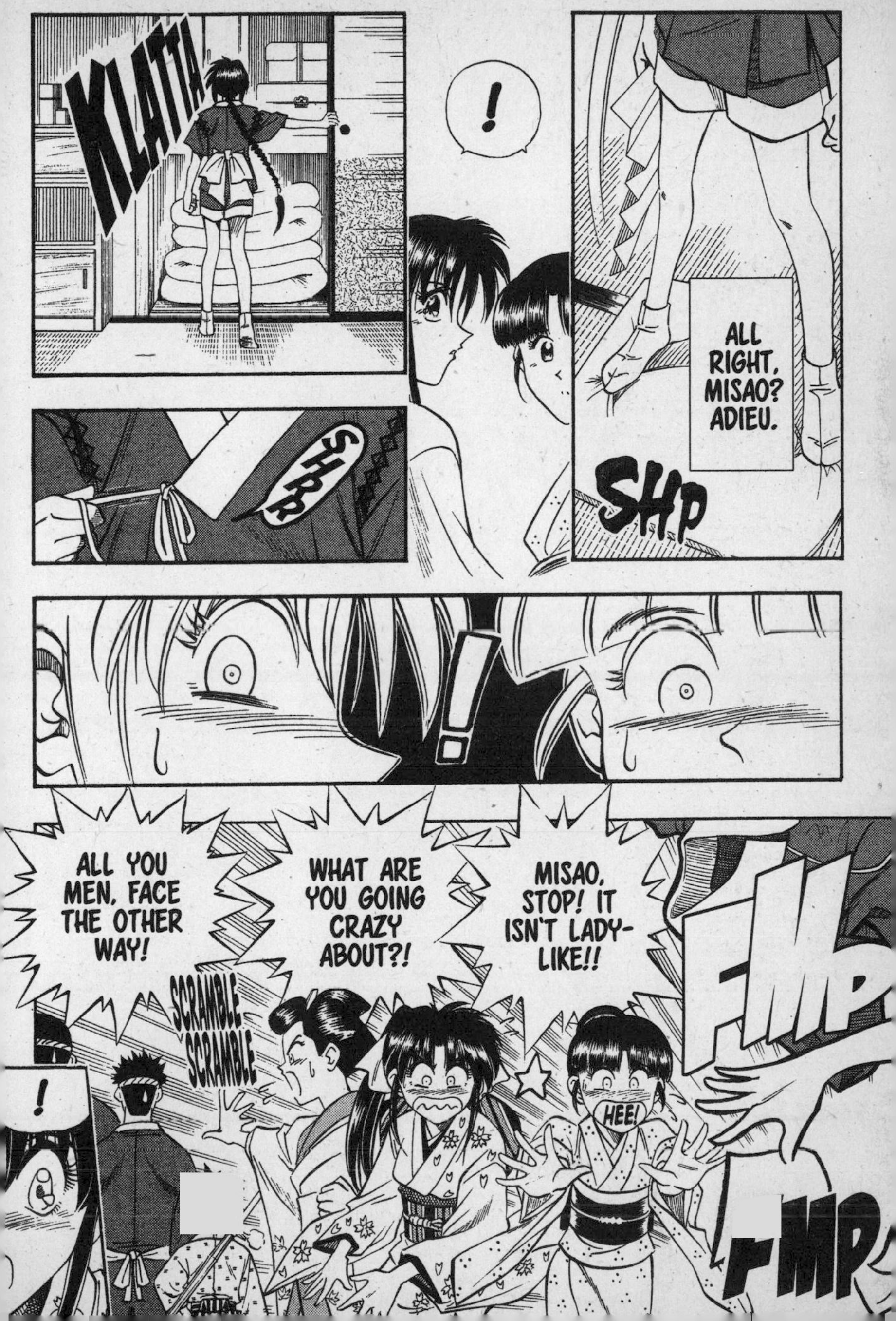
ALL RIGHT, MISAO? ADIEU.
SHP
!
KLATTA
SHRR
!
FMP
MISAO, STOP! IT ISN'T LADY-LIKE!!
WHAT ARE YOU GOING CRAZY ABOUT?!
ALL YOU MEN, FACE THE OTHER WAY!
HEE!
SCRAMBLE SCRAMBLE
!
FMP

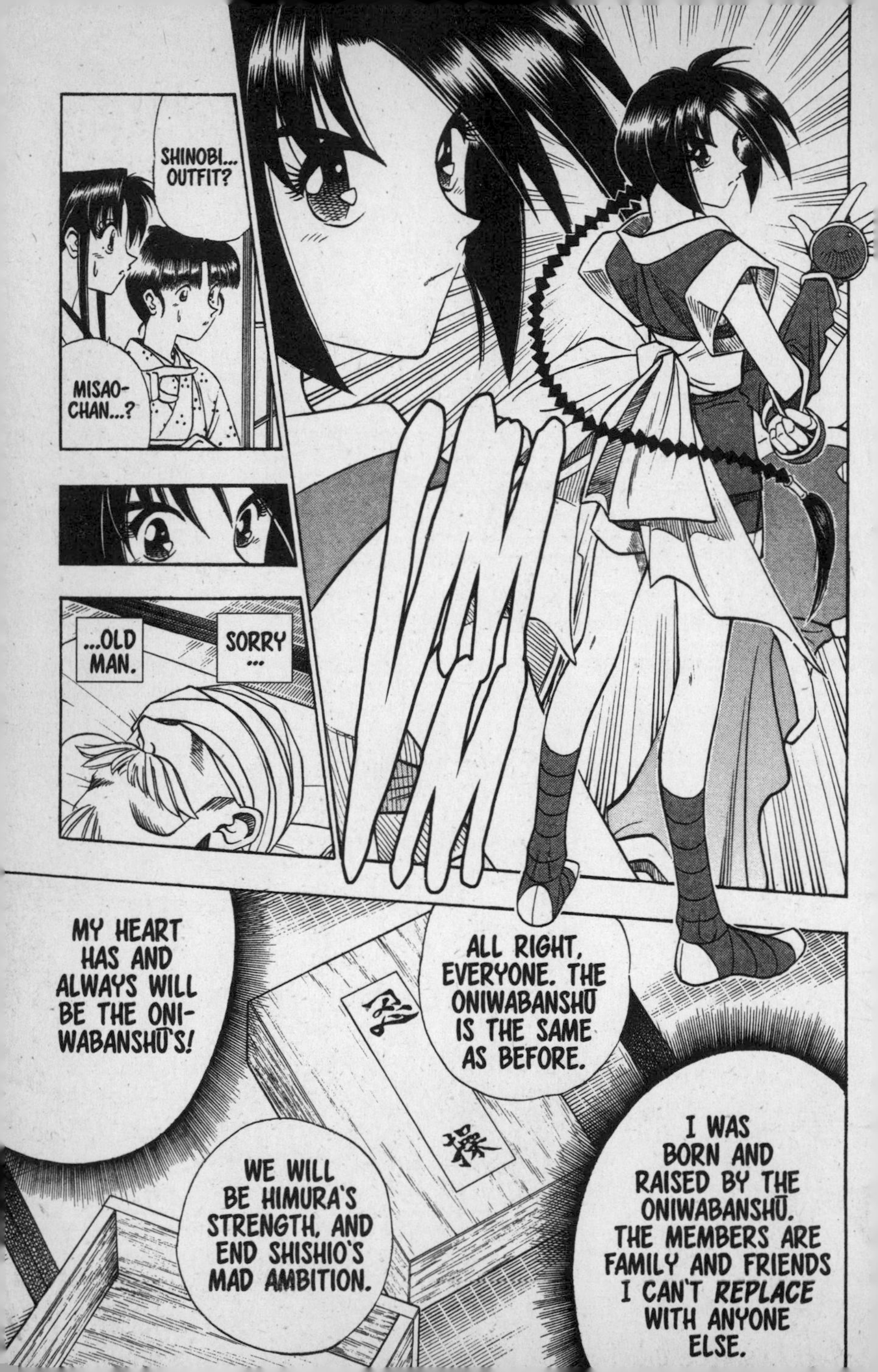
SHINOBI... OUTFIT?
MISAO-CHAN...?
SORRY...
...OLD MAN.
ALL RIGHT, EVERYONE. THE ONIWABANSHŪ IS THE SAME AS BEFORE.
I WAS BORN AND RAISED BY THE ONIWABANSHŪ. THE MEMBERS ARE FAMILY AND FRIENDS I CAN'T *REPLACE* WITH ANYONE ELSE.
MY HEART HAS AND ALWAYS WILL BE THE ONI-WABANSHŪ'S!
WE WILL BE HIMURA'S STRENGTH, AND END SHISHIO'S MAD AMBITION.
忍
操

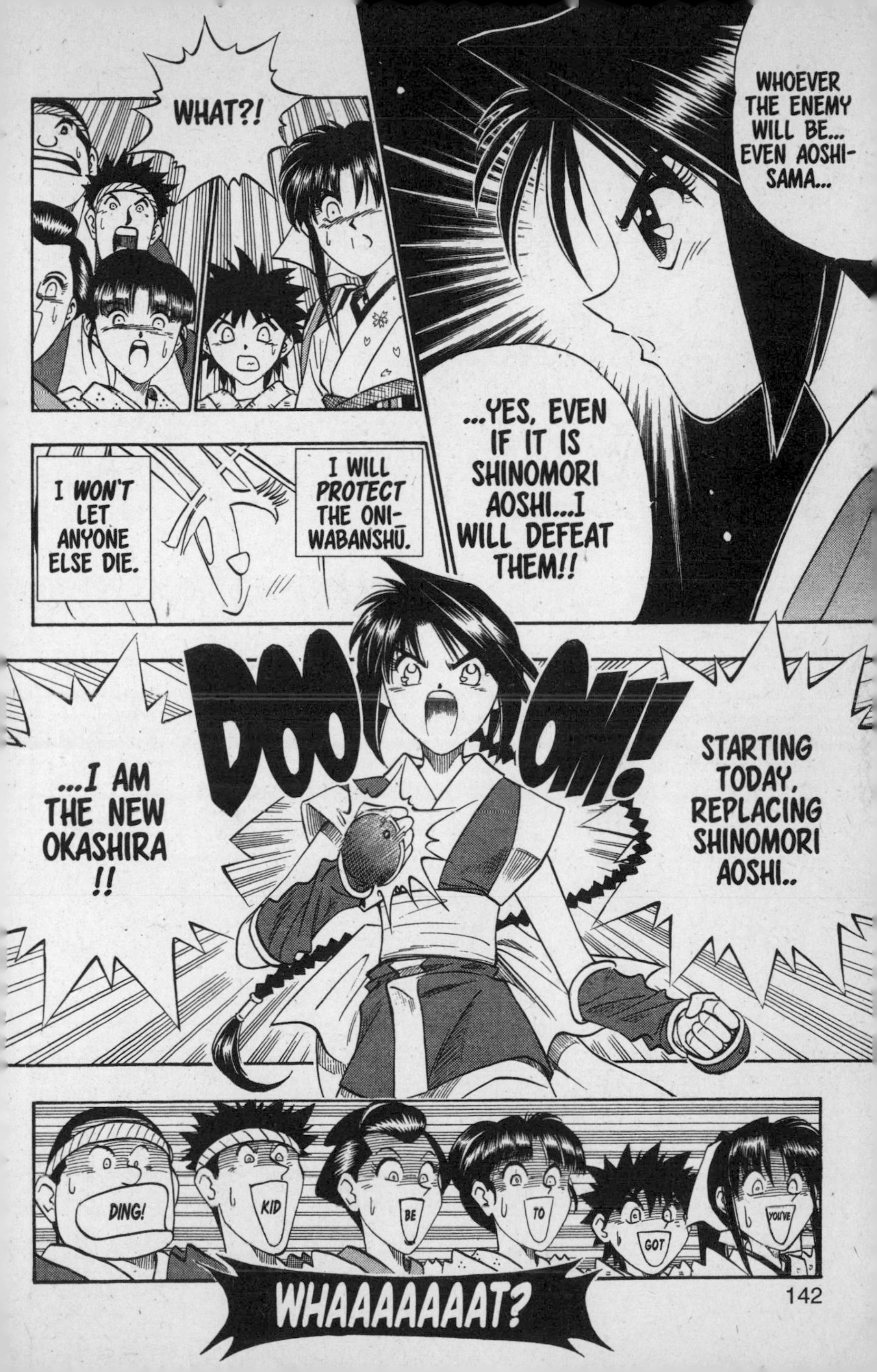
WHOEVER THE ENEMY WILL BE... EVEN AOSHI-SAMA...
...YES, EVEN IF IT IS SHINOMORI AOSHI...I WILL DEFEAT THEM!!
WHAT?!
I WILL PROTECT THE ONI-WABANSHŪ.
I WON'T LET ANYONE ELSE DIE.
STARTING TODAY, REPLACING SHINOMORI AOSHI..
DOOOM!
...I AM THE NEW OKASHIRA !!
YOU'VE
GOT
TO
BE
KID
DING!
WHAAAAAAAT?

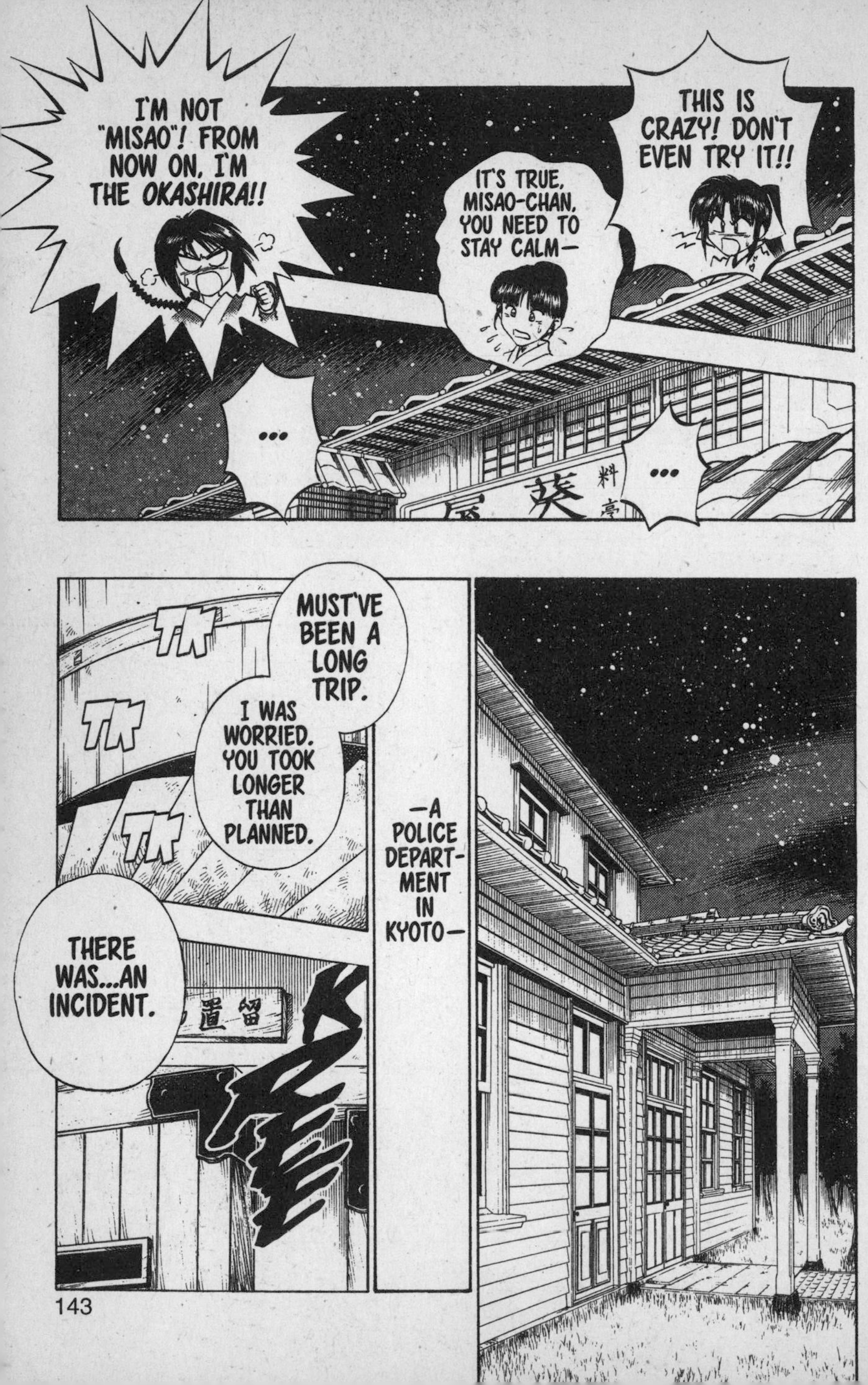
THIS IS CRAZY! DON'T EVEN TRY IT!!
IT'S TRUE, MISAO-CHAN, YOU NEED TO STAY CALM—
I'M NOT "MISAO"! FROM NOW ON, I'M THE *OKASHIRA*!!
...
...
—A POLICE DEPARTMENT IN KYOTO—
MUST'VE BEEN A LONG TRIP.
I WAS WORRIED. YOU TOOK LONGER THAN PLANNED.
THERE WAS...AN INCIDENT.

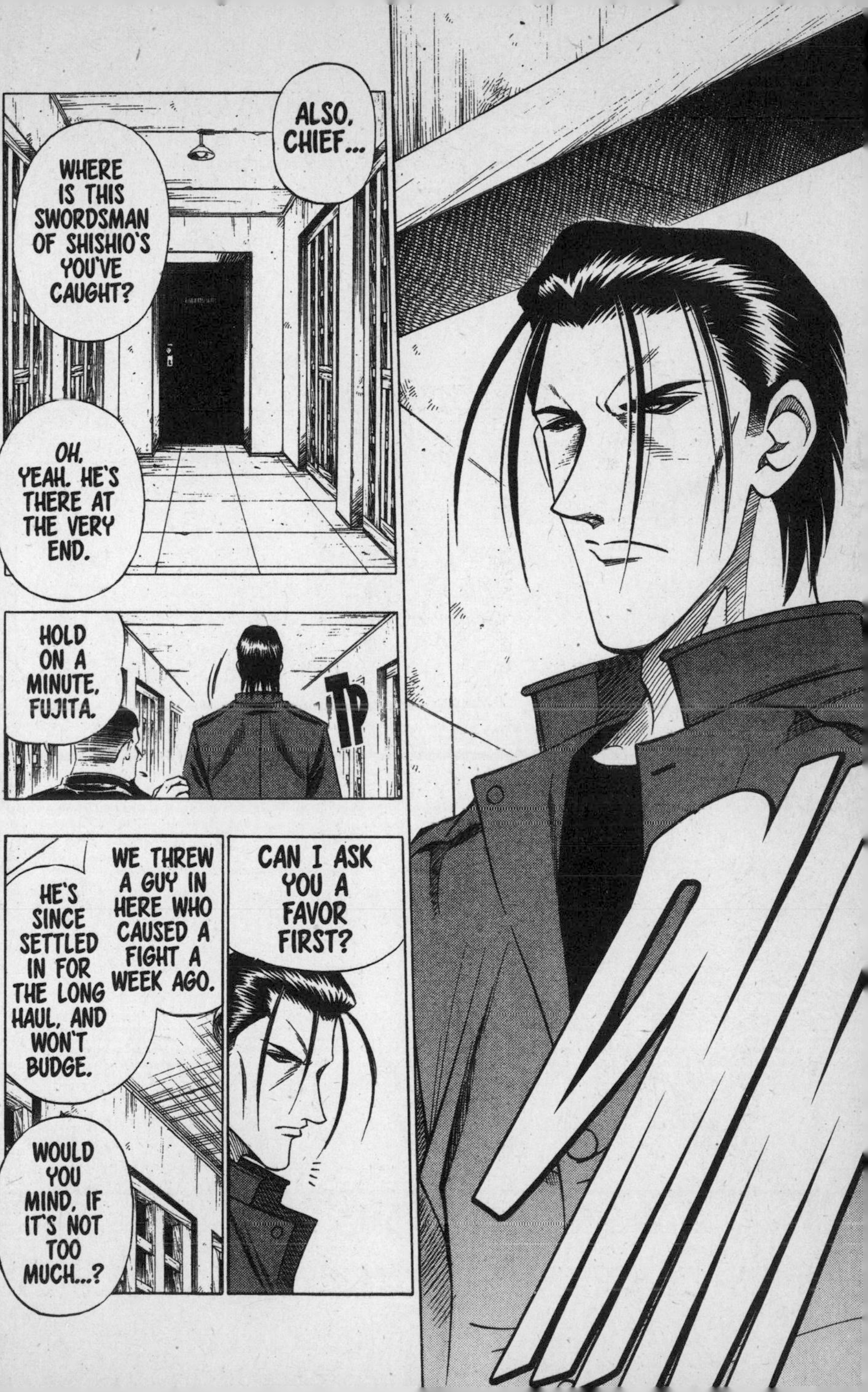
ALSO, CHIEF...
WHERE IS THIS SWORDSMAN OF SHISHIO'S YOU'VE CAUGHT?
OH, YEAH. HE'S THERE AT THE VERY END.
TP
HOLD ON A MINUTE, FUJITA.
CAN I ASK YOU A FAVOR FIRST?
WE THREW A GUY IN HERE WHO CAUSED A FIGHT A WEEK AGO.
HE'S SINCE SETTLED IN FOR THE LONG HAUL, AND WON'T BUDGE.
WOULD YOU MIND, IF IT'S NOT TOO MUCH...?

READ THIS WAY

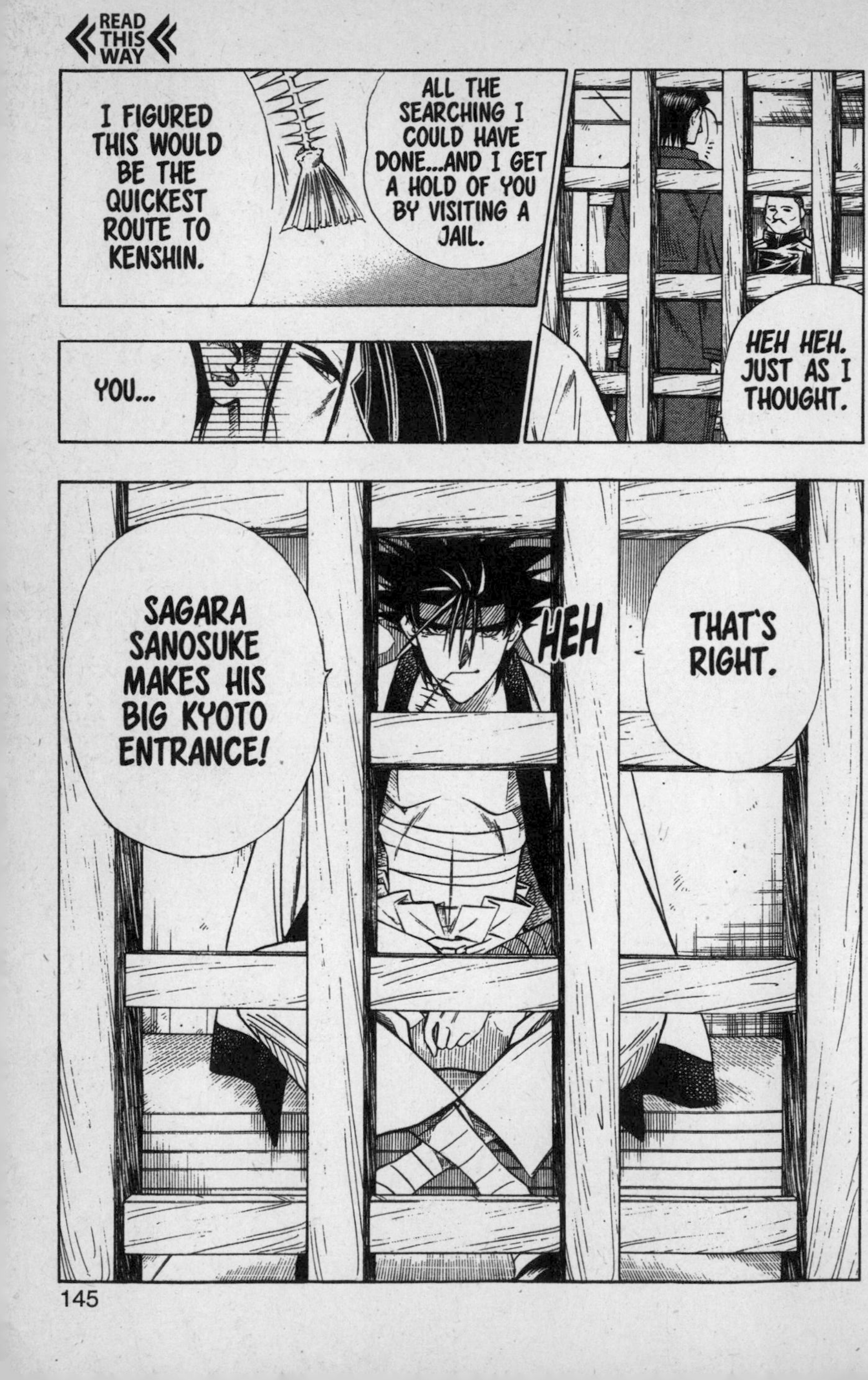
HEH HEH. JUST AS I THOUGHT.
ALL THE SEARCHING I COULD HAVE DONE...AND I GET A HOLD OF YOU BY VISITING A JAIL.
I FIGURED THIS WOULD BE THE QUICKEST ROUTE TO KENSHIN.
YOU...
THAT'S RIGHT.
HEH
SAGARA SANOSUKE MAKES HIS BIG KYOTO ENTRANCE!

Rurouni Kenshin

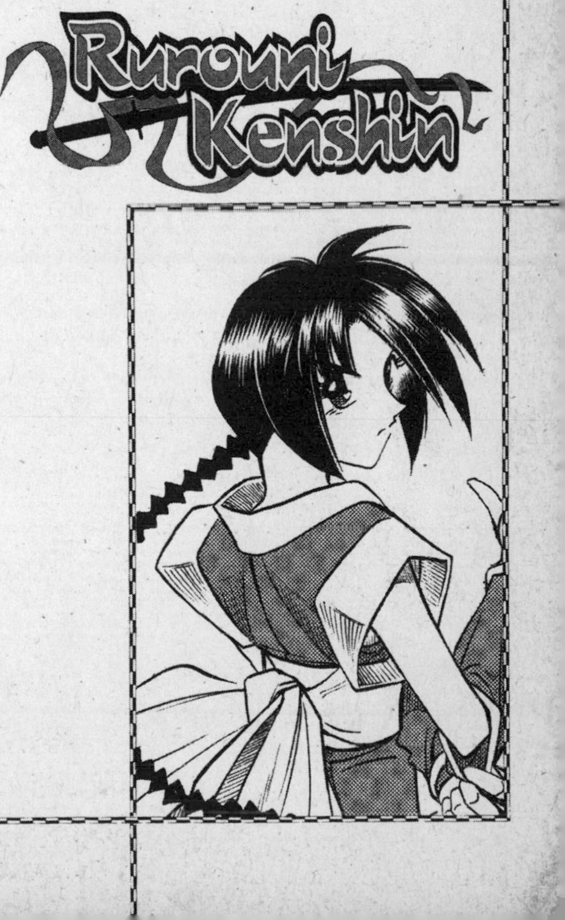

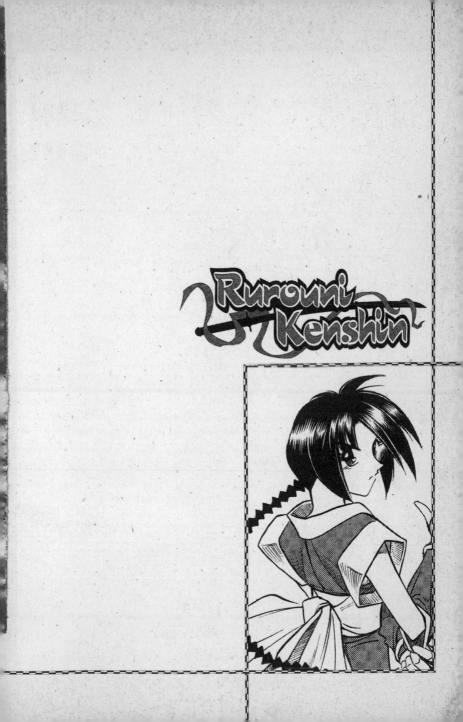

Act 92
A Bird and a Broom

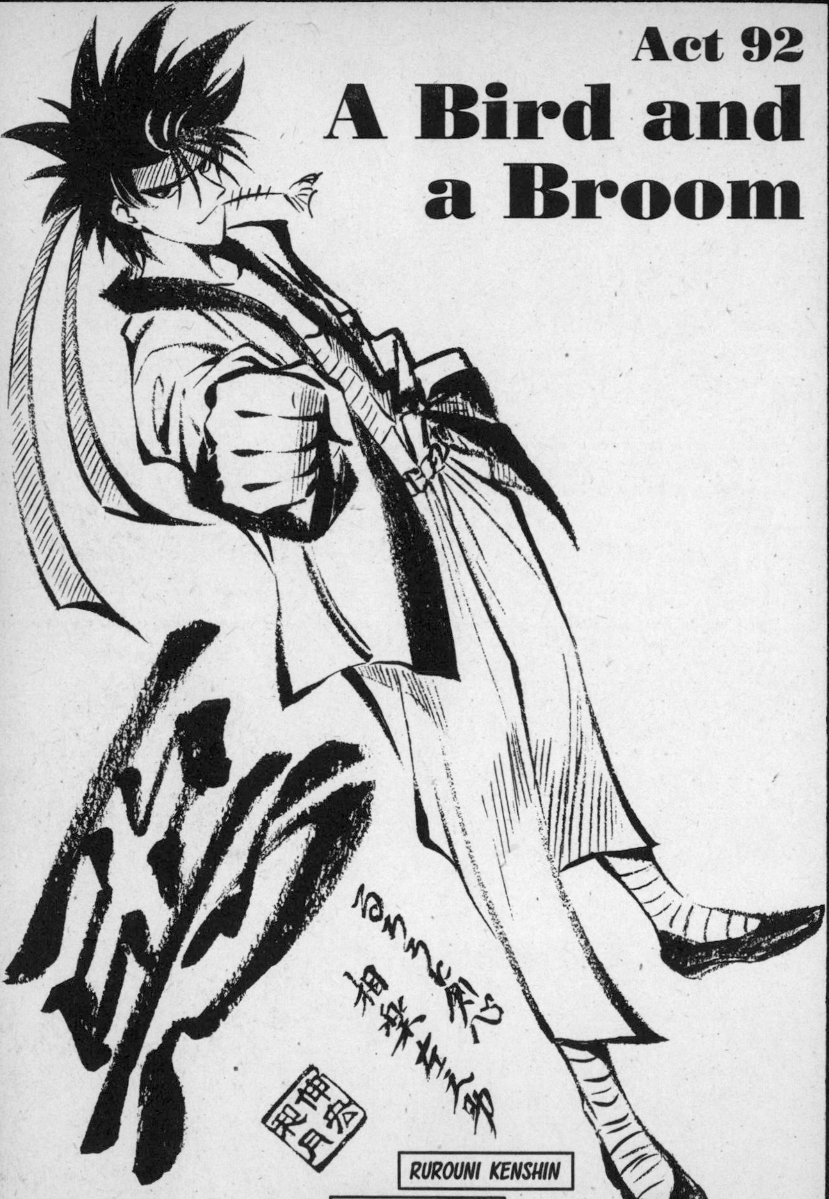
RUROUNI KENSHIN
SAGARA SANOSUKE

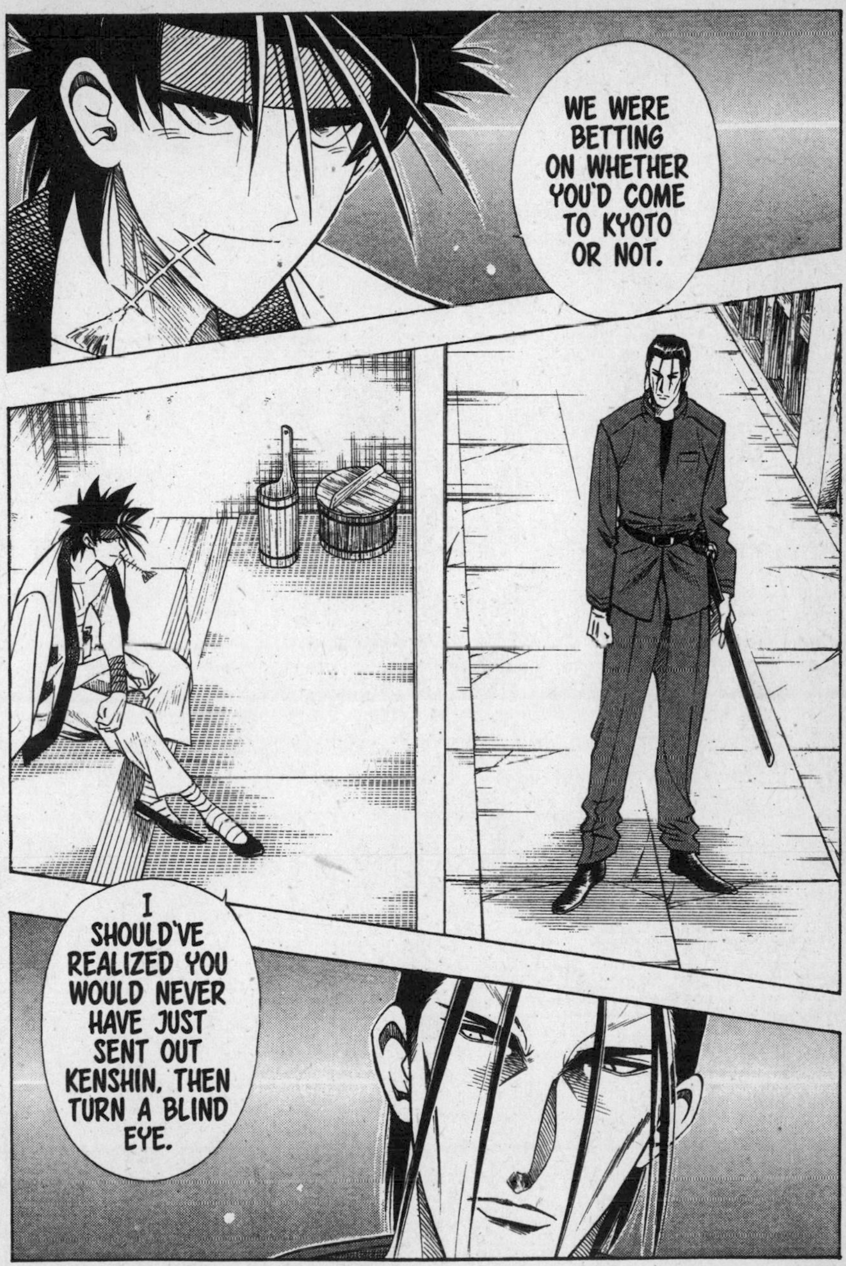
WE WERE BETTING ON WHETHER YOU'D COME TO KYOTO OR NOT.
I SHOULD'VE REALIZED YOU WOULD NEVER HAVE JUST SENT OUT KENSHIN, THEN TURN A BLIND EYE.

READ THIS WAY

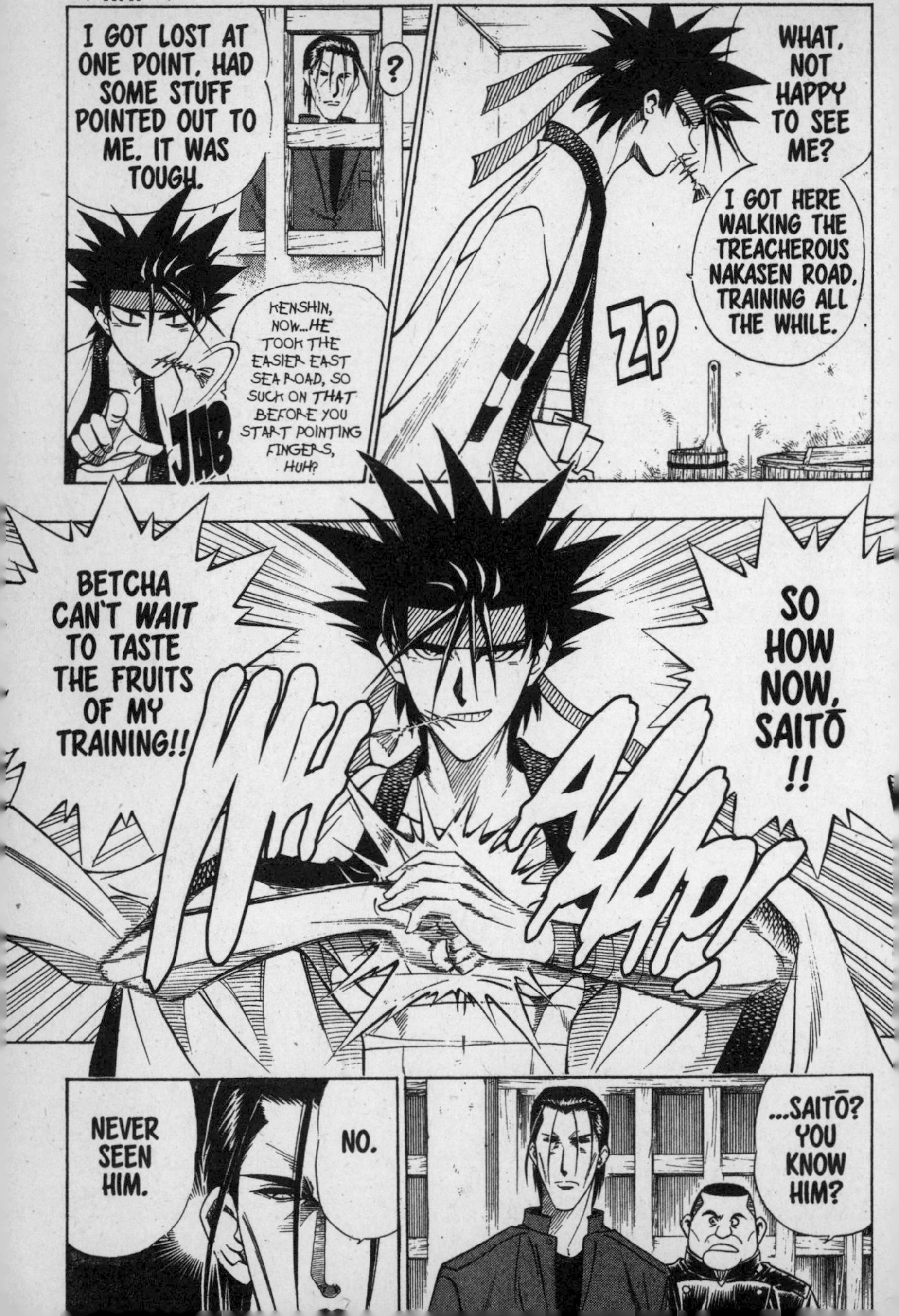
WHAT, NOT HAPPY TO SEE ME?
I GOT HERE WALKING THE TREACHEROUS NAKASEN ROAD, TRAINING ALL THE WHILE.
ZP
?
I GOT LOST AT ONE POINT, HAD SOME STUFF POINTED OUT TO ME. IT WAS TOUGH.
KENSHIN, NOW...HE TOOK THE EASIER EAST SEA ROAD, SO SUCK ON THAT BEFORE YOU START POINTING FINGERS, HUH?
JAB
SO HOW NOW, SAITŌ!!
BETCHA CAN'T WAIT TO TASTE THE FRUITS OF MY TRAINING!!
WHAAP!
...SAITŌ? YOU KNOW HIM?
NO.
NEVER SEEN HIM.

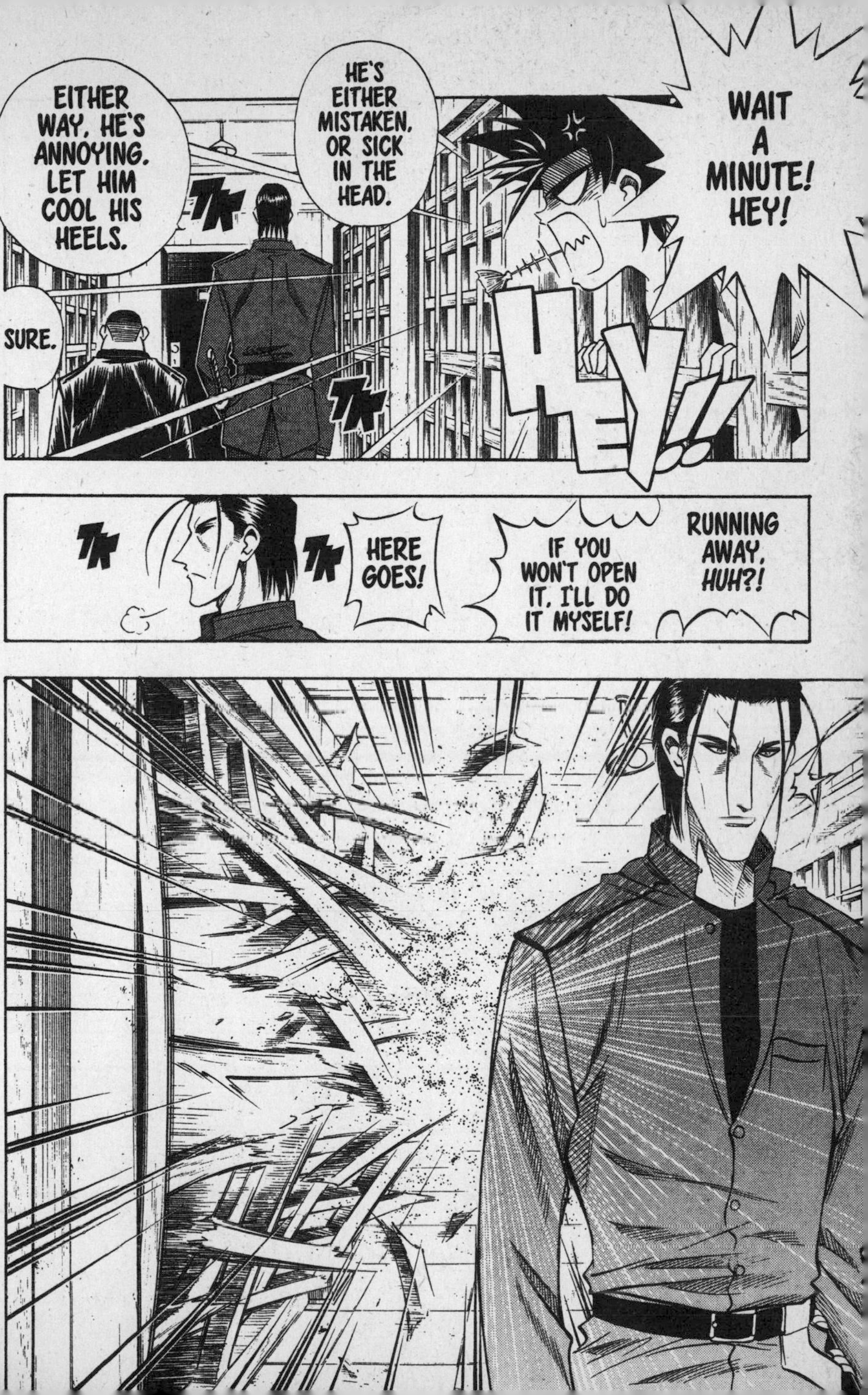
WAIT A MINUTE! HEY!
HEY!!
HE'S EITHER MISTAKEN, OR SICK IN THE HEAD.
EITHER WAY, HE'S ANNOYING. LET HIM COOL HIS HEELS.
SURE.
RUNNING AWAY, HUH?!
IF YOU WON'T OPEN IT, I'LL DO IT MYSELF!
HERE GOES!

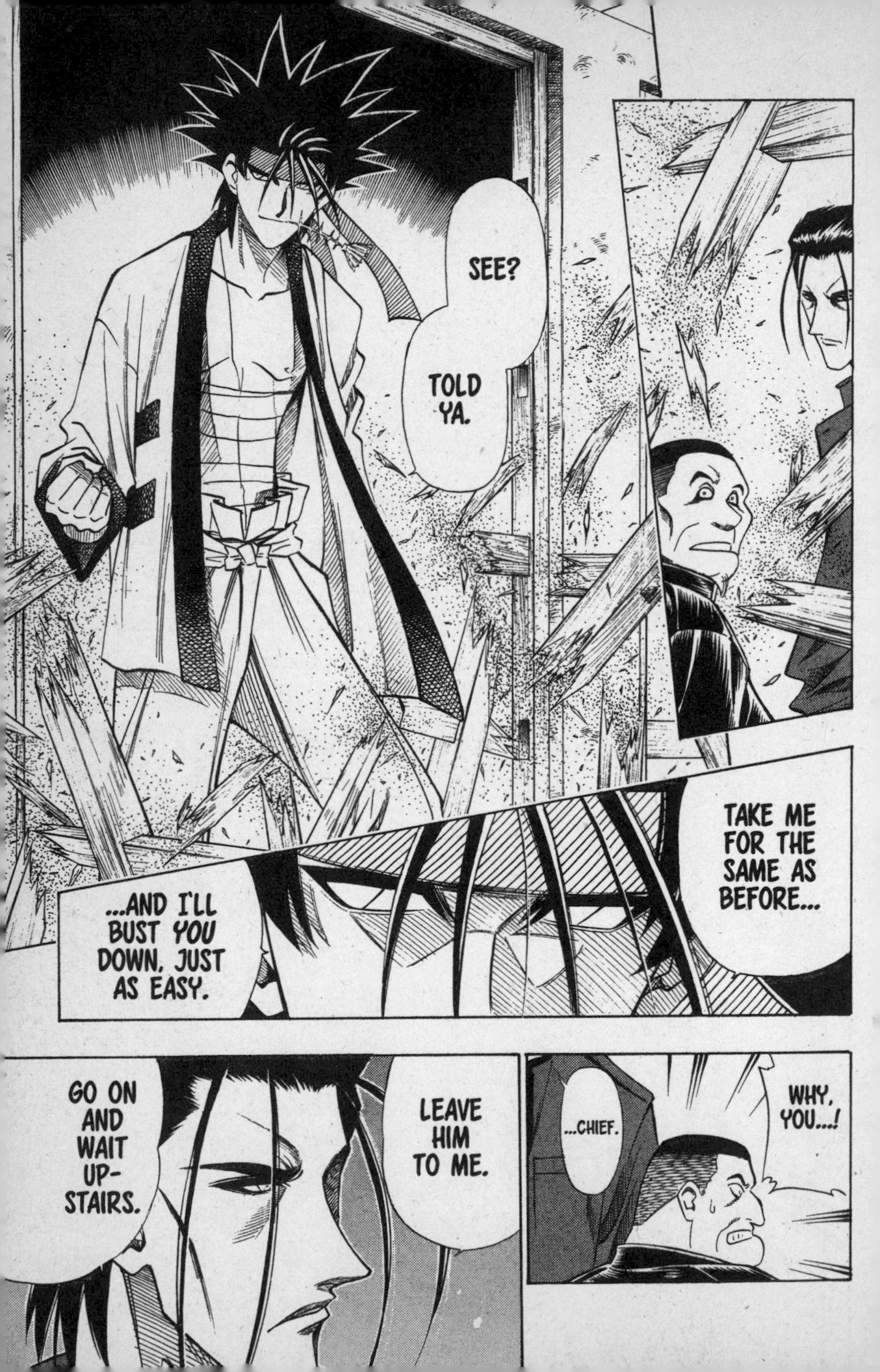
SEE?
TOLD YA.
TAKE ME FOR THE SAME AS BEFORE...
...AND I'LL BUST YOU DOWN, JUST AS EASY.
WHY, YOU...!
...CHIEF.
LEAVE HIM TO ME.
GO ON AND WAIT UP-STAIRS.

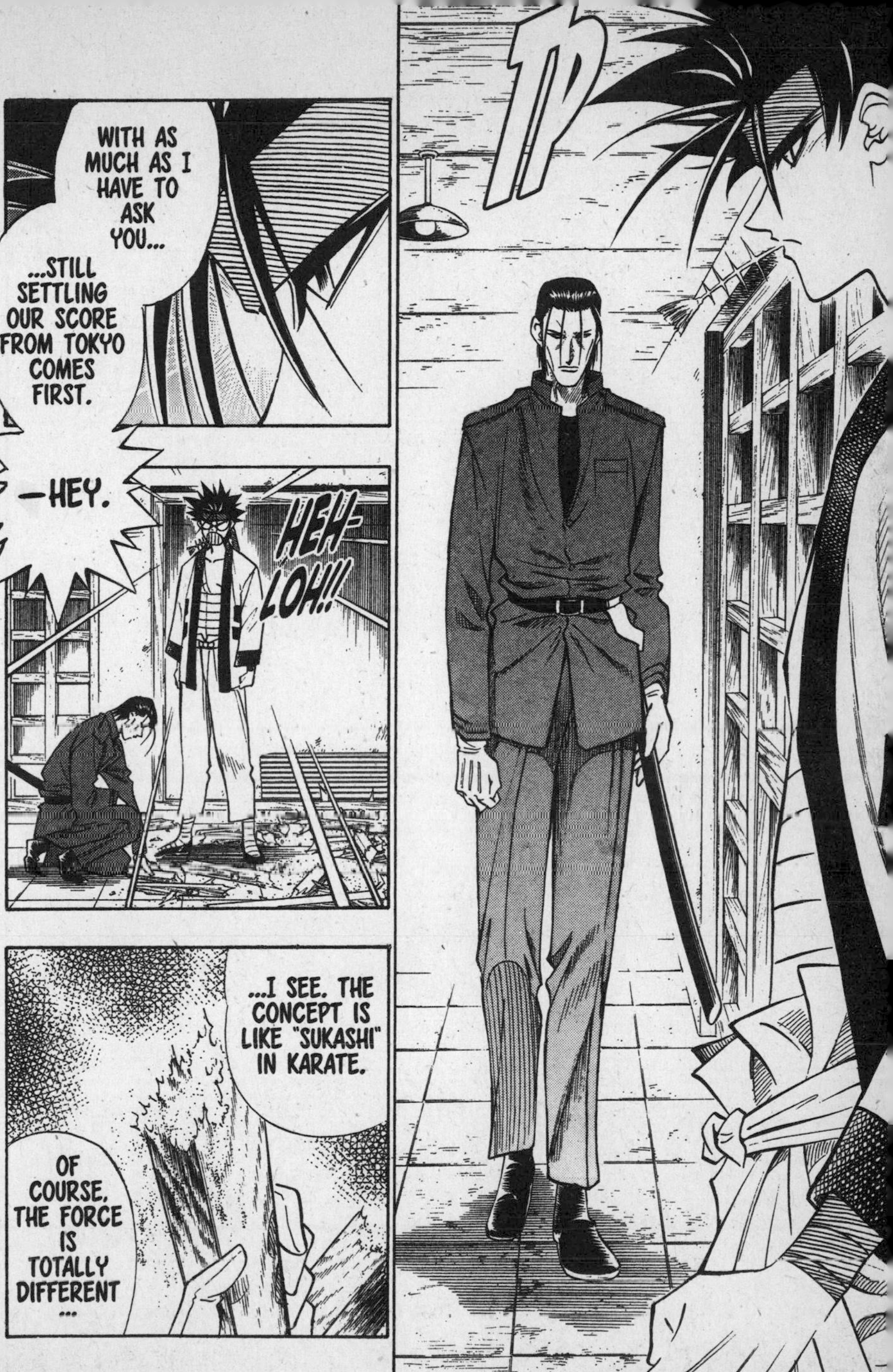
TP
WITH AS MUCH AS I HAVE TO ASK YOU...
...STILL SETTLING OUR SCORE FROM TOKYO COMES FIRST.
—HEY.
HEH-LOH!!
...I SEE. THE CONCEPT IS LIKE "SUKASHI" IN KARATE.
OF COURSE, THE FORCE IS TOTALLY DIFFERENT ...

READ THIS WAY

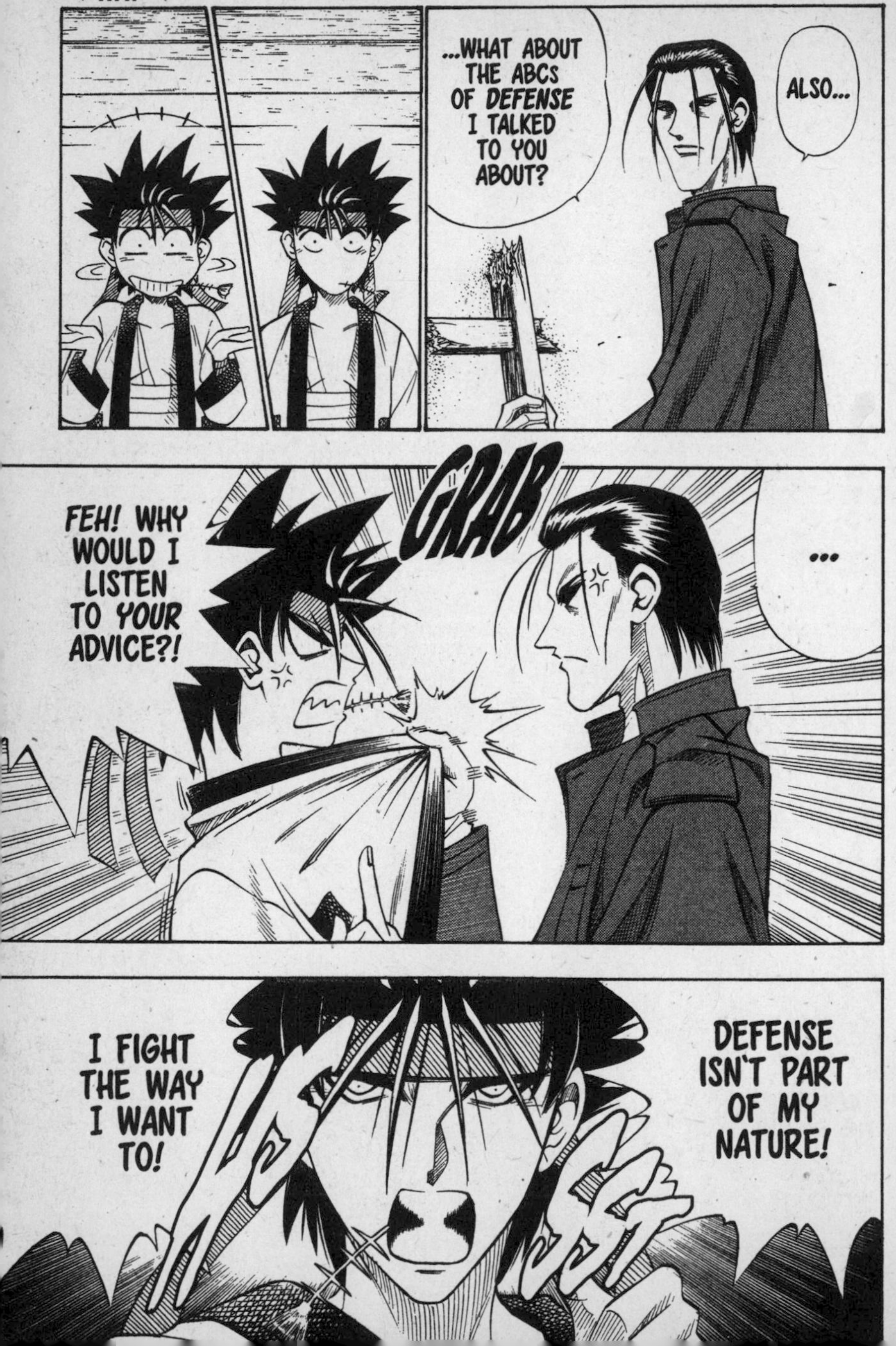
ALSO...
...WHAT ABOUT THE ABCS OF DEFENSE I TALKED TO YOU ABOUT?
...
GRAB
FEH! WHY WOULD I LISTEN TO YOUR ADVICE?!
DEFENSE ISN'T PART OF MY NATURE!
I FIGHT THE WAY I WANT TO!

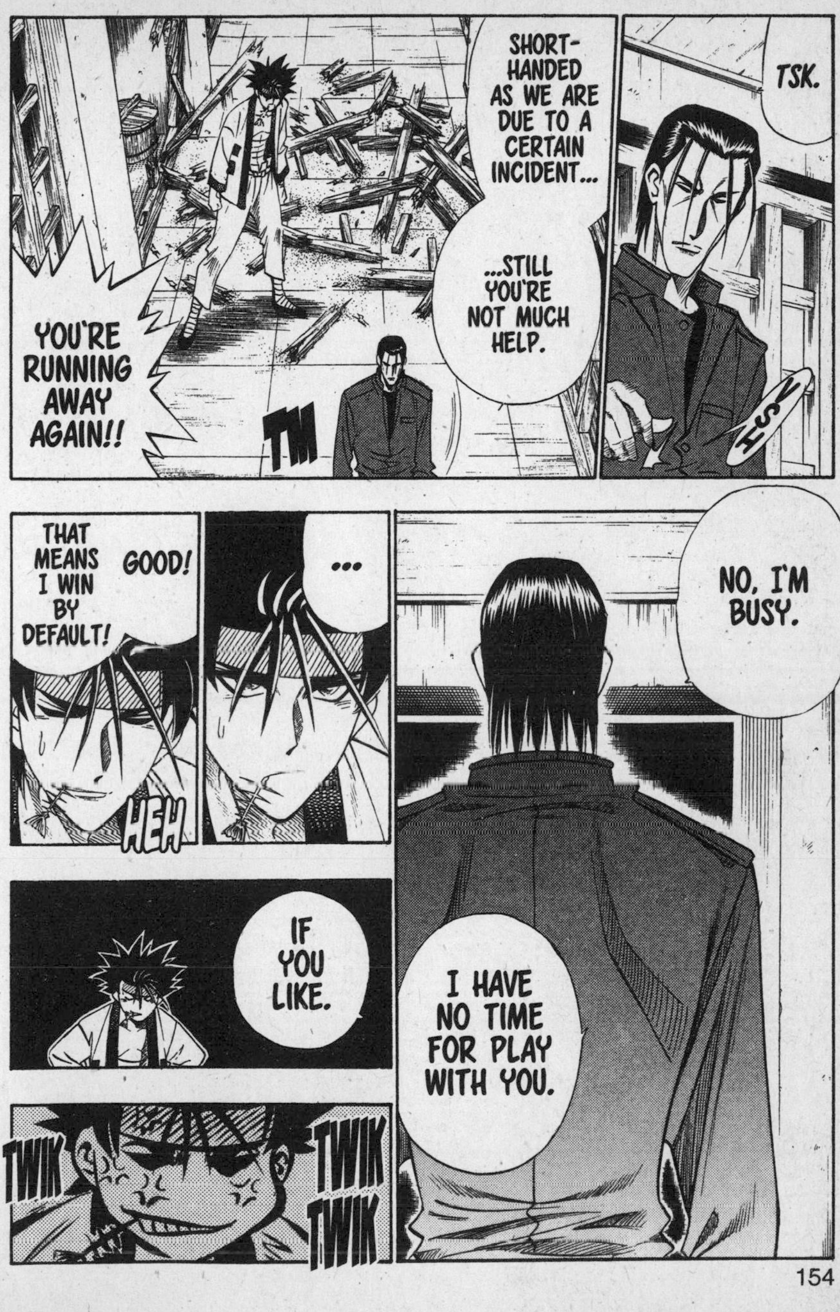
TSK.
VSH
SHORT-HANDED AS WE ARE DUE TO A CERTAIN INCIDENT...
...STILL YOU'RE NOT MUCH HELP.
TM
YOU'RE RUNNING AWAY AGAIN!!
NO, I'M BUSY.
I HAVE NO TIME FOR PLAY WITH YOU.
...
GOOD!
THAT MEANS I WIN BY DEFAULT!
HEH
IF YOU LIKE.
TWIK TWIK
TWIK

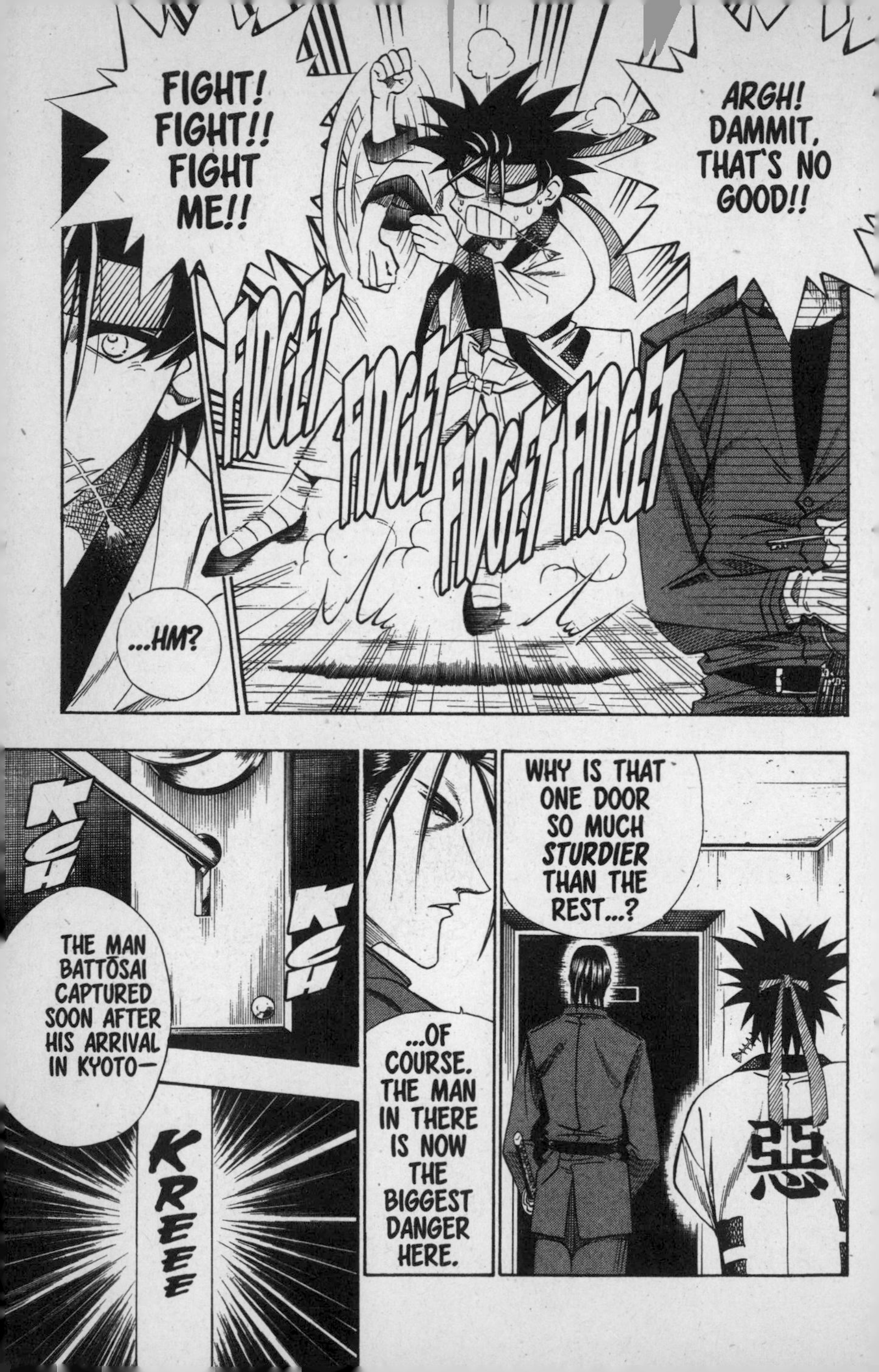
ARGH! DAMMIT, THAT'S NO GOOD!!
FIGHT! FIGHT!! FIGHT ME!!
FIDGET FIDGET FIDGET FIDGET
...HM?
WHY IS THAT ONE DOOR SO MUCH *STURDIER* THAN THE REST...?
...OF COURSE. THE MAN IN THERE IS NOW THE BIGGEST DANGER HERE.
KSH
KSH
THE MAN BATTŌSAI CAPTURED SOON AFTER HIS ARRIVAL IN KYOTO—
KREEE

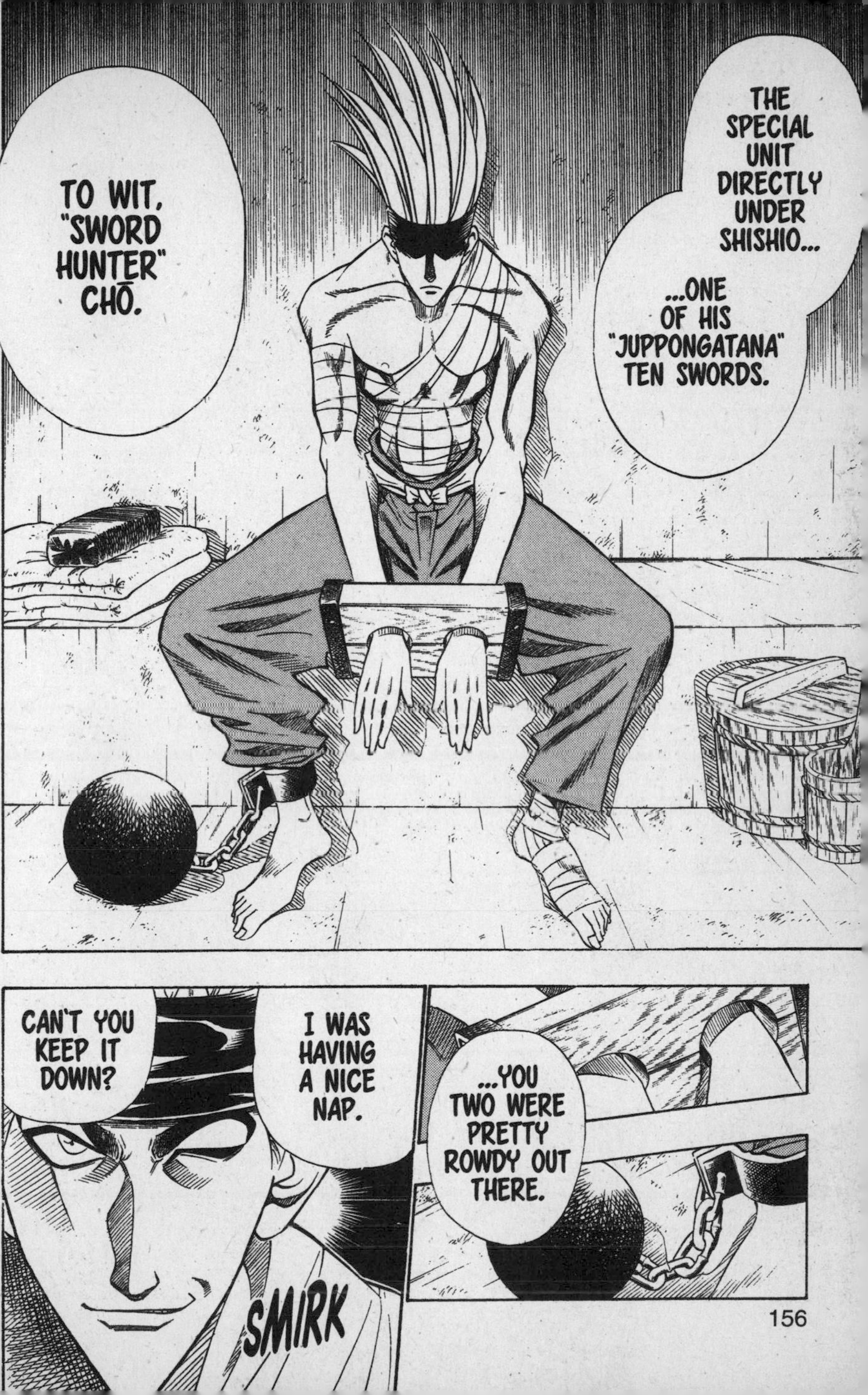
THE SPECIAL UNIT DIRECTLY UNDER SHISHIO...
...ONE OF HIS "JUPPONGATANA" TEN SWORDS.
TO WIT, "SWORD HUNTER" CHŌ.
...YOU TWO WERE PRETTY ROWDY OUT THERE.
I WAS HAVING A NICE NAP.
CAN'T YOU KEEP IT DOWN?
SMIRK

READ THIS WAY

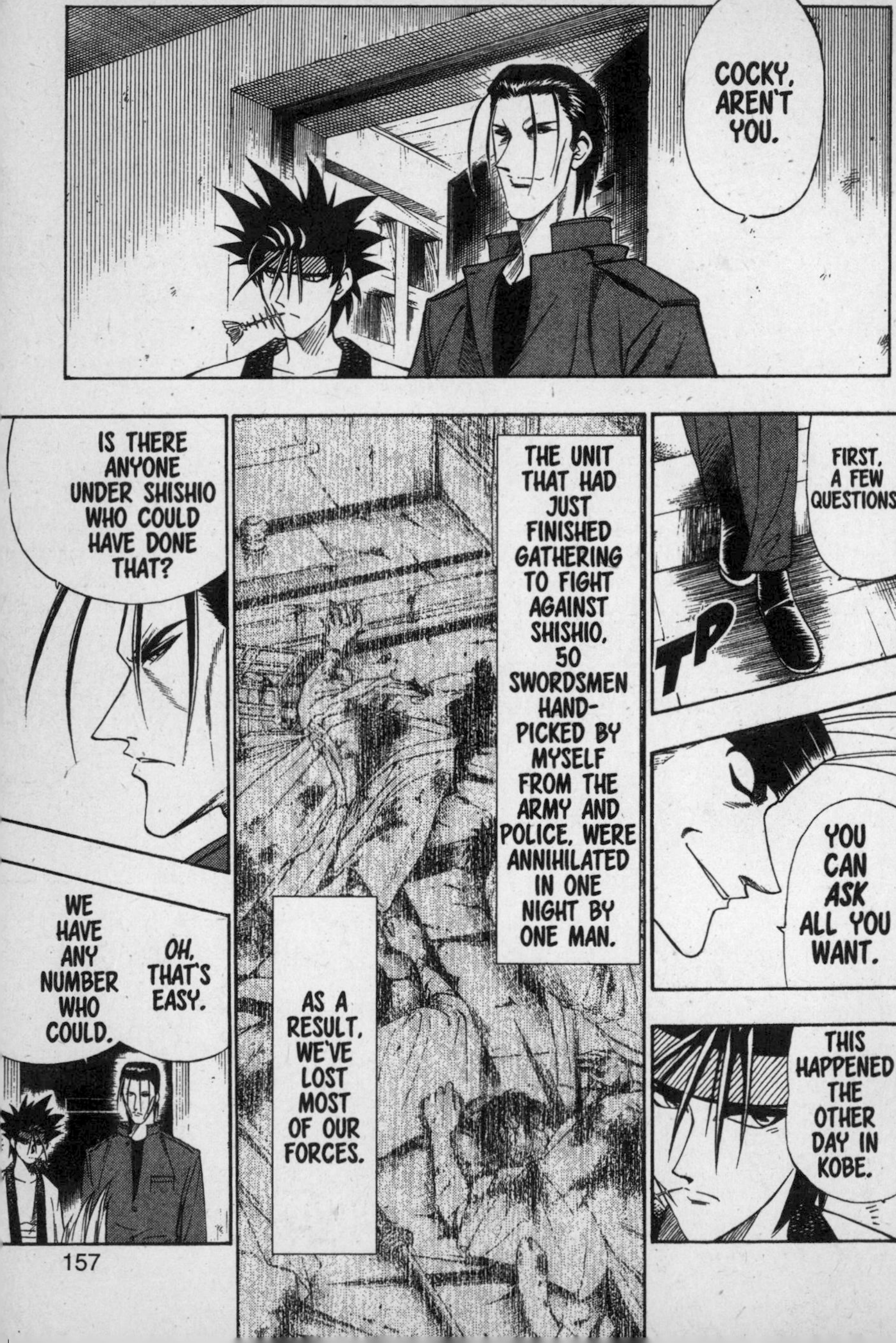
COCKY, AREN'T YOU.
FIRST, A FEW QUESTIONS.
TP
YOU CAN ASK ALL YOU WANT.
THIS HAPPENED THE OTHER DAY IN KOBE.
THE UNIT THAT HAD JUST FINISHED GATHERING TO FIGHT AGAINST SHISHIO, 50 SWORDSMEN HAND-PICKED BY MYSELF FROM THE ARMY AND POLICE, WERE ANNIHILATED IN ONE NIGHT BY ONE MAN.
AS A RESULT, WE'VE LOST MOST OF OUR FORCES.
IS THERE ANYONE UNDER SHISHIO WHO COULD HAVE DONE THAT?
OH, THAT'S EASY.
WE HAVE ANY NUMBER WHO COULD.

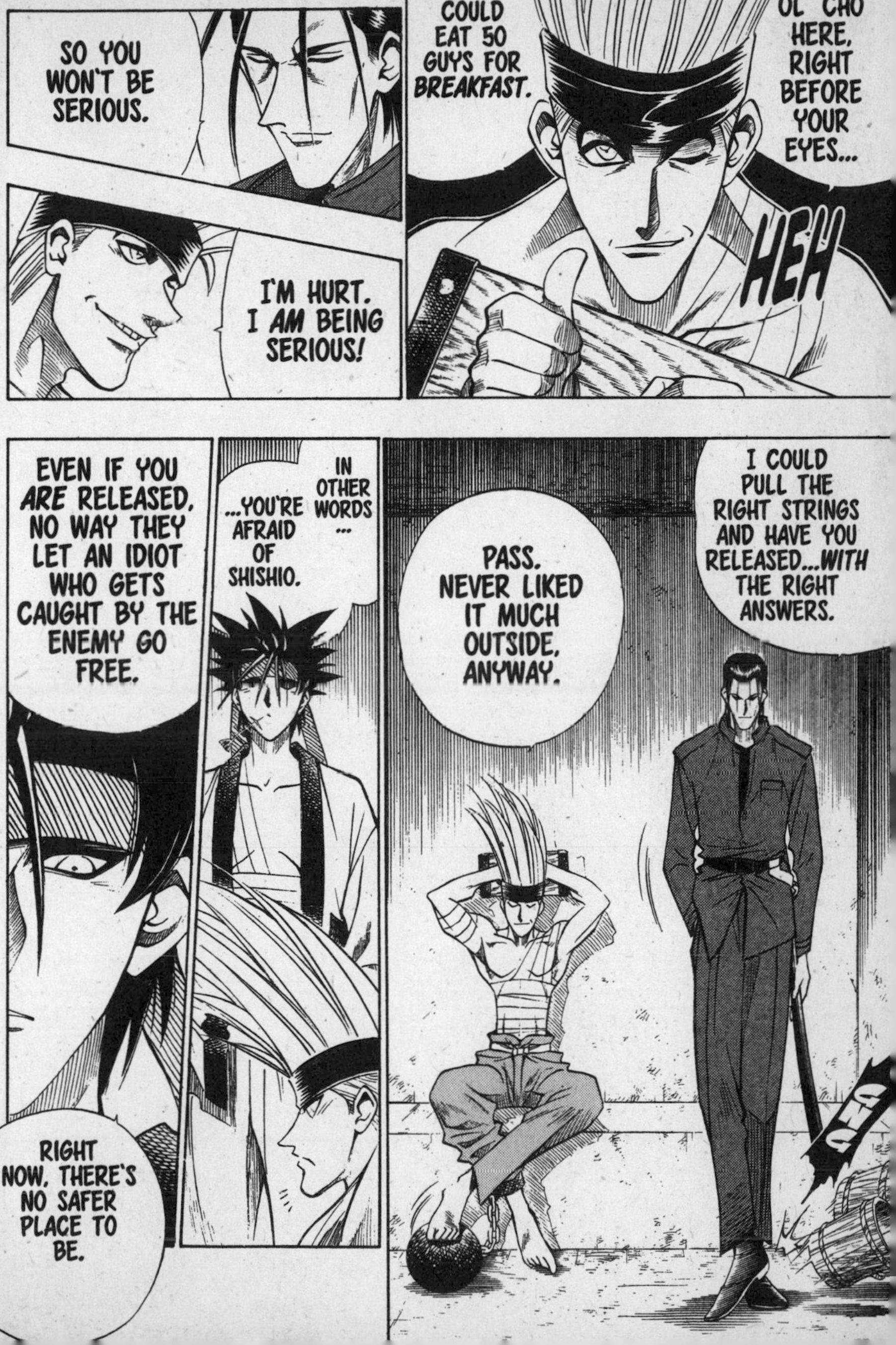
OL' CHŌ HERE, RIGHT BEFORE YOUR EYES...
...HE COULD EAT 50 GUYS FOR BREAKFAST.
HEH
SO YOU WON'T BE SERIOUS.
I'M HURT. I AM BEING SERIOUS!
I COULD PULL THE RIGHT STRINGS AND HAVE YOU RELEASED...WITH THE RIGHT ANSWERS.
PASS. NEVER LIKED IT MUCH OUTSIDE, ANYWAY.
IN OTHER WORDS...
...YOU'RE AFRAID OF SHISHIO.
EVEN IF YOU ARE RELEASED, NO WAY THEY LET AN IDIOT WHO GETS CAUGHT BY THE ENEMY GO FREE.
RIGHT NOW, THERE'S NO SAFER PLACE TO BE.

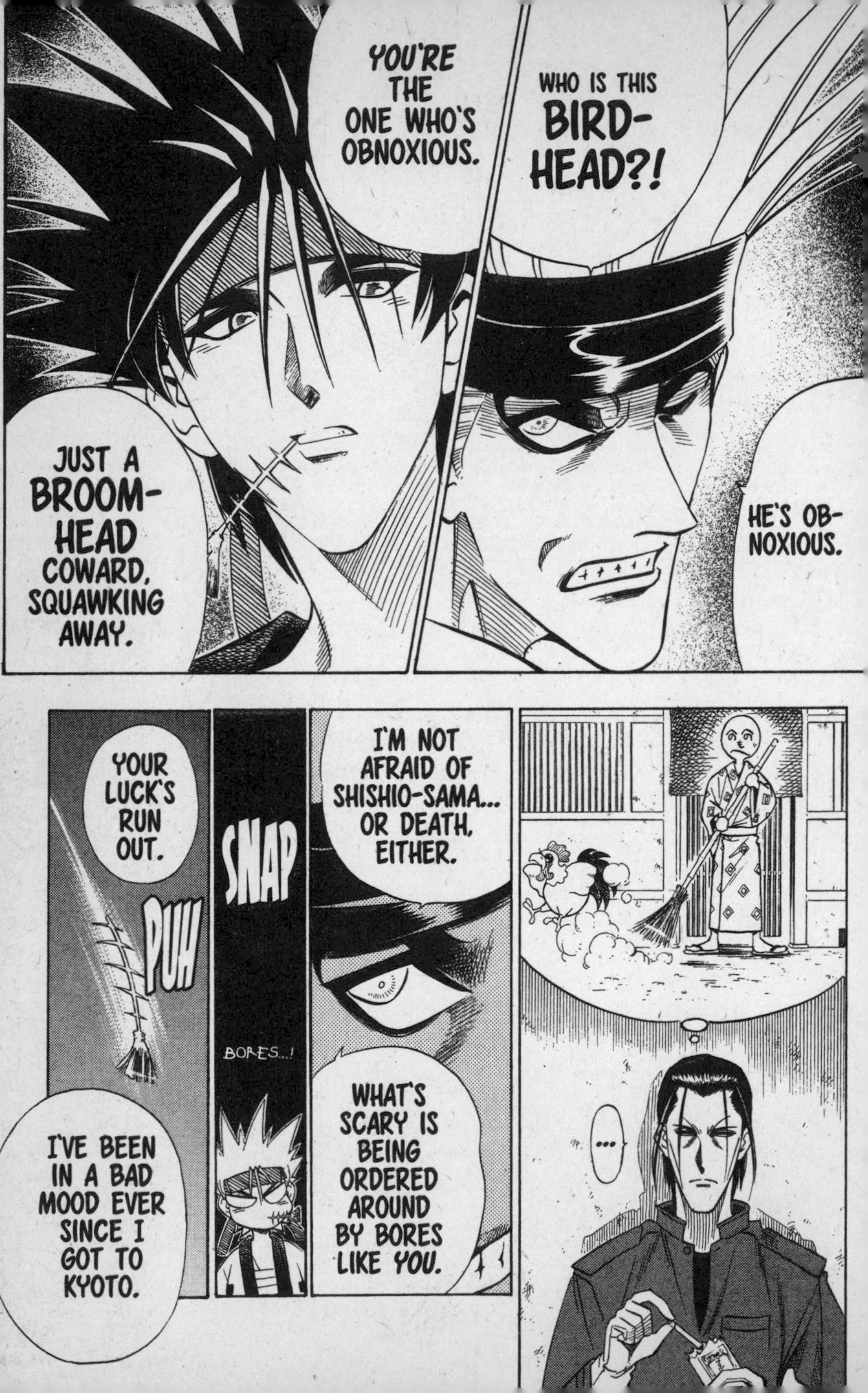
WHO IS THIS BIRD-HEAD?!
HE'S OBNOXIOUS.
YOU'RE THE ONE WHO'S OBNOXIOUS.
JUST A BROOM-HEAD COWARD, SQUAWKING AWAY.
...
I'M NOT AFRAID OF SHISHIO-SAMA... OR DEATH, EITHER.
WHAT'S SCARY IS BEING ORDERED AROUND BY BORES LIKE YOU.
SNAP
BORES...!
YOUR LUCK'S RUN OUT.
PUH
I'VE BEEN IN A BAD MOOD EVER SINCE I GOT TO KYOTO.

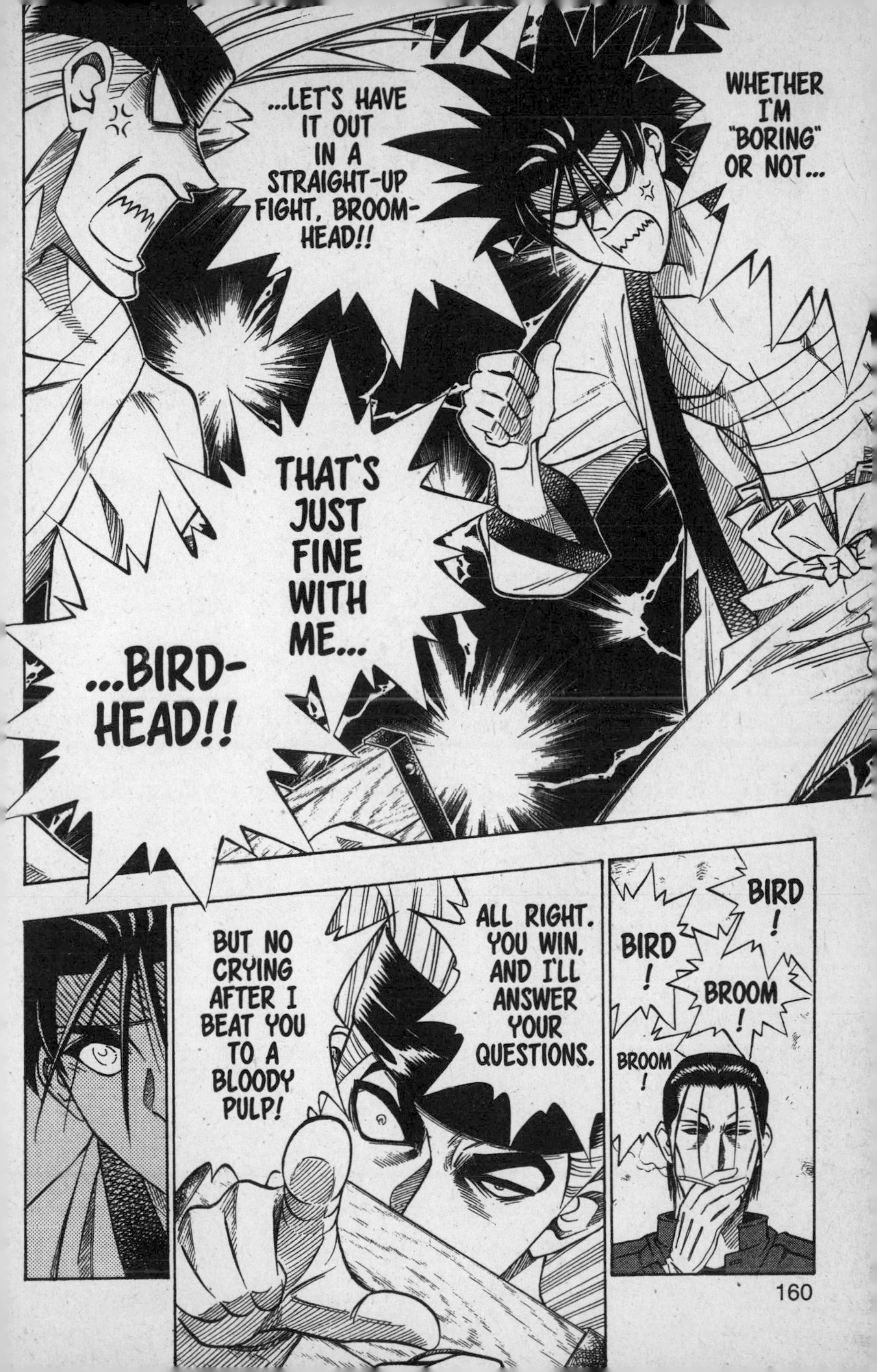
WHETHER I'M "BORING" OR NOT...
...LET'S HAVE IT OUT IN A STRAIGHT-UP FIGHT, BROOM-HEAD!!
THAT'S JUST FINE WITH ME...
...BIRD-HEAD!!
BIRD!
BROOM!
BIRD!
BROOM!
ALL RIGHT. YOU WIN, AND I'LL ANSWER YOUR QUESTIONS.
BUT NO CRYING AFTER I BEAT YOU TO A BLOODY PULP!

READ THIS WAY

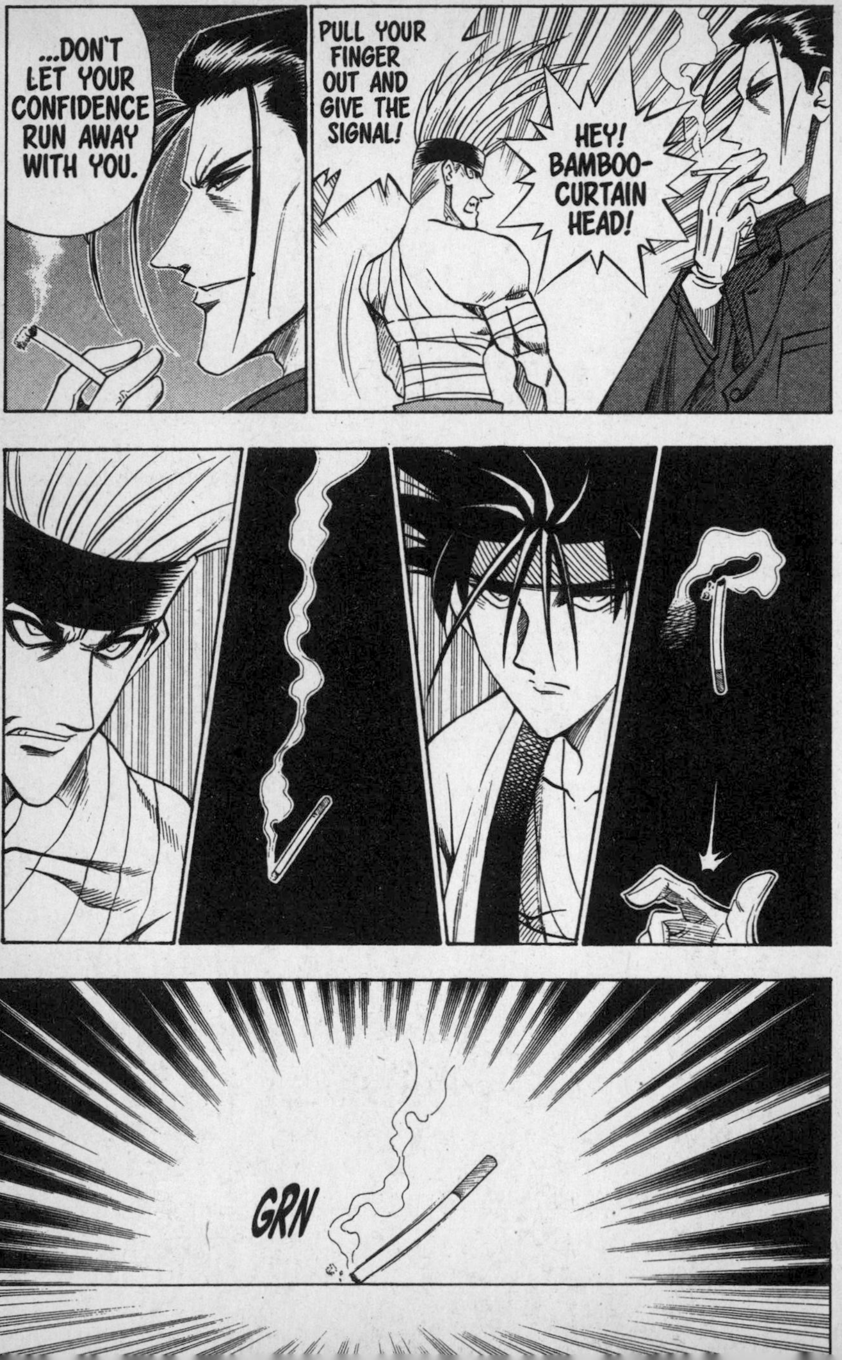
HEY! BAMBOO-CURTAIN HEAD!
PULL YOUR FINGER OUT AND GIVE THE SIGNAL!
...DON'T LET YOUR CONFIDENCE RUN AWAY WITH YOU.
GRN

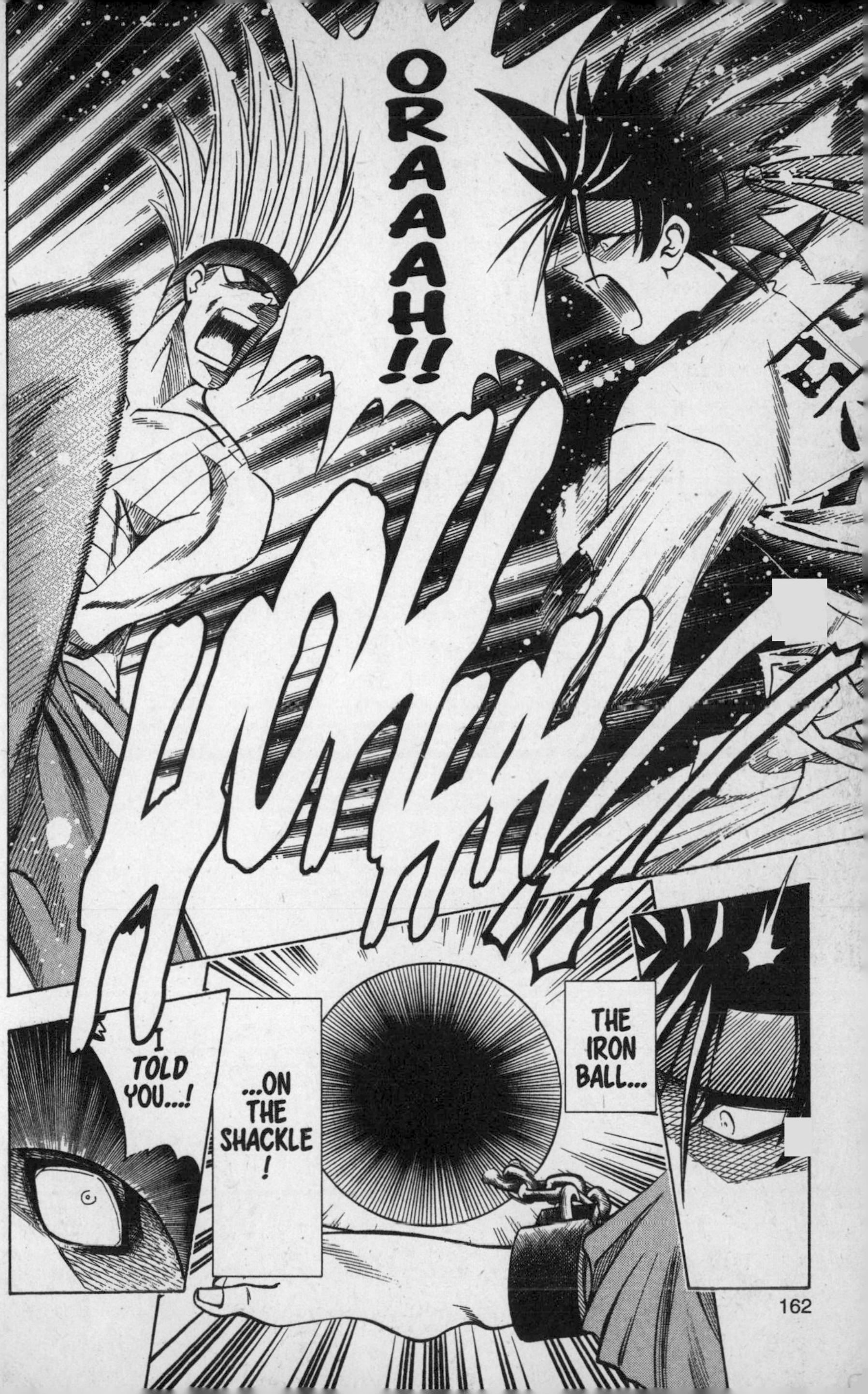
ORAAAAH!!
THE IRON BALL...
...ON THE SHACKLE!
I TOLD YOU...!

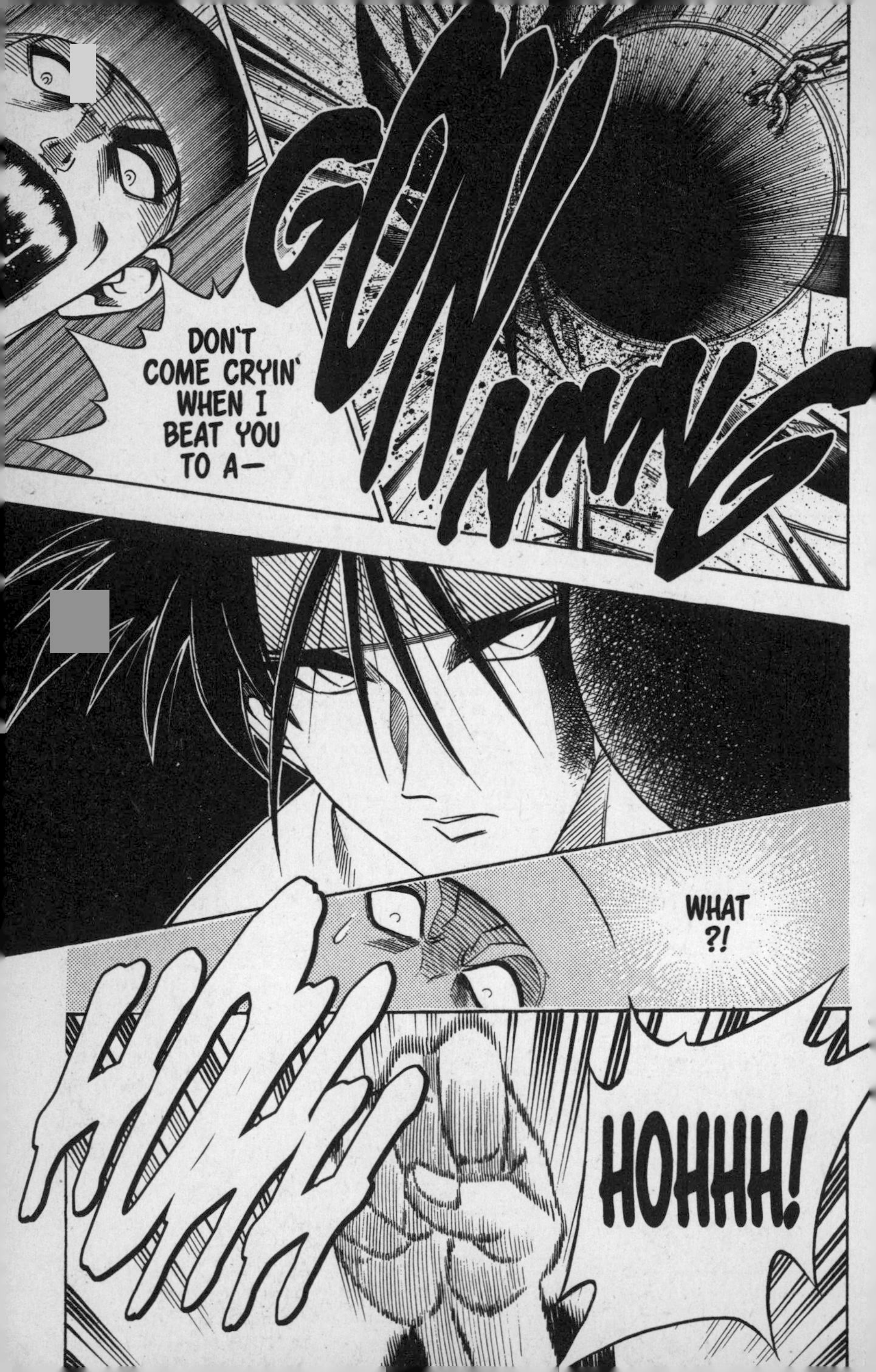
DON'T COME CRYIN' WHEN I BEAT YOU TO A—
WHAT ?!
HOHHH!

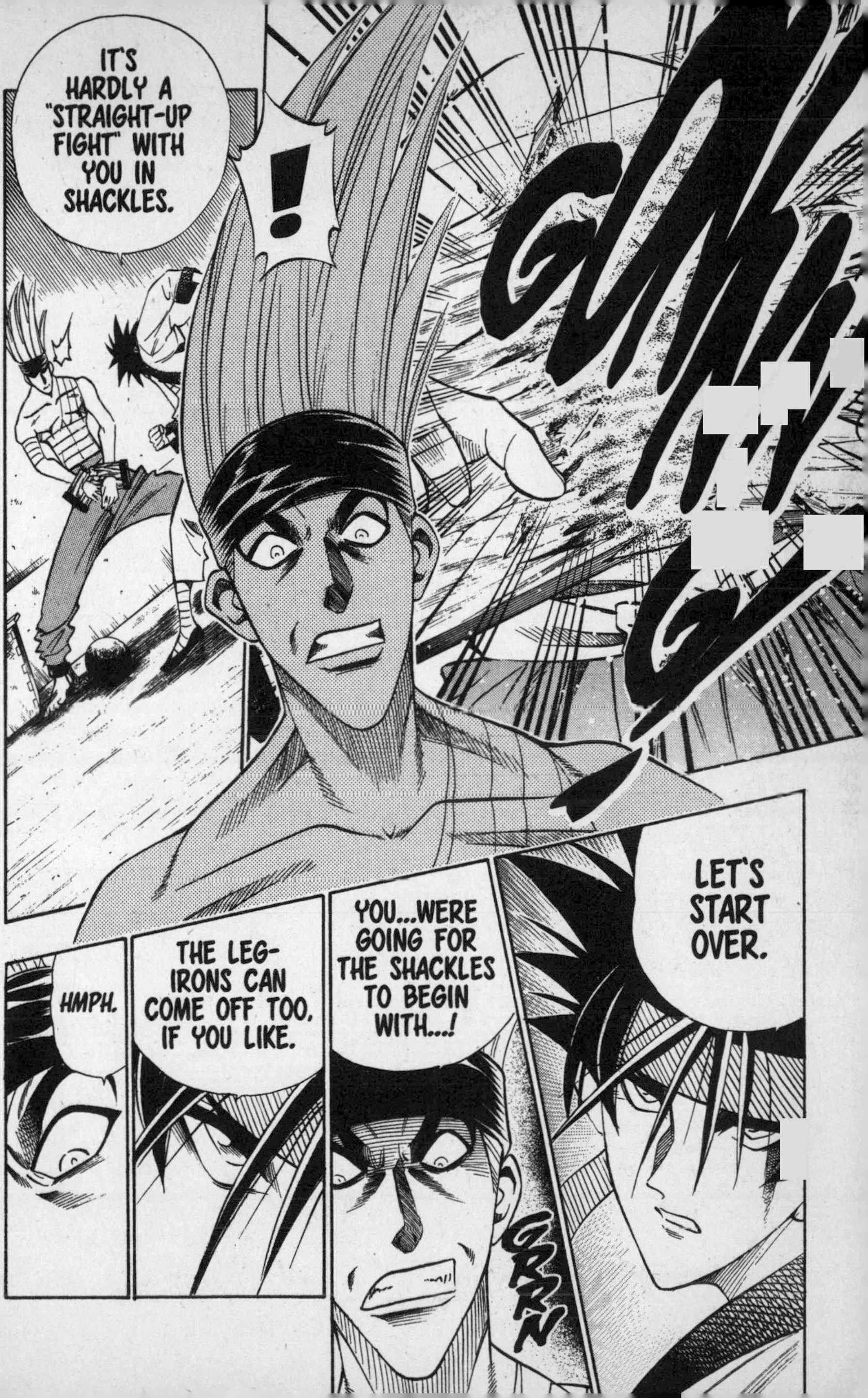
IT'S HARDLY A "STRAIGHT-UP FIGHT" WITH YOU IN SHACKLES.
!
LET'S START OVER.
YOU...WERE GOING FOR THE SHACKLES TO BEGIN WITH...!
THE LEG-IRONS CAN COME OFF TOO, IF YOU LIKE.
HMPH.

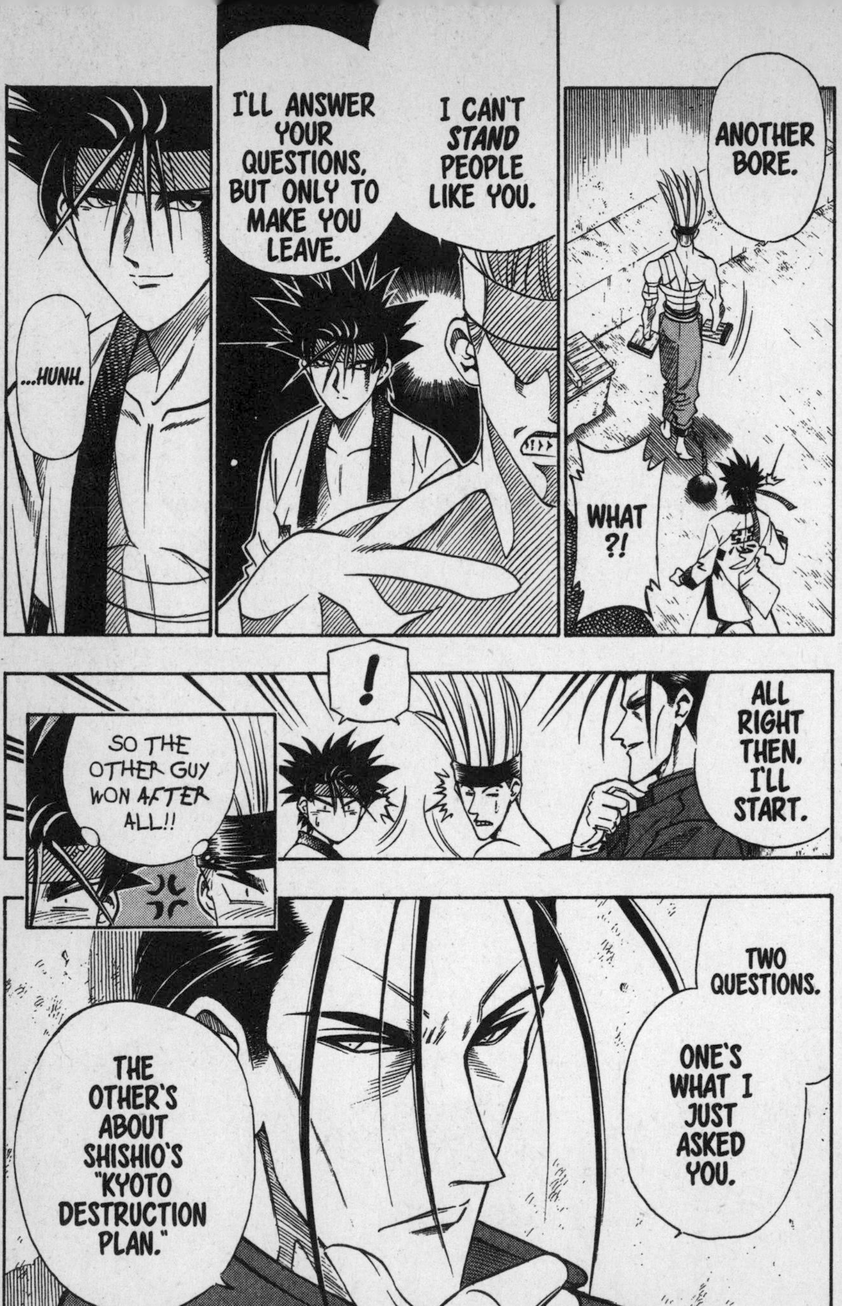
ANOTHER BORE.
WHAT?!
I CAN'T STAND PEOPLE LIKE YOU.
I'LL ANSWER YOUR QUESTIONS, BUT ONLY TO MAKE YOU LEAVE.
...HUNH.
ALL RIGHT THEN, I'LL START.
!
SO THE OTHER GUY WON AFTER ALL!!
TWO QUESTIONS.
ONE'S WHAT I JUST ASKED YOU.
THE OTHER'S ABOUT SHISHIO'S "KYOTO DESTRUCTION PLAN."

Rurouni Kenshin

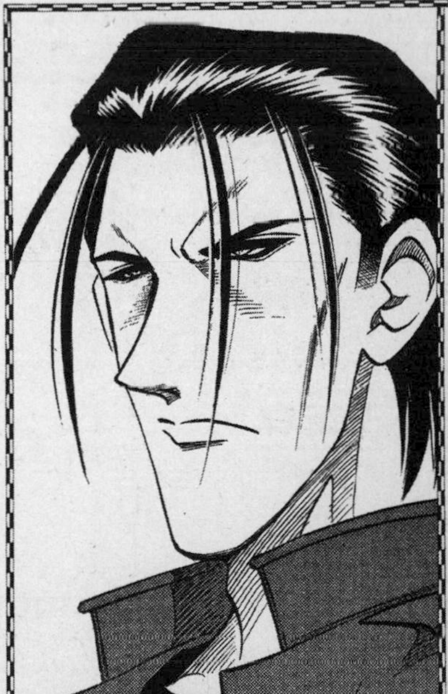

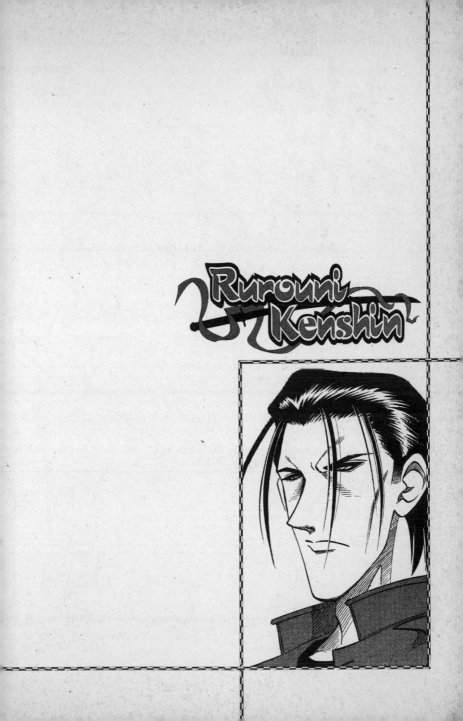

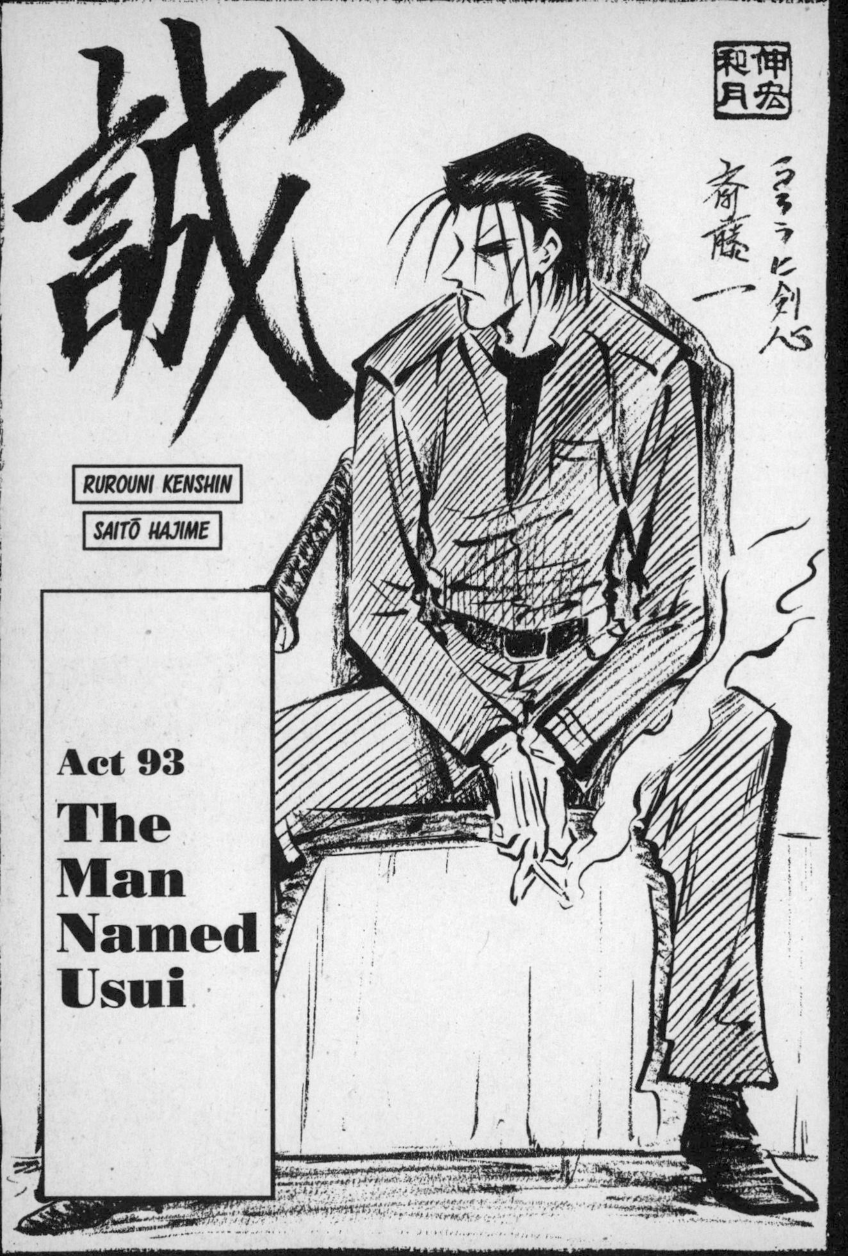
誠
るろうに剣心
斎藤一
RUROUNI KENSHIN
SAITŌ HAJIME

Act 93

The Man Named Usui

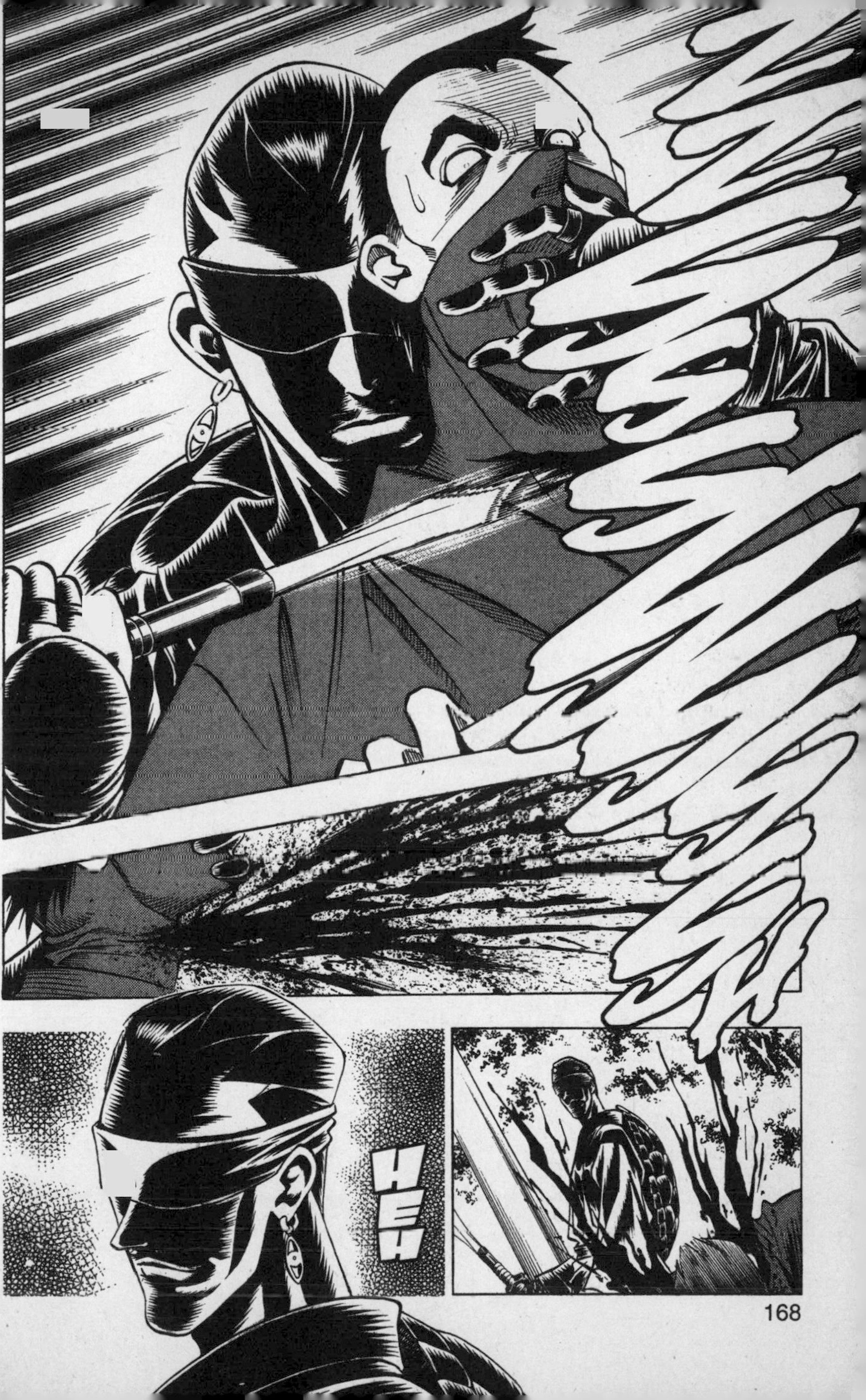
HEH

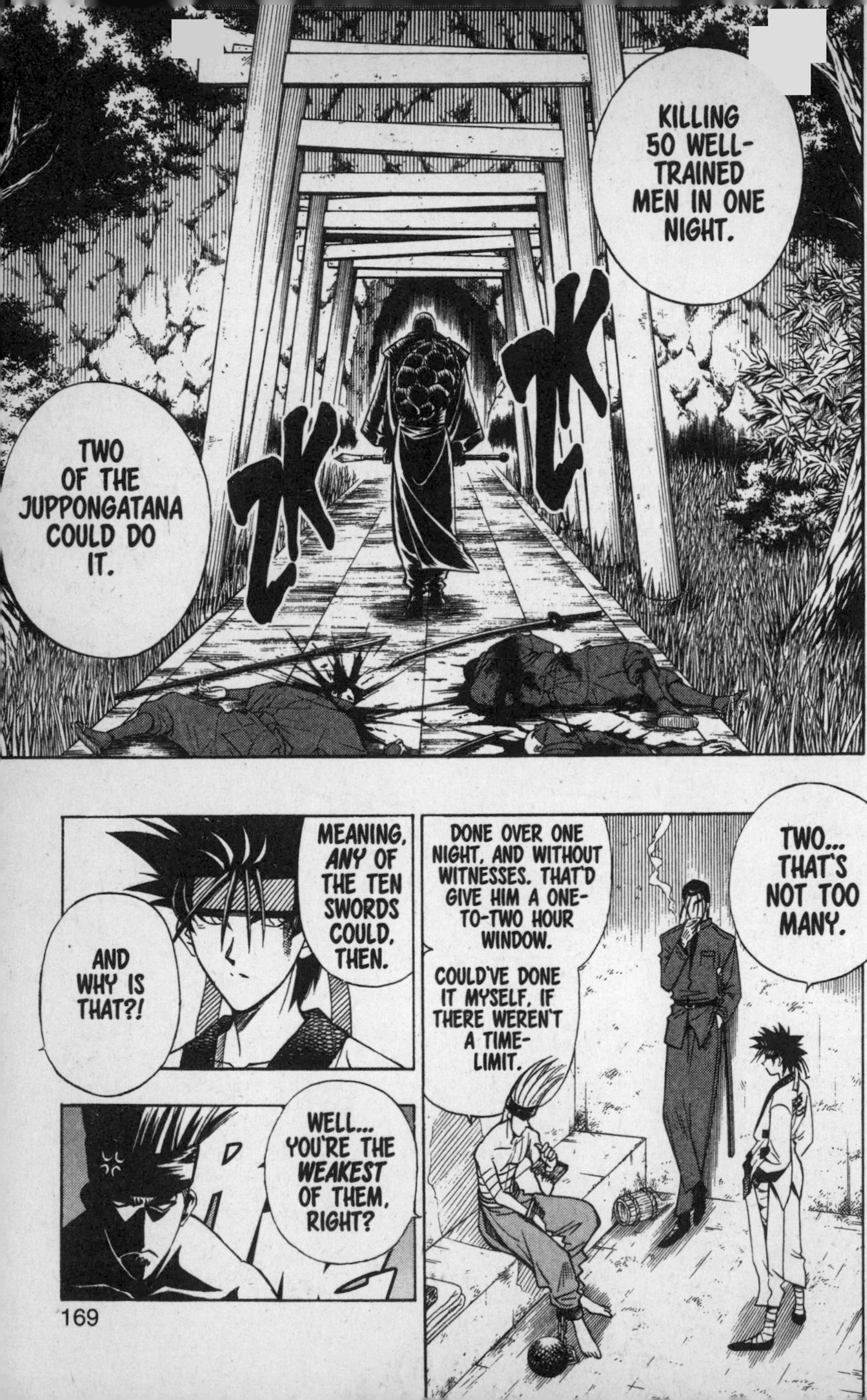
KILLING 50 WELL-TRAINED MEN IN ONE NIGHT.
TWO OF THE JUPPONGATANA COULD DO IT.
TWO... THAT'S NOT TOO MANY.
DONE OVER ONE NIGHT, AND WITHOUT WITNESSES. THAT'D GIVE HIM A ONE-TO-TWO HOUR WINDOW.
COULD'VE DONE IT MYSELF, IF THERE WEREN'T A TIME-LIMIT.
MEANING, ANY OF THE TEN SWORDS COULD, THEN.
AND WHY IS THAT?!
WELL... YOU'RE THE WEAKEST OF THEM, RIGHT?

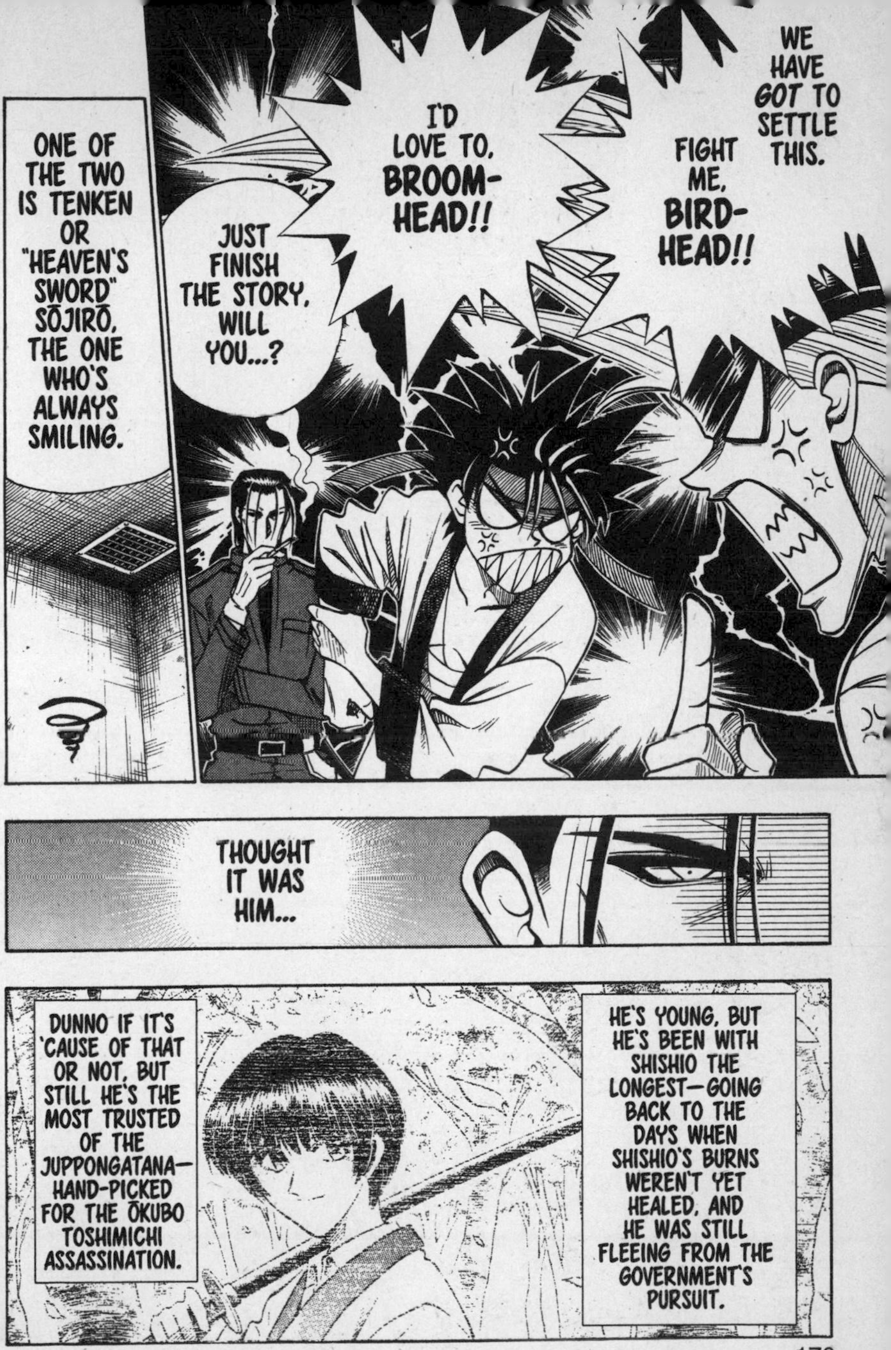
WE HAVE GOT TO SETTLE THIS.
FIGHT ME, BIRD-HEAD!!
I'D LOVE TO, BROOM-HEAD!!
JUST FINISH THE STORY, WILL YOU...?
ONE OF THE TWO IS TENKEN OR "HEAVEN'S SWORD" SŌJIRŌ, THE ONE WHO'S ALWAYS SMILING.
THOUGHT IT WAS HIM...
HE'S YOUNG, BUT HE'S BEEN WITH SHISHIO THE LONGEST—GOING BACK TO THE DAYS WHEN SHISHIO'S BURNS WEREN'T YET HEALED, AND HE WAS STILL FLEEING FROM THE GOVERNMENT'S PURSUIT.
DUNNO IF IT'S 'CAUSE OF THAT OR NOT, BUT STILL HE'S THE MOST TRUSTED OF THE JUPPONGATANA—HAND-PICKED FOR THE ŌKUBO TOSHIMICHI ASSASSINATION.

READ THIS WAY

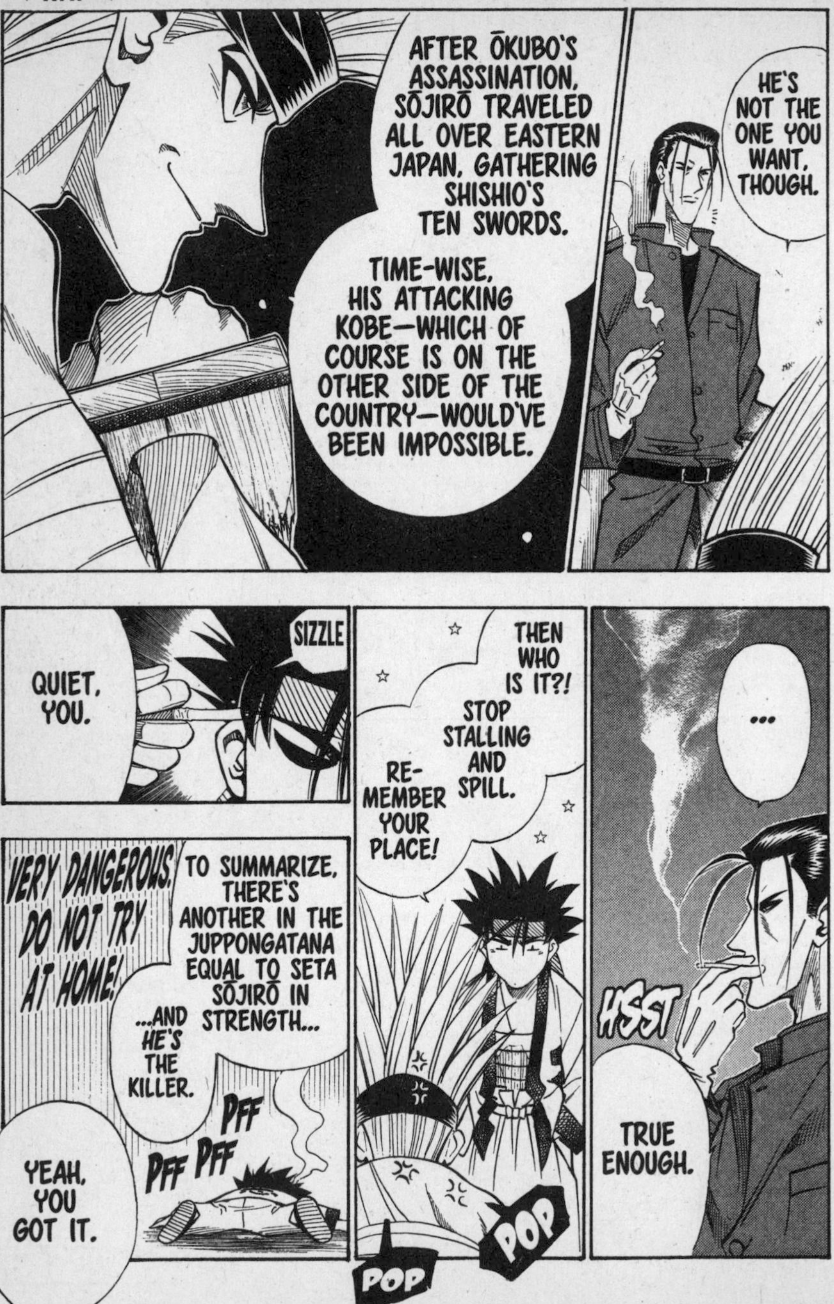
HE'S NOT THE ONE YOU WANT, THOUGH.
AFTER ŌKUBO'S ASSASSINATION, SŌJIRŌ TRAVELED ALL OVER EASTERN JAPAN, GATHERING SHISHIO'S TEN SWORDS.
TIME-WISE, HIS ATTACKING KOBE—WHICH OF COURSE IS ON THE OTHER SIDE OF THE COUNTRY—WOULD'VE BEEN IMPOSSIBLE.
...
HSST
TRUE ENOUGH.
THEN WHO IS IT?!
STOP STALLING AND SPILL.
RE-MEMBER YOUR PLACE!
POP
POP
SIZZLE
QUIET, YOU.
TO SUMMARIZE, THERE'S ANOTHER IN THE JUPPONGATANA EQUAL TO SETA SŌJIRŌ IN STRENGTH...
VERY DANGEROUS. DO NOT TRY AT HOME!
...AND HE'S THE KILLER.
PFF
PFF PFF
YEAH, YOU GOT IT.

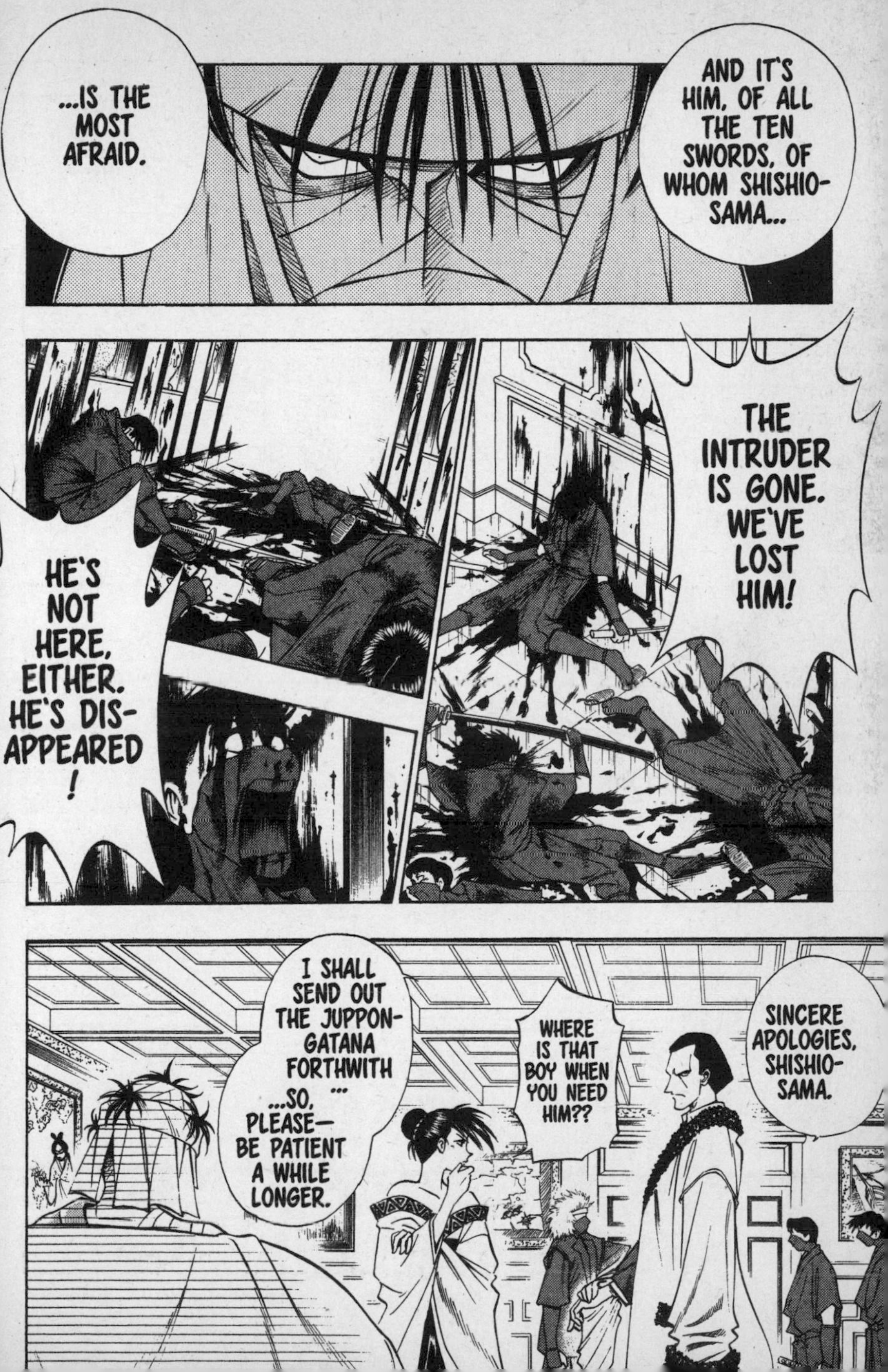
AND IT'S HIM, OF ALL THE TEN SWORDS, OF WHOM SHISHIO-SAMA...
...IS THE MOST AFRAID.
THE INTRUDER IS GONE. WE'VE LOST HIM!
HE'S NOT HERE, EITHER. HE'S DIS-APPEARED!
SINCERE APOLOGIES, SHISHIO-SAMA.
WHERE IS THAT BOY WHEN YOU NEED HIM??
I SHALL SEND OUT THE JUPPON-GATANA FORTHWITH ...
...SO, PLEASE— BE PATIENT A WHILE LONGER.

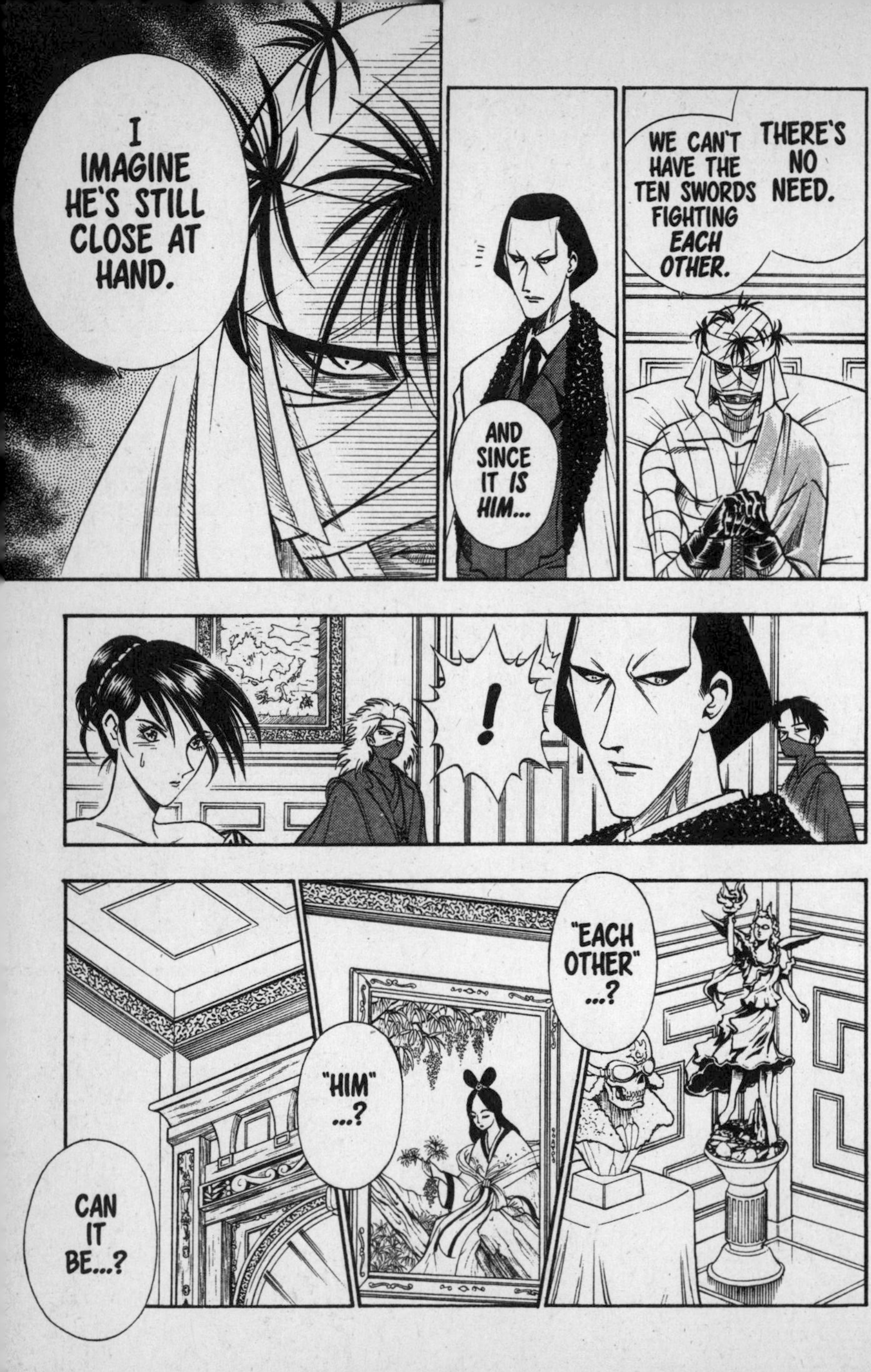
THERE'S NO NEED.
WE CAN'T HAVE THE TEN SWORDS FIGHTING EACH OTHER.
AND SINCE IT IS HIM...
I IMAGINE HE'S STILL CLOSE AT HAND.
!
"EACH OTHER" ...?
"HIM" ...?
CAN IT BE...?

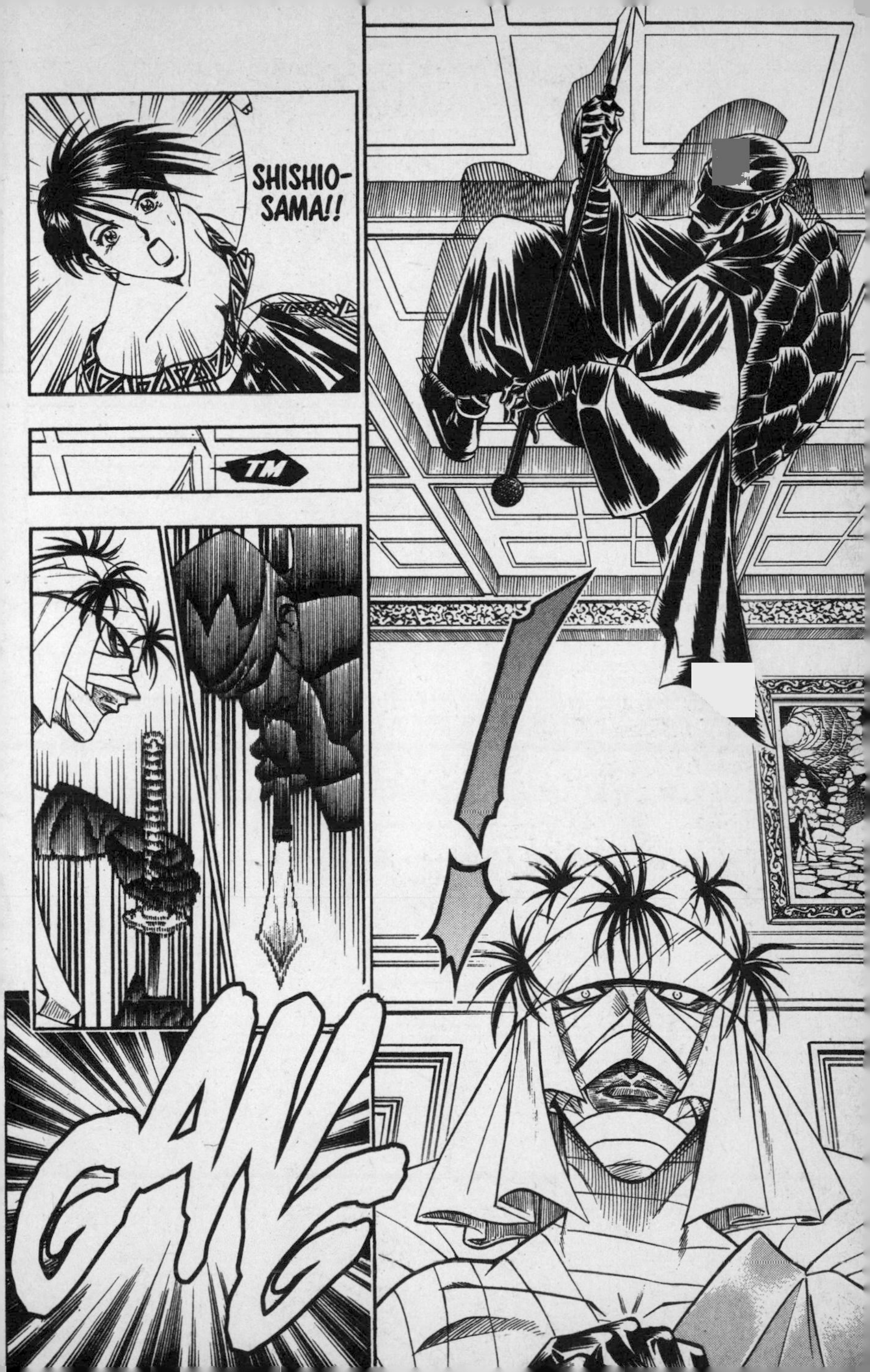
SHISHIO-SAMA!!
TM
GAN

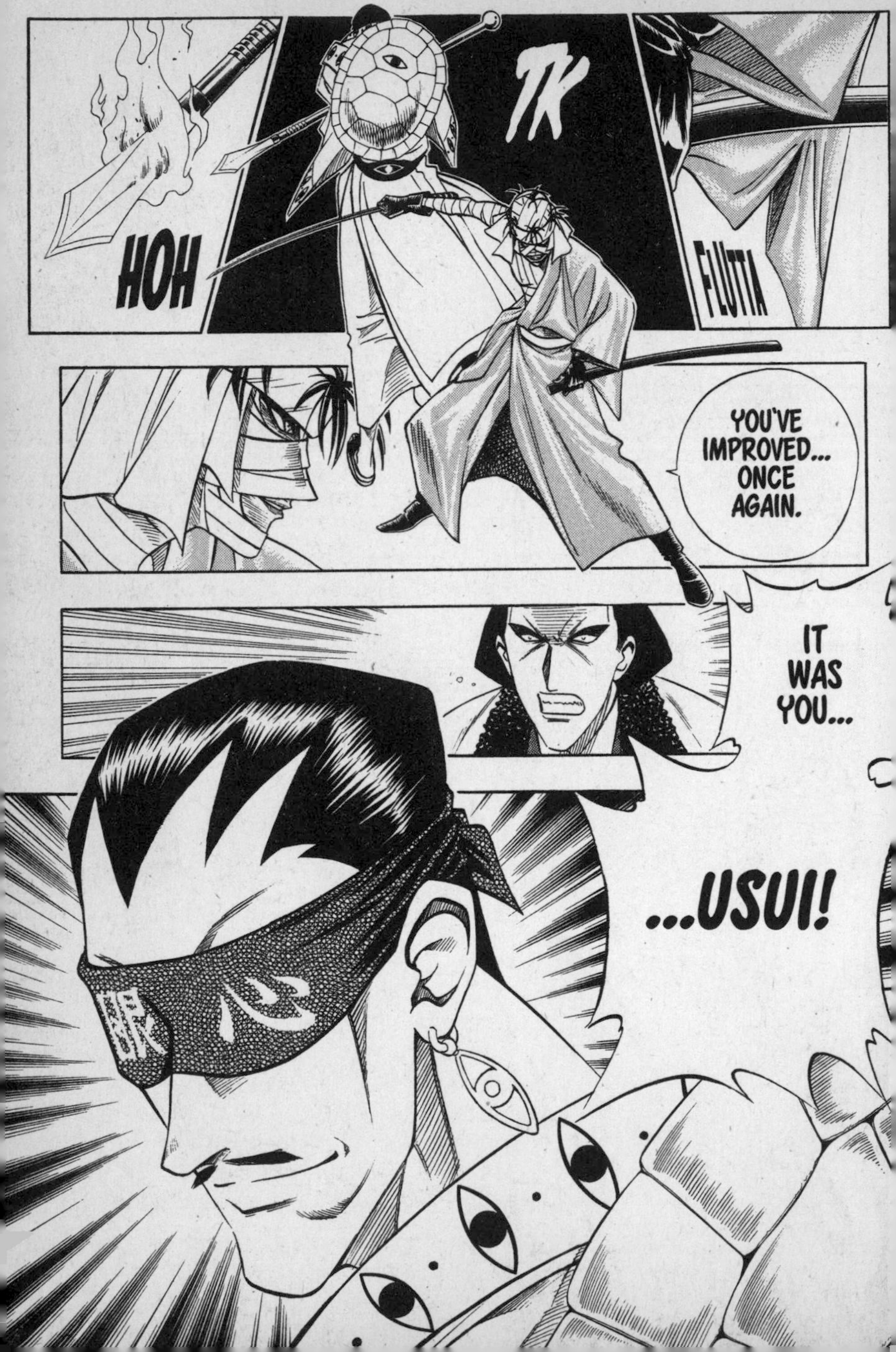
FLUTTA
TK
HOH
YOU'VE IMPROVED... ONCE AGAIN.
IT WAS YOU...
...USUI!

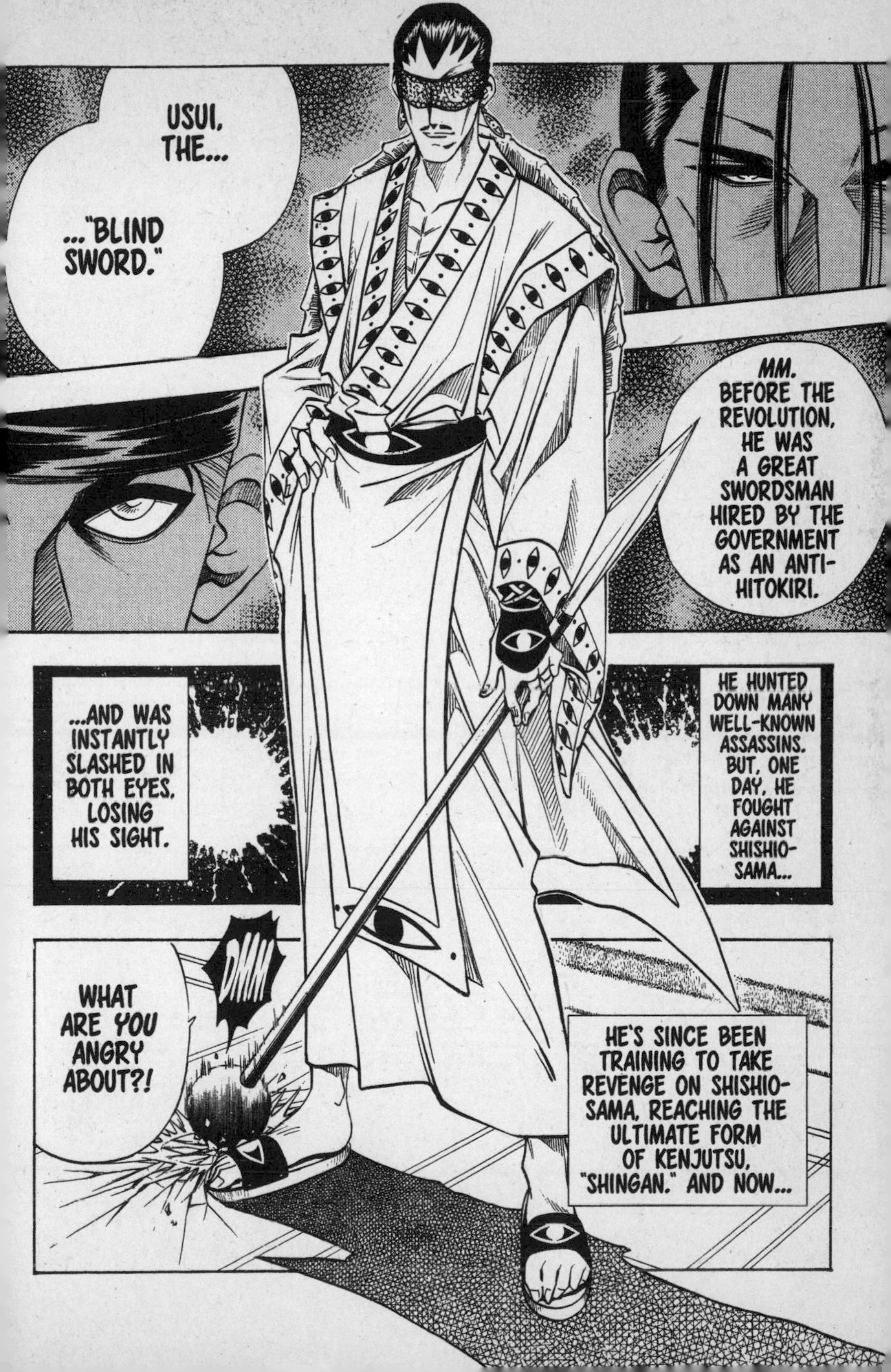
USUI, THE...
..."BLIND SWORD."
MM. BEFORE THE REVOLUTION, HE WAS A GREAT SWORDSMAN HIRED BY THE GOVERNMENT AS AN ANTI-HITOKIRI.
HE HUNTED DOWN MANY WELL-KNOWN ASSASSINS. BUT, ONE DAY, HE FOUGHT AGAINST SHISHIO-SAMA...
...AND WAS INSTANTLY SLASHED IN BOTH EYES, LOSING HIS SIGHT.
HE'S SINCE BEEN TRAINING TO TAKE REVENGE ON SHISHIO-SAMA, REACHING THE ULTIMATE FORM OF KENJUTSU, "SHINGAN." AND NOW...
DMM
WHAT ARE YOU ANGRY ABOUT?!

READ THIS WAY

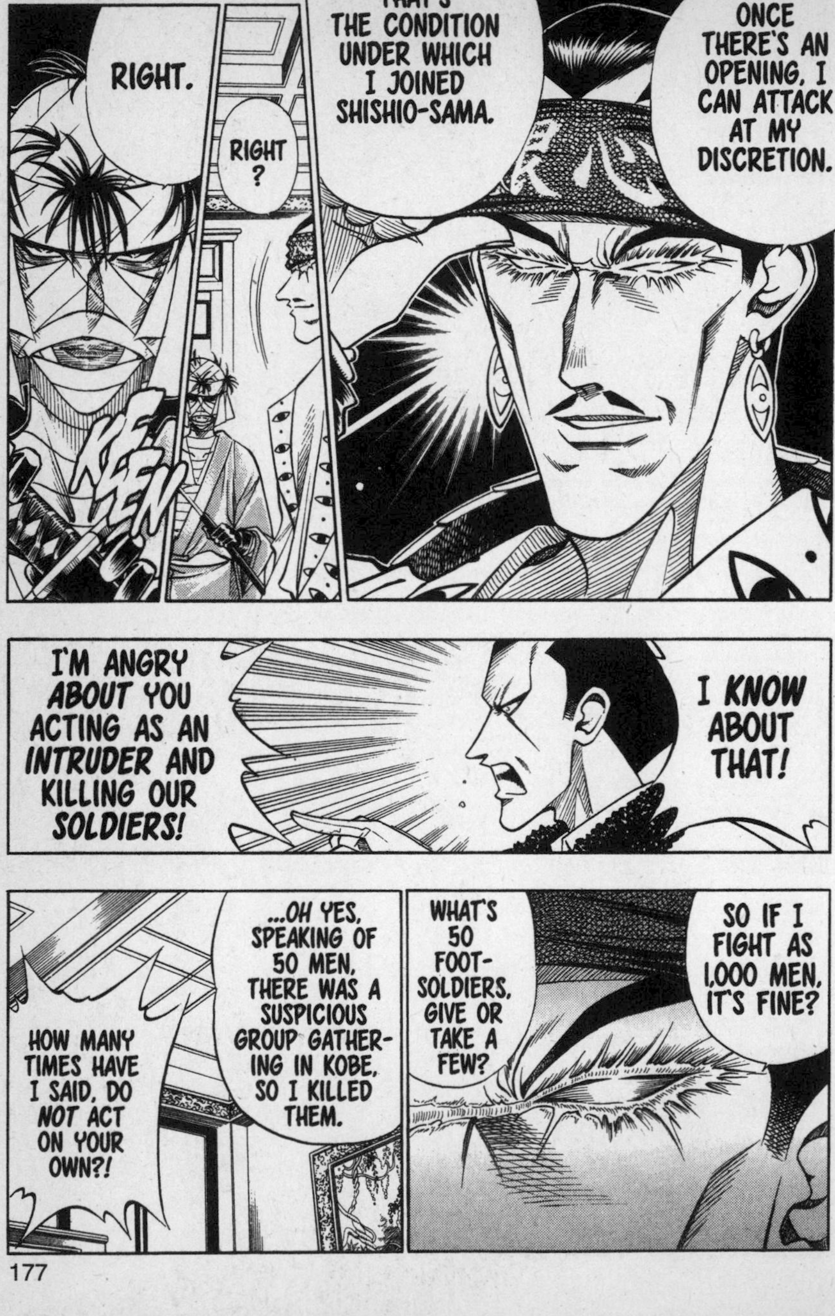
ONCE THERE'S AN OPENING, I CAN ATTACK AT MY DISCRETION.
THAT'S THE CONDITION UNDER WHICH I JOINED SHISHIO-SAMA.
RIGHT?
RIGHT.
KEN
I KNOW ABOUT THAT!
I'M ANGRY ABOUT YOU ACTING AS AN INTRUDER AND KILLING OUR SOLDIERS!
SO IF I FIGHT AS 1,000 MEN, IT'S FINE?
WHAT'S 50 FOOT-SOLDIERS, GIVE OR TAKE A FEW?
...OH YES, SPEAKING OF 50 MEN, THERE WAS A SUSPICIOUS GROUP GATHERING IN KOBE, SO I KILLED THEM.
HOW MANY TIMES HAVE I SAID, DO NOT ACT ON YOUR OWN?!

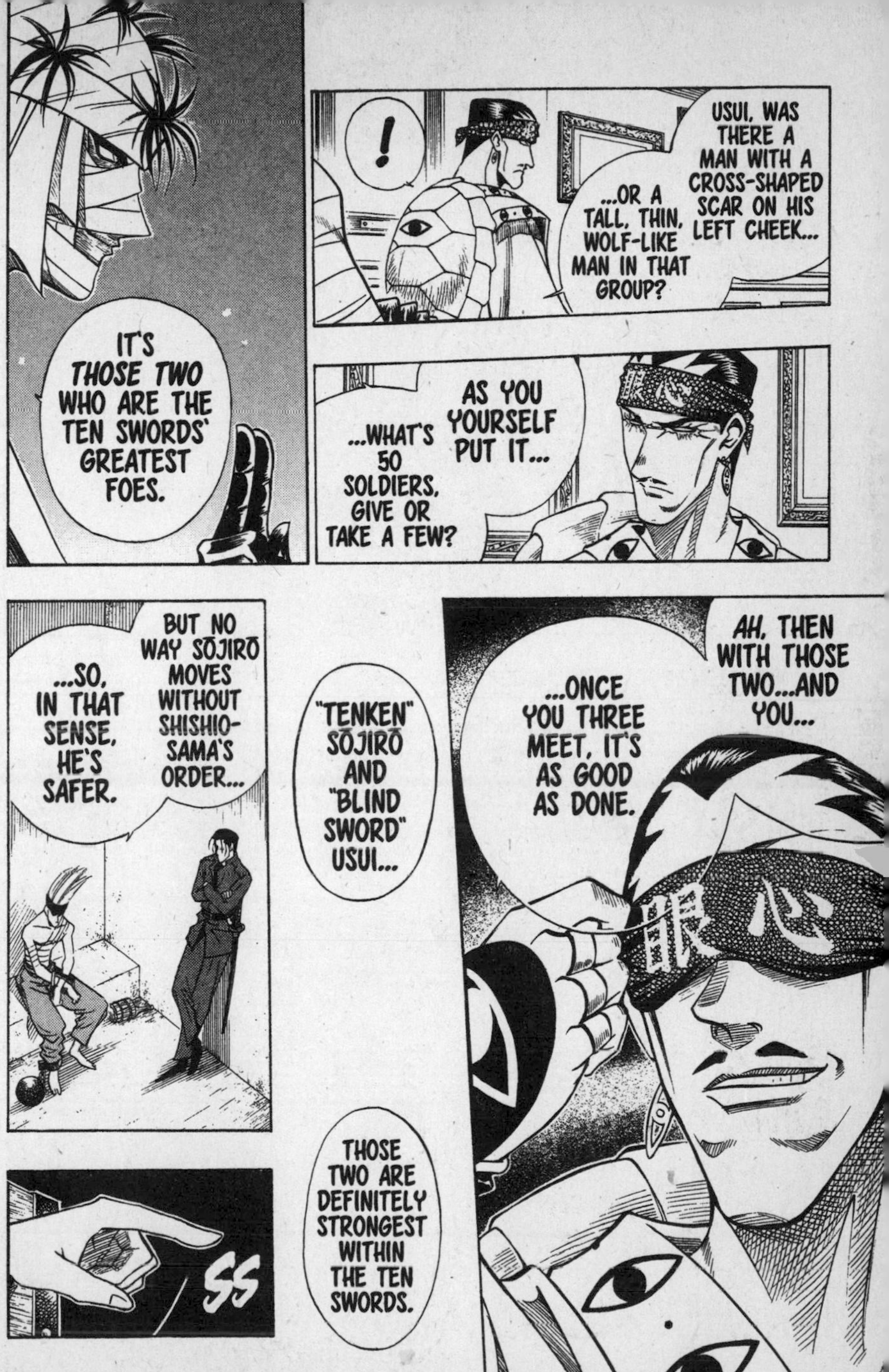
USUI, WAS THERE A MAN WITH A CROSS-SHAPED SCAR ON HIS LEFT CHEEK...
...OR A TALL, THIN, WOLF-LIKE MAN IN THAT GROUP?
!
AS YOU YOURSELF PUT IT...
...WHAT'S 50 SOLDIERS, GIVE OR TAKE A FEW?
IT'S *THOSE TWO* WHO ARE THE TEN SWORDS' GREATEST FOES.
AH, THEN WITH THOSE TWO...AND YOU...
...ONCE YOU THREE MEET, IT'S AS GOOD AS DONE.
"TENKEN" SŌJIRŌ AND "BLIND SWORD" USUI...
THOSE TWO ARE DEFINITELY STRONGEST WITHIN THE TEN SWORDS.
BUT NO WAY SŌJIRŌ MOVES WITHOUT SHISHIO-SAMA'S ORDER...
...SO, IN THAT SENSE, HE'S SAFER.
SS

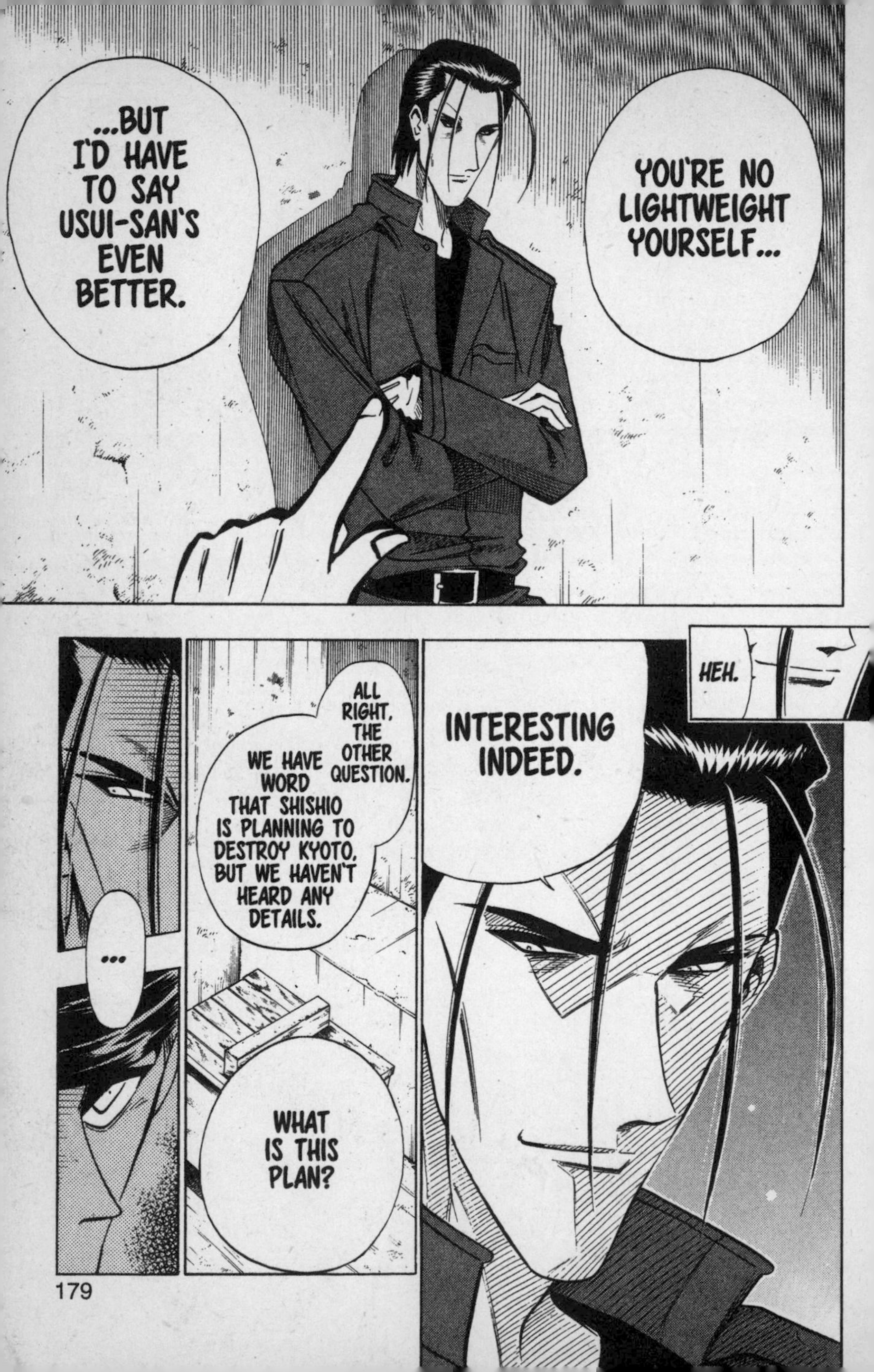
YOU'RE NO LIGHTWEIGHT YOURSELF...
...BUT I'D HAVE TO SAY USUI-SAN'S EVEN BETTER.
HEH.
INTERESTING INDEED.
ALL RIGHT, THE OTHER QUESTION.
WE HAVE WORD THAT SHISHIO IS PLANNING TO DESTROY KYOTO, BUT WE HAVEN'T HEARD ANY DETAILS.
WHAT IS THIS PLAN?
...

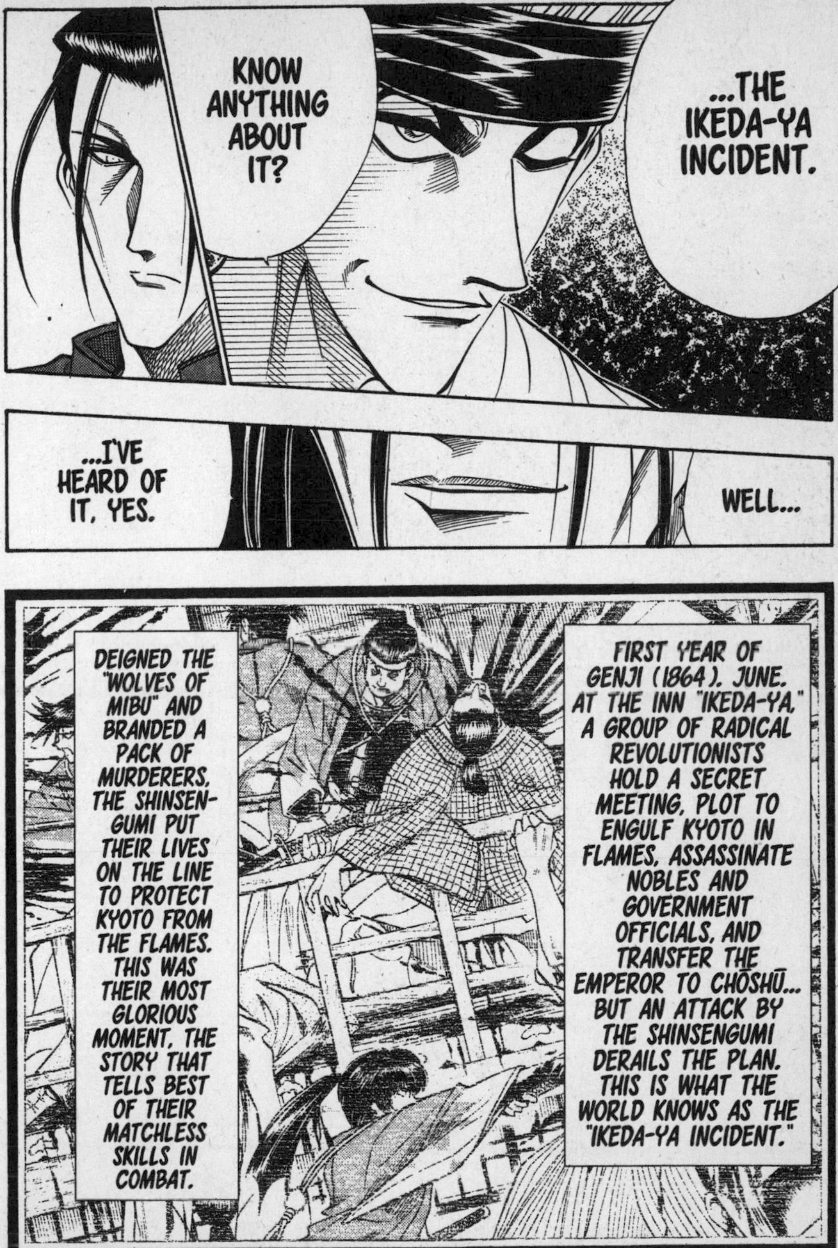
...THE IKEDA-YA INCIDENT.
KNOW ANYTHING ABOUT IT?
WELL...
...I'VE HEARD OF IT, YES.
FIRST YEAR OF GENJI (1864), JUNE. AT THE INN "IKEDA-YA," A GROUP OF RADICAL REVOLUTIONISTS HOLD A SECRET MEETING, PLOT TO ENGULF KYOTO IN FLAMES, ASSASSINATE NOBLES AND GOVERNMENT OFFICIALS, AND TRANSFER THE EMPEROR TO CHŌSHŪ... BUT AN ATTACK BY THE SHINSENGUMI DERAILS THE PLAN. THIS IS WHAT THE WORLD KNOWS AS THE "IKEDA-YA INCIDENT."
DEIGNED THE "WOLVES OF MIBU" AND BRANDED A PACK OF MURDERERS, THE SHINSEN-GUMI PUT THEIR LIVES ON THE LINE TO PROTECT KYOTO FROM THE FLAMES. THIS WAS THEIR MOST GLORIOUS MOMENT, THE STORY THAT TELLS BEST OF THEIR MATCHLESS SKILLS IN COMBAT.

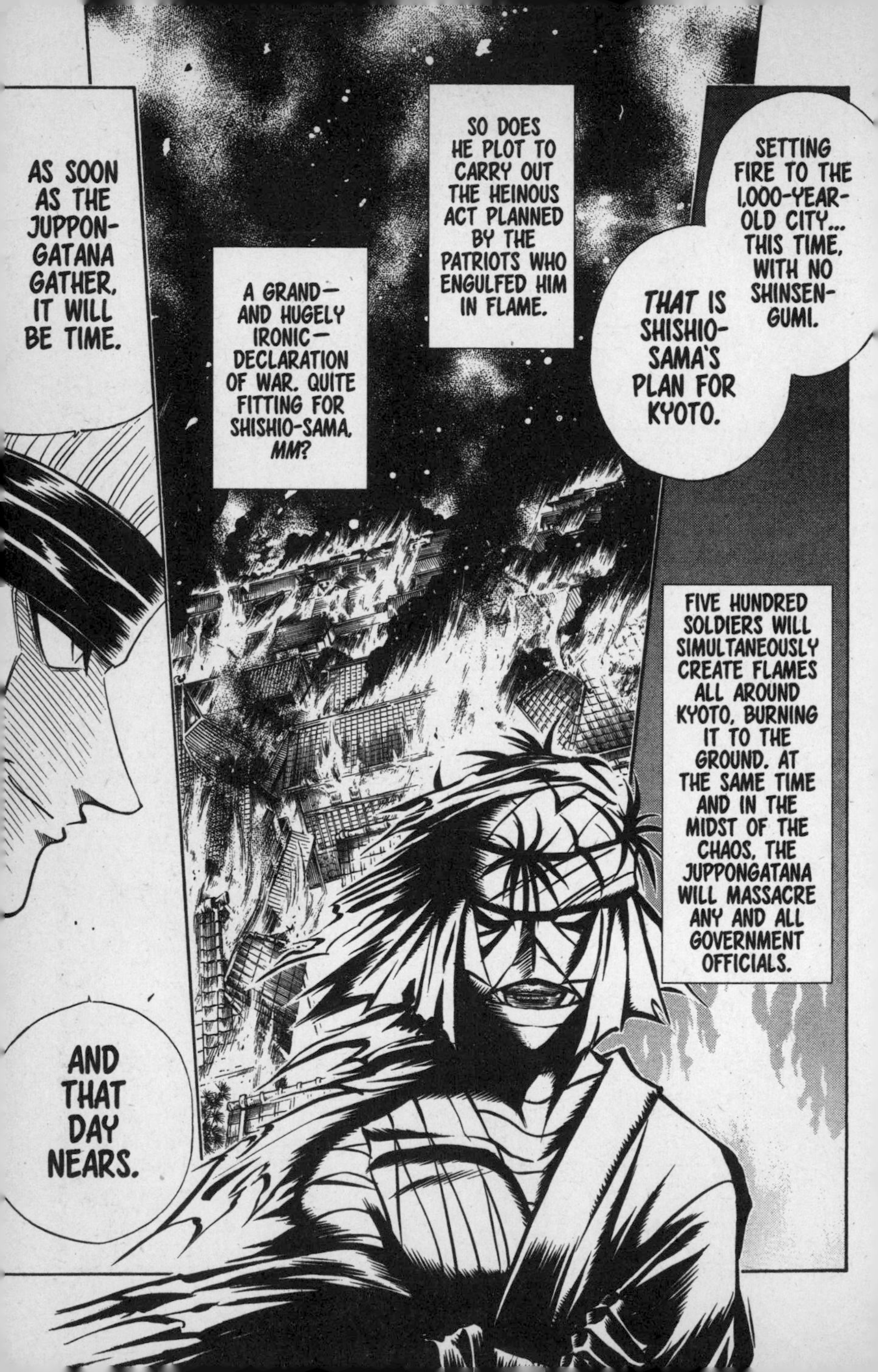
SETTING FIRE TO THE 1,000-YEAR-OLD CITY... THIS TIME, WITH NO SHINSENGUMI.
THAT IS SHISHIO-SAMA'S PLAN FOR KYOTO.
SO DOES HE PLOT TO CARRY OUT THE HEINOUS ACT PLANNED BY THE PATRIOTS WHO ENGULFED HIM IN FLAME.
A GRAND—AND HUGELY IRONIC—DECLARATION OF WAR. QUITE FITTING FOR SHISHIO-SAMA, *MM?*
AS SOON AS THE JUPPONGATANA GATHER, IT WILL BE TIME.
FIVE HUNDRED SOLDIERS WILL SIMULTANEOUSLY CREATE FLAMES ALL AROUND KYOTO, BURNING IT TO THE GROUND. AT THE SAME TIME AND IN THE MIDST OF THE CHAOS, THE JUPPONGATANA WILL MASSACRE ANY AND ALL GOVERNMENT OFFICIALS.
AND THAT DAY NEARS.

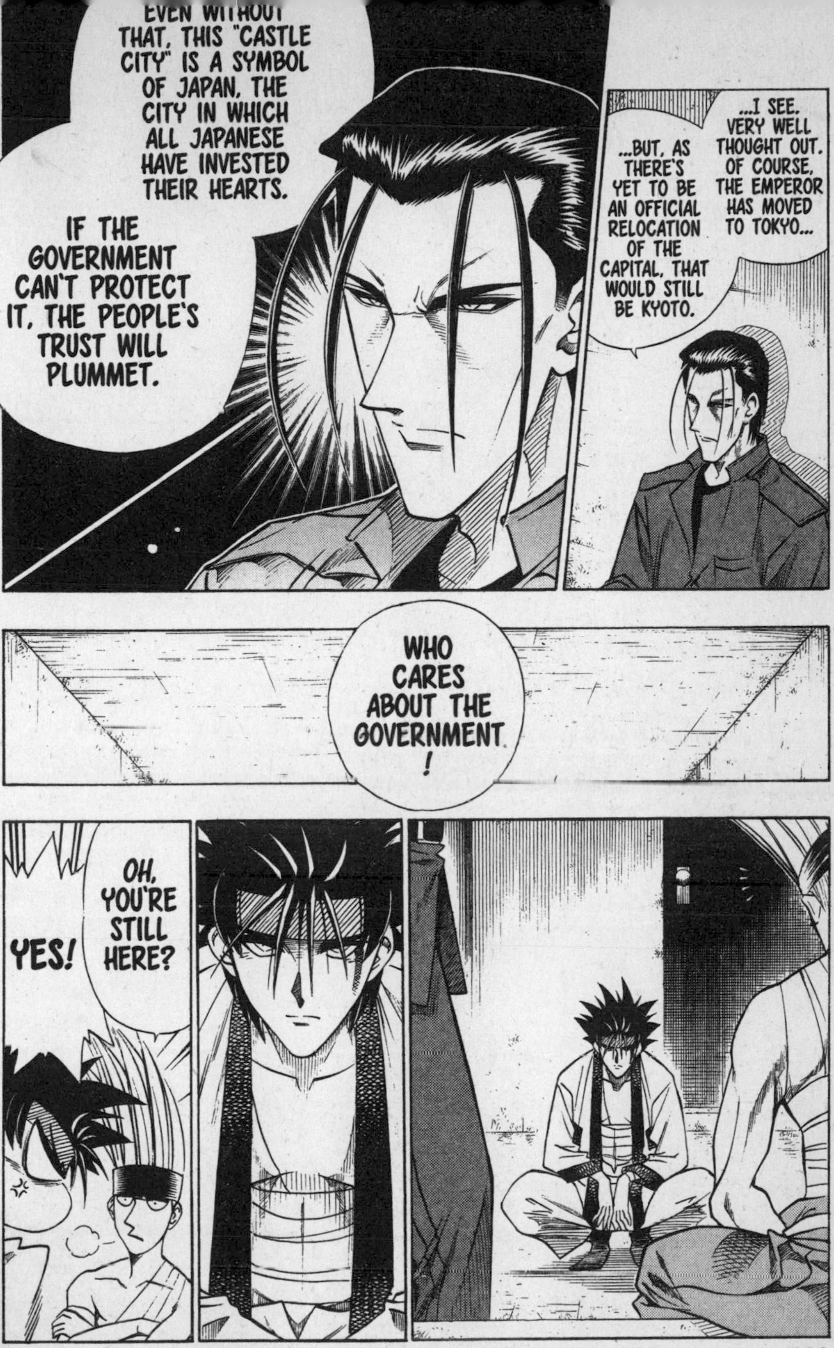
...I SEE. VERY WELL THOUGHT OUT. OF COURSE, THE EMPEROR HAS MOVED TO TOKYO...
...BUT, AS THERE'S YET TO BE AN OFFICIAL RELOCATION OF THE CAPITAL, THAT WOULD STILL BE KYOTO.
EVEN WITHOUT THAT, THIS "CASTLE CITY" IS A SYMBOL OF JAPAN, THE CITY IN WHICH ALL JAPANESE HAVE INVESTED THEIR HEARTS.
IF THE GOVERNMENT CAN'T PROTECT IT, THE PEOPLE'S TRUST WILL PLUMMET.
WHO CARES ABOUT THE GOVERNMENT !
OH, YOU'RE STILL HERE?
YES!

READ THIS WAY

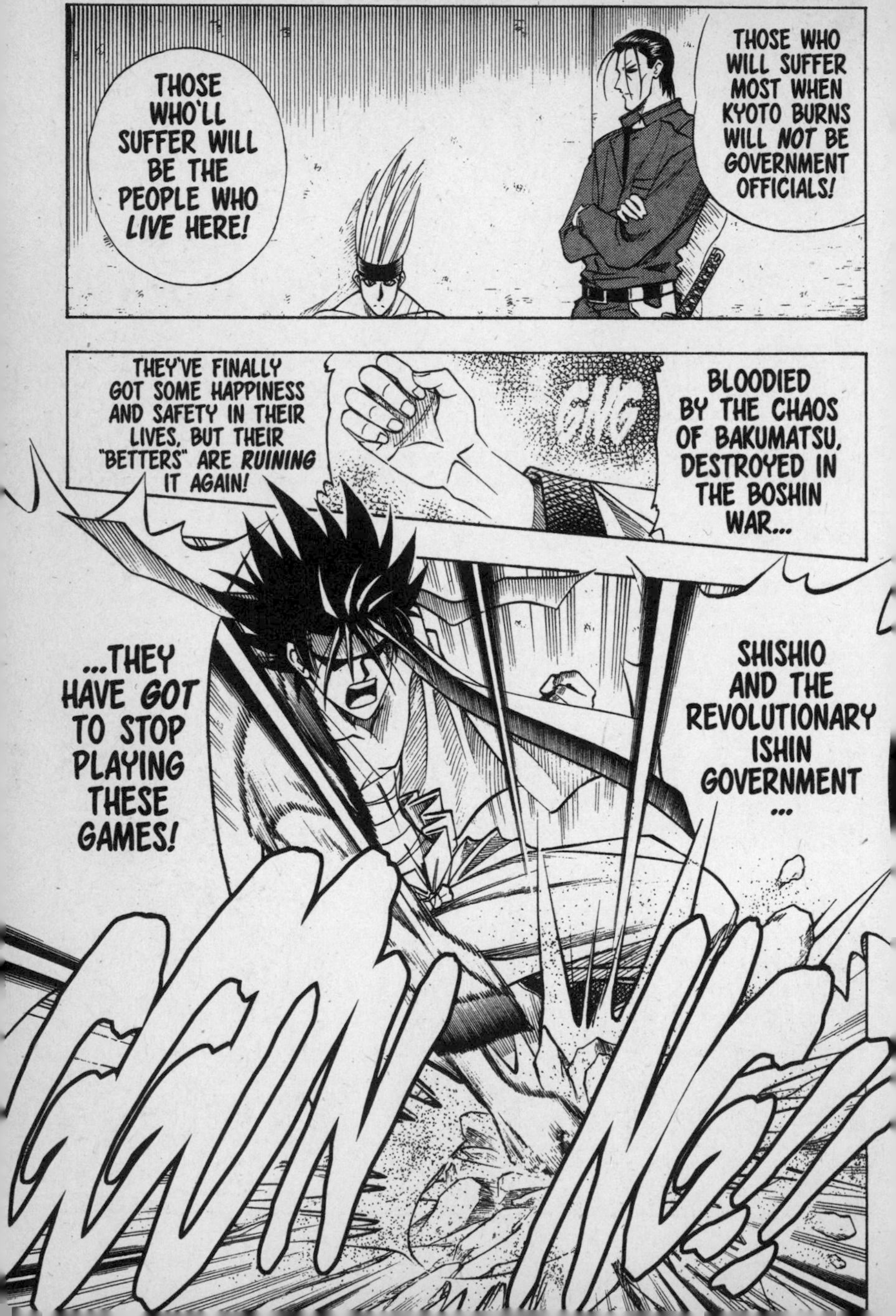
THOSE WHO WILL SUFFER MOST WHEN KYOTO BURNS WILL NOT BE GOVERNMENT OFFICIALS!
THOSE WHO'LL SUFFER WILL BE THE PEOPLE WHO LIVE HERE!
GNG
BLOODIED BY THE CHAOS OF BAKUMATSU, DESTROYED IN THE BOSHIN WAR...
THEY'VE FINALLY GOT SOME HAPPINESS AND SAFETY IN THEIR LIVES, BUT THEIR "BETTERS" ARE RUINING IT AGAIN!
SHISHIO AND THE REVOLUTIONARY ISHIN GOVERNMENT ...
...THEY HAVE GOT TO STOP PLAYING THESE GAMES!

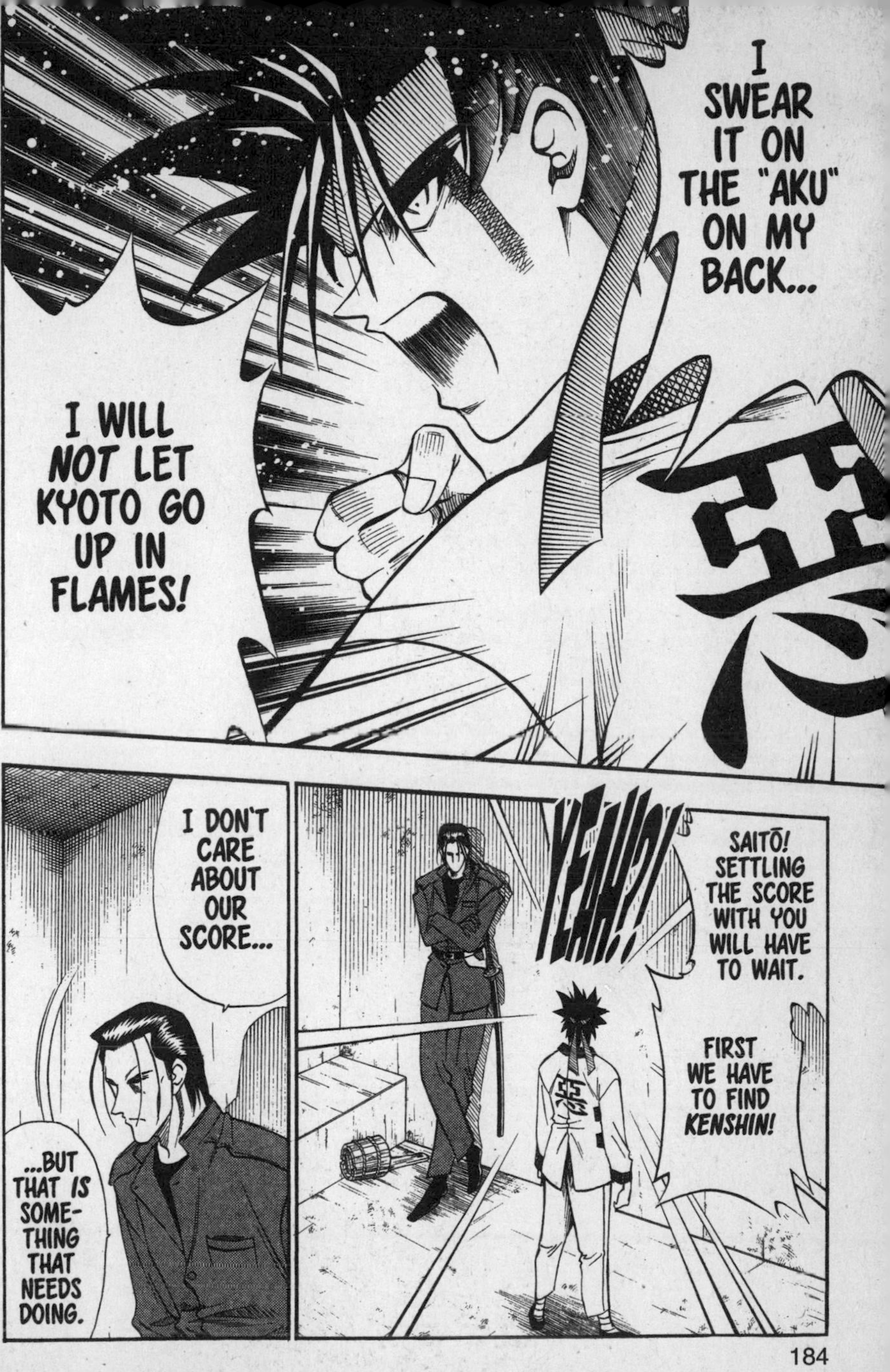
I SWEAR IT ON THE "AKU" ON MY BACK...
I WILL *NOT* LET KYOTO GO UP IN FLAMES!
SAITŌ! SETTLING THE SCORE WITH YOU WILL HAVE TO WAIT.
FIRST WE HAVE TO FIND *KENSHIN!*
YEAH!?
I DON'T CARE ABOUT OUR SCORE...
...BUT THAT *IS* SOMETHING THAT NEEDS DOING.

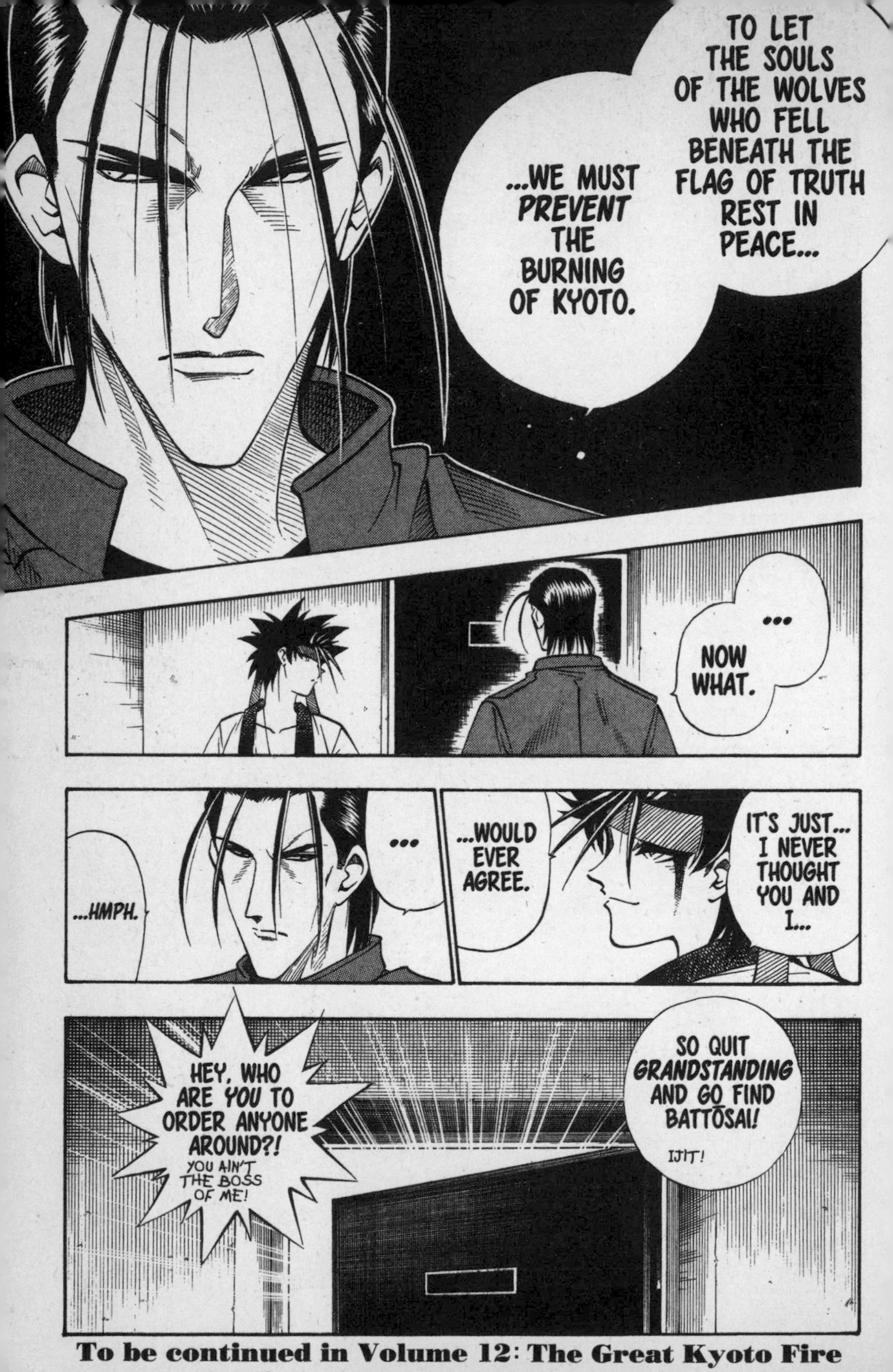
TO LET THE SOULS OF THE WOLVES WHO FELL BENEATH THE FLAG OF TRUTH REST IN PEACE...
...WE MUST *PREVENT* THE BURNING OF KYOTO.
...
NOW WHAT.
IT'S JUST... I NEVER THOUGHT YOU AND I...
...WOULD EVER AGREE.
...
...HMPH.
SO QUIT *GRANDSTANDING* AND GO FIND BATTŌSAI!
IJIT!
HEY, WHO ARE *YOU* TO ORDER ANYONE AROUND?!
YOU AIN'T THE BOSS OF ME!

To be continued in Volume 12: The Great Kyoto Fire

GLOSSARY of the RESTORATION

A brief guide to select Japanese terms used in **Rurouni Kenshin**. *Note that, both here and within the story itself, all names are Japanese style—i.e., last or "family" name first, with personal or "given" name following. This is both because* **Kenshin** *is a "period" story, as well as to decrease confusion—if we were to take the example of Kenshin's* sakabatô *and "reverse" the format of the historically established assassin-name "Hitokiri Battôsai," for example, it would make little sense to then call him "Battôsai Himura."*

Ishin Shishi
Loyalist or pro-Imperialist **patriots** who fought to restore the Emperor to his ancient seat of power

Juppongatana
Written with the characters for "ten" and "swords," Shishio's Juppongatana are literally that—the ten "swords" or generals he plans to use in his overthrow of Japan

Kamiya Kasshin-ryû
Sword-arts or **kenjutsu** school established by Kaoru's father, who rejected the ethics of **Satsujin-ken** for **Katsujin-ken**

katana
Traditional Japanese longsword (curved, single-edge, worn cutting-edge up) of the samurai. Used primarily for slashing; can be wielded either one- or two-handed.

Katsujin-ken
"Swords that give life"; the sword-arts style developed over ten years by Kaoru's father and founding principle of **Kamiya Kasshin-ryû**

Kawakami Gensai
Real-life, historical inspiration for the character of **Himura Kenshin**

kenjutsu
The art of fencing; sword arts, kendô

kodachi
Medium-length sword, shorter than a **katana**. Its easy maneuverability also makes for higher defensive capability.

-kun
Honorific. Used in the modern day among male students, or those who grew up together, but another usage—the one you're more likely to find in Rurouni Kenshin—is the "superior-to-inferior" form, intended as a way to emphasize a difference in status or rank, as well as to indicate familiarity or affection.

aku
Kanji character for "evil" worn by Sanosuke as a remembrance of his beloved, betrayed Captain Sagara of the Sekihô Army

Bakumatsu
Final, chaotic days of the Tokugawa regime

-chan
Honorific. Can be used either as a diminutive (e.g., with a small child—"Little Hanako or Kentarô"), or with those who are grown, to indicate affection ("My dear...").

dojo (dôjô)
Martial-arts training hall

-dono
Honorific. Even more respectful than **-san**; the effect in modern-day Japanese conversation would be along the lines of "Milord So-and-So." As used by Kenshin, it indicates both respect and humility.

Edo
Capital city of the **Tokugawa Bakufu**; renamed **Tokyo** ("Eastern Capital") after the Meiji Restoration

Himura Battôsai
Swordsman of legendary skills and former assassin (**hitokiri**) of the **Ishin Shishi**

Himura Kenshin
Kenshin's real name

Hiten Mitsurugi-ryû
Kenshin's sword technique, used more for defense than offense. An "ancient style that pits one against many," it requires exceptional speed and agility to master.

hitokiri
An assassin. Famous swordsmen of the period were sometimes thus known to adopt "professional" names—**Kawakami Gensai**, for example, was also known as "Hitokiri Gensai."

shinobi
Another word for "ninja"

Shinsengumi
"True to the old ways and risking their lives to preserve the old *shôgunate* system," the popular view of the *Shinsengumi* ("newly elected group") was that of swordsmen as charismatic as they were skilled

shôgun
Feudal military ruler of Japan

shôgunate
See *Tokugawa Bakufu*

sukashi
In karate, *sukashi* is defined as "attack-avoiding evasive action"

Tokugawa Bakufu
Military feudal government which dominated Japan from 1603 to 1867

Tokyo
The renaming of *"Edo"* to *"Tokyo"* is a marker of the start of the *Meiji Restoration*

tonfa
In effect a two-handed weapon (because one is held in each hand), traditional *tonfa*—that is, without ball-bearings or other mechanisms in the handle that allow increased rotation—were a favored weapon among Japanese police of the time, as an officer was said to be able, with relatively little training, to defend himself against unarmed or even (with more training) sword-wielding opponents. In Okina's case, his steel *tonfa* allow him to block Aoshi's nitô-ryû or "double-blade" *kodachi* attacks...although not, unfortunately, forever.

Wolves of Mibu
Nickname for the *Shinsengumi*, so called because of the town (Mibu) where they were first stationed

kunoichi
Female ninja. In that they are not referred to as simply "onmitsu" (ninja), their special name suggests their relative scarcity.

loyalists
Those who supported the return of the Emperor to power; *Ishin Shishi*

Meiji Restoration
1853-1868; culminated in the collapse of the *Tokugawa Bakufu* and the restoration of imperial rule. So called after Emperor Meiji, whose chosen name was written with the characters for "culture and enlightenment."

patriots
Another term for *Ishin Shishi*...and when used by Sano, not a flattering one

rurouni
Wanderer, vagabond

ryûshôsen
Sometimes translated as "Soaring Dragon Flash," the *ryûshôsen* of Kenshin's Hiten Mitsurugi school is one of his special moves, and is also known as "Dragon Flight"

ryûkansen
Also translatable as "Winding Dragon Flash," Kenshin's Hiten Mitsurugi school special move *ryûkansen* is given in here as "Dragon Spiral Strike"

sakabatô
Reversed-edge sword (the dull edge on the side the sharp should be, and vice versa); carried by Kenshin as a symbol of his resolution never to kill again

-sama
Honorific. Even more respectful than *-dono*. Used to show extreme respect—and when in reference to Shishio—extreme fear.

-san
Honorific. Carries the meaning of "Mr.," "Ms.," "Miss," etc., but used more extensively in Japanese than its English equivalent (note that even an enemy may be addressed as "-san").

Satsujin-ken
"Swords that give death"; a style of swordsmanship rejected by Kaoru's father

IN THE NEXT VOLUME...

As Kenshin looks back to the first, early years of his training at the hand of Hiko Seijûrô, his Hiten Mitsurugi master, the remaining members of the Juppongatana or "Ten Swords" arrive in Kyoto—the first phase of the mad Shishio Makoto's master plan for Japan finally underway. While Misao (now Okashira or "head" of the Kyoto-based spy clan) and the members of her Oniwabanshû onmitsu try and decide how best to prevent Shishio from setting the entire city ablaze, Kenshin, Sano, and Saitô consider their next course of action....

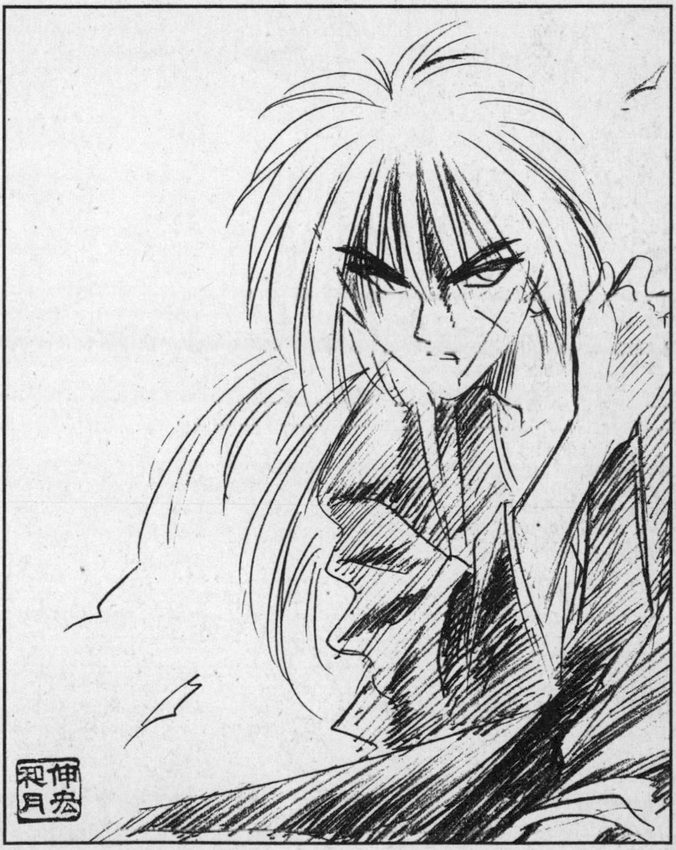
伸宏
和月

Available in March 2005

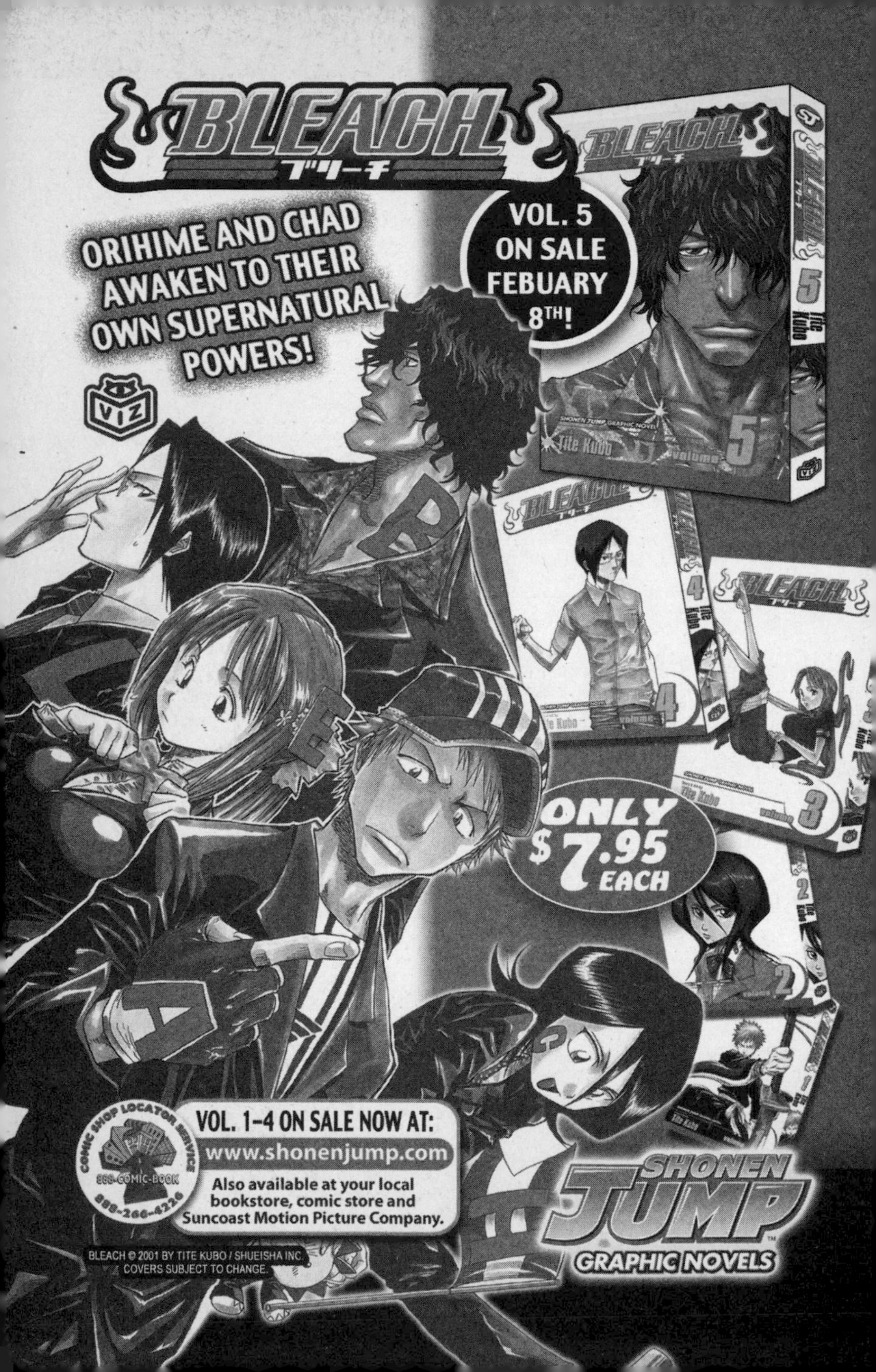
BLEACH
ブリーチ
ORIHIME AND CHAD AWAKEN TO THEIR OWN SUPERNATURAL POWERS!
VIZ
VOL. 5 ON SALE FEBUARY 8TH!
ONLY $7.95 EACH
VOL. 1–4 ON SALE NOW AT:
www.shonenjump.com
Also available at your local bookstore, comic store and Suncoast Motion Picture Company.
COMIC SHOP LOCATOR SERVICE
888-COMIC-BOOK
888-266-4226
BLEACH © 2001 BY TITE KUBO / SHUEISHA INC.
COVERS SUBJECT TO CHANGE.
SHONEN JUMP
GRAPHIC NOVELS

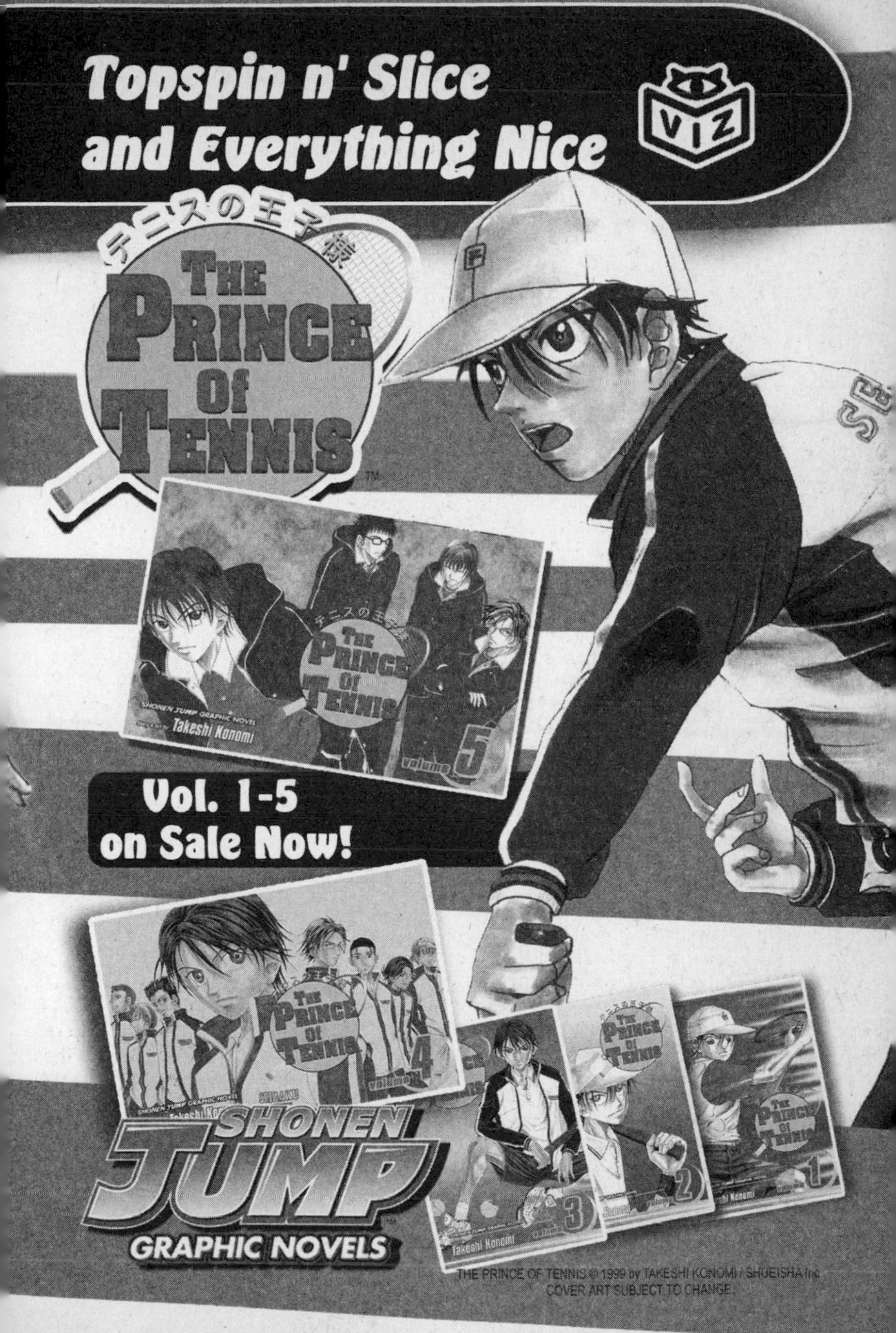
Topspin n' Slice
and Everything Nice
テニスの王子様
THE PRINCE OF TENNIS™
Vol. 1-5
on Sale Now!
SHONEN JUMP
GRAPHIC NOVELS
THE PRINCE OF TENNIS © 1999 by TAKESHI KONOMI / SHUEISHA Inc.
COVER ART SUBJECT TO CHANGE.

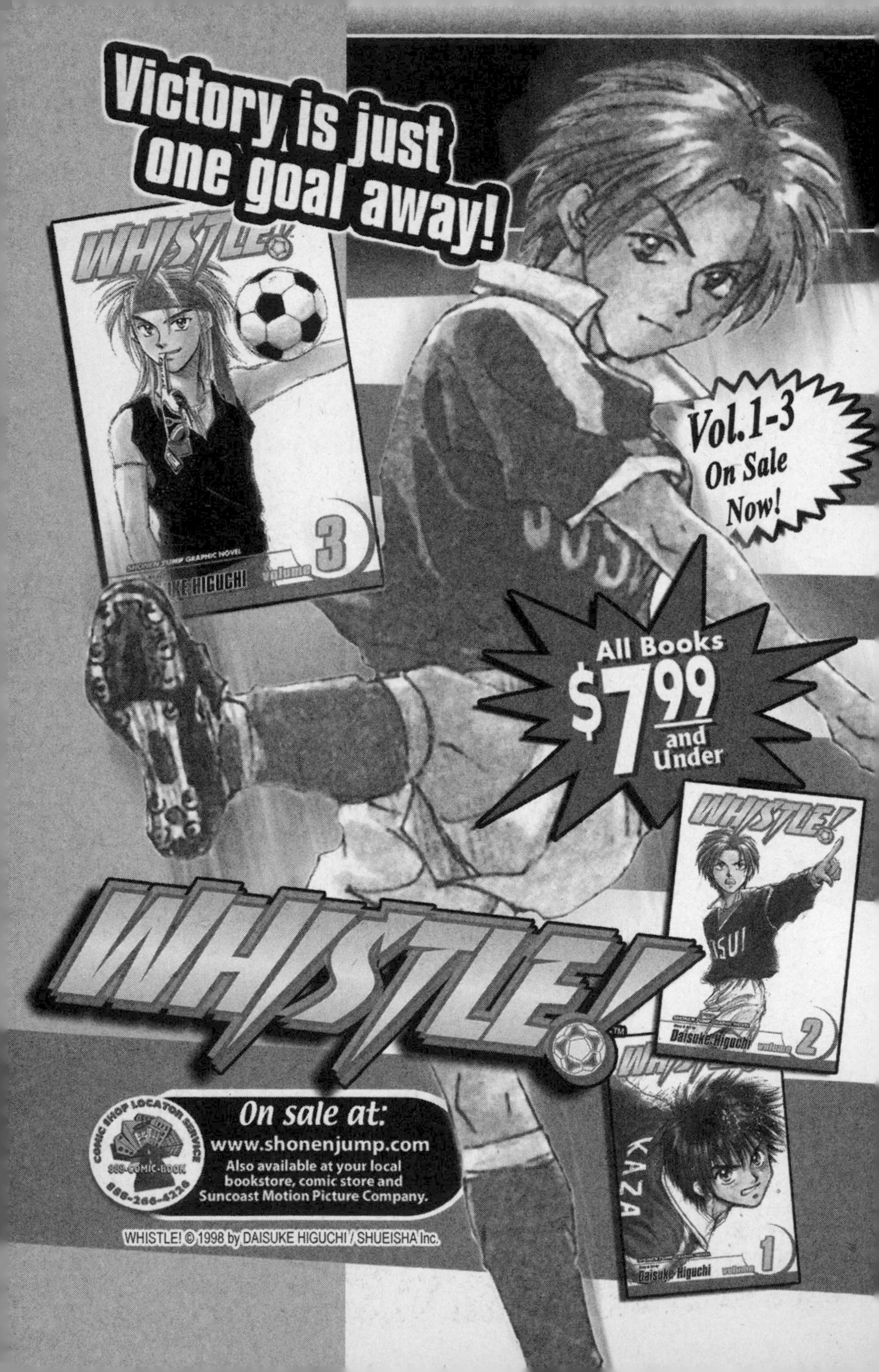

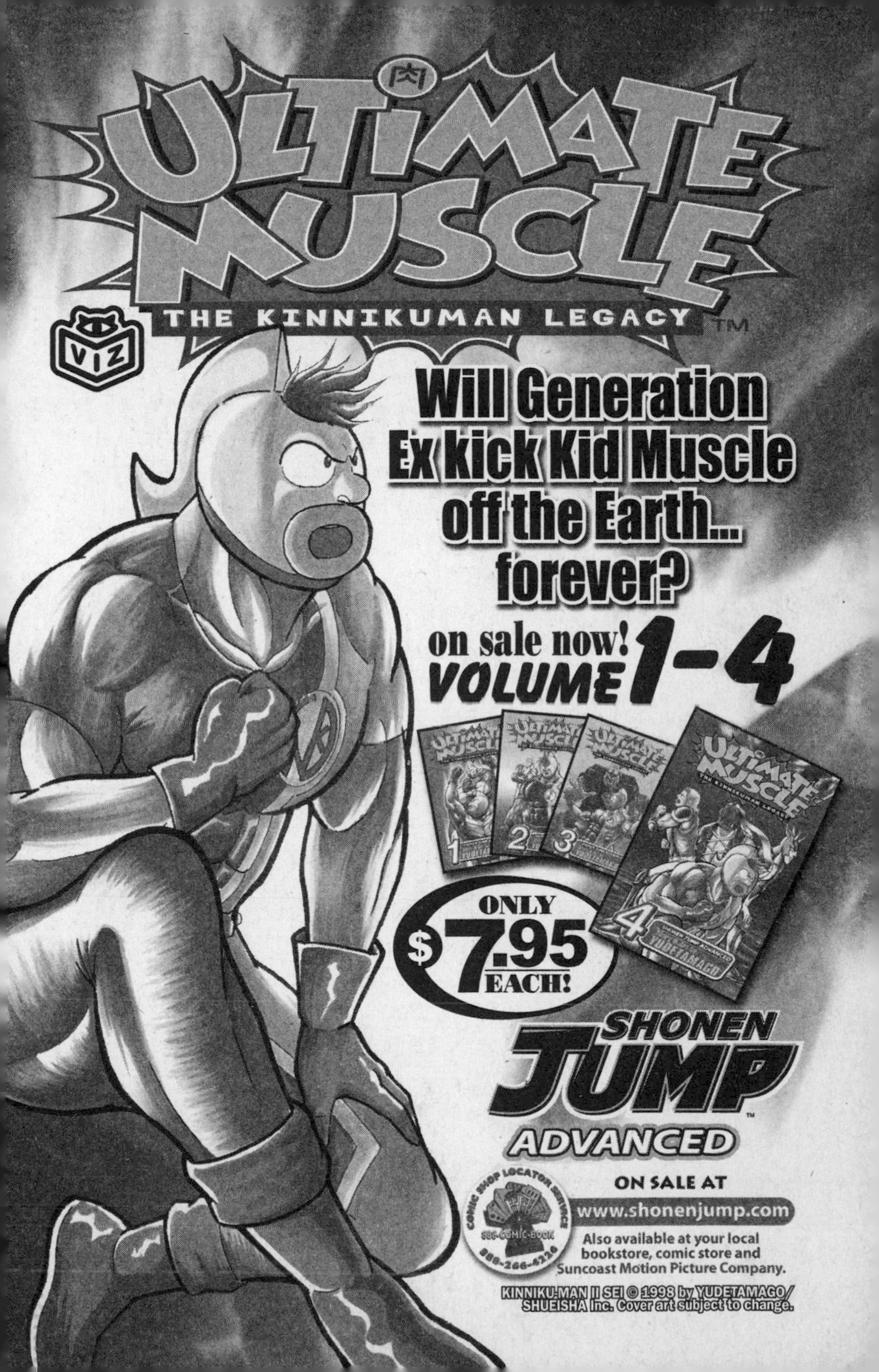
ULTIMATE MUSCLE
THE KINNIKUMAN LEGACY ™
VIZ
Will Generation Ex kick Kid Muscle off the Earth... forever?
on sale now! VOLUME 1-4
ONLY $7.95 EACH!
SHONEN JUMP ADVANCED
ON SALE AT
www.shonenjump.com
Also available at your local bookstore, comic store and Suncoast Motion Picture Company.
COMIC SHOP LOCATOR SERVICE
888-COMIC-BOOK
888-266-4226
KINNIKU-MAN II SEI © 1998 by YUDETAMAGO/ SHUEISHA Inc. Cover art subject to change.

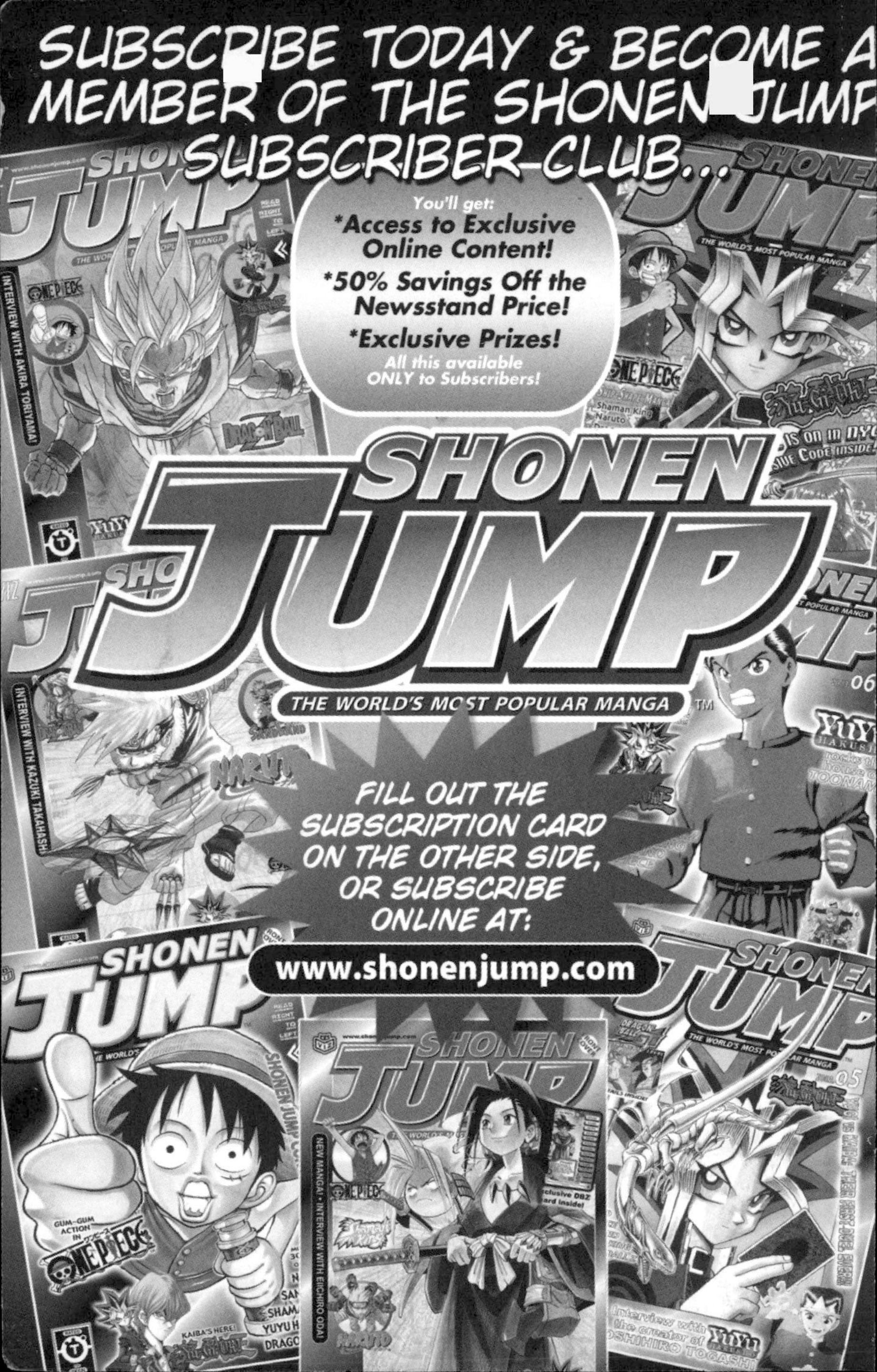
SUBSCRIBE TODAY & BECOME A MEMBER OF THE SHONEN JUMP SUBSCRIBER CLUB...
You'll get:
*Access to Exclusive Online Content!
*50% Savings Off the Newsstand Price!
*Exclusive Prizes!
All this available ONLY to Subscribers!
SHONEN JUMP
THE WORLD'S MOST POPULAR MANGA TM
FILL OUT THE SUBSCRIPTION CARD ON THE OTHER SIDE, OR SUBSCRIBE ONLINE AT:
www.shonenjump.com

Save 50% off the newsstand price!

SHONEN JUMP

THE WORLD'S MOST POPULAR MANGA

Subscribe today and save 50% OFF the cover price, PLUS enjoy all the benefits of the SHONEN JUMP SUBSCRIBER CLUB, exclusive online content & special prizes.
ONLY AVAILABLE to SUBSCRIBERS!

☑ **YES!** Please enter my 1 year subscription (12 issues) to *SHONEN JUMP* at the INCREDIBLY LOW SUBSCRIPTION RATE of $29.95, and sign me up for the Shonen Jump Subscriber Club.

$29⁹⁵

NAME

ADDRESS

CITY   STATE   ZIP

E-MAIL ADDRESS

☐ MY CHECK IS ENCLOSED   ☐ BILL ME LATER

CREDIT CARD: ☐ VISA   ☐ MASTERCARD

ACCOUNT #   EXP. DATE

SIGNATURE

CLIP AND MAIL TO ➡

SHONEN JUMP
Subscriptions Service Dept.
P.O. Box 515
Mount Morris, IL 61054-0515

Make checks payable to: **SHONEN JUMP.**
Canada add US $12. No foreign orders. Allow 6-8 weeks for delivery.

P5SJGN   YU-GI-OH! © 1996 by KAZUKI TAKAHASHI / SHUEISHA Inc.

SHONEN JUMP
THE WORLD'S MOST POPULAR MANGA

COMPLETE OUR SURVEY AND LET US KNOW WHAT YOU THINK!

☐ Please do NOT send me information about VIZ and SHONEN JUMP products, news and events, special offers, or other information.

☐ Please do NOT send me information from VIZ's trusted business partners.

Name: ______________________________

Address: ______________________________

City: ______________ **State:** ________ **Zip:** ______________

E-mail: ______________________________

☐ **Male** ☐ **Female** **Date of Birth (mm/dd/yyyy):** ___/___/______ (**Under 13? Parental consent required**)

1 Do you purchase SHONEN JUMP Magazine?

☐ Yes ☐ No **(if no, skip the next two questions)**

If **YES**, do you subscribe?

☐ Yes ☐ No

If **NO**, how often do you purchase SHONEN JUMP Magazine?

☐ 1-3 issues a year

☐ 4-6 issues a year

☐ more than 7 issues a year

2 Which SHONEN JUMP Graphic Novel did you purchase? (please check one)

☐ Beet the Vandel Buster ☐ Bleach ☐ Dragon Ball

☐ Dragon Ball Z ☐ Hikaru no Go ☐ Knights of the Zodiac

☐ Naruto ☐ One Piece ☐ Rurouni Kenshin

☐ Shaman King ☐ The Prince of Tennis ☐ Ultimate Muscle

☐ Whistle! ☐ Yu-Gi-Oh! ☐ YuYu Hakusho

☐ Other ______________________

Will you purchase subsequent volumes?

☐ Yes ☐ No

3 How did you learn about this title? (check all that apply)

☐ Favorite title ☐ Advertisement ☐ Article

☐ Gift ☐ Read excerpt in SHONEN JUMP Magazine

☐ Recommendation ☐ Special offer ☐ Through TV animation

☐ Website ☐ Other ______________________

4. **Of the titles that are serialized in SHONEN JUMP Magazine, have you purchased the Graphic Novels?**

- [ ] Yes
- [ ] No

If **YES**, which ones have you purchased? (check all that apply)

- [ ] Dragon Ball Z
- [ ] Hikaru no Go
- [ ] Naruto
- [ ] One Piece
- [ ] Shaman King
- [ ] Yu-Gi-Oh!
- [ ] YuYu Hakusho

If **YES**, what were your reasons for purchasing? (please pick up to 3)

- [ ] A favorite title
- [ ] A favorite creator/artist
- [ ] I want to read it in one go
- [ ] I want to read it over and over again
- [ ] There are extras that aren't in the magazine
- [ ] The quality of printing is better than the magazine
- [ ] Recommendation
- [ ] Special offer
- [ ] Other

If **NO**, why did/would you not purchase it?

- [ ] I'm happy just reading it in the magazine
- [ ] It's not worth buying the graphic novel
- [ ] All the manga pages are in black and white unlike the magazine
- [ ] There are other graphic novels that I prefer
- [ ] There are too many to collect for each title
- [ ] It's too small
- [ ] Other ______________________

5. **Of the titles NOT serialized in the Magazine, which ones have you purchased?**
(check all that apply)

- [ ] Beet the Vandel Buster
- [ ] Bleach
- [ ] Dragon Ball
- [ ] Knights of the Zodiac
- [ ] The Prince of Tennis
- [ ] Rurouni Kenshin
- [ ] Whistle!
- [ ] Other ____________
- [ ] None

If you did purchase any of the above, what were your reasons for purchase?

- [ ] A favorite title
- [ ] A favorite creator/artist
- [ ] Read a preview in SHONEN JUMP Magazine and wanted to read the rest of the story
- [ ] Recommendation
- [ ] Other

Will you purchase subsequent volumes?

- [ ] Yes
- [ ] No

6. **What race/ethnicity do you consider yourself? (please check one)**

- [ ] Asian/Pacific Islander
- [ ] Black/African American
- [ ] Hispanic/Latino
- [ ] Native American/Alaskan Native
- [ ] White/Caucasian
- [ ] Other

THANK YOU! Please send the completed form to:

VIZ Survey
42 Catharine St.
Poughkeepsie, NY 12601

All information provided will be used for internal ... We promise not to sell or otherwise divulge your inform...